Small Town
in Mass Society

SMALL TOWN
IN MASS SOCIETY

Class, Power, and Religion
in a Rural Community

Arthur J. Vidich and Joseph Bensman

Revised Edition

With a Foreword by Michael W. Hughey
and an Afterword by Arthur J. Vidich

University of Illinois Press
Urbana and Chicago

First Illinois paperback edition, 2000
© 1958, 1968, 2000 by Arthur J. Vidich and Marilyn Bensman
Reprinted by arrangement with the copyright holders
All rights reserved
Manufactured in the United States of America
♾ This book is printed on acid-free paper.

Library of Congress Cataloging-in-Publication Data
Vidich, Arthur J.
Small town in mass society : class, power, and religion in a
rural community / Arthur J. Vidich and Joseph Bensman.–
Rev. ed., 1st Illinois pbk. ed. / with a foreword by Michael W.
Hughey and an afterword by Arthur J. Vidich.
p. cm.
Originally published: Rev. ed. Princeton, N.J.: Princeton
University Press, 1968.
Includes bibliographical references and indexes.
ISBN 0-252-06890-4 (pbk. : acid-free paper)
1. Villages–United States. 2. United States–Rural conditions.
3. Mass society. I. Bensman, Joseph. II. Title.
HT431.V5   2000
307.72'0973–dc21   99-053655

P 5 4 3 2 1

TO HANS H. GERTH
whose ideas and example have
made this book possible

Contents

Foreword to the Illinois Paperback Edition
Michael W. Hughey

———◆———

Small Town in Mass Society is an ethnographic study of Springdale, a small rural town in upstate New York in the early 1950s. As such, at one level, this book belongs to a tradition of American community studies that includes the Lynds' Middletown books, W. Lloyd Warner's Yankee City series, scores of Chicago School studies, and numerous literary treatments by such writers as Sinclair Lewis, Thomas Wolfe, and Sherwood Anderson. Collectively, these works provide us with a detailed understanding of the institutional structure, organization of power, ethnic and racial dimensions, class structure, and overall cultural patterns of American small towns, which arguably were the dominant social institutions in American life until well into the twentieth century.

The contributions that *Small Town in Mass Society* makes to our understanding of small-town life are critically significant. Indeed, its depictions of the organization and psychologies of social classes, for example, or of the ideologies and symbols of town cohesion are perhaps the most insightful to be found anywhere in the literature. The book also contains detailed descriptions of aspects of small-town life that rarely appear elsewhere–for example, the political role of the school principal or the tacitly accepted rules by which local churches regulate themselves in their competition for members. Although the details are unique to Springdale, the book also confirms the typical small-town pattern of general dominance by the local business community and real control by only a few of its members.

In other of its emphases, however, due to the analytic skill and also partly to the excellent timing of its authors, this book occupies a unique niche in the community studies literature, in some ways moving beyond the genre entirely. Vidich and

Bensman recognized that their examination of Springdale was undertaken at a decisive point in the history of the town and the nation, at the moment of transition between two fundamentally different institutional and cultural orderings of life, between an America that was and an America that was becoming. In this sense, *Small Town in Mass Society* presents Springdale not only as the object of a community study but also as a case study of the social and cultural intersection at which a declining traditional order meets and contends with the increasingly apparent agencies and institutions of an ascendant modernity. Collectively and individually, Springdale's residents are confronted in myriad ways with external forces over which they have little control and of which they are often only dimly aware, even as they cope with the implications and consequences of these forces for their lives. By deftly stitching together the details of local life in Springdale with the broader historical changes and social transformations of the larger society, Vidich and Bensman elevate what is at bottom an ethnographic study into a broader, insightful analysis of fundamental social change in American life.

Most of the social transformations that eventually culminated in the "mass society" of the book's title began early in this century and, in some cases, late in the preceding one. Main Street businesses, consisting mainly of private farms, retail stores, and local or regional banks, were pushed gradually toward the peripheries of an economy that was increasingly dominated by nationwide markets and giant corporations. Political life moved inexorably toward greater dependence on political decisions, organizations, and monies that concentrated at the state and, increasingly, at the national level. Large-scale, centralized bureaucratic organizations steadily overrode local autonomy to extend a network of impersonal rules and standardized procedures into virtually every corner of national life. Mass transportation began connecting once remote areas to the new urban centers of power and opportunity. Radio and especially television disregarded all local boundaries, integrating virtually all individuals and communities into a larger community of shared visual imagery, prefabricated sitcom values, and consumer longings. Taken together, these various developments began shifting the cultural and institutional center of American life away from the countryside and to the cities, eroding local cultural styles, standards, and organizational patterns in favor of styles, standards, and patterns that originated in the urban metropolis.

These and other structural developments continued in the same directions following World War II, but in the postwar expansion of that period, they deepened so dramatically and accelerated so rapidly that it seemed a more profound change had occurred. In some ways it had, for by completing the institutional transformation that had already been well under way, postwar America appeared to be a qualitatively different society than it had been. Postindustrial society, new industrial state, new American society, monopoly capitalism, mass society–these and other labels represent various intellectual efforts to comprehend the contours of what American society had suddenly become.

Of course, the structural transformations of American society were neither monolithic nor uniform. They progressed more rapidly in the larger cities, where political and economic power was centralized and where the need for bureaucratic organization and administration was greatest. These changes penetrated into the small towns and rural areas at different rates and speeds and with differing local effects, depending on the specific forms the penetration took, the degree of acceptance of or resistance to it by different groups in the local community, or dozens of other factors that might or might not be shared with other towns. As these changes extended into the countryside, small towns throughout the United States became social and cultural hybrids, containing some combination of both traditional and more modern cultural and institutional patterns.

Small Town in Mass Society examines these transformations of American life not in terms of abstract theory or even with specific reference to the emerging agencies and institutions of the mass society itself. Its focus is instead on the consequences of these changes "on the ground," as they penetrated into the life of one small town and as they were refracted in the perceptions, experiences, reactions, and adjustments of its residents. Given these emphases, the book's title would be no less accurate if it were inverted to read *Mass Society in Small Town*. By the early 1950s, when the field work for *Small Town* was carried out, Springdale had, of course, already changed considerably from its nineteenth-century, country-town origins. Even so, residues of traditional cultural and institutional patterns remained very much in evidence, despite often being altered or diminished in practice. For example, even though political policies in the town were decided almost exclusively by a handful of men, who themselves were answerable on important issues to external political officials, parties, and agencies, residents insisted that the older ideologies of populism and agrarian grass-roots democracy continued to describe the town's operation and governance. As a result, town leaders were required to observe the forms and trappings, although not the substance, of popular democracy. Also surviving was a public ideology of personal equality, a deeply rooted feature of American political culture that appeared nearly unchanged from Tocqueville's descriptions of it in the 1830s. Springdale residents insisted on an assumption of equality as an ethical obligation in social relations, disdaining class-based exclusivity and pretentiousness even though the local class hierarchy was well established. In Springdale, as throughout the United States since its inception, the democratic ideal of equality has coexisted uneasily with fundamental economic disparity.

The Protestant ethic also survived in Springdale, although generally not as the coherent ethos that Max Weber found still operational, if somewhat secularized, in the United States in the late 1910s. In Springdale, the Protestant ethic had been broken into an ensemble of smaller parts, each containing a narrowed set of normative ideals, conceptions, and motivations. These fractured remains found selective expression in the economic psychologies of the town's social classes, depending on which remnant of the older ethos best addressed the economic circumstances and ideological needs of each class. For example, as Vidich and Bensman indicate, the traditional farmers, for whom farming was a way of life rather than a business opportunity, emphasized hard work as a virtue, but not rational investment for expansion and growth. Defensive-minded small businessmen similarly eschewed entrepreneurial investment in favor of saving and accumulating whatever wealth they could muster. Some groups among the middle classes emphasized the importance of work, but only as a means to further their consumption of leisure time and luxury items. As a broader economic orientation, the Protestant ethic continued to survive only among "rational farmers," who alone among Springdale's classes combined hard work, frugality, and self-denial in order to reinvest accumulated funds in business expansion and improved efficiency.

By contrast, the traditional emphases of the Protestant ethos did not resonate at all among educated professionals and white-collar workers, Springdale's "new" middle classes. These groups deemphasized the inherent value of work, focusing instead on leisure and personal consumption that were consistent with the stylized "good life" defined in advertising images. These new middle classes, though at the time small in number, were cultural revolutionaries who imported into Springdale cultural life styles, consumption patterns, and values that were not restricted by local norms and not connected to traditional cultural styles. Politically liberal, religiously unenthusiastic or at least moderate and tolerant in belief, sexually more "liberated" and sophisticated, more intellectually inclined, and much more varied in their consumption and life-style choices, they were the representatives of mass society in the small town, a living challenge to the traditions and ideologies around which Springdalers organized their lives.[1]

The new middle-class presence, as well as the increasing local importance of outside experts, policy decisions, and agencies and institutions of the larger society, affected community life in Springdale in ways that constantly violated residents' ideological conceptions of themselves, their town, and their way of life. The inescapable problem that residents faced, therefore, was to somehow come to terms with the widening gap between their political, economic, and cultural ideals and self-conceptions and the social and institutional realities affecting their lives.

In a section that should be required reading for students of social psychology, Vidich and Bensman examine Springdalers' responses as a valuable case study and analysis of some of the connections between personal psychology and social structure. For the most part, Springdale residents defended their values, ideals, and sense of autonomy by avoiding the recognition that they were threatened. Their strategies of avoidance, examined in detail in the book, included repressing, disregarding, and particularizing "inconvenient" facts; reconstructing memories, histories, and biographies to make them more consistent with ideological conceptions; tacitly colluding with other residents to collectively uphold necessary illusions about community life; and embracing various forms of self-externalization to prevent serious scrutiny of oneself and one's situation. For some, even the tattered remnants of the Protestant ethic offered a way to avoid recognition of "objective" realities by offering immersion in work as a positive activity in which one could lose oneself, thus upholding much-needed illusions by means of self-distraction. In these and other ways, Springdalers were able to continue living in an imagined nineteenth-century town that was maintained by collective illusions and personal dreamworlds. "Because they did not recognize their defeat," Vidich and Bensman suggest, "they are not defeated."

But neither could they long remain victorious, for their traditional normative conceptions of personal and community life were opposed by fundamental and seemingly inexorable changes in the very structure of American society. As the institutional reorganization and cultural redefinition of American life were further elaborated and extended throughout the society, Springdalers–and the small-town, old middle classes in general–had little choice but to slowly and often grudgingly recognize the decline of their values, traditions, and ways of life. (In Springdale, the publication of *Small Town in Mass Society* itself aided in that recognition.) As this recognition grew, so did their belief that the costs of social change extended far beyond their own eroding importance in the society. Since, by virtue of their own social, political, and cultural dominance over the previous one-and-a-half centuries, the old middle classes had successfully defined *their* values and traditions as those of Americanism itself, they could only perceive their own decline as a threat to the most fundamental conceptions of what America is and should be.

It is no exaggeration to suggest that, in the decades since the initial publication of this book, the major themes and defining points of contention in American politics have been directly shaped by the deepening politicization of old middle-class defensiveness, resentment, and cultural self-consciousness. The stages of their political awakening have included Nixon's "silent majority" in the 1970s, Reaganesque social and moral conservatism in the 1980s, and the more heated "family values" concerns of the 1990s. Generally, they have consistently sought to conserve and, ultimately, to reassert the primacy of the populist and Protestant cultural values of traditional American life, even if they have lately endowed these values with a nostalgic purity they never possessed in practice. With growing urgency, they have also resisted and attacked values and practices regarded as inconsistent with their own idealized standards, including abortion rights, homosexuality, the prohibition of prayer in public schools, evolutionary science, welfare indolence, pornography, and, as a general summation, liberalism. These issues are, of course, the familiar markers of the contemporary "culture wars," the most general expression of class conflict between old and new middle classes. In this book's analysis of the interpenetration of the distinct institutional frameworks to which each stratum's class standing and ways of life are connected, Vidich and Bensman reveal for us the primary social sources of these culture wars. More broadly, given the social and political primacy of the middle classes in American life, they offer us a deeper understanding of the formative development and emerging contours of contemporary American political culture in general.

That culture is not, of course, a finished product. The United States is not done with transitions, and Americans have not fully relinquished their inherited ideals and illusions about the nation's historic mission to be an emulative model for the rest of the world—a "city upon a hill"—or, in more muscular versions, to save the world from itself and for democracy. These ideals, in some ways confirmed in this "American Century" by the postwar emergence of an "American Empire," presuppose a sense of national greatness and power and a right to manage many of the world's affairs in accord with the nation's interests and self-image. Yet, today the United States finds itself ever more deeply enmeshed in a geopolitical context and global economy. We are increasingly made aware that internal democratic rule is mitigated by decisions made elsewhere in the world and that American economic performance–directly experienced by individuals in the form of jobs, salaries, opportunities, and purchasing power–can be powerfully affected by external decisions, incomprehensible circumstances, and impersonal forces that are not subject to American control. Possible responses to this situation include jingoistic nationalism, ground swells of sensitive patriotism, political and military aggressiveness, internal and external scapegoating, the collaborative maintenance of national ideals and illusions, all of the strategies of avoidance and self-externalization resorted to by Springdalers, and no doubt scores of other possibilities. The parallels between small-town residents facing the intrusions of the mass society and contemporary Americans confronting globalization and the decline of empire are obviously not exact. Nonetheless, should anyone rigorously examine the effects of globalization on the American psyche, they will find in *Small Town in Mass Society* a valuable analytic model and scholarly example. In this regard, the book remains relevant in a way that its authors probably neither intended nor anticipated.

In the final analysis, the test of enduring significance for this or any sociological work lies in how well it illuminates the unfolding complexity of history, deepens our understanding of the substantive issues raised by our changing society, and identifies the social, cultural, and institutional trends that most decisively shape and define the society's development. In its analysis of transformative social and historical change and of ongoing human efforts to comprehend and confront it, *Small Town in Mass Society* clearly passes that test. Today, more than forty years after the book's initial publication, it continues to inform our understanding of the richness, complexity, dynamism, and tenacity of American life and culture.

Note

1. Vidich and Bensman later developed a broader sociology of these new middle classes and their political and cultural roles in *The New American Society: The Revolution of the New Middle Classes* (Chicago: Quadrangle, 1971), revised and republished in 1987 as *American Society: The Welfare State and Beyond* (South Hadley, Mass.: Bergen and Garvey).

Introduction to Revised Edition

IT IS NOW ten years since Princeton University Press originally published *Small Town in Mass Society*. In these ten years, the book like a child entering the world has had to make its own way. Its career has included some troubles as well as a share of minor victories. Oddly enough, the book was first recognized by rural Protestant ministers and by teachers and principals in "country" schools. After a paperback edition was published in 1960 it became quite widely accepted. It was used as a supplement in introductory courses in sociology as well as in courses in the community and urban and rural sociology. At about the same time, schools of political science, higher education, philosophy and theology began to use chapters of the book that were of interest to them. In the last several years various chapters have been reprinted in a number of anthologies. In point of fact, the book has had considerable recognition, though as its authors we have not always been able to accept this recognition on the terms in which it was given.

It is true that by and large the central message of the book which described the penetration of the "isolated" community by the agencies and culture of mass institutions has been understood in the terms originally intended. Because of this understanding, students of the community are now able to study the community within the framework of large-scale, bureaucratic mass society rather than as the polar opposite of urban society. *Small Town in Mass Society* seems to have been successful in helping to abolish the notion that there is a dichotomous difference between urban and rural, sacred and secular, mechanical and organic forms of social organization. Though this central point has been accepted, we have a number of reservations about other interpretations that have been made of the book.

We have noted with some sense of amusement as well as bemusement that once a book becomes an objective fact by virtue of its publication, its authors lose control over how it is to be understood, misunderstood, interpreted, and misinterpreted.

A book stands on its own and presents itself to its readers in terms of its intrinsic meaning. If it communicates to its readers it does so by virtue of its ability to supplement or illuminate their experience. To the extent that the readers' world or images of the world change because of that communication, the book itself contributes to a remaking of the reality that it originally described. In a small way this book had this effect in Springdale itself: in the village election following publication people voted in larger numbers than they ever had before.

If the image of reality portrayed by a book is different from that intended by the authors because the reader sees it from his own angle of perception, there is nothing the authors can do about it. Still again, the reality and image conveyed by a book may at some points be more accurate than the authors themselves had realized. At other times, the authors do not understand the imminent meanings contained in their work, leaving it to reviewers or readers to tell the author what it was he really intended.

For the above reasons, as well as others, it is impossible for authors, ourselves included, to control the destiny of their own creations. Once the "creation" has entered the objective public world, it begins to have a life of its own. Thus in presenting this revised edition of *Small Town in Mass Society*, we are well aware of the limitations entailed not only in authorship but in revising the original work. As a result, we have made no attempt to rewrite any of the material in the main body of the original book except to add to footnote two on page 52 a sentence that was inadvertently omitted from the original manuscript.

Though we are republishing the book in its original form, we are adding a variety of essays and other published materials that we hope will help to clarify questions and problems that have been raised in connection with its public life. By adding these somewhat more private and inaccessible materials, we hope to add new dimensions to the book's public career. Before describing these new materials, we wish to comment briefly on certain attitudes that have been attributed to us concerning the meanings in the book.

Some students, especially those from urban areas, have interpreted the book as validating the urbanite's sophistication and snobbishness when he views the values of the small town resident. In our experience with urban students in New York City, we have found them only too willing to laugh at and scorn the Springdalers for their "narrow provinciality" and "illusions about life." In Chapter 4 we deal with the responses of Springdale residents to their powerlessness in the face of the domination they experience by the agencies and institutions of the larger society. The defenses that they have erected against this sense of powerlessness took the form of a reaffirmation of the very same values that were denied by their reality. They seem to hold values that are quixotic in both the romantic and "unrealistic" sense of the term. But, as we have indicated, these defenses were also realistic in that they enabled the Springdaler to survive in a world over which he had no control. As teachers and occasional lecturers we have been forced to counter the attitudes of superiority which students and other sophisticated urbanites have too easily adopted toward the residents of Springdale whose community only accidently happened to become the object of our study.

We have observed that the urbanite and the student of sociology are remarkably insightful when it comes to understanding the structure of psychological defenses that apply to the rural dweller. We have also observed, however, that this insight and knowledge of the Springdalers' defenses frequently serves as a source of support for the urbanite's and the student's own defenses. By assuming a snobbish and condescending attitude toward the Springdaler, the urban sophisticate implies that the situation of powerlessness does not apply to him.

When we studied and wrote about Springdale, we did not explicitly make comparisons between it and urban society. Because we did not make these comparisons, many urban readers could easily conclude that the social-psychological defenses of the Springdaler were unique. However, in writing *Small Town in Mass Society*, we did not feel free to extend our interpretation beyond the specific data of the Springdale study; doing so would have placed an excessive burden on the single case with which we were dealing. Nevertheless, it was clear to us at that time that the centralization, bureaucratization and dominance by large-scale organizations that was the controlling condition for Springdale characterizes to an even greater degree the situation of both urban society and the underdeveloped world. The only unique aspect of the Springdale condition was the particular way in which Springdalers responded to it.

The Springdaler and other rural dwellers like him is in many ways in a fortunate situation. He can and does identify himself with the traditions of democratic, frontier populism. Insofar as he has this source of identification with an earlier tradition no matter how outmoded and obsolete it may be, he at least has a mechanism with which he can psychologically defend himself against the dominance of a mass society. The resident of the underdeveloped world finds himself in the same position vis-à-vis the centers of world power and control. For him nationalism, tribalism and anti-Westernism serve the same psychologically defensive purposes. However, the psychological defenses of the inhabitants of the underdeveloped world are more vulnerable than those of the rural dwellers within America because in contrast to the latter they cannot feel pride in the fact that they are a part of the agencies and institutions that are defeating them.

The situation of the urban dweller is different from both the Springdaler and the inhabitant of the underdeveloped world. Though he faces the same problems of powerlessness, he finds it hard to disidentify from the agencies of dominance because he shares the same geographical and cultural milieu of the agencies and institutions which dominate him. However, like the others, he too, if he is to assert his identity and individuality, must develop defenses that will allow him to cope with his situation. Because the modern urban condition does not provide him with an independent cultural tradition, his defenses cannot be those of the Springdaler who at least still feels he is connected to the values of the late nineteenth century. The urban dweller has had to invent a new set of defenses which consist of the cultivation of privacy, of leisure, of "style" and of culture. In our new conclusion to this book, Chapter 12, we describe the processes and functions of these new urban styles. But even at the time we did the Springdale study we discovered the tentative emergence of a similar life style among the professional classes. Even in the mid-1950's, the professional middle class in Springdale found it difficult to identify with rural, populist values. At that time some Springdalers were not too different from urbanites in the new ideologies they had absorbed. Moreover, it cannot be argued that even though the Springdaler's defenses rest on nineteenth-century values that this response is intrinsically inferior to the defensive responses of the urbanite. In doing our work in Springdale we were concerned with the research, description and analysis of one particular town and not at all with making invidious judgments and comparisons between Springdalers and their self-selected superiors.

Just as some students smugly cast themselves in a role superior to the Springdaler, so in the same sense did some professional sociologists interpret Springdale as an archaic and amusing survival of an older age. In their view, *Small Town in Mass Society* "did away with Springdale" so that it could now be forgotten in the light of the modernization and newer social forms that contemporary society exhibits. In this interpretation *Small Town* was an epitaph for the American past. While it is no doubt historically true that the *culture* described in our book is an ever-decreasing part of the total American scene, it was not our purpose or our main point to write an epitaph or eulogy for Springdale and its culture. Our central concern was with the processes by which the small town (and indirectly all segments of American society) are continuously and increasingly drawn into the central machinery, processes and dynamics of the total society. With respect to this point, *Small Town* is not a study of a rural community. It is a study of how some of the major institutions of a society work themselves out in a particular community. To the best of our knowledge, Springdale still exists as a territorial entity and it is absolutely certain that it will continue to be there as part of a larger problem no matter how many epitaphs are written for it by sociologists.

Shortly before *Small Town* was published, Barrington Moore, Jr. suggested that we write an additional final chapter which would place the findings of our study of Springdale in the context of American society as a whole. While we thought at that time that his idea was a good one, we were not then prepared to accept his suggestion. At that time we felt that, because we were involved in the detailed work of a microscopic monographic study, we could not shift the focus and the pattern of our thinking sufficiently to locate Springdale in a macroscopic framework. Though we did not then accept Professor Moore's suggestion, we have in this new edition tried to place Springdale in the context of American history and contemporary American society. Chapter 12 which we have added to the book attempts to locate Springdale in the spectrum of all American communities as they have evolved in response to changes in the economic, political, social and demographic character of our society. This interpretation is linked to other work we have done since the publication of *Small Town* and is aimed at drawing explicit connections between Springdale and the mass society at a macroscopic level. The larger framework for this interpretation will be presented in our forthcoming book, *The Third American Revolution*.

One of the continuous criticisms we have heard of *Small Town* is that it does not contain an explicit statement of its theory and methodology. When we originally wrote the book, we thought that it ought to stand on its own feet without the benefit of supplementary methodological justifications. In our original Preface we simply stated that our methods and models had been described elsewhere. We still feel that that original decision was correct and that the substantive results and meaning contained in the book should be presented in plain English, insofar as we are capable of such expression.

To defend a book on methodological or theoretical grounds is to say that the meaning of the book is not contained in what it states. By definition, methodology and theory must be secondary to the attempt to directly comprehend the substance of an issue. It is only in rare instances that abstract theoretical and methodological concerns can be useful to the student who wishes to understand his world. Yet in spite of this, we have received innumerable requests from students in our own classes and from other schools around the country to reconstruct the methodology and formal theory of the book. We have felt that in our work we have been by necessity both methodologists and theoreticians, but since we have not wished to make this a conscious object of our concern, these aspects of the book have been implicit rather than explicit.

As a matter of fact, we had written several methodological and theoretical essays about the research contained in the book. During the time we were writing the book and after we had finished it, we asked ourselves what it was we were doing. Our reply to that question was contained in three essays which dealt with participant observation, the validation of field data and the relationship between field research and social theory. While these essays do not wholly describe the process by which the research was conducted and the book written, they are as good an approximation of a description of our work as we think we can achieve without making our methodology and theory more important than our substantive findings. We are certain that these essays do not entirely describe the processes of our research. Everyone is now increasingly aware of the personal and subjective factors that are a part of all research. No matter how much one might wish to control the research process, the self intrudes and projects itself on the research enterprise. Moreover, in attempting to reconstruct both the conscious and unconscious intellectual process that governed our thought at the time, we could falsify the description of the actual work by reading into it thoughts, rationalizations and responses that occurred much later, based on both the passage of time and on "new evidence." Our methodological and theoretical essays are published here as Chapter 13.

When *Small Town* was first published, it produced a minor scandal, not unlike the scandals that accompanied the publication of the Lynds' *Middletown* and the earlier volumes of W. Lloyd Warner's *Yankee City* series. The Springdale scandal involved not only the reaction of the community to the book, but also the reaction of Cornell University which had sponsored the project upon which our book was based. The scandal involved such issues as the invasion of respondent's privacy, the ethics of the researcher, and the responsibilities of the researcher to his data, his sponsoring institution and his problem. When we wrote and published the book, we had expected that Springdale "rightly" would be scandalized by our analysis. We had not, however, expected the indignant and scandalized reaction of Cornell University and some of its officers and professors. We became aware of Cornell's reaction to our work through a journal called *Human Organization* whose offices happened at that time to be located at Cornell. *Human Organization*, then edited by William F. Whyte, devoted several issues to the discussion of "The Springdale Case." Most of this discussion took place during 1959 and 1960, shortly after the book was published. It involved not just the authors and Cornell University, but a number of sociologists who were moved to take pen in hand and write letters to the editor. This reaction by *Human Organization* and Cornell University was in itself partly a sympathetic response to Springdale's sense of moral indignation about the book. For the officers and relevant professors at Cornell University, Springdale was a constituency that could not easily be ignored.

Contrary to the bureaucratic and public relations quality of the University's response, Springdale reacted to the book with a sense of existential vitality. On various occasions Springdalers hanged us in effigy, portrayed us as manure spreaders and as violators of small town codes of etiquette. The local picture in Springdale was complicated by the fact that one of the deans of the University was a resident of the town. This perhaps made it more necessary than it would otherwise have been for the University to identify with Springdale. As a result several University "sponsored" lectures and speakers in classrooms and on public platforms developed one or another aspect of the Springdale case. Though we were not present at any of these lectures, we have inevitably been informed of their content by friendly third parties. In one instance we were provided with a tape recording of a full-scale condemnation of our study. There is little question that the book had a jarring and irritating effect on its most immediately relevant audiences. *Small Town* made us controversial figures not only in the Ithaca area but in the profession: in several cases we were not considered for jobs (that we had not applied for) because of the controversies aroused by our work.

Since the Springdale case, issues of ethics and of the implications of "official" sponsorship of research have increased in importance. We can no longer be innocent because we are all now aware of the scandal concerning project Camelot and the penetration of the C.I.A. into the academic, youth and intellectual worlds: all social scientists are now aware of at least the public relations if not the ethical issues involved in problems of sponsorship. Because the Springdale case raised many of the issues that are now being widely discussed among social scientists, we felt it would be worthwhile to bring together the discussion of research ethics which it evoked. In Chapter 14 we have presented the entire debate concerning ethics, freedom and research as it appeared in *Human Organization*. In 1964 we wrote an essay called "The Springdale Case: Academic Bureaucrats and Sensitive Townspeople" as part of our book, *Reflections on Community Studies*, with Maurice Stein. That essay is reprinted in Chapter 14 and describes, at least from our point of view, the organization and history of the research and the writing of our book and emphasizes the ethical issues involved in research in modern bureaucracies. By publishing all this material in the present volume we hope not only to provide a broader basis for understanding the Springdale research but also to contribute to the current discussion of ethics in the social sciences.

This new and revised edition of *Small Town* thus brings together all of the publications connected with our research and the reactions to it, excluding reviews of the book and other secondary interpretations. For the first time the interested reader can have convenient access to the various "sides" of the issues and conflicts related to our work.

In presenting these materials in one volume, *Small Town in Mass Society* is now able to complete its own career on its own terms. The reader can now draw his own conclusions without prejudice or special handicaps. Henceforth no judgments need be made on incomplete information or on biased perspectives

provided by defensive authors with a vested interest in with-
holding information. With this we hope that this particular
aspect of our work will conveniently become some small part
of the passing scene.

ARTHUR J. VIDICH, Graduate Faculty,
New School for Social Research
JOSEPH BENSMAN, City University of New York

New York City
1968

Preface

IT IS PERHAPS easiest to describe the purpose of this book by first describing what it is not. The authors have not attempted to present a general description and analysis of all aspects of the life of a community. This is not a study of a community "whole" because all effort at total description must necessarily remain illusory if only for the reason that the multiplicity and complexity of observable facts belie comprehensive description. Moreover, by the act of attention implied by the selection of a problem, whole ranges of data lose their salience and importance. In this study a number of conspicuous areas of community life such as marriage, courtship and child-rearing are either not mentioned or are presented only as a necessary background to the discussion of other issues which the authors regard as more central to the focus of the study.

This study views the community as a limited and finite universe in which one can examine in detail some of the major issues of modern American society. The dynamics of these major issues, then, can be placed under a microscope in the setting of one rural community.

We have selected the following as central and significant issues:

1. The specific character of the relationship between the rural community and the dynamics of modern, mass, industrial society.

2. The social and economic bases of rural class structure as these are determined by both internal and external processes.

3. The relationship between the overt public life of the community as enacted by its members in public situations *and* the individual's private actions and experiences.

4. The analysis of mechanisms of community integration and techniques of personal adjustment as these occur in the face of social, institutional and cultural cleavages and conflicts which continuously threaten those social and cultural

values which have served as bases of integration and adjustment in the past.

In summary, this study is an attempt to explore the foundations of social life in a community which lacks the power to control the institutions that regulate and determine its existence. It is in this sense that the community is viewed as a stage on which major issues and problems typical of the society are played out.

If the above outline of problems suggests that the study has emerged from the very beginning as the result of conscious and controlled planning, the reader would be deceived. In view of the reader's possible interest in how the study developed, we should like to describe the sequence of ideas that have led to the book's present form.

Originally the study was designed to trace in detail the relationships between the rural community and the various agencies and institutions of American mass society that affect rural life. However, in analyzing the data relevant to this design, we quickly discovered that such an analysis required detailed examination of both the community's social classes and its political connections to a wide range of external social, economic and political institutions. Internal class and political arrangements, partly determined by outside forces, act to screen and funnel the very forces which determine them.

The class and political analysis opened our perception to a number of sharp contradictions in the community's institutions and values. The public enactment of community life and public statements of community values seemed to bear little relationship to the community's operating institutions and the private lives of its members.

This observation was so striking that it led to a reformulation of the basic questions asked of the data: What are the integrating psychological and institutional factors that make the community's social life possible? What are the major cultural systems which make it possible for the members of a community to continue to function as individuals in spite of the demonstrated negation of their basic beliefs by their immediate social environment? Finally, what techniques of personal and social adjustment enable the community members to live constructive and meaningful lives in the face of an environment which is hostile to their values, aspirations and illusions?

This book is only a description and social analysis. It is not a prescription or a prognosis. We feel that it is possible to provide an adequate description and diagnosis of the problems of the local community in a mass society only by neither involving oneself in the attempt to provide social and political solutions nor committing oneself to *any* "solutions."

We should like to add that in presenting the data we have not felt it necessary to draw explicit attention to the underlying theoretical models and schemes used in the analysis; the professional reader, however, will have no difficulty in noticing the use and implications of such schemes and models as are employed. We have done this because we believe that formal theoretical models are important only insofar as they contribute to the systematic gathering and understanding of a body of data.

The broader professional relevance of our methods and models to other existing methods and models in the social sciences has been considered in articles and papers which have appeared elsewhere.

* * *

The authors express their gratitude to the University of Puerto Rico for providing the travel funds, the secretarial aid and the time which made it possible not only to write this book but to do so as a joint enterprise. We especially wish to thank Jaime Benitez, Pedro Muñoz Amato and Adolfo Fortier for their consideration and encouragement in facilitating the completion of the manuscript.

The data employed in the study are a by-product of the research project, Cornell Studies in Social Growth, sponsored by the Department of Child Development and Family Relationships, New York State College of Home Economics,

Cornell University, with the aid of funds from the National Institute of Mental Health, United States Public Health Service, and the Social Science Research Council. While the present study is entirely independent of Cornell Studies in Social Growth and in no way reflects its views or policies, we should like to acknowledge the cooperation extended to us by the following persons affiliated with the project: Robert Dalton, Urie Bronfenbrenner, Edward Devereux, Richard Lawrence, Paul Dempsey, Helen Faigin, Mary Gallway, Jacqueline Goodchilds, Arthur Gravatt, Arthur Kover, Harold Feldman, Howard Chevron, Richard Suchman.

For helpful encouragement in the course of the analysis of the data and in the preparation of the book we wish to express our gratitude to Barrington Moore, Jr., Melvin Tumin, Floyd Hunter, Hans Gerth, Ben Nelson, Reinhard Bendix, John Useem, C. Wright Mills, Hans Speier, Beate Salz, Evon Z. Vogt, Robert N. Wilson, Clyde Kluckhohn, Reuben Hill, Héctor Estades, Gordon Lewis, Irving Howe, Bernard Rosenberg and Israel Gerver.

We wish to thank Ernestina Ferrer de Ballester and her staff in the secretarial office of the College of Social Sciences, University of Puerto Rico, for the patience and care which they gave to the typing of the manuscript in its several revisions.

We wish especially to thank our wives, Virginia Wicks Vidich and Marilyn Bensman, for assistance in all phases of our work.

ARTHUR J. VIDICH
JOSEPH BENSMAN

I

The Appearance of Public Community Life: The Integrating Symbols

Chapter 1

──────────◄◉►──────────

Social, Economic and Historical
Setting of the Community

A First Impression

SPRINGDALE is located in upper New York state about twenty-five miles from three different commercial-industrial centers, medium in size, in a region that is ordinarily regarded as primarily agricultural. From Springdale it is an easy trip over modern highways to both New York City and Washington, D.C.

A motorist who passes through Springdale would hardly notice it except, perhaps, as a possible speed trap. There is a heavy volume of intercity truck traffic that goes through the community every night, carrying milk, gasoline, farm produce and new cars from points north and west to the eastern seaboard. On summer and fall weekends the community's highway is congested with passenger cars headed for nearby recreation areas and the football stadium in University Town.

A closer look at the community quickly brings forth the image of the typical New England town: a well-kept, clean, neat place; a small shopping center; white colonial style, freshly painted houses, interspersed with houses of each of the architectural eras up to the ranch house. One cannot escape the impression of the small town with one main street that has largely escaped the general hustle and turmoil of American life. Springdale supports no movie house, no supermarket and no outside industry.

In order to see the substance of the community, one has to leave the main highway. The beauty of the village rests on a picturesque stream that is so important to the people that they have organized a large-scale cooperative effort to rebuild its dam. Near the stream stands the community school, an imposing modern building that is a visible representation of the whole trend to centralized education in the past fifty years. Though the school is large and new, in recent years Springdale has had to face the problem of insufficient classroom space. There is, however, no disagreement on the importance of the school to the life of the community. Many of the social and cultural activities of the people take place within its halls.

Not far from the school is a railroad station, the only other conspicuous public building in the town. Railroading, however, is not important to the community since the road consists of a single set of tracks representing a spur line that ends twenty miles away. A small diesel engine makes a daily round trip to the end of the spur and back, but for the past few years has not stopped at Springdale.

The village appears to be singularly free of activity. Indeed, on an ordinary weekday few people and only very few cars will be seen on the streets. The greatest amount of visible activity centers around the school when children and teachers come and go. Activity is more visible in the late afternoon when people do their shopping on their way home from work.

There are times when the community becomes noticeably alive. Rainy days bring a large number of farmers who come to do their accumulated shopping. Saturday morning is always a day of high commercial activity; village business reaches its peak in volume. On Sunday morning the tone of village life changes completely; this is a time of sedate church activity when people dress up in their best clothing. The religious basis of rural life is symbolized by well-filled church parking lots.

Much of the community's social life is not externally visible at all. To see the community in action one must be aware of the organizations and social groups that attend to the affairs of community life. These activities take place in the churches, in private homes and particularly in the school. Innumerable planning and committee groups discharge their duties and keep the organized life of Springdale in motion.

Social and Economic History

The history of Springdale reveals a number of decisive changes in the social and economic past of the community. For example, the community as it existed in 1900 or 1870 is quite different from the community which the observer confronts today. But the unequal development and change of particular segments of community life mean that at some points the community is more intimately linked to its own past than at others. Each of the community's historical periods contributes a set of conditions which are woven into the fabric of current community life. It would be difficult to comprehend Springdale as it exists today without presenting its historical background. Moreover, the attention to a time dimension provides an important mechanism for seeing the community in dynamic rather than static terms.

THE EARLY PERIOD

Springdale was first settled in 1793 by ex-soldiers of the Indian wars. By 1800 there were more than one hundred settlers, most of whom were deeply religious Congregationalists who had migrated from Connecticut. The chief economic enterprise of this group was lumbering and subsistence agriculture based on corn and wheat. By 1811 Springdale township had been formed and at about the same time, due to the construction of a turnpike which connected northern points and the Susquehanna drainage system, a number of villages and hamlets were established which were then equal in size to what was later to become Springdale village.

At that time the present-day village consisted of two definite settlements, one above and one below the creek which bisected them, and this distinction remains in a limited way today. Two fire companies, two shopping centers and the "social feuding" of older inhabitants remain as remnants of this division. Old-timers tell stories of gang wars between adolescent peer groups from different sides of the creek. Such reminiscing emphasizes the quaintness of a social division which no longer has meaning to most of today's residents.

Between 1825 and 1855 lumbering had become an important industry. Timber was exported and abundant supplies of hemlock supported a number of tanneries that had grown up in the community. General farming, though still based on primitive methods and crude hand machinery, became more important and maple syrup became a prime cash crop. In 1825, 8,350 acres of land were under cultivation; in 1855, 30,769 acres or three-fifths of the town's area were farmed.

A railroad, completed in 1834 and cutting through the heart of the village, stimulated commercial activity and increased the importance of Springdale village; Springdale became a post-village entitled to regular deliveries of mail and newspapers, and an iron works dependent on outside markets was set up. The township population between the years 1820-1850 had increased from 1,665 to 3,433.

THE GROWTH OF VILLAGE INDUSTRY AND GENERAL FARMING, 1855-1880

By 1880 lumbering had virtually disappeared as the primary economic base of the community. Most of the tanneries which had coexisted with the lumbering industry had closed their doors. In their place new methods of agriculture—the plow, and horses instead of oxen as draft animals—made farming the chief economic enterprise of the community. More than five-sixths of the total acreage of the township was farmed by 1875.

The average acreage of the 501 farms then in operation was 101. Butter stored in barrels in the cellars became an important cash crop, shipped to the market twice a year. Shipping facilities for milk did not exist beyond the local market so that butter production tended to be limited to the excess milk production of a farmer's few "family" cows.

Although farming became a dominant enterprise, it was not prosperous. Prices of farm commodities in the post-civil-war period were generally low and continued so for many years, a fact which may be related to the later shift to dairy husbandry. However, because of this intensive interest in farming, several agricultural societies grew up. The first, in the 1840's, was replaced in 1855 by the County Agricultural Society, which spread information and gave fairs and races until 1866. A third society was started in 1871 and lasted until the beginning of the twentieth century.

By 1880 the village had expanded to 1,050 people, a population larger than at present. New churches were established and a bank, chartered in 1864, serviced a growing and prosperous village industry which included three hotels, a wool factory, two flour mills, two blacksmith shops, two wagon repair shops, a foundry and so forth. Along with the specialization that was beginning to take industry out of the home, an increasing emphasis was placed on a cash economy and on more specialized farming.

In 1880 the population of the township increased to 4,323, its highest point in history, with more than three-fourths of the people living on farms where hand labor was still a valuable economic asset.

The small-town press and the county "directory" reached their highest development during this period. Springdale's first newspaper, *The Press*, was published in 1867. It was followed by the *Free Press* in 1873 and the *Independent* from 1876 to 1879. The *Review* led a short existence during 1874 to 1875. Several gazetteers and county directories, all large and fat volumes, chronicled the social and commercial events of the day. Today these have become collectors' items for those whose family names are memorialized on their pages. Hardly noted by the chroniclers is the appearance of a telegraph operator on the occupational rolls of 1875. He inconspicuously opened up a new era in communications and just as inconspicuously became obsolete a few years ago when the service was discontinued in a new age of communication.

THE DECLINE OF FARMING AND GENERAL PROSPERITY IN THE VILLAGE, 1880-1910

Due to soil exhaustion and the farmers' inability to adapt new machines and farming methods to the rolling hills of the area, general farming became outmoded and unprofitable in the latter part of the 19th century. Under these circumstances farming could not compete effectively with the cheap lands and high productivity of the Middle West. As one observer noted, "Farming in the East, conducted as our husbandmen understand it, is no longer a profitable pursuit, for the lands valued at from $20-$100 an acre, with labor at from $1.50-$2.00 a day, cannot be made to compete with lands in the great West worth from $2.00-$6.00 an acre, with labor at from 75¢ to $1.00 a day." With this decline in general farming, farmers increasingly turned to cheese and butter production.

While farming was declining, the village was consolidating its industry and experiencing a high prosperity. The 1896 assessment records list a total of 56 business enterprises in the village. Of these, 26 were stores or shops, 4 were hotels and the remainder small-scale industries including 3 foundries, a blanket factory, a glove factory, 2 carpenter shops, 3 saw mills and several other types of mills. Village assessments rose rapidly between 1903 and 1910 while farm assessments remained the same or declined. To indicate the expansive attitude of the town, Springdale was incorporated in 1900 and several years later installed a central water-supply system. Two new newspapers, *The Standard* and *The Gleaner* were competing for local subscribers.

Despite this village prosperity, the population of the village and township was declining, primarily as a result of migrations to surrounding cities undergoing industrial expansion. The migrants continued to maintain close contacts with their rural cousins and frequently came back to visit or to stay during periods of industrial unemployment. The local hotels catered to the more prosperous visitors as well as to traveling businessmen and vacationers. Of the four hotels then in the town, one remained in the 1920's and 1930's, and now there are none.

MASS MIGRATION AND THE GASOLINE ENGINE, 1910-1930

Two reliable indices of farm prosperity are the value of farm land and the percent of farms occupied by tenants, the richest land having the highest tenancy rate. In 1920, farm land in Springdale was valued at $26 per acre and only 8 per cent of the farms were operated by tenants. The mechanized and competitive farming of the mid-West had devalued the land and destroyed the price structure of Springdale's farms and their commodities during the farm boom of World War I. Between 1875 and 1930 the number of operating farms had decreased from 510 to 365 in spite of the fact that there is hidden in these figures a large in-migration of farmers shortly before and during the 1920's. Depressed farming conditions and industrial opportunities during World War I had caused an upheaval in the social composition of the population of Springdale.

In 1920 only 67 percent of the males and 60 percent of the females brought up on Springdale farms remained to live on farms. Moreover, only 54 percent of those men living on farms were under 35 years of age. Inheritance practices made it difficult for sons to acquire farms and tenancy was economically unfeasible. As a consequence of these two factors, the farm population was an aging one which tended increasingly to a subsistence type of farming. As many as 20 percent of Springdale's farms were deserted in 1920 while many more were up for sale by farmers who could not afford to leave them.

As land prices declined, farm ownership came within the economic reach of Polish and Ukrainian industrial workers in the industrial cities and coal regions to the south. To this group land was the fulfillment of a European dream made possible by land agents who mediated between them and the "old Yankee stock." By 1920 they made up 10 percent of the farm operators and had already established their own religious, fraternal and social organizations.

The period from 1910 to 1930 was one in which there was a mass turnover of farm owners. More than half of all farm operators were first generation settlers on the farms which they then occupied; less than 3 percent occupied farms that had been in the family for four generations. There was a considerable movement of farmers within the township and a still greater number of farmers who were new to the community. These new farmers were the Poles and Ukrainians, a group of unsuccessful Midwestern German farmers and local merchants whose business failed during this period. A major reconstitution of the settlement pattern of the farm population had taken place.

In the meantime other forces in combination with the farm decline had caused a major upheaval in the organization of the village. Modern industrial methods drove local industry off the market. Factories, craft specialists and mills almost disappeared from the local scene. The disappearance of the local market and the influx of modern merchandizing methods such as the mail-order house drastically reduced the number of shops and stores. Merchants whose fathers before them had been farmers turned to farming in a desperate effort to make a living. Business property was left to deteriorate or, as in some cases, literally to crumble to the ground. Little or no new construction was begun during the years 1910-1930.

The development of the mass-produced gasoline engine formed the basis around which a social and economic reconstitution of Springdale took place. The automobile established an intimate social connection between Springdale and the outer world and provided new business and occupational opportunities in the form of gasoline stations, repair shops and road construction and maintenance. It made possible the R.F.D. and, in conjunction with the radio, a comprehensive daily contact with events and happenings as reported in the mass media.

The farm tractor, the milk truck and the mechanized accessories of milk processing procedures all combined to set the framework for the development of dairy farming and fluid milk production. Butter and cheese production gave way to the specialized production of fluid milk delivered daily to urban markets. Buckwheat, maple syrup, hay and sheep, previously important sources of cash income, declined in importance. The farm family, previously a large work unit, was reduced in size and organized itself around new work processes and a new work routine.

It is obvious that the severe depopulation and large-scale resettlement of Springdale township caused an upheaval in the organization of the social life of the community. Many churches and schools closed their doors. Civic and social organizations became moribund for lack of an active membership and economic resources. New ethnic groups and other "outsiders" began the process of finding or making a place for themselves in the organized life of the community. New neighbors had to accommodate to each other and new friendships and social groups were formed along new and different lines in a rapidly changing social environment.

THE GREAT DEPRESSION AND THE GREAT WAR, 1930-1950

Springdale's farmers remained indebted throughout the 1920's and the general boom in building bypassed the village. The depressed conditions of the Twenties were extended into the Thirties in more intensified form. Farmers who had made the conversion to fluid milk production and who had abandoned hay and buckwheat as cash crops (the transformation of fields to pasture lands and feed grains) saw the bottom fall out of the structure of fluid milk prices. Milk wars and milk dumpings became institutions in the early 1930's. The farm community itself was split along several lines according to the several political solutions proposed to solve the milk dilemma. Only the better operators and producers and those not too heavily indebted survived under these circumstances. Some farmers eked out a living on almost a non-cash basis while others sold or abandoned their farms. The state conservation department bought up large tracts of once farmed land and turned them back into a wilderness. Many of the Polish and Ukrainian farmers, accustomed to the hard life of European peasantry, managed to retain holdings and in some cases even improved the depleted soil. Some of this group lost or sold their holdings and moved to the village to start from scratch in a new social environment.

Business in the village had reached a new low beyond its previous low in the 1920's. Business failures and business turnovers, which had been high since 1910, reached a new high. Some businessmen, however, with cash or a sound operating base, turned their money into local real estate investments and have since seen the value of their holdings skyrocket. These were few, for of some thirty store or shop keepers now in business, only five were operating these same businesses in the Thirties. The relief check, relief work, pension checks and various welfare measures were important features of the local economy. Day laborers were plentiful during the harvest season and gardening became an economic necessity for a great many families. The "family cow," a pig or two and some chickens might be kept in the back yard—even in the stables standing behind fine houses whose occupants once kept horses.

Organized social life became segmented and fractionalized. The Grange Hall, the home of a once powerful town and village organization, showed unmistakable signs of weathering from the lack of maintenance. The Masons, with high initiation fees, found it difficult to conduct a program. Churches, once proud and vigorous symbols of religious faith, showed signs of disrepair even when they could support a minister. The combined businessmen's organization, called Ro-Ki, once important in formulating local business practices and ethics and a staunch supporter of community activities, vanished from the local scene, never to return in its old form. The American Legion, along with several fraternal orders, continued to hold meetings in the hall above the grocery store on the basis of new rental arrangements designed to "suit the times." The Poles succeeded in maintaining their own organizations.

By the late 1930's the Federal Milk Price Order had become law. The agricultural and credit policies of the New Deal were being felt in the community. Milk had been given a stable price structure. Amid an uproar of opposition a new central school was organized, twenty-six independent school districts disappeared, and, hence, an important industry which attracted state capital-subsidies had been added to the village.

During the decade of the Thirties the local population increased from 2,564 in 1930 to 2,601 in 1940, a two percent gain which hardly reflects the actual volume of population movement. While city cousins returned to the township to live off the land or double-up in the old homestead, some of their own cousins left for the city in search of better prospects. Some farmers moved to the village while villagers moved to the farms. Strangers and outsiders bought up small plots of land over the countryside and built shacks to live in. The shack people became a social element in the town. Some were villagers who went into the country and squatted on untended land. Others were descendants of old and once proud "farm families" who never left the land: the old homestead had become a shack through a slow and gradual process of economic poverty and social decline.

Organized milk marketing and the sharp rise in price of farm commodities associated with World War II opened up a new era of prosperous agriculture. Farmers who survived the previous decades began to expand and mechanize their farms. Some who had gone to the cities in the depression came back and bought farms with industrial earnings. New farmers, some of them Finnish, attracted by the cheap although marginal land, came to the township from nearby localities. A few went into part-time chicken farming while other farmers added chickens as a secondary crop. A few brought up on farms went back to farming to avoid the draft. Veterans, returning from the war and aided by federal legislation and training programs, swelled the ranks of the new and prosperous farm community. Inevitably, economic processes claimed their toll of farm losses, but the large majority of farmers, for the first time in their lives, were debt-free by the end of the decade. Some, indeed, felt hemmed in by the state land that surrounded their farms.

Meanwhile, regional industries were expanding and booming to meet the industrial needs of a nation at war. To the ranks of a small group of village industrial workers was added the labor pool left over from the Thirties—village as well as rural non-farm—that now found a place in industry.

Commuting to industrial work became a social pattern. Women, widows and the disabled could find work if not in industry then in the local glove factory which almost in spite of its management was caught up in the war effort. Even before the end of the war, but particularly after it, industrial workers moved into the township in search for places to live. Abandoned farm dwellings were reoccupied. Houses attached to farms bought up by expanding farmers were sold along with a few acres of land to workers "hungry for the soil." New houses were built in the village and every man had his own plans for renovation and improvement. Even the shacks took on a new gleam as electricity reached the remoter areas in advance of the television aerials which were soon to protrude from their roofs.

In the late Forties a new wing was added to the central school "not ten years old." There were now more children, more teachers, nine school buses and a school budget of several hundred thousand dollars. It was difficult to find a store front that was left unoccupied for more than several weeks at a time. The American Legion, its ranks swelled by returning veterans and new migrants, bought itself a "big old house and installed a bar and bartender" in spite of "raised eyebrows." Churches were rebuilt and redecorated on almost a debt-free basis and each one supported its own minister. The Masons and Grangers painted and renovated their halls. Stemming from an effort to revive the old Ro-Ki, a "Community Club" was organized ("open equally to all") which incorporated within itself many activities and organizations previously defunct or organizationally crippled. What oldsters remembered as the recreation of youth now became Youth Recreation, an organized program financially supported by the state. There was talk of the need for a new library, a new community center and a new educational program for the town.

The social life of the community took on new dimensions and was revitalized. "Newcomers" with new ideas, many of whom worked in other places, sat side by side with newcomers of a generation ago and descendants of original settlers. Polish sons had married Yankee daughters. Farmers and industrial workers and socially outcast shack people were neighbors side by side. Teachers who "pulled their shades when they had a party" lived next door to matronly ladies on main street. One could buy a hard drink on either end of main street. In the "better" homes one played bridge and enjoyed refreshments with one's own social group on Saturday night; poker games were played on the same night in the back room of the filling station. Two bars, one of which catered to "no-goods" and which was apt to receive the attention of the constable, did a brisk business. Innumerable people of all types left the village to find entertainment and gratification in other places—friends in other towns, drive-in theaters, movie houses and hot-rod races. Still many others stayed home for an evening of televised entertainment. New as well as old Springdalers were living through a new world of experiences in an environment whose social past is documented by abandoned country graveyards and one-room schoolhouses. Beneath this resurgence of community life lay a new set of social problems based upon a socially reconstituted community.

An Informal Census

About 3,000 people live in Springdale township. One thousand of these live in Springdale village and the remainder, except for those who live in five hamlets of about 100 people each, live in the open country, always near a road. Approximately 500 of those who live outside the village are people who are not socially or commercially oriented to Springdale village. They are the residents of two of the hamlets and those who live in the open country areas which surround these hamlets. They live closer to larger settlements in other townships and, though they vote and pay taxes in Springdale, they send their children to other schools and tend not to participate in the social and economic life of the town. Hence, the effective social membership of the community is about 2,500 people. This is the population which came under observation in this study and, except when otherwise specifically mentioned, is the group with which this book is concerned.

The adult population of Springdale—those between twenty and eighty years of age—consists of about 1,700 persons who are organized into approximately 700 households. A household may consist of one aged person living alone or a husband and wife with ten children. In general any living unit that does its own cooking on separate facilities is a household.

A little more than three-quarters—about 78 percent—of the adult population is married. Of the remainder about 6 percent say they have never married while 14 percent are widowed. Two percent admit to being separated and, in a community where it is a sign of disrespect to be divorced, only three people say they are divorced.

Those who are currently married have on the average about two and a half children living at home. The range of children per family is broad, however, and extends from none to ten. Springdale, like other rural areas, exports its youth to the urban centers and on the whole produces more children than local opportunities can accommodate. Almost all families who have post-school-age children have a son or daughter in the city or in the armed forces.

Few individuals in Springdale are totally without education. On the other hand about 40 percent have had eight or less years of schooling. These are largely older residents and immigrant groups who grew up in an era or under conditions which did not offer the educational facilities available today. Another 40 percent is composed of persons who have graduated from high school or have had some high-school education. About 15 percent have had college or technical training and 10 percent of these have graduated from college. Most of the college graduates are not native Springdalers, but, at the same time, many original Springdalers have college educations but no longer live there.

It is a sign of the economic times that of all household heads only three were unemployed. Eighty-three percent had jobs, of which 37 percent were self-employed and 46 percent were employed as wage or salary workers. About 7 percent, made up of widows, youth and un-employables, were non-employed, and 7 percent were retired. The retired represent many types—an ex-Marine Corps sergeant, an old railroad conductor and the hermit with an odd-job youth—but primarily they are farmers who left the farm to "live out their years" in the village.

Exact incomes in a rural community made up of many farmers and businessmen are difficult to secure. Farmers tend to underestimate their incomes because they deflect living costs onto farm operation costs and because, in producing their own food, they tend not to be aware of its cost. Farmers and businessmen do not like to talk about their incomes to interviewers and, if they do, they tend to devalue it.

In terms of stated incomes, percentages of households are distributed in income categories roughly as follows:

Stated Income Categories	*Distribution of Households by Percentages*	
Less than $2,000		29%
$2,000 to $3,999	56%	35
$4,000 to $5,999		21
$6,000 to $7,999		4
$8,000 to $9,999		2
Over $10,000		1
Ambiguous response or refused to say		8
	Total	100%

There is probably no distortion in the fact that 29 percent of the families in Springdale in 1952 should claim incomes of less than $2,000 since any close inspection of the community reveals considerable poverty and marginal living. The 56 percent who claim incomes between $2,000 to $6,000 probably come close to averaging between $4,500 and $4,800. If there is a dominant standard of living, it falls within the $2,000-$6,000 income range, and the total of those who have incomes in this range is probably less than 50 percent rather than 56 percent since it is in this range that those who underestimate their incomes are apt to fall. More people earn over $6,000 than will admit. Springdalers do not like to think of their community and themselves in it as too broadly differentiated in economic terms. It is quite likely that the one who claimed an income over $10,000 did not have it and that those who actually have such incomes gave lower figures. In very rough terms, however, the ranges and percentages of incomes represent a reasonably accurate general picture. About 25 percent of the present population were born in the community, though some of these have lived in other places for periods of their lives. The remaining 75 percent are immigrants to the community. Immigrants still residing in the community arrived in about the following percentages during the following periods of time:

Time Period	Percentage of Immigrants
1870-1909	11%
1910-1919	7
1920-1929	10
1930-1939	12
1940-1945	10
1946-1952	25
	Total 75%

The thirteen years from 1940 through 1952 account for the influx of more than one-third of the population. The depression decade of the Thirties was, of course, a period of urban migration to rural areas. But even before this, migration rates were high, higher than indicated in the percentages, since each receding decade reflects the percentages of survivors only. It is apparent that there is a considerable exchange of people between Springdale and other places, a fact which comes as a surprise to Springdalers, who like to think of their community as predominantly made up of a stable native population.

Only one segment of Springdale, the Polish, mixed with some Ukrainians who make up about 15 percent of the population, is given a separate ethnic group identity by Springdalers. They represent the major portion of the migration of the decade of the Twenties. There are other ethnic groups represented, but so small in numbers that they are not easily visible. These include a few Finns who represent an offshoot of a nearby Finnish settlement, a few Germans who moved into the community from the Midwest during the First World War, a few Italians and always "quite a few Irish teachers." There is one Negro family which stems from a Civil War settlement in a neighboring town but this family lives on the periphery of the township and is never seen in the village or in the social life of the community. These groups, with the occasional exception of the Finns, are not regarded as separate ethnic groups.

The Economic Basis of Community Life

Springdale has no significant machine industries. The leather goods factory, which expanded to more than one hundred employees under wartime pressures, now supports six workers. Next to agricultural products, lumber is the chief economic resource of the community, but it is exploited by only one commercial sawmill which is owned and operated by two families. Village business, for the most part, consists of retail establishments and service facilities. "Big business" is composed of several farm implement dealers and grain merchants who service the surrounding agricultural area. Farm merchandise in stores and the presence of a milk collecting plant in the village indicate the importance of the farm trade to local business. Economically the village functions as a farm trading center.

Agricultural enterprise is based on dairy farming organized around the family farm as the unit of production. Farms range in size from 50 to 1,000 acres and differ considerably in the degree to which work processes are mechanized. Some farmers own only a tractor and a few accessories, while others have mechanized almost all work processes. Out of about 200 farmers, only 20 to 30 are tenants or renters and only 2 or 3 of these farms are owned by absentee owners. While farm ownership is high, there is also a high incidence—more than half—of indebtedness in the form of mortgages and credit purchases of farm machinery.

Farm land in Springdale township, except for a small proportion located in the valleys, is hilly and heavily wooded, and the productive capacity of the land varies greatly from farm to farm according to the care with which the land is treated by the farmer. On the whole these topographical considerations mean that pasture lands exceed grain lands. Farmers in this area tend to determine their optimum size of herd by available pasture land, and supplement the grain needs of their herds by direct purchases from feed mills in the village. This fact makes their connection to the village economy particularly intimate.

Farmers purchase anywhere from 30 to 70 percent of their feed grains and, hence, operate with relatively high fixed costs. Their level of fixed costs makes their farm operations more sensitive to small fluctuations in the price of milk. In this sense, in contrast to other agricultural areas in the state, a greater proportion of farms are marginal production units. To the extent that village business depends on farmers, these facts of agriculture are of concern not only to farmers but also to the merchants.

Less socially noticeable but economically very important are a sizeable group of commuting industrial and other wage workers who make up approximately one-third of the employed residents of the township. Their income is derived from industrial wages and constitutes a direct support to the local economy in the form of consumption and taxability. As a group, however, industrial workers are settled inconspicuously throughout the township. Since they are potentially mobile and not tied to the community by investments in businesses or farms, they are generally not recognized as constituting an important basis of the local economy.

Residents of the community are themselves apt to refer to the centralized school as the major industry of the village. It operates on a budget of a quarter of a million dollars and provides employment for about sixty persons. It represents a capital investment of several million dollars and plays the economic function for all families of training the youth for future employment.

The family garden, the mason jar and the deep-freeze are important parts of Springdale's economy. For many families, in the village as well as in the country, the garden represents an important income supplement. A small garden can easily produce a family's annual vegetable needs, and in this way the diligent housewife can make a direct contribution to the household economy. There are, of course, a number of enterprising persons who produce garden surpluses and offer them for sale on the local market.

Seventy percent of all Springdalers own their own homes. The rest who rent are largely apartment dwellers in the village who have not yet acquired sufficient capital to make a down payment on a house of their own. The community places a high value on the economic independence which is implied by home ownership. The poor as well as the well-to-do, those who live in shacks and those who live in the colonial mansions, like to be free of a monthly rent commitment which does not lead to the security of home ownership for old age. About 40 percent of the owned homes are under some type of mortgage—veteran, F.H.A. or personal loans—but this is regarded as preferable to the uncertainties of a relationship with a landlord.

A wide spectrum of occupations is represented in the community. There are on the one hand business proprietors, farm owners and professionals; on the other hand, clerks, salesmen, farm laborers, skilled and semi-skilled workers, manual workers and the odd-job men of many skills and no specialty. To a certain extent the type of occupations Springdalers are engaged in determines their place of work. A little less than a third of those who are employed—mostly the businessmen, the professionals and a scattering of clerks and laborers—work in the village. Another third work outside the village but in the township; these largely comprise the farm owners and the farm laborers. Somewhat more than a third of the employed population commute to work in neighboring towns and cities. This group includes most of the skilled and unskilled industrial workers and a few sales and clerical workers.

More striking, however, is the amount of work Springdalers do. Contrary to the impression of the lackadaisical slow-moving community that the casual observer is apt to get,

Springdalers are hard-working people who keep themselves busy at constructive work. The casual observer gets his initial impression partly because the people are not easily visible in their work environment and partly because the work force is dispersed over wide areas. One is apt to see the merchant chatting with a passer-by on the street, a few farmers standing around the feed mill or someone painting a house and from this get the impression of a low level of work activity.

In about 65 percent of Springdale's households, at least one person is engaged in a full-time job. In another 25 percent two or more persons are working at full-time jobs. The remaining 10 percent who give no occupation are the retired, the widowed and the shiftless whose incomes are derived in ways other than work. In addition to this, however, from 15 to 20 percent of all heads of households hold down more than one job. In some instances, a household may have as many as three or four sources of income from work. Some of those who hold two jobs combine industrial work with a part-time business or part-time commercial farming. Others do part-time selling, repair work, clerking or odd-jobs in connection with some other full-time occupation. Merchants spend long hours in their stores and professionals are as devoted to their work as professionals elsewhere.

In addition, the householder is apt to turn his efforts to constructive work after working hours. Home improvements, canning, auto repairs, sewing and repairing—all such efforts contribute to the economic welfare and income of the community.

Social and Organizational Life

In Springdale, informal social gatherings take many forms, ranging from parties which can be attended only by invitation to reunions of local kinship-based clans. Within this range there are gatherings of the filling station crowds, bridge parties, baby showers, the unexpected social "drop-in" and the like. There is, of course, a great range in the volume of social participation of different individuals. Some individuals organize almost all of their non-work time around such gatherings and may participate in several different social groups. Others socialize in a very limited way with relatives or a few close friends or neighbors. Still others do their socializing entirely outside the community with friends or relatives in other places. There are those, too, who prefer their privacy and isolate themselves from all such contacts. These social groupings do not randomly include anyone who wishes to participate in them. Patterns of exclusion and preference tend to bring together the like-minded. It is a feature of Springdale, however, that such social distinctions are rarely noticed and never verbalized. There is, instead, the common belief that "anybody can visit anybody" and "everybody can join any club he wants to."

Purely social gatherings in homes and in other places of meeting have direct extensions into the formally organized life of the community. It is a characteristic of community life, which is consistent with De Tocqueville's observations of more than a century ago, that a heavy emphasis is placed upon organized group activities. Such organizations, of which in a strict accounting there are more than two hundred, serve a wide range of purposes and functions. They deserve more detailed description simply because they comprise such an important part of the public life of the community.

The Masons and the American Legion and their auxiliaries, the Eastern Star and the Legion Auxiliary, have arisen, particularly since World War II, as important community organizations. Both maintain substantial "homes" and both are connected to vigorous national organizations which support local activities. Each has a membership of about one hundred and each maintains vigorous auxiliary programs which multiply the number of those engaged.

The Masons offers its members an intimate, warm and ritualized relationship with other members. It offers an opportunity to achieve status by progression through a series of orders in a sphere of activity not directly linked to the social forces of the community, and provides psychological security to its members in the form of old-age homes, orphanages, and in the extension of a quasi-kinship bond with all "brothers" to whom at any time one need not be a stranger. In the community, Masons, as Masons, call upon each other in times of family and financial crisis.

The Legion program includes a vast range of activities— the provision of hospital beds, wheelchairs and crutches, weekly suppers and parties, a continuously open recreation center and bar, a monthly newsletter, participation of uniformed members in public ceremonies, organized baseball for youth and so on. All these activities require a relatively large budget—perhaps the largest of any private organization in the community—and a continuous devotion to money-raising ventures. Membership dues contribute only a minor share of operating expenses. The clubhouse bar, a constant source of irritation to the Methodist and Baptist churches and to temperance supporters, is an important source of revenue. Special projects like buying baseball uniforms or hospital beds involve public canvasses. The Legion's major source of income is a July 4th parade and carnival. On this day the community is organized by the Legion—each neighborhood as a matter of patriotic duty prepares a float. The festivities of the day which culminate in the carnival—the sale of carnival concessions, Legion-managed soft-drink and eating stands, raffles and bingo—provide the Legion with an opportunity to maintain its solvency.

Although the Legion is connected to a national organization with a broader political program, local members have nothing to do with higher levels of organizational activity. Sometimes they hold offices at the district level, but no one from Springdale has ever held a state office. By and large on a daily operational basis the local chapter does not impinge on the state and national levels.

The Legion does not command the respect of the respectable groups in the community. Though some of its means and methods are acceptable, it symbolizes "loose-living" and an unwillingness to cooperate with the churches.

The Grange, which was originally begun as a fraternal order with a political purpose, has been transformed at the local level into a fraternal order with a social purpose. In the process it has gained a high respectability in community life—Grangers are thought of as reputable people. To a certain extent this is a reflection of the age of the membership which consists largely of older persons who have lived in the community a long time. Many of the members are retired or ex-farmers now residing in the village, and others have never had any connection with farming.

The program of a Grange meeting is based on a ritual which prescribes the actions of all members according to status position attained. After such formal proceedings, the group may hear a speaker or engage in recreational activities —quoits, checkers, chatting and the like. These activities provide a basis for conversation in contexts outside of meetings; amusing incidents such as a glaring mistake in ritual performance will be remembered and talked about. The Grange maintains its own home and, except for an occasional bake sale, does not orient itself to outside activities.

Springdale has three mutually exclusive book clubs to which membership can be secured only by invitation. Membership in the Monday Club, which was organized about thirty or forty years ago, is determined largely by heredity. The Tuesday Club is fifteen or twenty years old and was founded by a group of excluded dissidents. Since it includes ministers' wives it has a certain amount of regular turnover and is less difficult to get into. The Wednesday Club was founded within the last ten years and accommodates the community's newcomers. Each book club has sixteen members and each member buys a book a year; hence each member has an opportunity to read fifteen books other than her own each year. Some of these books are reviewed at meetings, but programs may also include speakers. These clubs socially differentiate the "cultured group" of ladies in the community.

The fire companies originated as free associations of firefighting volunteers in the days when fire fighting was a manual affair. The two companies came into existence because the village creek at one time prevented reliable and quick movement from one end of town to the other. Though the cause has long since disappeared, and even in the face of strong pressures for consolidation, the two companies remain. Consolidation has taken place at the higher level of the fire district—a regional state-supported agency—and in the form of an annual joint meeting which elects a community fire chief whose function it is to direct joint fire-fighting operations. Although both companies jointly fight all fires, there is considerable hostility between the two concerning proper methods of fire fighting and over the allocation of honor for meritorious service and bravery after each fire. The two companies have retained their social competitiveness and their clublike characteristics even in the face of technological and organizational advance.

One company is made up of older men who by virtue of age and conservative-mindedness are alleged not to possess the daring and courage necessary to the fire fighter. They are known as the "card and checkers club." The other company is made up of "young and daring fire fighters" who are sometimes regarded as reckless, too interested in heroic action and in personal aggrandizement. This latter group provides the manpower and organization and is given the modern equipment necessary to effective fire fighting. It, too, has social aspects but they are organized around the fire-fighting process. The hose rooms act as a clubhouse where past fires are discussed and analyzed and where honors in the form of social recognition are bestowed on those who demonstrate excellence of performance in fire-fighting action. Instead of cards and checkers, this group occupies itself with the care and maintenance of equipment and with periodic checks of equipment.

Some community organizations are not directed to specialized avocational interests, have no formal rules of exclusion and are community-wide in scope and purpose.

The Community Club, formed after the last war, is open to everyone. It features a monthly social meeting, "an evening of fun and entertainment," and is attended by 50 to 150 persons. Dues are $1.00 a year, but their payment is not a requirement for attendance nor, in practice, for voting. Meetings are held in the school cafeteria and, in addition to a "pass-the-dish" supper, ice-breaker games, group stunts and impromtu skits, include a business meeting and an outside speaker who talks on an entertaining or educational subject.

When first organized the club brought under its scope a whole range of organizations which had previously led separate but marginal existences. These included the community choir, the dramatics club and a businessmen's bureau to substitute for the old Ro-Ki. There are also membership, program and publicity committees, and other committees such as town affairs, village affairs, school affairs and community beautification which concern themselves with community affairs.

The membership is made up of country dwellers as well as villagers, but only about five percent of those who attend are farmers. Its members are chiefly villagers who have been in the community less than ten years, with the remainder consisting of older village residents who like the social unity for which the club stands.

Other major community-wide organizations are those connected with the extension program of the land grant college —the Farm and Home Bureaus. These are vocation-linked groups and in this sense they are restrictive. However, all farmers can be members of the Farm Bureau and all homemakers are eligible for membership in the Home Bureau. The youth branch of this agency, the 4-H, extends to all youth in the community, farm as well as village. These groups have utilitarian programs—production problems, efficiency in home management, gardens—but also provide opportunities for social intercourse. They do not recognize age or status differences in their membership and they tend to be organized within neighborhood boundaries. These groups probably have the largest membership of any organization in the community and their programs are guided by professional organizers.

In the past Springdale has had an athletic association whose purpose was to provide public support for sporting activities. It concerned itself with backing town athletic teams, giving athletic banquets and cooperating with the state conservation department in restocking local streams.

With more recent changes in sports habits, local sporting activities do not hold the interest they once did and the athletic association has ceased to exist. Sports have become more individual in character and are pursued in more expensive ways. Community baseball teams are no longer able to recruit players in a systematic way. Fishermen who once fished local streams now make long trips to fishing resort regions. Springdalers have now organized their own bowling and rifle teams which compete in regional circuits; golf and tennis enthusiasts drive thirty miles to play.

Organized sports are now largely limited to the high school athletic program and to youth recreation. High-school teams, American Legion Little League Baseball, Youth Recreation handicraft programs and swimming instruction—these are the major areas of organized sporting and athletic activities and they provide the basis for spectatorship in the community.

There are a great number of organizations which exist only temporarily or for a specialized occasion. All the charitable fund-raising groups—Red Cross, Cancer, Cerebral Palsy, Heart Fund, March of Dimes, etc.—find expression in local committees which are organized from above and outside. The composition of these committees varies from year to year and the committees disband upon completion of the drive. Civil defense and air defense organizations reflect the national emergency of the postwar period.

The major organizations with which we will be systematically concerned in later chapters are the governing bodies and the churches. The town board has jurisdiction over the village and the open country which surrounds it while the village board deals only with village affairs. The centralized school is governed by an elected school board which covers educational matters for the whole school district. There are four Protestant churches in Springdale village and these serve as the focal points of the community's religious life. A Polish Catholic church in the country serves the Polish group and has practically no impact on this predominantly Protestant community.

Chapter 2

Springdale's Image Of Itself

"Just Plain Folks"

WHEN one becomes more intimately acquainted with the people of Springdale, and especially with the more verbal and more prominent inhabitants, one finds that they like to think of themselves as "just plain folks." The editor of the paper, in urging people to attend public meetings or in reporting a social event, says, "all folks with an interest" should attend or "the folks who came certainly had a good time." Almost any chairman of a public gathering addresses his audience as folks—"all right folks, the meeting will get underway"—and the interviewer in his work frequently encounters the same expression—"the folks in this community," "the townfolk," "the country folk," "good folks," and "bad folks." Depending on context, the term carries with it a number of quite different connotations.

First and foremost, the term serves to distinguish Springdalers from urban dwellers, who are called "city people," an expression which by the tone in which it is used implies the less fortunate, those who are denied the wholesome virtues of rural life. City people are separated from nature and soil, from field and stream, and are caught up in the inexorable web of impersonality and loneliness, of which the public statement in Springdale is: "How can people stand to live in cities?" In an understandable and ultimate extension of this valuation one may occasionally hear references to the rural or country folk, in contrast to the villagers, the former being regarded by Springdalers as the "true folk."

The self-designation as "folk" includes everyone in the community; by its generality of reference it excludes neither the rich nor the poor, for everyone can share equally in the genuine qualities ascribed by the term. This is not to say that the community does not recognize scoundrels and wastrels in its own environment; quite the contrary, the scoundrel and allied types become all the more noticeable in the light of the dominant genuineness of rural life. It is rather to say that the standard of judgment by which character is assessed in Springdale includes no false or artificial values. To be one of the folks requires neither money, status, family background, learning, nor refined manners. It is, in short, a way of referring to the equalitarianism of rural life.

The term also includes a whole set of moral values: honesty, fair play, trustworthiness, good-neighborliness, helpfulness, sobriety, and clean-living. To the Springdaler it suggests a wholesome family life, a man whose spoken word is as good as a written contract, a community of religious-minded people, and a place where "everybody knows everybody" and "where you can say hello to anybody." The background image of urban society and city people gives force and meaning to the preferred rural way of life.

Rural Virtues and City Life

The sense of community-mindedness and identification has its roots in a belief in the inherent difference between Springdale and all other places, particularly the nearby towns and big cities. For the Springdaler surrounding towns all carry stigmata which are not found in Springdale: the county seat is the locus of vice and corruption, the Finnish settlement is "red," University Town is snobbish and aloof, and Industrial Town is inhuman, slummy and foreign. In the big city the individual is anonymously lost in a hostile and dog-eat-dog environment. Being in the community gives one a distinct feeling of living in a protected and better place, so that in spite of occasional internal quarrels and the presence of some unwholesome characters, one frequently hears it said that "there's no place I'd rather live . . . there isn't a better place to raise a family . . . this is the best little town in the whole country." In the face of the outer world, Springdalers "stick up for their town."

The best example of community identification occurs when newspapers of neighboring towns choose to publicize negative aspects of Springdale life: making banner headlines over the dismissal of a school principal, publishing the names of youthful criminal offenders who come from good families. In such instances, irrespective of issue or factional position, anyone with an interest in the community comes to its defense: "We may have our troubles, but it's nothing we can't handle by ourselves—and quicker and better if they'd leave us alone." A challenge to the image of Springdale as a preferred place cuts deep and helps to recreate the sense of community when it is temporarily lost.

It is interesting that the belief in the superiority of local ways of living actually conditions the way of life. Springdalers *"make an effort* to be friendly" and *"go out of their way* to help newcomers." The newspaper always emphasizes the positive side of life; it never reports local arrests, shotgun weddings, mortgage foreclosures, lawsuits, bitter exchanges in public meetings, suicides or any other unpleasant happening. By this constant focus on warm and human qualities in all public situations, the public character of the community takes on those qualities and, hence, it has a tone which is distinctly different from city life.

Relationships with nearby towns, in spite of the occasional voicing of hostility, also have a sympathetic and friendly competitive aspect. No one in Springdale would gloat over another town's misfortunes, such as a serious fire or the loss of an industry. Athletic rivalries have long histories and although there is a vocabulary of names and yells for "enemies," these simply stimulate competitiveness and arouse emotions for the night of the contest. No one takes victory or defeat seriously for more than a day or two and only in very rare instance is there a public incident when outsiders visit the town. "Nobody really wants trouble with other towns."

When one goes beyond neighboring communities, the Springdaler leaps from concrete images of people and places to a more generalized image of metropolitan life. His everyday experiences give him a feeling of remoteness from the major centers of industry, commerce and politics. His images are apt to be as stereotyped as those that city people hold concerning the country. Any composite of these images would certainly include the following:

1. Cities breed corruption and have grown so big and impersonal that they are not able to solve the problems they create.
2. Cities are an unwholesome environment for children and families, and have had an unhealthy effect on family morals.
3. Urban politicians and labor leaders are corrupt and represent anti-democratic forces in American life.
4. Washington is a place overridden with bureaucrats and the sharp deal, fast-buck operator, both of whom live like parasites off hard-working country folk.
5. Industrial workers are highly paid for doing little work. Their leaders foment trouble and work against the good of the country.
6. Cities are hotbeds of un-American sentiment, harbor the reds and are incapable of educating their youth to Christian values.
7. Big universities and city churches are centers of atheism and secularism and in spite of occasional exceptions have lost touch with the spiritual lesson taught by rural life.
8. Most of the problems of country life have their origin in the effects which urban life has on rural ways.

What is central, however, is the feeling of the Springdaler that these things do not basically affect him. While he realizes that machinery and factory products are essential to his standard of life and that taxation and agricultural policy are important, he feels that he is independent of other features of industrial and urban life, or, better, that he can choose and select only the best parts. The simple physical separation from the city and the open rural atmosphere make it possible to avoid the problems inherent in city life. Personal relations are face-to-face and social gatherings are intimate, church-going retains the quality of a family affair, the merchant is known as a person, and you can experience the "thrill of watching nature and the growth of your garden." Springdalers firmly believe in the virtues of rural living, strive to maintain them and defend them against anyone who would criticize them.

"Neighbors are Friends"

Almost all of rural life receives its justification on the basis of the direct and personal and human feelings that guide people's relations with each other. No one, not even a stranger, is a stranger to the circumambience of the community. It is as if the people in a deeply felt communion bring themselves together for the purposes of mutual self-help and protection. To this end the community is organized for friendliness and neighborliness, so much so that the terms "friends" and "neighbors" almost stand as synonyms for "folk."

In its most typical form neighborliness occurs in time of personal and family crisis—birth, death, illness, fire, catastrophe. On such occasions friends and neighbors mobilize to support those in distress: collections of money are taken, meals are prepared by others, cards of condolence are sent. A man whose house or barn has burned may unexpectedly find an organized "bee" aiding in reconstruction. Practically all organizations have "sunshine" committees whose sole purpose is to send greeting cards. These practices are so widespread and ultimately may include so many people that an individual, unable to acknowledge all this friendliness personally, will utilize the newspaper's "card of thanks" column to express his public appreciation.

Borrowing and "lending back and forth" is perhaps the most widespread act of neighborliness. Farmers say they like to feel that "in a pinch" there is always someone whom they can count upon for help—to borrow tools, get advice, ask for labor. In spite of the advent of mechanized and self-sufficient farming and consequently the reduction of the need for mutual aid, the high public value placed on mutual help is not diminished. Though a farmer may want to be independent and wish to avoid getting involved in other peoples' problems and, in fact, may privately resent lending his machinery, it is quite difficult for him to refuse to assist his neighbor if asked. Even where technological advance has made in-roads on the need for the practice, to support the public creed remains a necessity.

For housewives in a community where "stores don't carry everything" domestic trading and borrowing is still a reality; they exchange children's clothing and *do* borrow salt and sugar. In Springdale they say "you never have to be without . . . if you need something bad enough you can always get it: of course, sometimes people overdo it and that makes it bad for everybody, but after a while you find out who they are." The process of selectively eliminating the bad practitioners makes it possible to keep the operation of the practice on a high plane.

Neighborliness has its institutional supports and so is given a firm foundation. Ministers and church groups make it a practice to visit the sick in hospitals and homes and to remember them with cards and letters, and all other organizations—The Legion, Masons, Community Club, book clubs—designate special committees to insure that remembrance is extended to the bereaved and ill. The Legion and Community Club "help our own" with baskets of food and clothing at Christmas time and organize fund drives to assist those who are "burned out." The ideology of neighborliness is reflected in and reinforced by the organized life of the community.

To a great extent these arrangements between friends and neighbors have a reciprocal character: a man who helps others may himself expect to be helped later on. In a way the whole system takes on the character of insurance. Of course some people are more conscious of their premium payments than others and keep a kind of mental bookkeeping on "what they owe and who owes them what," which is a perfectly permissible practice so long as one does not openly confront others with unbalanced accounts. In fact, the man who knows "exactly where he stands" with his friends and neighbors is better advised than the one who "forgets and can't keep track." The person who is unconsciously oblivious of what others do for him and distributes his own kindness and favor without thinking is apt to alienate both those whom he owes and doesn't owe. The etiquette for getting and giving in Springdale is an art that requires sensitive adjustments to the moods, needs and expectations of others. This ability to respond appropriately in given situations is the sign of the good neighbor. That this sensitivity is possessed by large numbers of people is attested to by the fact that friendliness and neighborliness contribute substantially to the community's dominant tone of personalness and warmth.

Of course, everyone does not participate equally or at the same level in being a good friend and neighbor. Deviations and exceptions are numerous. Neighborliness is often confined to geographical areas and to socially compatible groups. The wife of the lawyer is on neighborly terms with others like herself rather than with the wife of a carpenter. Farmers necessarily have less to do with people in the village and teachers are more apt to carry on friendly relations with each other. Those who are not willing to both give and take find themselves courteously eliminated from this aspect of local life. "People who are better off" simply by possessing sufficient resources do not find it necessary to call on friends and neighbors for help, though "everyone knows that if you went and asked them for something, they'd give it to you right away." Others have a more "independent turn of mind" and "will get by with what they have, no matter what, just to be free of mind"; the ideology of neighborliness is broad enough to include them "so long as they don't do anyone harm." The foreign elements, particularly the Poles, limit their everyday neighboring to their own group, but still by community definitions they are good neighbors because "you can always trust a Pole to deal square . . . if they owe you anything, they will always pay you back on time." Some folks are known as "just good people" who by choice "keep to themselves." By isolating themselves within the community they neither add nor detract from the neighborly quality of community life and so do not have an effect on the public character of the town.

The only group which does not fall within the purview of the conception of friend and neighbor is the 10 percent of the population that live "in shacks in the hills." The people who live in shacks "can't be trusted"; "they steal you blind"; "if you're friendly to them, they'll take advantage of you"; "if you lend them something you'll never see it again"; "they're bad . . . no good people . . . live like animals." Hence by appropriately extending the social definition to give it a broader base than mutual aid, all groups in the community, except the shack people, fulfill the image of good friend and neighbor. The self-conception then reinforces itself, serves as a model for achievement and adds to the essential appearance of community warmth.

Good Folks and Bad Folks

"Of course, there are some people who just naturally have a dirty mouth. You'll find them anywhere you go and I'd be lying if I said we didn't have a few here." The "dirty mouth" is a person who not only fabricates malicious gossip about his enemies but also wantonly and carelessly spreads his fabrications. He commits the double *faux pas* of being deliberately malicious and of not observing the etiquette of interpersonal relations, and he is perhaps the most despised person in the community.

There are a whole range of personal qualities which are almost unanimously disapproved in Springdale. These are identified in the person

"who holds a grudge . . . who won't ever forget a wrong done to him."

"who can't get along with other people . . . who won't ever try to be friendly and sociable."

"who gives the town a bad name . . . always raising up a ruckus . . . always trying to stir up trouble."

"who trys to be something he isn't . . . the show-off . . . the braggart."

"who thinks he's better than everybody else . . . who thinks he's too good for the town . . . who thinks he's a cut above ordinary folks."

"who is bossy . . . thinks his ideas are always the best . . . tries to run everything . . . wants to be the center of attention all the time without working for it."

"who makes money by cheating people . . . who hasn't made his money honestly . . . you can't figure out where he got all that money."

"whom you can't trust . . . whose word is no good . . . who doesn't do what he says he was going to do . . . who doesn't carry through on anything."

In almost the exact reverse, the qualities of a good member of the community are found in the person who

"forgives and forgets . . . lets bygones be bygones . . . never dredges up the past . . . lets you know that he isn't going to hold it against you."

"is always doing something for the good of the town . . . gives willingly of his time and money . . . supports community projects . . . never shirks when there's work to be done."

"gets along with everybody . . . always has a good word . . . goes out of his way to do a good turn . . . never tries to hurt anybody . . . always has a smile for everybody."

"is just a natural person . . . even if you know he's better than you, he never lets you know it . . . never tries to impress anybody just because he has a little more money . . . acts like an ordinary person."

"always waits his turn . . . is modest . . . will work along with everybody else . . . isn't out for his own glory . . . takes a job and does it well without making a lot of noise."

"worked hard for what he's got . . . deserves every penny he has . . . doesn't come around to collect the first day of the month . . . you know he could be a lot richer."

"stands on his word . . . never has to have it in writing . . . does what he says . . . if he can't do it he says so and if he can he does it . . . always does it on time."

Springdalers affirm that on the whole most people in the community have these qualities. They are the qualities of "average folk" and "we like to think of ourselves as just a little above the average." "Average people can get things done because nobody has any high-blown ideas and they can all work together to make the community a better place to live."

What is interesting about the usual definitions of good and bad people are the types that are excluded entirely. At this level those who go unrecognized, even in the negative statements, are the intellectuals, the bookish and the introverts. In a community that places a high premium on being demonstrably average, friendly and open, the person who appears in public and "doesn't say much" is a difficult character to understand: "he's a good fellow, but you never know what he's thinking." "Book reading and studying all the time," while they have a place, "shouldn't be carried too far . . . you have to keep your feet on the ground, be practical." The intellectual is respected for his education, is admired for his verbal facility and sometimes can provide the right idea, but nevertheless he is suspect and "shouldn't be allowed to get into positions of responsibility." It is apparent that where stereotyped public definitions do not easily fit, non-conformity is still tolerated so long as it does not seriously interfere with the workings of the town.

In the community setting the test case of the toleration and sympathy for non-conformity lies in attitudes toward cranks, psychotics and "odd" personalities: the ex-minister who writes poetry, the hermit who lives in the woods, the woman obsessed with the legal correctness of her husband's will, the spinster who screams at callers, the town moron and the clinical catatonic. Needless to say these represent only a small percentage of the population. The point is that Springdale is able to absorb, protect and care for them; when in the infrequent instance they intrude on the public scene, they are treated with the same sympathy and kindness accorded a child. So long as non-conformity does not interfere with the normal functioning of the town, no price is exacted from the non-conformist. At the worst, the non-conforming types are surrounded by humor. They become local "characters" who add color and interest to the everyday life of the community; because they are odd and different, they are always available as a standard conversational piece. In this way the community demonstrates its kindness and "lives and lets live."

"We're All Equal"

With the exception of a few "old cranks" and "no goods," it is unthinkable for anyone to pass a person on the street without exchanging greetings. Customarily one stops for a moment of conversation to discuss the weather and make inquiries about health; even the newcomer finds others stopping to greet him. The pattern of everyone talking to everyone is especially characteristic when people congregate in groups. Meetings and social gatherings do not begin until greetings have been exchanged all around. The person who feels he is above associating with everyone, as is the case with some newcomers from the city, runs the risk of being regarded a snob, for the taint of snobbishness is most easily acquired by failing to be friendly to everyone.

It is the policy of the Community Club to be open to "everyone, whether dues are paid or not" and hardly a meeting passes without a repetition of this statement. Those who are the leaders of the community take pride in this organization specifically because it excludes no one, and this fact is emphasized time and again in public situations. Wherever they can, community leaders encourage broad participation in all spheres of public life: everyone is urged and invited to attend public meetings and everyone is urged to "vote not as a duty, but as a privilege." The equality at the ballot box of all men, each according to his own conscience, in a community where you know all the candidates personally, where votes can't be bought and where you know the poll-keepers, is the hallmark of equality that underpins all other equality. "Here no man counts more than any other"; this is stated in every affirmation of rural political equality—"if you don't like the rascals, use your vote to kick them out."

The social force of the idea finds its most positive expression in a negative way. The ladies of the book clubs, the most exclusive and limited membership groups in Springdale, find themselves in the ambiguous position of having to be apologetic for their exclusiveness. Because they are select in a community which devalues standoffishness, they are the only groups that are defensive in meeting the rest of the public. To the observer, they explain, "It's not that we want to be exclusive. It's just that sixteen is all you can manage in a book club. If anybody wants to be in a book club, she can start her own, like the Wednesday Group." By the same token they receive a large share of resentment; any number of vulgar expressions refer to this feminine section of the community.

The public ideology of equality has its economic correlates. One must not suppose that inequalities in income and wealth go unnoticed; rather, they are quite closely watched and known in Springdale. However, such differences, as in the image of the frontier community, are not publicly weighed and evaluated as the measure of the man.

In everyday social intercourse it is a social *faux pas* to act as if economic inequalities make a difference. The wealthiest people in town, though they have big homes, live quite simply without servants. The serviceman, the delivery boy and the door-to-door canvasser knock at the front door and, though they may feel somewhat awkward on carpeted floors, are asked to enter even before stating their business. A man who flaunts his wealth, or demands deference because of it, is out of tune with a community whose "upper class" devalues conspicuous consumption and works at honest pursuits. "What makes the difference is not the wealth but the character behind it."

It is not a distortion to say that the good man is the working man and in the public estimation the fact of working transcends, indeed explains, economic differentials; work has its own social day of judgment and the judgment conferred is self-respect and respectability. Work, in the first instance, is the great social equalizer, and the purest form of work which serves as a yardstick for all other work is farm work. By this mechanism the "hard-working poor man" is superior to the "lazy rich man." The quotation marks are advised and indicate the hypotheticalness of the case because in common usage the two, work and wealth, go together. Where they don't it is because of misfortune, catastrophe, bad luck or simply because the man is young and work has not yet had a chance to pay its dividends. But even wealth is the wrong word. Work is rather juxtaposed beside such terms as rich, solvent, well-off; wealth implies more economic differentiation than Springdalers like to think exists in their community. Thus, the measure of a man, for all public social purposes, is the diligence and perseverance with which he pursues his economic ends; the "steady worker," the "good worker," the "hard worker" in contrast to the "fly-by-night schemer," the "band-wagon jumper," and the "johnny-come-lately." For the Springdaler the test case is the vulgar social climber, the person who tries to "get in with the better people" by aping them in dress and possessions which only money can buy. In spite of the social and economic differences visible to the outside observer, the pervading appearance of the community is that of a social equality based on the humanness of rural life.

The Etiquette of Gossip

Like other small rural communities Springdale must face the classic problem of preserving individual privacy in the face of a public ideology which places a high valuation on positive expressions of equalitarianism and neighborliness. The impression of community warmheartedness which is given by the free exchange of public greetings and the easy way "everybody gets along with everybody else" has its counterpart in the absence of privacy implied by the factor of gossip. The observer who has been in the community for a length of time realizes that "everybody isn't really neighborly . . . that some people haven't talked to each other for years . . . that people whom you might think are friends hate each other . . . that there are some people who are just naturally troublemakers . . . that he'd skin his own grandmother for a buck." However, such statements are never made in public situations. The intimate, the negative and the private are spoken in interpersonal situations involving only two or three people. Gossip exists as a separate and hidden layer of community life.

That is why it is at first difficult for the observer to believe the often-repeated statement that "everybody knows everything about everybody else in Springdale," or, as stated otherwise, "in a small town you live in a glass house." It develops that the statements are true only to a degree: while one learns intimate and verifiable details of people's private lives, these never become the subject of open, public discussion.

In the private sphere—at what is commonly regarded as the level of gossip, either malicious or harmless—Springdalers tend to emphasize the negative and competitive qualities of life. One learns about domestic discords, sexual aberrations, family skeletons, ill-gained wealth, feuds, spite fences, black sheep, criminal records and alcoholism. The major preoccupation, however, is reserved for "what he's worth" in the strictly monetary and material meaning of the expression. The image of the sharp trading farmer, the penny-wise homemaker and the thrifty country folk is reflected in reverse in this concern with the state of other people's finances and possessions. All men, from the bartender to the clergyman, are capable of such concern typically expressed as follows:

> "I'd say he's worth at least $30,000. Why the cows and buildings are worth that alone."

> "You'd think a man with his money would give more than $50 to the church."

"The reason he's got so much is because he never spends any, hasn't taken a vacation for thirty years, never contributes a cent to anything."

"There's a man who's got a fortune and you'd never guess it."

"What I couldn't do with his dough."

"The way they spend money, you'd think it was like picking leaves off a tree."

"There's a guy making $2,800 and he's got a new Pontiac."

"Up to his neck in debt and he walks around like he had a million."

"Lend him a cent and you'll never see it again."

"He cleaned up during the war."

"There isn't anything he can't turn into a dollar."

"Figure it out. He's working, his wife's working, they haven't got any kids and they're collecting rent on two houses besides."

"He could be doing well if he stopped drinking."

"He may be taking in more than me, but then he's killing himself doing it."

"If he'd loosen up and be human, this town would be a better place for everybody."

"But, then, I haven't done so bad myself. There's the car, only four years left on the house and two kids through school."

These and similar statements, however, serve the function of enabling a person to calculate his relative financial standing. They are encountered almost everywhere in private gossip, but remain unspoken and hidden in ordinary public situations.

What is interesting about gossip is that in Springdale it seldom hurts anyone. Because it occurs in small temporarily closed circles and concerns those who are not present, the subject of the gossip need never be aware of it. Moreover, the *mores* demand, or better still one should say that it is an iron law of community life, that one not confront the subject of gossip with what is said about him. For this reason, though everyone engages in the practice, no one *has* to learn what things are being said about him. In the rare instance where one hears about gossip about oneself, it comes as a distinct shock "to think that so-and-so could have said that about me."

In a way, then, it is true that everyone knows everything about everyone else but, because of the way the information is learned, it does not ordinarily affect the everyday interpersonal relations of people; in public view even enemies speak to each other. When the victim meets the gossiper, he does not see him as a gossip and the gossiper does not let the privately gained information affect his public gestures; both greet each other in a friendly and neighborly manner and, perhaps, talk about someone else. Because the people of the community have this consideration for other people's feelings ("we like to think of ourselves as considerate and kind, not out to hurt anybody . . . that's one of the main reasons you live in a small town") relationships between people always give the impression of personalness and warmth.

The etiquette of gossip which makes possible the public suppression of the negative and competitive aspects of life has its counterpart in the etiquette of public conversation which always emphasizes the positive. There are thus two channels of communication that serve quite different purposes. In public conversation one hears comments only on the good things about people—"a man who has always done good things for the town"; "a swell guy"; "she's always doing good things for people"; "a person who never asks anything in return." More than this, the level of public conversation always focuses on the collective success of the community and the individual successes of its members. People comment on the success of a charitable drive, on the way a money-raising project "went over the top," on "what a good program it was," on the excellence of the actors' performance. These same themes become the subject of self-congratulatory newspaper articles. When failures occur, when the play "was a flop," as of course must happen from time to time, one senses what is almost a communal conspiracy against any further public mention of it. So too with the successes of individuals—the man who after many years of diligence finally gets a good job, the person who completes a correspondence course, the local girl who gets a college degree, the local boy who makes good in the city, the man who finally succeeds in establishing himself in business, the winner of a contest, the high scorer, the person who has his name in a city newspaper—all such successes are given recognition in conventional conversation and in the press. At the public level all types of success are given public recognition while failure is treated with silence. It is because of the double and separate set of communication channels that negative gossip seldom colors the friendly ethos and the successful mood of the public life of the community.

II

Major Institutional Realities

Chapter 3

———————————◆———————————

The Major Dimensions of Social
and Economic Class

The Meaning of Work, Wealth
and Economic Activities

EQUALITY, industriousness, improvement and optimism, all of which gain meaning and substance through the pursuance of hard work, comprise the central features of the dominant ideology in Springdale. Hard work means more than simply keeping busy, for in order for a man's work to be respected and esteemed it must be directed wholeheartedly to the specific demands of his occupation and other useful ends. The respect attached to hard work, therefore, is given not only to the work as such but also to the goals which the work is designed to fulfill. These goals are not ordinarily short term; they consist of buying a house, setting up a business, raising a family, sending children to college, planning and preparing for self-support in old age or any economic objective which requires the greater part of a lifetime to accomplish and which implies a serious effort at self or family improvement. To achieve full respect a man must pursue his goal with great personal sacrifice to comfort and leisure, which he must postpone to a time in life when economic goals are largely fulfilled. The respect which this hypothetical man receives is enhanced if he is a regular and devoted churchgoer and if it is known or believed that he has money which he himself has made, saved and accumulated in his own lifetime by virtue of his own hard work and the frugality of his wife. If by local standards this man has a large sum of money which he spends in "useful" and not "foolish" ways, he is on the way to becoming the most respected and honored man in the town.

Although, needless to say, few if any men fulfill this standard of respectability, it is the standard by which all men are judged. A calculus exists and is employed by which it is possible to evaluate one man against another with respect to how well or poorly the standard is fulfilled. The chief items in this calculus are, in the order of their importance, hard work, self improvement and money. In any actual evaluation these three items of judgment are inseparable since any specific evaluation is a relatively unconscious act.

Hard work in the ideal pattern means work to the point of physical exhaustion. The farmer working in the heat of summer at the peak of the harvest season from five in the morning when he must milk his cows to late in the evening when he loads his hay by spotlight is given his due respect. The only way the professional man can show that he works hard is by working long hours. Teachers, to receive respect, must spend their time in the school after four o'clock, and must not have secondary occupations and preoccupations. The office light of the lawyer must burn late into the evening; the doctor who takes a vacation is the object of resentment. The businessman thinks little of keeping his store open from ten to twelve hours a day and when he complains that his trade has left for the city supermarket, he is told to keep his store open longer. Industrial work with its regulated work day and work week is viewed as offering a man little basis for respect except in combination with other types of activity.

Self-improvement, according to the ideal pattern, is less connected with any idea of self-fulfillment than it is with the idea of self-enhancement or striving for the rewards offered by society. Self-improvement is taken at its simplest level to refer to the acquisition of new skills and new possessions or to the development and further elaboration of old ones. In addition to the various schemes people undertake to improve themselves personally, such as extension and correspondence courses and the wide range of "how to" and "self-improvement" literature, a man basically improves himself by maintaining an expansive economic orientation. That is, activity which is directed at contributing to the enhancement of possessions (paying off the mortgage, adding acreage, increasing proprietary equity) contributes most directly to self-improvement.

Through the judicious manipulation and exercise of a combination of hard work and self-improvement a man improves his social position. Literally he mobilizes all his resources for a chance to move upward in the social estimation of others. His position at any given time is most easily, although by no means exclusively, measured by money. People who seem to be able to make money are known simply as "moneymakers" and for this group there is easy envy and resentment. These who are known as "spenders" become targets of a moderate derision which borders on pity; and should economic calamity befall the spender he is assumed to have received his logical and inevitable reward. "Pennywatchers" are the cautious and the miserly. They are not altogether the object of disdain or laughter, for it is always remembered that "pennies make dollars." Lastly, there are the reliefers and the "bums" who are the degraded and declassed, with neither money nor the willingness to work—with no possibility, even by their own admission, for self-respect.

In reality, the above-stated public ideology is not held equally by all segments of the population of Springdale. It is, however, the publicly stated ideology and the one with the oldest and most respected tradition. Its particular locus is the middle class, which in a small town represents a broad and differentiated segment of the population.

There are other ideologies held and acted out either voluntarily or involuntarily by other groups of people in the community. Since ideologies concerning work, wealth and economic activities are so central to the way of life of an individual, individuals and groups who differ from the central and dominant ideology in a similar way exhibit entirely different styles of living both from each other and from the publicly dominant ideology. Where such differences in styles of living are exhibited, we use them to construct classes and on this basis distinguish one class from another.[1]

---

[1] By the word "class" the authors mean typical configurations of social and economic behavior which make it possible to distinguish groups of individuals from each other. That is, classes are identified

In Springdale it is possible to identify five class groups, two of which contain distinct sub-groups. These are: (1) The middle class, made up of independent entrepreneurs (13 percent),[2] prosperous farmers (25 percent), and professionals and skilled industrial workers (9 percent); (2) the marginal middle class made up of aspiring investors (10 percent), economically and socially immobile ritualists (10 percent), and psychological idiosyncratics (2 percent); (3) traditional farmers (10 percent); (4) "old aristocrats" (1 percent); and (5) shack people (10 percent).

The Classes

THE MIDDLE CLASS

Independent Entrepreneurs. The businessmen (all small in Springdale) are largely those whose business constitutes their sole source of income. The range of businesses includes grocery stores, restaurants, filling stations, household appliances, farm implements, feed mills, a hardware store, a television shop and so forth. In an environment with a limited market, competition characteristically takes two forms: keeping the business establishment open for long hours, and the elaboration of overlapping inventories from store to store.

---

in terms of productive activity, patterns of consumption and other forms of social and economic behavior. The term does not necessarily imply a recognition of "belonging together" by the members of the class, though in some cases such a recognition may exist. Nor does it imply a single unidimensional rating scale within which all individuals fall, since it is an observation of the authors that whole groups of individuals simply have no social existence for other individuals, even in the small rural community with which we are concerned. In addition, the class grouping does not necessarily imply a rating according to prestige, status or honor since, again, it has been the observation of the authors that there is no common social prestige scale which includes all other individuals from the point of view of any particular individual. In short, the word "class" is used to distinguish particular groups of individuals who exhibit specified social and economic life styles. Where prestige, social status and social recognition are used in this presentation, they will be described as specifically applicable to and between given groups and individuals.

[2] This and the following percentages refer to the approximate percentage of households out of a total of 750 which fall in each group. The total adds up to 99 percent because 1 percent of the sample was unclassifiable.

A single operator in cooperation with his wife or another member of the family typically keeps his business open from ten to twelve hours daily.[3] The threat of buying elsewhere—in neighboring city stores—where prices may be cheaper and where service is more efficient is held over the merchant's head.

In response to his predicament the businessman engages in fewer and fewer risk ventures. He is geared to the maximum utilization of his existing facilities, eschews measures which would moder ize his plant at capital expense and, instead, tries to develop a clientele whose loyalty is based on personal considerations. He conducts his business in an atmosphere of scarcity; he shies away from products which do not have an established market, fears large inventories and avoids such merchandizing methods as "loss leaders."

The Better Business Bureau attempts to protect the limited market to which its members appeal. Transient peddlers and traders are resented and every effort is made to control their activities through licensing and other restrictive measures.

Although local competition is rigorous, the source of greatest competition lies in retail outlets in nearby cities and the surrounding region. As these large centers of retail distribution become more elaborate and efficient, the local merchant loses a greater share of the trade of the mobile segments of the population. His trade becomes more limited to the aged, the loyal, the infirm and those who must buy on credit.

The general business conditions of the merchant are largely determined by forces outside his control. The goods and commodities which he sells are provided by mass distributors who also set price scales. In the case of many commodities, profit margins are specified and, in the case of franchise businesses, other business practices as well are more or less rigidly specified.

These circumstances lead the small businessman to a nonexpansive attitude toward his enterprise. Only six out of

[3] The psychological disposition to work is an important variable in distinguishing the life styles of the various classes. See Max Weber, *The Protestant Ethic and the Spirit of Capitalism*, N.Y., 1948.

approximately fifty businessmen are in process of investing capital. However, these are all new businessmen whose investment represents necessary expenditures toward establishing the business rather than a policy of continuous reinvestment and expansion. In the absence of efforts directed toward increasing his profits by increased capital investments and increased inventories (a more favorable merchandizing climate), he directs his efforts at a niggardly cutting of costs. This ideology is illustrated by the folklore of the business community which typically attributes the cause of local business failures to excessive spending for consumption and equipment, and to the excessive utilization of potential labor for unprofitable leisure-time pursuits.

The businessman places a high value on the retention of money in the form of cash deposited in the bank or, as in some cases, hidden on his premises in a cigar box or the like. When he reaches a certain level of accumulation, he invests savings in real property or in mortgages on real property. Securities, bonds and the like are suspected where tangible property is not immediately visible.

The individual businessman is apt to be torn between maintaining the utmost secrecy about his net worth and a desire to boast about his financial well-being and success. In part he is afraid to let the community know how "rich he is," in the fear that jealousies aroused will affect his business; simultaneously, he wants to collect the esteem which he feels is his due.

In their relations with each other, businessmen are highly suspicious and distrustful. They scrutinize each other's business activities and practices so as to be able constantly to evaluate each other's standing and competition. All this is done with a minimum of social contact; businessmen do not socialize much with each other or with the rest of the community.

Their participation in community affairs is largely limited to supporting a great number of organizations without being active in any of them. The private life of the family tends to take place in the semi-public environment of the business premises, a fact which is frequently made possible by the absence of children (there is a high frequency of single child families).

The only businessmen who deviate in any significant sense from this description are those involved in farm-connected businesses, grain and farm machinery sales and milling operations. Since their business chances are closely linked to the farm economy, they along with the successful farmers exhibit quite different social characteristics.

Rational Farmers. "Rational farmers" are those who conceive of and work at farming as a business. Cost, including labor and capital costs, are carefully calculated and related to the prices received, and costs and energy are distributed in such a way as to produce the maximum yield. Rationality rather than sentiment or tradition govern the work and mentality of rational farmers. The rationally operated farm requires at a minimum fifteen to twenty head of milking stock and is geared to maximum productivity. Each increase in size of herd (up to eighty head in Springdale) requires the farmer to recalculate all variables that enter into production efficiency. That is, the farmer must recalculate his total cost/gross income ratio as related to net income. The significant variables in this economic calculus are price levels of milk, additional labor and machinery required, the cost of building materials (he builds his own buildings) and additional feed costs, since in Springdale it is relatively difficult to expand land holdings. Fifty milking cows and the machinery, land and buildings required to support them have a total capital valuation ranging from $40,000 to $60,000 at price levels in 1953. Obviously, few independent farmers possess either the capital or the credit standing to enter farming at this level. Typically the farmer enters his enterprise at a much lower level of capital investment and over a period of time "builds his farm up." The last ten years of agricultural prosperity have provided an ideal environment for the expansion of farm enterprise. Indeed, many of the farmers prosperous at the time of this study entered farming in Springdale within the last ten to fifteen years, while the rest include practically all the Polish farmers who entered the community thirty years ago.

It is the distinctive and typical feature of these farmers that they return their profits into the expansion of their enterprise. They do not save for the purpose of saving. Instead, they save for the purpose of reinvestment, i.e., modernization of equipment and plant expansion.

The farmer gears his enterprise to the production of fluid milk which is marketed in the New York Metropolitan Milk Marketing Area, a market controlled by law by a market administrator. He can determine his income from milk (the milk check) by his volume of production and its butter fat content, the only two variables in the price structure which he is able to control directly. Depending on the price structure and on his calculation of his position in relation to it, the farmer may deliberately decide to increase volume at the expense of butter fat content (poorer feed) or vice versa; or he may decide to decrease milk production by selling stock and investing feed in pigs. These suggest the level at which alternatives are open to him.

The rational farmer offsets his position of vulnerability and lack of power in relation to the determination of prices by concentrating on the reduction of production costs. However, his cost cutting is not done at the expense of production efficiency; he cannot skimp on commercial fertilizers or machinery replacement and it is to his perceived advantage to install labor-saving devices. The farmer cuts his costs by making the most efficient use of his own and his family's labor. In so doing, the style of living of the family of the rational farmer is linked to the productive enterprise.

The labor of children, especially boys, is highly valued and utilized. A child of seven or eight years is capable of operating a tractor in the organized work routine required for hay loading. A son in high school can be calculated as half-time labor—a farmer may plan an expansion program in coordination with the life cycle of his children. The farmer's wife, it is observed in Springdale, is capable of making or breaking a successful farm operation by whether she works in the barn, the fields or garden at critical moments and in critical seasons. The family as a productive unit has extensions into the home. Investments which will enhance the productive efficiency of the kitchen—modern appliances, modern kitchen plans, various labor saving devices—are viewed on almost the same plane as investing in a new manure spreader. It is only after the productive plant has been expanded and the kitchen modernized that the external beautification and internal decoration of the farm home takes place. It is a commonplace to see shabby or neat but extremely modest farm dwellings attached to large-scale and prosperous farm enterprises. Personal or luxury consumption gives way to the investment of money in avenues which will yield further returns through production efficiency and the efficient utilization of labor. The emphasis on work and efficiency, using the clock as a standard, leaves little scope for rituals or ceremonials in the farmer's style of work. Social activities and participation, except in churches, play no or only a minor part in his life. At best, for him, such activities are a "waste of time."

The class position of the farmer relative to other segments of the middle class is most directly dependent on price structures and markets whose dynamics are determined in the society at large. Alterations in these dynamics affect him immediately and force him to respond to the alterations in both the operation of his business and his style of living. Within this dependence, he gears his style of living to economic mobility—economic expansiveness and hard work—but he achieves his mobility from a position of economic independence of the local community in which he lives.

Professionals and Skilled Industrial Workers. Professionals, quasi-professionals, managers and skilled industrial workers, to be sure, do not constitute a class entity with a common social consciousness but, nevertheless, they exhibit a uniform and consistent style of living. Their central characteristic is their status as employees who have fixed ceilings on their incomes. Income is derived from the sale of professional services or a fixed number of hours of labor. The arbitrary fixing of the length of the work day by forces outside the individual's control makes this group the leisured section of the middle class. The manner in which this leisure time is allocated and expended separates them from the marginal middle class to be discussed below.

Their level of fixed income effectively prevents the accumulation of savings for investment purposes. Characteristically, total income is devoted to consumption purposes. In the absence of opportunities for capital expansion and the full utilization of labor, the central feature of their style of living may be described as a problem in consumption choices. The opportunity to spend thought and study in the expenditure of income is provided by the leisure available to them.

In rough order of priorities, income is devoted to home ownership, automobile ownership, children, home improvements and home decoration. Home ownership occupies a central place because it is viewed as a type of security and as the accumulation of equity. The gradual accumulation of equity over the course of a lifetime constitutes a major psychological substitute for an expansionist psychology.

The car, the home and children are the main outlets for the expression of consumption and serve as a common basis for social competition, a fact which in this sense at least gives the group a psychological unity, although they may have little in common occupationally. They can and do, in their social intercourse, talk at length about consumption problems—comparing car models, furniture, rugs, color combinations, the dress and achievements of children, etc., etc.

Children, whatever other gratifications they may serve, are an important part of a *social* mobility calculus. Intellectual and competitive ability in school are highly esteemed, for the child is being groomed for higher education which will lead to a professional or at least a white-collar career. All manner of personal achievement is emphasized and rewarded in the hope that achievement will become a firmly fixed motive in the child. In a real sense parents project their own mobility strivings onto their children and in so doing perhaps minimize the conflicts that could arise from a conscious or unconscious perception of the limits placed on their own economic mobility.

Children, however, do not constitute a completely adequate substitute for mobility since they are at best a vicarious substitute and subliminally, at least, are recognized as such. The indirect drive for mobility has its corollary in a direct drive for security. In the case of the teacher, it is a tenure appointment; for the industrial worker, it is employment in a stable industry and the careful guardianship of his seniority; for other types of professionals, it is maintaining good personal relations with their professional superiors; for the fee-professional, it is the protection of a clientele. In all instances retirement plans, unemployment insurance, sickness benefits and all types of personal and medical insurance programs assume a central importance. Major decisions in the life plan are made with respect to assuring the possession of such deferred-gratification contractual arrangements.

Taxation on income, contrary to the practice with farmers and businessmen, is automatically withheld by the employer and this system is passively accepted as a condition for receiving income. Their focus of attention is placed on the possibility of a tax rebate which, when received, is viewed as a windfall and stands as a symbol of what is perhaps the major degree of freedom in an otherwise totally allocated income. Viewed as unexpected income, it can be spent without regard to fixed plan on an "expensive night out," a weekend in New York city or as a down payment on a household appliance. This stylization of attitude toward taxes is not found in any other group.

Like the businessmen and farmers, the fee professionals experience no technical ceiling on the utilization of labor. Their income is determined by the number of clients they are willing or able to accommodate. Characteristically, however, they make a conscious decision to underemploy themselves. That is, a high value is placed upon leisure-time activities.

Their self-determination of their work/leisure ratio to accommodate for leisure is a decision which partly reveals their psychological orientation to economic mobility.

Teachers are accorded prestige because of the formal schooling they have completed, but their salary schedules in a small town are low. In Springdale their average salary is between $3,000 and $3,400, hardly sufficient to attain the level of consumption expected of them by themselves and by others. Typically this income is supplemented by secondary jobs. Due to the teachers' direct dependence on locally controlled resources (the attitude of the town that teachers are hirelings), the acquisition of capital holdings, except for a house (after tenure has been granted) and a car, arouses the hostility of other groups in the community. Hence the teacher is a total consumer not only by virtue of his income level but also by virtue of the purely social pressures which play upon him in the local community.

The leisure available to these middle-class segments enables them to provide the active support for many of the community's organizations. Whether or not they hold offices, they plan and execute most of the community's non-political organizational life and it is in this context that the various occupational types who make up this class have an opportunity to meet. However, this does not mean that all participate equally in community organizations since level of activity is open to individual choice. It is here that industrial workers are socially differentiated. Because they work outside the community and because many live in the open countryside, they are relatively socially invisible to the rest of the community. By self-selection, however, some of them through social, religious and organizational activities establish ties within the community. When these ties occur they connect these industrial participators with the professional group and not with the businessmen or farmers.

The social status of the professionals is based only partly on their education. All of the professionals gain status from the real or imputed connections which they are believed to have with the institutions and tastes of the outside society. The "college bred" are the culture carriers of the town and adhere to standards of taste and consumption which are not indigenous. Lawyers, teachers, ministers, etc., mediate between local institutions and those in the mass society to which they are connected. They are the functionaries who run the town. It is these facts, irrespective of size and source of income, which support their social position in the community.

The middle class more than any other class is concerned with social activities. Their concern with social activity is reflected in the one exclusive activity which is related to pretensions of social superiority—the book clubs. The book clubs are quite unique in Springdale because there is a definite implication that the Monday Club is superior to the Tuesday Club, which in turn is superior to the Wednesday Club, and all three by implication are superior, at least culturally, to everyone else. At the same time the more dominant ideology of social equality, defined in part as anti-snobbishness, places the would-be snobs on the defensive and causes them to be resented by everyone else in the community, including members of the economically and politically more powerful classes. All of the book club *social aspirants* are drawn from the middle class, but specifically they are drawn from the wives of professionals and skilled workers and to a lesser extent from the wives of businessmen. Within the group of aspirants, ratings of superiority are made primarily on the basis of length of residence in the community. It is for this reason that the members of the Monday Club include the wives of the old aristocratic families. No wives of any rational farmers, the economically most successful group in the community, are members of book clubs. Moreover, since membership is restricted, not all wives of even the preferred segments of the middle class are members, though there are many who would like to be. Book club membership serves to distinguish "social" status and prestige differences among middle-class women.

Although such *social* class does exist in the community, the numbers involved are relatively small and their importance is diminished by the public ideology of equality. This, however, does not mean that class is unimportant. Class, defined as differences in life styles rather than as differences in social snobbery, is all-important. In fact it is so important that to consider class only as social snobbery would grossly underestimate the importance of class in the community, particularly as it affects the dynamics of community life.

THE MARGINAL MIDDLE CLASS

Surrounding the middle class proper are an equally large number of individuals who can be described as only marginal to the middle class. That is, their aspirations and behavior are oriented to one of the middle-class patterns described above, though, for reasons described below, they do not fully exhibit the life styles of the segments of the middle class. In this respect they are not a homogeneous group, but their differences demonstrate the polarization of middle-class life styles.

Aspiring Investors. These are families who are *in process* of attempting to establish an economic basis in private business or independent farming. Typically their economic basis is rooted in some type of relatively steady, semi-skilled or unskilled job—factory work, service occupations, manual labor or white-collar clerical work. Most frequently the husband holds a full-time job while the wife manages the business or farm in his absence.

However, irrespective of such efforts, these part-time business or farming ventures are marginal because the aspiring investor has insufficient capital, is inexperienced, lacks time or is unable to use successfully proved business and farming techniques. They compete with established business for a limited market which prefers to deal with proved businesses with good business reputations. Or, as farmers, they compete in a highly competitive commodity market which rewards efficient production. Slight downward fluctuations in consumer buying or farm prices have an immediate negative effect on their business chances. They are the first to be forced out of business in a declining market.

Family life is organized around making the business a success; work knows no limits and a portion of job income is used for capital investment—truck, livestock, equipment, etc. Immediate consumption wishes are deferred and social participation is devalued.

This group enjoys a certain degree of prestige and deference from the *middle-class businessmen*. Their affirmation of the middle-class virtues of hard work, industriousness and frugality calls forth an emotional reaction of respect from the businessmen, who see such efforts as possibly leading to success and fulfillment. The prosperous farmers tend to laugh at the clumsy, inefficient efforts they put forth and clearly see the extent of their business vulnerability, even though a high proportion of these successful farmers arrived in this direction themselves, perhaps even under similar market conditions.

As individuals they may go in one of two directions. A very small number may successfully gain entry to the business or farm segments of the middle class, and these represent living evidence of the conceivability of achieving the middle-class status. The great proportion do not. Instead, their style of living becomes based on a perpetual attempt to achieve the goal without ever decisively reaching it.

Hard-working Consumers. Occupationally this group pursues a great variety of types of wage work (factory, service, manual) or commission selling (specialized merchandizing of specialized products). Typically, the husband and wife both work at full-time jobs, a fact which assures a secure income and set hours, and permits the planning of other segments of family living and social activities along fixed and predictable lines.

The work and the consequent organization of family living which it entails assures an income permitting a desired level of consumption which includes fixed home mortgage costs and monthly payments on an automobile, kitchen appliances and a television set, recreation, membership dues, etc. Living standards are routinized to a level of income which requires multiple employment, but since all income is derived from work, ceilings on mobility are clearly seen.

This is a ritualization of the middle-class style as seen in the externals of consumption and social participation rather than savings or business investment. It is an affirmation of middle-class respectability achieved by the over-exploitation of physical resources in a direct effort to maintain "standards." This group is different from the middle-class professionals and skilled workers only in degree, but the difference in degree is sufficient to make them different in kind.

Economically and Socially Immobile Ritualists. Occupationally this group is similar to the above, but for reasons of lack of physical stamina or motivation they are not engaged in multiple employments. Yet in a fumbling way they attempt to emulate the middle class.

Houses are well kept, lawns are weedless and laundry is white. There is a pride in modest property which provides an outlet for individual expression, and this largely represents the limits of the social horizon. Religious participation is taken seriously, but is expressed in the socially inferior denomination, while social participation, usually segregated by sex, does not follow any middle-class pattern.

Their style of living represents a rejection of hard work and social mobility and results in a modest but respectable middle-class consumption pattern. The various elements of respectability, as defined in the small rural community—neatness, morality, sobriety—are detached from economic behavior and take on a central and autonomous importance.

Psychological Idiosyncratics. Their occupations are similar to the above and, again, there is only one job per family. Although they maintain a modest standard of consumption they do not obviously and publicly fulfill the respectability standards of neatness, morality and sobriety in any significant psychological sense. Their outstanding characteristic is the private or personal way in which they find an outlet, either as individuals or as families, for psychological expression. Effort outside of work is directed to activities which have individual and private meanings that lead to their social isolation. For instance, one such person keeps baseball records in great detail on all major league baseball players who have been active for the past fifteen years. Another owns a horse and a pony which he keeps less for the purpose of riding than for grooming, corraling, feeding and petting. Still another keeps innumerable pets and makes bird houses, all identical, which he has no intention of selling. Such activities tend to be compulsive and form the core around which life is patterned.

On the whole the marginal middle class, except for the idiosyncratic segment, is a group of serious "church people." Aside from its meaning as a religious experience, attendance at the Sunday morning service is an artifice of respectability, yet non-attendance could easily lead to feelings of guilt. Active participation in community organizations tends to be limited to one organization at most, largely because the work load or other domestic and property duties prevents broader participation. They may mix socially in the P.T.A. and other school events in which there is a common basis of interest arising from children, but on the whole the American Legion and the fire companies tend to exist for them. Their mode of participation itself tends to reflect the stabilization of their style of living at a level marginal to the middle class. Moreover, they exclude themselves from middle-class acceptance by their pattern of "sociability." Spouses do not act as a "social team"; characteristically the husband belongs to men's organizations and associates with select cronies. The wife works or is simply a housewife and cares for children.

The various segments of this group realize, according to their pattern, that hard work, savings and respectability are important and that it is through the exercise of these virtues that a middle-class status can be achieved. But simultaneously they realize, at least subliminally, that there are limits to achieving the middle-class goal. As a consequence of this recognition, they endeavor to achieve this goal by grasping one or another or a combination of the various elements that make up the middle-class ideology. This results in a dual psychology: their desperate attempt to achieve their goal is caused by their awareness of their position, and this awareness results in a compulsive affirmation of the select segment of the middle-class pattern which gives meaning to their social existence.

THE "OLD ARISTOCRACY"

This is not the "upper class" of Springdale. It is a group of about ten families who are a vestige of a former business and commercial elite which fifty or seventy-five years ago was an upper class. On the basis of historical and genealogical factors, these few families occupy the highest prestige positions in the community. Their ancestors are remembered as the founders of both the community and its most respected institutions, particularly the churches and the bank.

The prestige which they possess is partly rooted in the economic success and accumulated wealth of their ancestors. For it is on the basis of inherited wealth that they have been able to maintain the appurtenances necessary to respectability. Their inherited wealth is supplemented by incomes, usually small, from a variety of occupations, including the operation of the traditional family business, small and frequently deviant type farming operations on the "old homestead," or by holding poorly remunerated semi-public jobs such as a clerkship in the bank. Their inherited wealth exists in the form of a home, the ownership of securities and various types of annuities. Due to their limited current incomes in relation to high current prices and to the ravages of the depression, their economic history is characterized by a slow and gradual depletion of capital reserves.

Almost irrespective of the current value of the legacy left them, they base their style of living on a scarcity outlook. Modern appliances, modern modes of interior decoration and new cars tend to be absent. Instead, a great emphasis is placed upon the preservation of the old homestead—in "keeping it up," but not necessarily modernizing it. The home is the repository of family heirlooms, antique furniture and the family Bible, which records the genealogical connections of illustrious ancestors. Its style of architecture and its contents stand as symbols of class identification recognized and supported by the professional segment of the middle class, which places a high value on and attempts to emulate this segment of their life style by acquiring similar type houses and furnishings (antiques). The old families serve to emphasize the symbols of continuity and the degree of "Americanization" of the town.

Characteristically they seclude themselves from the rest of the community. They do not participate in community affairs or activities to any significant degree. Church participation is at a minimum and is reduced to attendance at Christmas and Easter services. Their personal associations tend to be limited to other individuals within their own group; they do not associate on a broad basis but rather, on the basis of old ties, limit their friendships and acquaintanceships to individuals whose social backgrounds are similar to their own. By their social seclusion and their abdication of positions of prominence in community affairs, they neither possess power nor influence the daily course of community affairs.

TRADITIONAL FARMERS

Traditional farmers have been by-passed by the social and economic changes of the past twenty years. For them farming is a way of life to be practiced in all its ceremonial and ritual complexity. They exist as an anachronism on the modern scene.

Even though they have shifted to dairy farming within the past fifteen or twenty years, they have done so on a small scale. Some, for sentimental reasons or out of habit, may still "put in" hay or buckwheat or view their maple trees as an important source of income, but these are secondary crops. Typically they have between ten to fifteen milking cows, one of which may be kept for sentimental reasons, or between 400 and 800 laying hens along with a collection of "show" chickens. These farmers do not have secondary jobs.

Capital investments are kept low by not investing in modernization and mechanization. Machinery is apt to be second-hand and limited in quantity (a tractor and one or two accessories) and usually includes a few pieces which have been in use for 30 or 40 years. Stock and storage buildings are unimproved and by their design require the inefficient utilization of labor in the work process. In short, the traditional farmer manages to survive by cost cutting rather than by increased capital investment, a process which requires full but inefficient utilization of labor.

This group represents a closed frontier psychology—a psychological inability or unwillingness to adapt to the requirements necessary to seize opportunity—which results partly from following an older tradition of family farming and partly from the psychological impact of the depression. They survived the depression only because they were able to cut costs, expenditures and personal consumption to a minimum, and they have since become habituated to this method of farming.

The closed frontier psychology of this group permeates other aspects of their style of living. The family tends to become a social enclave which provides its own social stimulation. Education for children is deemphasized; instead, children are viewed as a valuable source of labor and the inheritors of the farm. Where there are many children, some may migrate to surrounding cities for unskilled jobs only to return at frequent intervals during periods of unemployment or between jobs. Consumption within the family tends to be limited to the necessities of life; modern manufactured products are absent and little emphasis is placed upon personal adornment.

By and large this group tends to be socially isolated from the rest of the community. A few may maintain a traditional connection with organizations such as a church or the Grange or they may maintain social contacts with family friends of long standing. Their family names and their place of residence are known by many who would find it difficult to recall when they last saw them.

Interestingly, many of the prosperous farmers envy their seeming independence from the economic forces of modern society. Their low fixed operating costs and their marginal consumption standards make them almost invulnerable to fluctuations in the price structure; by their method of operation and their style of living they have immunized themselves against violent upheavals in the market. This the prosperous farmer idealizes as the fulfillment of "old fashioned freedom" and independence. Indeed, in periods of high prosperity their formula brings a relatively high return on their labor while their low costs act as a form of insurance against dropping prices. Hence, they avert the rational farmer's central problem of the cost/price squeeze in a period of declining prices and so serve as an object of envy.

THE SHACK PEOPLE

Shack people represent a relatively wide range of incomes —$1,500 to as high as $3,500 per year—but irrespective of their income they are the object of universal derision in Springdale, a declassed group. By the style of their dwelling —the jerry-built shack, the converted barn, the abandoned tenant house—they implicitly reject the whole complex of middle-class life styles. In the status evaluation made of them by others in the community, it matters little whether they consciously reject the middle-class patterns or whether they simply fail to understand the importance of housing styles.

The range of occupations includes unskilled factory work, all types of unskilled manual labor and farm labor. The rate of job turnover is apt to be high, due to dissatisfaction on the employer's part, quarrels with co-workers or boredom with the work as such. In some instances their work is apt to be seasonal, making for regular periods of unemployment, or they may choose to be unemployed for portions of the year when the weather is suitable for hunting and fishing. In other cases the wage-earner may be permanently adjusted to a state of semi-permanent unemployment due to invalidism, alchoholism or lack of work incentive.

Irrespective of source of income there is usually a great variation in family income from year to year. As a consequence of this variability in income, the shack people do not plan consumption in long-range terms and it is this fact which shapes their daily living as well as family organization. Income tends to be spent on immediate needs as defined by individual tastes. A high proportion of income may be spent on recreation, sporting equipment or some object of personal or home adornment which momentarily captures their fancy. Even where income is technically adequate, no economic plans are laid for future contingencies such as ill health and security, nor is consideration apt to be given to such matters in job selection.

A multitude of family arrangements exist which have the frequent common characteristic of being composed of a large number of individuals. Roughly speaking, two modal types of what might be termed "composite" families occur. On the one hand there is the family consisting of the father, mother, children and one or more relatives (grandparents, uncles, informally adopted children) who live together on a relatively permanent basis. On the other hand there is the family consisting of a shifting group of related individuals which at times includes transient members like uncles, married daughters with children, etc. The family, like consumption, represents an accommodation to immediate circumstances.

The shack people are largely segregated from the rest of the community and, except for friendship circles comprising two or three such families, they are largely segregated from each other. They do not participate in community affairs at any level, including voting. They live on the social fringe of the community and, by the perhaps unconscious choice of other groups, they are neither totally visible nor totally invisible. In the course of ordinary activities and social events in the village, there appears to be tacit agreement not to recognize or mention their existence. On the other hand, they are accepted as social realities when it is necessary to invoke an absolute negative basis for social comparison. Their social function, whatever else it may be, for the other classes is to serve as a "baseline" against which individuals in other groups can make favorable comparisons of themselves. Hence any other group is in a position to justify its life style and to receive psychological gratifications from making such an invidious comparison.

The Social and Economic Meaning of Class

The expanding farmers embody most fully the stereotype of the successful entrepreneur. By emphasizing hard work and savings for the purpose of reinvestment and expansion and accordingly by deemphasizing luxury, personal consumption and idleness and by, furthermore, adjusting their economic calculations to the controlled market, they have found a formula which has given them success. Their success in these operations and the high valuation of their holdings give them a powerful position in the community.

The shack class represents the other extreme of deemphasizing work and savings in favor of immediate consumption and gratification. Socially, the shack people represent the residual scrapheap of the competitive economic process, individuals who have been unwilling or incapable of meeting the demands of social and economic competition. They are the degraded, declassed element whose social existence is noticed by other groups only when a negative image of comparison is needed.

The old aristocracy are noted neither for wealth (though it may have existed in the past), consumption nor an expansionist attitude. Their dominant behavior patterns are centered on the hoarding of funds accumulated in the past and on the use of these funds for consumption purposes (though in this case consumption is important only because other economic functions are almost entirely non-existent). Thus, their incongruent position of holding prestige without power or wealth can be understood only in terms of ceremonial functions; economically and politically they are a threat to no one. Occupationally they hold such ceremonial and symbolic positions as bank clerk. Their social existence confers a sense of continuity to a non-expanding town which is as a whole as committed to the past as it is to the present and the future. The life styles of its members, in terms of architecture and heirlooms, are viewed as ideal consumption patterns by aspiring middle-class professionals and have the legitimacy of acceptance in the society at large.

For the foreign groups—a scattering of Finns, Italians, Germans, and especially the Polish farmers—the acceptance of the old aristocracy represents an attachment to the symbols of America, though the expansive behavior of the Polish farmers is perhaps more representative of the American tradition. However, the anxieties about being "foreigners" in a predominantly "American" community compels them as a group to embrace those elements which appear to them to be "really" American. The foreign groups fall short of being "socialized" to American non-economic patterns (language, associational patterns and separate lodges) and, as a consequence of this, their preoccupation with establishing their American basis results in the elevation to a position of great importance of those symbols which serve the purpose, and for them no other purpose, of defining "Americanism." Thus, the old families and the symbols which surround them serve this psychological and ceremonial function even when there is no social intercourse between the "deferent" group and the object of deference, and where the socially esteemed living ancestors wield no effective power in the community. In this manner the declining dominant class of the nineteenth century is accepted.

Neither the businessmen nor the traditional farmers invest expansion capital, and furthermore their deemphasis of business capital investments of any kind reflects a psychology of scarcity-mindedness. The non-expanding traditional farmers rationalize their emphasis on work rather than on investment by gearing their operations to possible declines in farm prices, wherein their low absolute, but not unit, costs put them in a favorable position for survival. The businessmen prefer accumulation to investment; that is, surplus funds are invested in highly liquid assets, particularly local real estate, which places them in a relatively advantageous position *vis à vis* deflationary movements, but in a disadvantageous position in a rising market and in an expanding economy.

In the case of the traditional farmers their psychological

orientation to work, savings and investment represents a traditional attitude which was reinforced by the depression of the Thirties. In carrying out such an approach, they were then unwilling or unable to take advantage of the price rises and agricultural expansion in the war and postwar period, a fact which differentiates them from the expanding farmers who were able to and did take advantage of price rises, expanding markets and federal agricultural policies.

The lack of expansion on the part of businessmen is conditioned by the existence of more efficient competition of more efficient out-of-town chain stores, super markets and large retail markets. In fact, their scarcity orientation reflects an attempt to deal with these long-term institutional trends.

Each of the segments of the marginal middle class exhibits a distinct set of characteristics. The aspiring investors affirm the virtues of work and emphasize investment, but due to high capital requirements or lack of sufficient local business, only a small minority achieve the status of full-time businessman or farmer. The multiple jobs and the investment of job income represents a ritualized effort to attain the status of businessman or farmer, when for the most part, due to larger institutional trends, the achievement is not possible. This failure leads to the point where work becomes an autonomous function and becomes meaningful in and of itself. It means that the hard-worker can affirm his respectability and his moral superiority, particularly over the shack people. Moreover, his efforts are recognized as being valuable in and of themselves by other hard workers in the community. The businessmen especially hold this group in high regard, though the expanding and successful farmers are apt to have only disdain for their awkward ways.

The hard-working consumers, while emphasizing the work ritual, emulate the middle-class professionals in their emphasis on stylized forms of consumption. The emphasis on work and having two jobs is only secondarily an affirmation of the work ethic, and much more the attempt to secure the wherewithal to accumulate the consumption items necessary to exhibit the preferred style of life.

The economically and socially immobile reject mobility and with it the work ideology, since they hold only one job. They retreat to modest but respectable middle-class consumption patterns. They emphasize neatness, sobriety and morality, the chief elements of respectability, as values to be especially highly estimated and as values which distinguish them decidedly from the *lumpen-proletariat*, the shack people.

The psychological idiosyncratics represent a category of disparate individuality and include individuals who have no socially stylized style of living. They exhibit consumption patterns similar to those of the socially and economically immobile group, but rely on personal idiosyncrasies to find a meaningful place for themselves and their lives. Thus their private hobbies are a means to fulfilling a social gap caused by their self-imposed isolation from the community.

The professional and skilled working class deemphasize work (because of fixed hours or because of voluntary under-maximum employment) and devalue savings except as a residual category. As a substitute for these elements, stylized consumption has become a source of prestige. This includes stylized taste, leisure, child-rearing, homemaking and vacations. In behaving in this manner, the professional group introduces new and alien elements into the town. Social participation and private life become a substitute for economic advancement. These factors are perhaps best explained by the fact that members of these groups perceive definite income ceilings. Their social and consumption behavior implies a recognition of these ceilings and an attempt to find alternative sources for a meaningful existence.

It is possible to isolate four variables which comprehend the profusion of life styles and life plans exhibited in Springdale. These variables are investment and reinvestment, hoarding, consumption and work. The differential emphasis given to these variables distinguishes the five classes and the subdivisions of the middle and marginal middle classes and provides a basis for examining the social and economic components of class distinctions.

The investment ideology implies almost all of the original tenets of the Protestant Ethic: the affirmation of work, saving, investment, limited personal consumption, optimism and expansiveness. Its sole representatives in Springdale are the expanding farmers. The aspiring investors of the marginal middle class act out these tenets but only in a ritualistic way since their economic position does not permit their realization; their investment represents the investment of non-business income and does not lead to expansion and reinvestment.

The hoarding ideology implies the substitution of labor for capital, the cutting of costs, economic pessimism and a relatively high liquidity preference. Its representatives in Springdale are the non-expanding traditional farmers, the small businessmen, and in a different way the old aristocracy. The adherence to this perspective implies a weakening of the public ideology and the search for halfway alternatives. Work and accumulation substitute for expansiveness, optimism and mobility-mindedness as the decisive elements of the ideology.

A primary emphasis on consumption represents a third perspective which is almost totally alien to the Protestant Ethic. Neither work nor expansiveness is decisive; economic mobility is seen as limited. Personal consumption and social rather than economic participation constitute almost the exclusive alternative to economic mobility. The shack people and the professional classes share in their rejection of the public ideology. The shack people reject any attempt to rationalize life, reject work as a means of mobility and express their life styles in terms of immediate, short-term consumption and other gratifications. The professional classes stabilize their consumption patterns at a much higher level, stylize and rationalize their consumption and in so doing present a claim for prestige in the community on the basis of these publicly devalued patterns. Their emphasis on leisure goes hand in hand with social and community participation and a high degree of cosmopolitanism—all these forms of behavior result in a high degree of public visibility and an increase in their social and political status in the community.

The hard-working consumers by virtue of their multiple jobs succeed in reaching the desired consumption levels but are not accorded the prestige of the professionals. The economically and socially immobile ritualists attempt to emulate the preferred consumption patterns, but succeed in doing so only insofar as they are able to distinguish themselves from the shack people, while the psychological idiosyncratics, though economically classifiable as consumers, represent a category of disparate individuality for which psychological rather than economic classifications are meaningful.

The professionals and skilled industrial workers, however, stabilize their levels of consumption at socially stylized patterns and levels and it is at this point that the social definition of consumption is a social as well as an economic fact. A high emphasis on consumption can result in quite different styles of living and life goals among different groups.

The basic class dimensions of the community, then, can be described in terms of different emphases on hoarding, investment and consumption. To the economist, of course, these are classic variables in Keynesian thought—consumption, unspent income and saving—regardless of more recent terminological usages and refinements. It is understood that in Keynesian terminology "saving" is investment. That is, it is not the saving here stressed as characteristic of the businessmen, but it is rather the investment characteristic of farmers. The saving of the businessmen, the old aristocrats and the traditional farmers can be classed as hoarding or as "unspent income."

It can be said that when Keynes describes the determinants of income he is also describing basic psychological orientations to the disposition of income and that those psychological orientations can be the basis of classes and the psychology of classes. Moreover, when these psychological orientations are acted out in the community, they have consequences for the dynamics of class. Any group that is successful in the investment function is likely, over the long run, to be transcendent over other groups. This is illustrated by the case of the rational farmers over the past twenty years. Any group that hoards, such as the businessmen or traditional farmers and in time too the old aristocrats, is likely to lose out in the competition for social dominance.

In addition, any set of social and economic facts which alter the hoarding, consuming and investment ideologies of particular groups will alter the structure of class predominance in the community. The larger institutional trends which have altered the conditions of small business had led to the businessman's hoarding psychology and to his loss of social prestige. The farmers and professionals, by their emphasis on the preferred life styles, have assumed class predominance.

Lastly, any group that in the past has achieved a certain degree of recognition in the community and then, later, finds limits placed on its economic mobility will attempt to buttress its position by making social rather than economic claims for its predominance. The emphasis on stylized consumption by the professionals and skilled workers, and the institutionalization of antiquarianism by the old aristocracy, reflect present and past ceilings placed on economic opportunities.

Paralleling the psychological variables of hoarding, consumption and investment are psychological attitudes toward work. The prosperous farmers work hard because they consider their work a form of investment. The hoarding groups may work equally hard but regard their work as a *substitute* for investment. The consuming groups cease to make work a major source of life meaning and substitute for it leisure-time pursuits which are highly stylized in terms of prestige.

The basic change in the underlying dimensions of social class, then, represents changes from an optimistic, expansion, investment economy to various forms of rejection of this ideology. This rejection is neither complete nor unidimensional. The expanding farmers still retain the open frontier perspective, but even this is changed in content since the frontiers for expansion are rational and sensitive adjustments to the specific forms and policies of state and federal agricultural policies.

Groups which affirm the ideology find that the condition for its attainment, the acquisition of capital, is exceedingly difficult. Their affirmation takes the form of ritualistic and compulsive behavior in which the end product is not available to those who practice its precepts.

For the small businessmen and traditional farmers the ideology of hard work and cost cutting become a substitute for investment, and the dominant psychological tone shifts from optimism and abundance to pessimism and scarcity.

The greatest shift in the dimensions of class is an increasing emphasis on stylized consumption and social activities as a substitute for economic mobility. "Social class," then, seems increasingly to be replacing "economic class" as a basis for community esteem.[4]

It thus appears that there are a plurality of alternative bases for class divisions and life stylizations in the rural community. Moreover, these life stylizations have their locus in different and specific segments of the community. The extent to which any one perspective predominates in the community at large depends on the relative success of the representatives of each of the ideologies. For this reason a definitive statement of the future of social stratification is not possible. If the present agricultural prosperity continues, the rational farmers and the farm-oriented businessmen will continue in ascendance and the small businessmen and the traditional farmers will continue their decline. If, however, an agricultural depression takes place, the scarcity-minded groups in the community are economically and psychologically prepared to cope with the problem of survival. But, in either case, the underlying secular trend indicates a shift from production to consumption values in the community.

[4] The recent emphasis on the social rather than the economic basis of class in the literature may represent not a purification of findings and a correction of errors but rather a new phenomenon in American life; as ceilings are perceived on economic mobility, purely social mobility and social value become emphasized as an alternative basis for prestige in the community.

Chapter 4

Springdale and the Mass Society

The Ambivalent Attitude
to Mass Society

SPRINGDALERS have a decided respect for the great institutions that characterize American society. The efficiency, organizational ability and farflung activities of giant government and business enterprise inspire them with awe. The military might of the nation and the productive capacity of industry lend a Springdaler a sense of pride and security, and the continuous development and successful application of science assure him that he is a participant in the most forward-looking and progressive country in the world. Anyone who would attack the great institutions of America would have no audience in Springdale: "Everybody knows this country wouldn't be what it is if it weren't for free enterprise and the democratic form of government." When the Springdaler is on the defensive he will tell the critic, "If you don't like it here you can go back to where you came from."

The Springdaler also sees that the urban and metropolitan society is technically and culturally superior to his own community. He sees this in his everyday life when he confronts the fact that his community cannot provide him with everything he needs: almost everyone goes to the city for shopping or entertainment; large numbers of people are dependent on the radio and television; and everyone realizes that rural life would be drastically altered without cars and refrigerators. Springdalers clearly realize how much of local life is based on the modern techniques, equipment and products which originate in distant places.

The community is constantly dependent on cultural and material imports and welcomes these as a way of "keeping up with the times." However, they believe that the very technical and cultural factors that make for the superiority of the "outside" also account for the problems of living that cities exhibit. The "city masses," while they have easier access to progress, are also the ready-made victims of the negative aspects of progress. In contrast, rural life, because it is geographically distant, can enjoy progress and avoid the worst features of the industrial mass society; Springdalers can believe that they are in a position to choose and utilize only the best of two worlds, that the importations, if properly chosen, need not affect the inner life of the community.

Because it is possible to choose only the best, the Springdaler can believe, that in spite of some disadvantages, his is the better of two worlds. This belief in the autonomy or, at worst, the self-selective dependency of rural life makes it possible for the community member publicly to voice the following conceptions concerning the relationships between his town and mass society:

1. That the basic traditions of American society—"grassroots democracy," free and open expression, individualism—are most firmly located in rural society. The American heritage is better preserved in the small town because it can resist bad city influences and thereby preserve the best of the past.

2. That the future hope of American society lies in rural life because it has resisted all "isms" and constitutes the only major bulwark against them.

3. That much of the progress of society is the result of rural talent which has migrated to the cities. In this way rural society has a positive influence on urban life; rural migrants account for the virtues of city life. "Everyone knows that most of the outstanding men in the country were raised in small towns" and Springdalers proudly point to several local names that have made good on the outside.

4. That "when you live in a small town you can take or leave the big cities—go there when you want to and

always come back without having to live as they do."
There is the belief that "if more people lived in small
towns, you wouldn't have all those problems."

These summarize the types of beliefs that are frequently
stated in public situations. The observer who is willing to go
beyond the public statements discovers that Springdale has
a great variety of direct and intimate connections with a wide
range of institutions of the mass society. Moreover, these
institutions affect many phases of the community, have consequences for its internal local functioning and in some ways
control the direction of social change within it.

Springdale is connected with the mass society in a variety
of different forms. The cumulative effect of these various connections makes possible the continuous transmission of outside policies, programs and trends into the community, even
though the effects of the transmission and the transmitting
agents themselves are not always seen. Outside influences
can be transmitted directly by a socially visible agent such as
the extension specialist who lives in the community for the
purpose of acting upon it. Outside interests and influences
can also be expressed indirectly through members of the
community: policies and programs of relatively invisible outside interests are transmitted by *heads* of local branches of
state and national organizations, by *heads* of local businesses
dependent on outside resources and by *heads* of churches
attached to larger organizations. In some instances the community is affected by the consequences of decisions made by
business and government which are made with specific reference to the community, i.e., the decision to build a state road
through the community or the decision to close down a
factory. Plans and decisions that refer directly to the community are made from a distance by invisible agents and
institutions. Perhaps most important are the mass decisions
of business and government which are transmitted to the
rural scene by the consequences of changes in prices, costs
and communications. These affect the town even though they
are not explicitly directed at it, and they comprise the invisible

social chain reactions of decisions that are made in centers of power in government, business and industry. The invisible social chain reactions emanating from the outside no doubt alter the life of the community more seriously than the action of visible agents such as the extension specialist.

These types of transmission do not represent mutually exclusive channels, but rather exist in complex interrelationship with each other. They merely suggest the major ways in which the community is influenced by dynamics which occur in the institutions of mass society. How these combined dynamics in their various combinations affect the fabric of life in Springdale can be seen by examining the way in which cultural importations and economic and political connections shape the character of community life. In their net effect they influence the psychological dimensions of the community.

Cultural Importations from Mass Society

The external agents of cultural diffusion range from specific observable individuals placed in the local community by outside institutions to the impact of mass media of communications and successive waves of migration. The consequence of these modes of diffusion lies in the effect which they have on local styles of living.

FORMAL IMPORTING ORGANIZATIONS

The adult extension program of the land grant college is mediated at the local level by the county agent and the home demonstration agent who respectively are concerned with farming methods and production, and patterns of homemaking and family life. These agents carry out their program through the Farm and Home Bureau organizations. In Springdale township these agencies have a membership of 300-400 adults. The county agent is primarily concerned with introducing modern methods of farm production and operation and with fostering political consciousness among the farmers. As a type of executive secretary to the local Farm Bureau whose officers are local farmers, the agent acts as an advisor in planning the organization's program, which includes such items as production and marketing problems, parity price problems and taxation problems.

The organizational structure of the Home Bureau parallels the Farm Bureau. From skills and techniques and personnel available at the extension center, local programs consist, for example, of furniture refinishing or aluminum working as well as discussions on such topics as child-rearing, nutrition, penal institutions and interior design. The Home Bureau extension specialist trains a local woman in information and techniques which are reported back to the local club. This program, geared as it is to modern home-making, child-rearing and the feminine role, has the effect of introducing new styles and standards of taste and consumption for the membership.

Other institutional connectors similar to the above in organizational structure account for the introduction of still other social values and social definitions. The 4-H Club, the Future Farmers of America and the Boy and Girl Scouts, as well as the Masons, Odd Fellows, American Legion, Grange and other local branches of national organizations and their auxiliaries, relate the Springdaler to the larger society through the social meanings and styles of activity defined in the programs, procedures and rituals of the national headquarters. State and national conventions, but not office holding, of these as well as church organizations directly link individuals to the outside. In effect these arrangements regularize and institutionalize the communication and organizational nexus between the small town and the point of origin of new ideas and values.

New cultural standards are also imported by agents who are not permanent residents of the town or who have only a transient relationship with it. These include the teachers at the central school, many of whom view their jobs as a temporary interlude in a progression of experience which will lead to a position in a city system. The other agents of contact are a wide variety of salesmen and "experts" who have a regular or irregular contact with business, government and private organizations. From the surrounding urban centers and the regional sales offices of farm implement and automobile manufacturers and nationally branded products, modern methods of merchandizing and business practice are introduced. Experts in civil defense, evangelism, fire-fighting, gardening, charity drives, traffic control and youth recreation introduce new techniques and programs to the local community. This great variety and diversity of semi-permanent and changing contacts in their cumulative effect act as a perpetual blood transfusion to local society. The net effect that these agents have as transmitters of life styles depends in a measure on their position and prestige in the community. The differential effect of these cultural contacts is treated below.

THE UBIQUITY OF MASS MEDIA

Social diffusion through the symbols and pictorial images of the mass media of communications has permeated the community, reducing the local paper to reporting of social items and local news already known by everyone. Few individuals read only the local weekly paper; the majority subscribe to dailies published in surrounding cities and in the large metropolitan areas. This press, itself part of larger newspaper combines, presents an image of the passing scene in its news and nationally syndicated features to which the population of an entire region is exposed.

The mass culture and mass advertising of television and radio reach Springdale in all their variety. Television, particularly, is significant in its impact because for the first time the higher art forms such as ballet, opera and plays are visible to a broad rural audience. National events such as party conventions, inaugurations and investigative hearings are visible now to an audience which was previously far removed from the national centers of action and drama. Because of the relative geographic isolation of Springdale, television has made available entirely new areas of entertainment, information and education. It has created new leisure-time interests, has introduced new modes of leisure-time consumption and has led to the acceptance of standardized entertainment models. Wrestling, Arthur Godfrey and Howdy-Doody are common symbols of entertainment. Equally available and pervasive among the classes and individuals to whom they appeal are pocket books, comic books, and horror and sex stories. Micky Spillane, Willie Mays, Davy Crockett and other nationally prominent personages as well as nationally branded products are as well known and available to the small town as they are to the big city. The intrusion of the mass media is so overwhelming that little scope is left for the expression of local cultural and artistic forms.

However, the diffusion of the printed word is not limited to the mass media; it is present also in the realm of education, both religious and secular. The state department of education syllabus defines minimum standards and content for subject matter instruction. Courses of Sunday School instruction are available for all age levels, and each faith secures its material from its own national religious press. In each of these major institutional areas the standards and *content* of instruction are defined in sources available only in standardized form.

THE IMMIGRANT AS CULTURAL CARRIER

Specific individuals are carriers of cultural diffusion, and the volume and extent of migration in and out of the community suggests the degree and intimacy of its contact with the mass society. In a community which is regarded as stable and relatively unchanging by its own inhabitants, only 25 percent of its population was born locally. Another 25 percent has moved into the community since 1946 and 55 percent are new to the community since 1920. Moreover, of the 45 percent who have moved to the community since 1932, more than 30 percent have lived for a year or longer in cities with populations in excess of 25,000; 7 percent in cities with populations in excess of one-half million.

Each decade and each generation introduces a new layer of immigrants to the community. The agricultural and business prosperity of the 1940's and early 1950's has brought city dwellers to farms and to businesses on main street, and the housing shortage has led workers to reclaim long-abandoned farm dwellings. The 12 percent of new people who moved into Springdale in the Thirties came in response to the effects of the depression. From 1918 to 1928 the Poles moved onto farms abandoned by descendants of original settlers. Indeed, the ebb and flow of migration extends back to such eras of political and economic upheaval as the depression of the 1890's, the civil war, the depression of the 1830's and the mass movement of people during the Indian Wars and the opening of the territory in the early 1800's. Each new wave of migrants, bringing with it the fashions and thought styles of other places, influences the cultural development of the community.

The cumulative consequences of these channels of diffusion and the quantity and quality of the "material" diffused denies the existence of a culture indigenous to the small town. In almost all aspects of culture, even to speech forms, and including technology, literature, fashions and fads, as well as patterns of consumption, to mention a few, the small town tends to reflect the contemporary mass society.

Basically, an historically indigenous local culture does not seem to exist. The cultural imports of each decade and generation and the successive waves of migration associated with each combine to produce a local culture consisting of layers or segments of the mass culture of successive historical eras. In the small town the remaining elements of the gay-ninety culture are juxtaposed against the modern central school. The newer cultural importations frequently come in conflict with the older importations of other eras. The conflict between "spurious" and "genuine" culture appears to be a conflict between two different ages of "spurious" culture.

The Economic Nexus: Occupational Gatekeepers to the Mass Society

Simply because individuals pursue given occupations, their interconnections with mass society follow given patterns. They may be direct employees of specific organizations of the mass society; they may be the objects and targets of the programs of mass organizations; they may be trained by and in great institutions or their skills may be utilized only in urban areas. Because of these occupational characteristics they are specially qualified, accessible and available as transmitters of specific organizational and cultural contacts and contents.

Because these individuals in their occupational roles as gatekeepers are treated as specialists by both the community and mass society, occupation even more than life style becomes a crucial dimension of community life. The content, quality and amount of cultural importation accounted for by an individual is a function of the specific occupational nexus which he has to both the community and mass society.

THE PROFESSIONALS

A number of institutional representatives who are residents of the town receive their position in the community by virtue of their connections with outside agencies. Their position in the community is secured in part by the institution to which they are connected and by the evaluation of the role they are imputed to have in the agency which they locally represent.

The group of individuals who possess a borrowed prestige based on their external affiliations fall largely in the professional category. They are individuals who uniformly possess a college education. Among their ranks are included lawyers, ministers, doctors, teachers, engineers, and a variety of field representatives of state and federal agencies who settle in the community for occupational purposes. All of these individuals, except one or two, have migrated to the community as adults. In addition to the prestige which they are accorded by virtue of being "educated," their overwhelming characteristic as a group lies in the influence which they have in mediating between the town and the larger society. They possess the knowledge and techniques necessary for connecting the small town to the intricate organization of the mass bureaucratic society. They possess "contacts" with outside agencies and their role requires an ability to understand "official" documents and forms, and to write appropriate letters to appropriate bureaus. Thus, for example, the lawyer is counsel to political bodies as well as to free associations and other local organizations, in which capacities he gains an extensive and intimate knowledge of affairs of the town and thereby acquires a position of influence. In like manner the technical knowledge of state educational regulations and policies possessed by the high-school principal is indispensable to the locally constituted school board.

In addition to the prestige and influence which segments of this group possess by virtue of their education and institutional role, they are accorded a respect and, in some cases, awe because of the power which they are imputed to have in manipulating the outside world; they can accomplish things for the community which no one else can.

Moreover, this professional group as a whole, including the relatively transient teaching staff, are felt to have access to styles of taste and consumption which are considered different from those available to the rest of the community. As a result these institutional connectors are considered outside the ordinary realm of prestige assignments and social stratification. That is, their social position in the community is not guaranteed by conforming to standards which are indigenous to the community but, rather, by imputed conformance to "alien" or "exotic" standards of urban life.

As a result of this dual position, individuals in this group, especially those who have come from or have resided for some time outside the community, are able to influence styles of consumption and thought in the community. They do this in three main areas of activity: in organizational activities, community projects and social fashions. They have been prime movers in setting up a formal program of youth recreation and in vigorously participating in and supporting local cultural activities such as plays, recitals and educational talks. In the P.T.A. they constitute the block favoring those modern methods and programs which bring the outside world to the small town—talks by foreign university students, race relations discussions and socio-dramas in dating and parent-child relationships. Ideas for the development of a community center and adult education programs emanate from and are supported by them. In terms of dress styles and personal adornment as well as home furnishings and styles of party giving, this group is in the forefront of innovation.

This innovating group of middle-class newcomers is supported by a group of college-educated locals who act as a bridge between the new standards and local society. In supporting these new standards, the local group absorbs some of the resentment which is directed at the innovating group by both the farmers and merchants.

It must be noted that the professionals' psychological orientation to accentuate the "elite" cultural values of mass society is more than merely a product of their residence, education or background in the mass society. The limitations on economic success and the limited professional opportunities in the community means that the drive toward success through work and investment is not fully available to them. The possession of alien cultural standards makes it possible for the professionals to reject the success drive by accepting meaningful standards alternative to those available to the rest of the community; they distinguish themselves in the community by their identification with external values.

BUSINESSMEN

For storekeepers, filling station operators, appliance dealers, automobile and farm equipment dealers and feed mill operators, the external world is a source of supply for the goods and commodities which they sell on the local market. Their position in relation to their source of supply and the overall condition of the national economy determines the level of their business activity, ceilings on their potential income, and hence indirectly their style of life. To analyze this group we must consider separately the position of the independent shopkeeper, the businessman who operates on a franchise and the feed mill and farm implement dealer.

The shopkeepers who make up the bulk of the business community have experienced a slow and gradual decline in their class position relative to other groups in the community. This is mainly due to the breakdown of their monopolistic position with respect to the local market, but it is also related to the rise of other groups. The development of the automobile, the appearance of the chain stores in surrounding areas and the expansion of mail order sales have placed them in a competitively disadvantageous position. Moreover, the nationally branded and advertised product, with its fixed profit margin determined by the producer, has tended in a general way to determine his volume/profit ratio in a way increasingly disadvantageous to him. His decrease in profits in relation to volume has driven him to a greater competition with other local shopkeepers—a competition which takes place in the form of despecialization, greater reliance on credit trade and keeping his shop open for long hours. The first two of these responses to his dilemma have further depressed his profit/volume ratio: in the one case by reducing his return on his investment and in the other case by increased losses due to bad debts. He keeps his business open in an effort to improve his investment/profit ratio and this he can do only by staying in the store himself.

The economic position of the small shopkeeper prevents him from reinvesting earnings in his own business. He sees little to be gained by modernizing and expanding his store in an effort to increase profits. Hence, the very basis on which the business group could achieve a class ascendancy are not open to it. Moreover, the long hours which he keeps in his store prevent him from holding a secondary occupation and limit his activities in community affairs. As a result he lives in an atmosphere of social and economic scarcity relative to his position thirty years ago and relative to other segments of the community. This accounts for the dominant psychology of scarcity-mindedness which is characteristic of this most numerous segment of the business class.

The position of the businessman who operates on a *franchise* is more obviously linked to the mass society. Usually he not only has a single source of supply, but also his source of supply (a petroleum company, for example) specifies the business practices and standards which must be maintained in order to retain the franchise. If the retail outlet is owned by the supplier (as with some filling stations) rents may be charged on a sliding scale according to volume of business— less volume, less rent—with the consequence that the profit margin of the local operator is not fixed.

More important, however, are the combined effects of the distribution policies of the petroleum products companies and appliance producers. Most of the big producers of these products maintain a local outlet; in some cases a single product may be retailed in two or three small-scale local outlets. In at least one line, household appliances, price cutting has become a standard form of competition. The effect of this proliferation of outlets is to depress the business chances of any single operator retailing a given branded product.

This group responds to its economic situation by increasing business hours, by carrying secondary lines and by intensive competition for "service" trade. Business is conducted at almost any hour of the day or night. Since these are one-man businesses, other members of the family are soon incorporated in the work process; children are helpers, wives act as secretaries and clerks. In the extreme case, the family life of the filling station operator orients itself almost completely to "keeping the business open"; the husband and wife are on duty together or the husband is absent from home except to sleep. This group is known to the community primarily through its occupational circumstances and its relationships are based upon being entrepreneurs and having a clientele. As individuals they are relatively unimportant to the community since there is a high rate of turnover of franchises.

There are three individuals in the business class who are exceptions. These are the feed mill operators and the farm implement dealers who in Springdale consist of one feed mill operator located on the periphery of the township, one implement dealer located in the village, and one large-scale combined feed mill, housing supply and farm implement partnership. Because they service an agricultural industry which since the early Forties has been prosperous, they are favorably situated in the local economy.

In terms of their customer relationships they are most intimately tied to the farmers, especially to the prosperous farmers who do most of the buying. Because of their market position their economic fate is intimately related to that of the farmers. In the period of farm ascendancy at the time of the study, they too were prosperous and exhibited all of the same aspects of expansion, investment and opportunity-consciousness already described for the farmer. In addition, however, because they are businessmen and the most successful businessmen, they have achieved the respect, admiration and enmity of the business community as well as of the town at large.

They are the most heavily capitalized group of individuals in the community and play an important credit function in the local agricultural economy. Because of the farmer's economic dependence on them and the interlocking character of their mutual fate, the feed mill and implement dealers identify themselves with the farmer's interests. In local politics they are in a position to provide the leadership in organizing the farmer's interests and frequently act as spokesman for the farm community. This is particularly true of the feed mill and implement partnership since it is the community's dominant enterprise; the other feed dealer is less important because his business is small and is located on the periphery of the town, and the other implement dealer is unimportant politically because being an Italian he is ethnically peripheral.

Thus two sub-groups of the business community, shopkeepers and franchise operators, experience a social and economic decline relative to a third, the feed and implement dealers.

These shifts in relative success are linked to accessibility to economic opportunity which is largely defined by external forces.

INDUSTRIAL WORKERS

Industrial workers represent a curious gap in the relationship of the rural community to mass society. Individuals who live in Springdale but work outside on products which are geared to a national market are not understandable to other members of the community because the rural community lacks the perceptual apparatus necessary to understand industry and the industrial process. The industrial worker lives in the community, but the occupational basis of his existence is not subject to the social pigeon-holing by others necessary to making judgments and assessments of him.

Industrial workers consist mainly of individuals and their families who have migrated to the community in an effort to escape city life and to seek cheaper housing as well as land for home gardens. Due to the ecological conditions of the rural community (a large number of abandoned farm dwellings and the breakup of large houses into apartments), in-migrating as well as native industrial workers live in a scattered pattern throughout the township. As a consequence of their work routine, which involves, in addition to their work in a factory, one or two hours of commuting plus, in many cases, the operation of an extensive garden, home improvements and the care of livestock or a secondary occupation, this group tends to be relatively socially isolated in its day-to-day contact with the rest of the community. Their work carries them to the city where they can do their shopping and engage in city activities. As individuals some of the industrial workers strive to become involved in community activities and many of them maintain an affiliation with one of the local churches.

This dependence on outside industry affects the internal stratification pattern of local society. There are apparently no fixed standards available to other groups in the community, especially the farmers and businessmen, by which a social class position can be assigned to industrial workers relative to their own class position. Industrial processes tend not to be understood by the non-industrial groups and, therefore, these latter groups are not able to assign evaluations of skill, workmanship and prestige to the various individuals engaged in industrial activity. There is some evaluation of industrial workers based on an evaluation of the shop in which they work since sharp differences in working conditions and security benefits exist from shop to shop, but this is insufficient to assign differential status to individuals who work at different jobs in the same shop. A rather minimal evaluation rests on the general attitude other groups have to industrial workers as a generic type. Local workers are viewed with a mixture of envy and pity: envied because they have what is regarded as a short work day, good pay and little responsibility to their jobs; pitied because their opportunities for economic advancement are "arbitrarily" limited.

Because of the paucity of data and criteria available to other groups for ranking individual workers, the problem of the social definition of their position is left in large measure to definitions of positions which individuals give to themselves. Thus the industrial worker in the small town, more than individuals in any other group, is in a position to create his own social standing. He can do this partly by church affiliation, but primarily through affiliation with auxiliary church organizations, participation in community organizations, association in social circles and by demonstrating his ability to work hard by improving his home and cultivating a respectable garden.

But even given these criteria, the bulk of the industrial group is not socially *visible* to the rest of the community. That is, they are not conceived as a group because there is no single framework available to other groups to give their perception a perspective.

Their major occupational role exists outside the framework of the local society. This would suggest that even in a relatively "simple" rural community there is no single standard for social stratification. That is, social stratification in this type of situation represents a plurality of unrelated dimensions, often in conflict or not even coherent, in the midst of which groups of individuals may exist as congeries. This has been pointed out in the literature of urban stratification, but it has always been assumed that the small-scale rural society could be stratified from top to bottom, an hypothesis which this observation suggests is not the case. A major reason why a single standard of stratification cannot be used is that a single standard presupposes knowledge which makes assessments possible. The Springdaler does not have the knowledge of the complex industrial commercial processes of modern society to be able to locate individuals in these processes.

FARMERS

As noted earlier, there are two classes of farmers, the rational and the traditional. A major difference between them is the way they organize their production in relation to the mass market and government regulations.

Those who gear themselves to the mass market address themselves to favorably pegged prices, subsidies and quotas. As a consequence when prices and regulations are favorable they accept the favorable environment as a condition for their operations. They invest and expand, work hard and are successful. Their success stimulates confidence and buoyancy and produces an expansionist psychology.

In a peculiar way the traditional farmers who as a group do not gear themselves to the mass market do this specifically because of their relations with the mass market. As older farmers they have learned from the depression that they can be economically vulnerable, and they have learned that they can survive in the community by being immune to the market. The depression experience was so bitter for them that they have learned nothing since. Thus it happens that at the time of the study they were still living in the market of the early Thirties.

To show how the internal status position of the farmer is related to the institutional structure of the larger society, account must be taken of the fluctuations in the agricultural economy over the past thirty years. The agricultural depression beginning after World War I and extending to the beginning of World War II placed the farmer in a depressed (indebted) economic position. The decline of the farmer in Springdale was more extreme than in the nation at large during this period because Springdale is a marginal agricultural area with relatively poor land and a high rate of feed purchases. Farmers were either dispossessed, displaced or they retrenched to a heavily indebted minimum standard of consumption and operation. In this period the farmer verged on being declassed or actually was declassed. Today the farmer is an important and ascendant segment of the rural middle class. From a position of near bankruptcy in 1933 he had risen (at the time of the field work for this study) to a position of heavy capitalization and social prominence. His rise coincided with the rationalization of marketing procedures (The Federal Milk Price Order in the New York Milk Shed), federal agricultural policies, and the rise in the market value of his products since the early 1940's. Specific agricultural policies which have contributed to his rise include the price support program, farm credit programs, and fertilizer and other land improvement give-aways. A little recognized source of preferential treatment given him by an outside agency lies in the structure of United States income tax laws, which allow for rapid depreciation of plant and equipment, little accountability on cash sales and a broad base of allowable operating expenses.

Although the status of all farmers is equally linked to decisions and policies of these larger institutional structures (the price structure and federal agricultural legislation), all farmers do not equally orient their operations to legislation and regulations oriented to them. At this point the rate of status ascendancy of the individual farmer is probably directly related to the extent to which he accepts the preferential treatment accorded him in these larger policy decisions. Those who have been most swift and efficient in adjusting to the changing conditions of the agricultural economy over the past twenty years constitute the most rapidly ascending segment of farmers.

As a consequence of the character of the institutional connectors which link the farmer to the great society, the status of the farmer relative to other local groups is relatively independent of local community forces. By the same token, his status is directly related to price structures and mass decisions and policies. Alterations in these external forces, such as a tumbling in farm prices, can cause an upheaval in the status structure of the local community. This analysis does not exhaust the class groups. Other groups are occupationally less directly connected with the mass society and its markets. The aristocrats are oriented to the market only by fixed interest rates established in previous economic periods; their income from annuities, insurance payments and fixed inheritances declines in an inflationary period. The shack people, with the exception of their consumption function, are separated from the market by their unwillingness to direct their attention to it for any sustained period of time, even though their consumption standards are inflated at those times when they do address themselves to the market. The marginal middle-class groups economically are not in a position to be directly and importantly related to the market except through the general price level. Their relationship to the market is mediated through their imitation of more prestigeful and successful groups which are located in the community.

Occupation, Class and Community

It will be noted that the above analysis of the impact of mass society, as stated in the framework of occupation, stands in contrast to the analysis of class which was stated as differences in style of life. The difference is understandable only in terms of the different economic and psychological functions of these two elements. Style of life is related to preferences in expenditure of time, energy and money. Occupation deals with source of income rather than its expenditure. Obviously there is a connection between the two: that is, it is difficult in the long run to spend in excess of one's income. The possession of income however does not by itself guarantee a style of living. In addition to income, the elements necessary to guarantee a style of living are taste, aspirations, habits and skills. This means that individuals in the same occupational class may be affiliates of different social classes as in the case of segments of the marginal middle class. In recognizing this, one sees that social class has an independent volitional character from occupational categories. However, one cannot forget that through time the means available for consumption are products of income and that those factors which affect the income of members of a given social class also affect an individual's class eligibility. It is specifically at this point that the relationship of occupational classes to the mass society is important in its effect on the internal social classes of Springdale and, moreover, on the cultural and psychological character of these social classes.

Those groups which are favorably linked to the mass society are in a position to be socially, economically and politically ascendant in the community; in Springdale these are the rational farmers. Those groups which are unfavorably linked—segments of the marginal middle class—find it difficult to achieve the wherewithal to practice the preferred styles of life. Moreover, a favorable position with respect to certain aspects of mass society can and does in the long run produce optimism, buoyancy, aggressiveness and high self-esteem among members of a given class. Thus the psychological foundation of the class of rational farmers has changed over time. On the other hand, a negative position *vis à vis* mass society produces feelings of penury, scarcity, defensiveness and defensive social snobbery. Each of these sets of attitudes becomes a basis for further social and economic orientations for the affected classes.

The Political Surrender to Mass Society

Local political institutions consist of a village board, a town board and local committees of the Republican and Democratic parties. The jurisdiction of the village board includes powers of control and regulation over a variety of community facilities and services—street lighting, water supply, fire protection, village roads, street signs and parks. To carry out the functions empowered to it, it possesses the power of taxation. The town board is concerned chiefly with fire protection, the construction and maintenance of roads; through its participation on the county board of supervisors, it participates in programs connected with welfare, penal and other county services.

However, at almost every point in this seemingly broad base of political domain the village and town boards adjust their action to either the regulations and laws defined by state and federal agencies which claim parallel functions on a statewide or nationwide basis or to the fact that outside agencies have the power to withhold subsidies to local political institutions.

Local assessment scales and tax rates are oriented to state equalization formulas which partially provide the standardized basis on which subsidies are dispersed by the state. State highway construction and development programs largely present local political agencies with the alternative of either accepting or rejecting proposed road plans and programs formulated by the state highway department.

The village board, more than the town board, is dependent on its own taxable resources (taxes account for almost half its revenues) and best illustrates the major dimensions of local political action. The village board in Springdale accepts few of the powers given to it. Instead, it orients its action to the facilities and subsidies controlled and dispensed by other agencies and, by virtue of this, forfeits its own political power. Solutions to the problem of fire protection are found in agreements with regionally organized fire districts. In matters pertaining to road signs and street signs action typically takes the form of petitioning state agencies to fulfill desired goals "without cost to the taxpayer." On roads built and maintained by the state there is no recourse but to accept the state traffic bureau's standards of safety. A problem such as snow removal is solved by dealing directly with the foreman of the state highway maintenance crew through personal contacts: "If you treat him right, you can get him to come in and clear the village roads." In other areas of power where there are no parallel state agencies, such as for garbage collection or parks, the village board abdicates its responsibility. As a consequence of this pattern of dependence, many important decisions are made for Springdale by outside agencies. Decisions which are made locally tend to consist of approving the requirements of administrative or state laws. In short the program and policies of local political bodies are determined largely by acceptance of grants-in-aid offered them—i.e., in order to get the subsidy specific types of decisions must be made—and by facilities and services made available to them by outside sources.

Psychologically this dependence leads to an habituation to outside control to the point where the town and village governments find it hard to act even where they have the power. Legal jurisdictions have been supplanted by psychological jurisdictions to such an extent that local political action is almost exclusively oriented to and predicated on seeking favors, subsidies and special treatment from outside agencies. The narrowing of legal jurisdictions by psychologically imposed limits leads to an inability to cope with local problems if outside resources are not available.

Power in local political affairs, then, tends to be based on accessibility to sources of decision in larger institutions. Frequently this accessibility consists merely of the knowledge of the source, or it may mean a personal contact, or an ability to correspond to get necessary information. Under these circumstances, power in the political arena is delegated to those with contacts in and knowledge of the outer world and to those who are experts in formal communication with impersonal bureaucratic offices. These are, on the individual level, the lawyer and, on an institutional level, the political party. The lawyer gains his paramountcy through technical knowledge and personalized non-party contacts up the political hierarchy with other lawyers. He is the mediator between the local party and the party hierarchy, and transforms his personalized contacts into political indispensability in the local community. His access to outside sources of power determines his power and predominance in the local community.

The Social Psychological Consequences
of the Rural Surrender

A central fact of rural life then, is its dependence on the institutions and dynamics of urban and mass society. The recognition of this dependence and the powerlessness associated with it give to the agents and institutions of the great society a degree of respect and admiration which, however, does not always connote approval. Rather, there is a high degree of ambivalence with respect to these agents and institutions. They have respect because of their power and wealth, and because their norms have the legitimacy of acceptance in wide areas of the society at large. On the other hand, the very dominance of the mass institutions causes resentments, since, in the light of this dominance, rural life in its immediacy is devalued. Hence, for example, although the standards of the land grant college are accepted, the institution and its agents may be resented for the role they play in innovation.

The phenomenon of psychological ambivalence to the mass society is particularly reinforced by the fact that slight changes in the policies and dynamics of the mass institutions can have profound effects on the rural way of life and on its major social and economic classes—i.e., parity policies, industrial relocations, new state roads and state subsidization formulas. In response to these conditions, the members of the rural community and their political spokesman resent their dependency and powerlessness and channelize it into anti-urban politics and policies. In relation to the outer world, there exist two types of political victory; when rural rather than urban areas get a disproportionately large share of the benefits of the state budget and when the city can be made the object of investigation on grounds of corruption or vice by politicians surrounded by a halo of rural images. At the same time a personal identification with important urban political officials lends an individual prestige in the rural community.

But this continuous transvaluation of the attitudes toward

urban life and its representatives are never so simple as the
dependence-resentment mechanism would suggest. For such
political and psychological currents are supported by intri-
cately articulated images of the mass society and rural self
images, described in Chapter Two, which for the purposes of
this discussion can be termed counterimages.

These images, themselves, are a product of complex institutional developments and reflect the process of urban penetration. For it is uniquely ironical that the self-image of the
rural community and its image of urban life are in part the
products of the penetration of urban mass media. Through
these media the people of Springdale see urban life dominated
by crime, dirt, filth, immorality, vice, corruption and anti-
Americanism. The urban center is seen as a jungle of man's
inhumanity to man; the large political center as a "dog-eat-
dog" world of investigations and counterinvestigations with
few clearly defined heroes. It sees the urban middle classes
confronted by apparently hopeless personal problems and
moving from crisis to crisis without end. It is because of the
mechanism of resentment that the Springdaler can see wide
class differences in urban society and be unaware of class in
his own environment.

Contrariwise, the mass media frequently present rural life
in idyllic terms. The *Saturday Evening Post* cover brings
forth the image of the cracker barrel, the virtues of life close
to soil and stream and of healthy, simple, family living. The
weekly press carries syndicated columnists who extol the
virtues of ruralism. Political as well as feature speakers who
come to town invariably reinforce the town's image of itself:
"The false life of cities," "If America were made up of small
towns like Springdale, this would be a better country." "The
goodness of America lies in the small town where life and
nature meet to make for genuine living." The urban man of
knowledge and the university scientist verbalize their own
image of rural life and in doing so shape the self-image of the
rural audience.

Separate urban images exist for the various segments which
epitomize the rural community. The farmer is strong, self-

reliant and capable. He is warm, affectionate and devoted but these characteristics are frequently hidden under a crusty, gruff exterior. He is a good businessman and a sharp trader capable in the final analysis of outwitting others, especially the city slicker. Outside of a few old gossips, community life is richly warm and filled with a wide variety of social interchange, gatherings and genuinely spontaneous self-expression. The rural dweller is religious, moral and upright, though capable of "cutting-up" in a way which is both amusing and tolerable. The villains, the sharp-dealers, the frauds, when not urban types, exist in order to provide the protagonist and the community with an effective demonstration of its values in action.

The above picture, of course, is only a profile of the images presented to the rural consumer of mass media. Numerous exceptions exist, as, for example, the image of rural corruption often present in the violent type of pocket novel. Another notable exception is the absence in the mass media of an image of the rural, commuting, industrial worker. His place in rural society is difficult to stereotype, particularly since it stands in sharp contrast to the image of the self-reliance and independence of the rural community as personified by the farmer. Thus the lack of definition of the rural industrial worker in the mass media corresponds to the lack of a definition of industrial workers held by the residents of Springdale, including the lack of a self-definition by the industrial workers themselves.[1]

The mass media then provide the raw materials out of which the rural resident can and does form personal images which enable him to approach the psychological demands of

[1] Industrial workers who live in the country are caught in the cross pressures which exist between their positions as workers and the dominant and hostile definitions which their culture gives to their position. They tend to be anti-union, yet desire the benefits which they think unions give to workers. But these desires are not frequently expressed at a verbal level. In the absence of alternatives and in the presence of a dominant cultural stand against unions, the industrial workers affirm the dominant values of the community, including personal pride in the paternalistic concern of their employers. This is done with no apparent psychological cost to the workers.

his situation. The rural target of the mass media thus can select·those elements of the total output which enable him to meet those psychological needs, ignoring both the materials and the implications which are not congruent with the manner in which he wishes to structure his perception and images.

From the standpoint of the producer of mass media, to complete the picture, the image presented of rural life and life in general reflects not only his estimate of his audience (since not all of the mass media are specifically aimed at the rural market) but also the psychological climate of the urban centers where images of rural life are produced. The romanticization of rural life in press and radio reflects the need of the urban dweller to conceive of rural life as simpler and freer from the complexities, tensions and anxieties which he faces in his own world. Rural life is thus conceived as a counter-image which highlights his own situation. However, when presented to the rural resident, it serves as an image which enables the rural dweller to form symbolic and ideological resistance to urban society. It is thus through the mass media that the negative reactions to mass society of both the rural and urban dweller are linked; and it is as sets of similar responses to the negative aspects of urbanism that both urban and rural dwellers find a common symbolic meeting ground.

In addition to images which may be the peculiar product of the mass media, Springdalers hold negative images of the major urban institutions. Washington is populated by corrupt politicians, influence peddlers and communists. Cities are hotbeds of radicalism and atheism. Industrial workers led by racketeers are lazy, highly paid and incapable of performing the complex managerial practices necessary to success in farm and small business management. Big universities and city churches are seats of secularism and the city influence is held responsible for local immorality and corruption. These images in their complex articulation enable the rural resident to take pride in his situation, to meet the psychological threat of his powerlessness in a mass society and to organize political action which expresses both his economic interest and his psychological needs.

It must be remembered, however, that the central fact of rural life is ambivalence: the negative image of urban life goes hand in hand with respect for the power, the wealth and the legitimacy of acceptance of urban values. The most contrary values are thus held in complex, psychologically balanced constellations. As a result, the response of rural residents to urban institutions is not stable through time. Slight shifts in their situations can cause the most varied responses. Their political loyalties are subject to sudden shifts in phase with shifts in farm income, price levels and the policies of state and federal governments. Anti-urban elements are held in check or can develop relatively easily. Furthermore, the balance of power and influence within the community can and does vary with relatively slight shifts in the external situation affecting these groups.

Hence, those factors which appear to be decisive in determining the action of the rural community are factors which originate in areas outside the rural community. Thus, even when the rural community attacks the urban mass society, the nature of the attack, its intensity and the situations which bring it forth are, in large part, the products of urban mass society. Rural life, then, can be seen as one area in which the dynamics of modern urban mass society are worked out.

There is always the danger of considering all aspects of mass society as responding only to the dynamics of mass society, so that when one completes one's analysis mass society dissolves into a response to itself. It must be remembered that there is a reciprocal relationship between Springdale and mass society in which Springdale, taken as one of thousands of similar communities, exerts itself upon and shapes the mass society. This reciprocal relationship is found primarily in the area of politics. The analysis of this relationship brings into focus an entirely new set of perspectives on the life of the community.

III

Class and Mass in Politics

Introduction

THERE are three major areas of politics in Springdale: village government, town government and school government. However they do not involve the same constituencies or the same political interests. The village government is excluded from jurisdiction over those who live in the country so that farmers do not participate in its affairs. The town government and the school district potentially include all residents of the township but because each encompasses different interests and purposes—road issues in the one and school issues in the other—quite different groups, especially leadership groups, are involved in the political processes of each.

Because of the differences in the class composition of the groups interested in politics in each of the major jurisdictions, each jurisdiction exhibits a social and psychological climate different from the others. Each exhibits different political processes, different issues and different connections to the mass society.

In addition to the local jurisdictional levels, the township is of course connected to county, state and national political jurisdictions. In this case, too, different combinations of groups and leaders are involved in the attempt which Springdale makes to come to formal and informal terms with the society of which it is a part.

The analysis of political processes is of a different order from the analysis of class processes. In politics a specific individual or a small number of individuals may serve as links connecting large groups of individuals and institutions. It therefore becomes necessary to trace the detailed specific actions and careers of specific political leaders and the detailed historical evolution of relevant political events. Without a recognition of the time dimension, it would be impossible to make a meaningful analysis of Springdale's political process. Politics, whatever the social and economic background of the groups involved, expresses itself through individuals.

Chapter 5

―――――――――――――⟨◉⟩―――――――――――――

The Business Character of Village Politics

The Ethos of Village Politics

ANY understanding of village politics demands a recognition of four major processes that affect and underpin rural political action: the pervasiveness of politics in rural life, the unanimity of decision making, the minimization of decision making and the surrender of jurisdictional prerogatives.

THE PERVASIVENESS OF POLITICS IN RURAL LIFE

Politics is a dominant theme of village life. Every man, from the politically impotent to the controlling figures of the community, talks politics. Long-standing issues such as town and village relations, past issues, dead issues, irrevocable decisions such as school consolidation and settled problems solved by time alone—all these in addition to local current affairs are discussed and rediscussed.

The recognition of politics as a major source of conversation contributes to a definite political ceremony. One makes it a point to speak to certain people at certain times and places and not at other times and places. In periods of local political crisis, one is careful to plan one's pattern of public association in such a way as to not reveal one's position with respect to a given controversy. Should two individuals assumed to be political rivals be seen together too frequently, gossip quite quickly has it that they are "hatching a deal" or are in some form of collusion directed at a third party. If these same rivals are not seen together (drinking coffee, passing time on a street corner) for a long period of time, this fact provides grounds for speculations concerning a "serious rift" between them. In consequence, such rivals through conscious design plan their intercourse so as to give the appearance of "normalcy," in order that extreme conclusions cannot be drawn from their daily public action. Individual action of central as well as marginal political figures as it occurs on the street or in meetings of organizations provides the grist for political gossip and discussion. Through gossip channels and the intricate network of connecting links which eventually join almost all individuals in the community except the shack people to each other, more or less directly or indirectly and with various intervening information dead-ends and speed-up points, news of the actions of individuals and organizations spreads with amazing rapidity. To be sure, the rapidity and extent to which information spreads depends upon its importance or its intrinsic interest, but this does not materially diminish the quantity of political "talk" in the small community.

The pervasiveness of political discussion is of special significance when one notes that it is focussed on personalities rather than on issues, and that it continues in the presence or absence of issues. Issues, then, are not an essential ingredient of village politics.

UNANIMITY IN DECISION MAKING

Within the formally constituted governing agency of the village, the village board, politics is conducted on the principle of unanimity of decision. In two years of observation of village board meetings in Springdale, all decisions brought to a vote were passed unanimously. The dissent, disagreement and factionalism which exist in the community are not expressed at board meetings. Through a process of consultation prior to an official meeting and by extended discussion involving the entire group during the meeting itself, a point is reached when it seems reasonable to assume that everyone will go along with the proposed action. Only then, as a final parry, will someone suggest that a motion be made to propose the action. After a short period of silence which provides a last opportunity for further discussion prior to the motion, the motion is made. Whereupon it is assumed that the motion is passed, or, if brought to a vote, as occasionally happens, it passes unanimously.

To illustrate the technique of unanimous decision making, one can look at the board's activities in investigating a second-hand pump to be used as a source of spare parts for the village water pump:

"Narry says quite emphatically, 'something's got to be done about that pump or there won't be any water, I'm telling you.' Smith suggests that a couple of board members might work along with Narry in appraising the old pump that is for sale. Monson picks up one of the points Narry had made previously on the possible fire hazard involved for the village if the pump were to fail and some fire broke out. There would just not be any water. Monson says that Narry has a good point. There is a pause. Monson says, 'To bring matters to a head, why not act on Ed's (Smith's) suggestion?' Smith responds, 'Give Narry some backing. We don't have to wait for the next meeting. (Narry had indicated that the pump may be sold rather quickly to someone else.) Let them use their own judgment.' Monson adds that they might have a pump repairman go with them so that they can have some expert opinion. The other members of the board are spontaneous in thinking this a good suggestion. Smith says, 'I suggest that Mr. Martin and Mr. Henderson be on the committee.' Henderson remarks half-jokingly that he knows nothing about pumps but he indicates his willingness to serve on the committee. Morris says rather quietly, 'There's a legal point. Can a trustee appoint the Mayor to a committee?' There is laughter. Flint (counsel) says, 'Why not?' Morris smiles silently. Monson wants to know who is for the motion (Smith's 'motion' appointing a committee). There is tacit agreement that the committee is appointed."[1]

[1] All personal names throughout the text are fictitious. Although this may not hide personal identities from those who are familiar with Springdale, our material could not be meaningfully presented without reference to individuals. Since political affairs are *public* in the broadest sense of the term, our procedure of using names and reports of *official public meetings* is necessary.

In other matters decisions may be reached through the process of simply making a motion: a board member makes a motion to "pay the bills" and it is assumed that the motion is carried without a vote or comment from the mayor that it is passed. Issues over which disagreements may exist among members are not brought before the board. In the official records of board proceedings, all decisions are recorded as unanimous.

At the formal level in the public meeting, then, on large or small issues and through the utilization of a number of techniques, decisions are reached by unanimous agreement.

MINIMIZATION OF DECISION MAKING

Although the principle of unanimity of decision is almost a requirement in Springdale politics, few items of business outside of routine and legally required action ever reach the decision-making stage. It is an outstanding characteristic of village government that it does not initiate new undertakings and new projects. The village board tends to limit its function to the conduct of routine "housekeeping" business: paying bills, collecting taxes, paying wages, keeping books and setting up committees. It is a common complaint among all groups in the community that the village board does nothing. The members of the board themselves in their actions and in their words demonstrate and state that they do not want to assume responsibilities for which there is no past tradition or precedent. For two years the board from time to time considered, discussed and dropped the subject of providing snow and garbage removal facilities for the community. Ultimately it was decided that: (a) There was no need for snow and garbage removal services. (b) "You have to pay for it." (c) "The more services you go into the more you have to do." (d) "Then there's taxes and depreciation."

Against this background of the avoidance of innovation and the minimization of decision, it is well to look at the potential functions of the board. The central functions of the board include broad powers of control and regulation over a variety of community facilities and services—street lighting, water supply, fire protection, police protection, village roads, street signs, licensing, parks, social welfare and garbage disposal. In addition, the board, in its articles of incorporation, is empowered to undertake new functions necessary to the maintenance of the community in the same manner that a small city assures itself adequate transportation or takes measures to maintain its economic base by protecting or encouraging economic development. To plan and execute its programs the village board possesses the power of taxation over real estate and water service located within the incorporated limits of the village and is privileged to set tax rates and evaluate the worth of taxable property. Without question, the legal jurisdictions of the board are broad, but this jurisdiction has been abdicated or compromised to county or state levels of government.

THE SURRENDER OF JURISDICTION

In almost every area of jurisdiction the board has adjusted its action to the regulations and laws externally defined by outside agencies which engage in functions parallel to its own. State police, regionally organized fire districts, state welfare agencies, the state highway department, the state youth commission, the state conservation department—these agencies and others are central to the daily functioning of the village. Though such agencies and their representatives are frequently resented by the community and though local officials talk bitterly of them, their services are accepted and sought because they are free or because acceptance of them carries with it monetary grants-in-aid for the local community. A high proportion of the village budget represents subsidies from the state government. The major social services of the community are either provided by or paid for by outside agencies. The acceptance of such aid or financial assistance carries with it the requirement of fulfilling the regulations and laws of the supporting agency. It is through a combination of these requirements and the acceptance of the aid that the local governing agency finds itself in a position of having surrendered its legal jurisdictions to outside agencies.

However, in addition to the objective fact of the surrender, there is a fundamental reason why no action is taken by the village board.

In certain respects, as we have suggested, board meetings have all the aspects of a ceremonial occasion. At a public level these meetings manifest the trappings and rituals of a primitive social ceremony. Meetings are set as they have always been set for the first Tuesday or the third Monday of the month, with a special annual meeting on the first Monday of April. To the uninitiated outsider, members convene as if by magic without prior communication and with the regularity of the phases of the moon. All arrive at the appointed time and at the appointed place whether there is business or no business. After the exchange of standardized greetings ("Good evening, Mr. Morris") and stylized jokes (shady gossip and salesman type jokes), the minutes and the treasurer's report (given by the same person) are formally called for. Committee reports, whose contents are known to all beforehand, are requested and presented (in most cases by the legal counsel). From this point on, all items of business are considered rather simultaneously as if in open discussion of whatever strikes the fancy. The careful observer will note that even in the absence of formal voting several decisions have been made. There is no response to the call for new business—our protocols do not record the formal introduction of any new business for a two-year period.

However, this ceremonialism is an outward manifestation of private actions which have meaning at an entirely different plane. The understanding of the political and psychological transvaluation of public ceremonies is the key to the comprehension of small-town politics.

Village Politics

SOCIAL COMPOSITION AND IDEOLOGY
OF THE VILLAGE BOARD

The elected officials of village government (three trustees, a mayor and a clerk) are with but few exceptions local businessmen, primarily owners and operators of retail stores.

However, not all businessmen qualify for public office and not all officials are businessmen. As a primary qualification for election an individual must have been a resident of the community for at least ten years; preferably and most frequently he has been a lifelong resident of the village. Hence his personal "character" and his ideology are well known to the community at large. To be selected as a candidate for public office he must subscribe to a low-tax, low-expenditure ideology and be relatively unsophisticated in the techniques of political analysis and public administration. These qualifications tend to reside in the business community.

When a village official is regarded as especially competent in the affairs of government, he is usually "coopted" or promoted to a position in the "invisible government," where his talents can be utilized to better advantage and where he has a greater opportunity to exercise power (the cases of Howard Jones, who was mayor for fifteen years, and Flint, the village counsel, both of whom as noted below hold key positions in machine politics).

If an official is not a shopkeeper, he must possess, in addition to the above, the qualifications of economic vulnerability or a kinship connection with one of the dominant figures of machine politics. Examples of such cases include a janitor, a relative of Howard Jones engaged in insurance selling; a school superintendent whose professional functions have largely been superseded by school consolidations; and a recent mayor who is a part-time school-bus driver, part-time chiropractor, part-time strawberry grower. When board members are not directly engaged in small business, their life circumstances are such that they are easily able to reflect the ideology of the businessmen and fulfill the qualification of political and administrative incompetence.

Trustees are almost completely unfamiliar with the routine procedures for conducting village business. Legal terminology and the formal vocabulary of the government form, so central to the conduct of their business, are alien to their manner of speech and their way of thinking. More important, however, their life activity, circumscribed within business or some other specialization, leaves them unprepared to comprehend village-state relations and prevents their acquiring a perspective broad enough to encompass the range of political sentiment represented in the community. Hence, in calculating potential reactions to their actions, they think in personal rather than interest-group terms. They are not, then, able to assess their relationship to a constituency, and this lack of skill leads to the indecision which results in incompetence. What is more, the picture of their performance which emerges to the public level is generally regarded as reflecting a do-nothing, incompetent governing agency. The incompetence of the board members is an open and widespread subject of public discussion among all groups in the community, and elected board members themselves are quick to admit to the outside observer that they "don't know much" about village government.

It thus happens that the incompetent, the economically vulnerable and the appropriately kinship-connected individuals are elected with a regularized consistency, as described below, to a village board on which they find they have nothing to do because, in their own perspective, the routine affairs of government are automatic. Meetings are routinized to fixed times and places and the ceremonies in which they participate are reduced to a pattern of talking which consumes time and accomplishes nothing.

The ceremony of talking while accomplishing nothing reflects the dominant psychology of those groups in the village which exist behind the scenes and control the processes and purposes of government. This group is composed of the small businessman who subscribes to the ideology of low taxes and low expenditures.

THE LOW-TAX IDEOLOGY AND BUSINESS DOMINANCE

The businessman exhibits the phenomenon of a psychology of scarcity. His private business operations are based on non-expansion and cost-cutting principles. Capital investment for the purpose of business expansion does not occur. Instead, the village businessman uses obsolete equipment and merchandizing methods. His business practices are based on the careful and jealous guardianship of a limited and local market. The primary appeal to the market is personal loyalty. Under these circumstances the businessman is concerned with minimizing the costs of operation and with accumulating savings. In his business as well as his private life he emphasizes the virtues of thrift, savings and the minimization of consumption. The virtues which he emphasizes result in accumulated savings which are partly hoarded as cash and partly invested in local real property. When this psychology of scarcity on the part of the businessman is translated into government operations, a premium is placed upon low government expenditures and low taxes.

In concrete personal terms, low expenditures mean low taxes and low taxes mean low fixed costs in business operations and the greater chance to accumulate as savings what might otherwise be "eaten up" in taxes. In the village board no expenditure is approved without a careful prior consideration of its consequences for the tax rate.

Hardly a meeting of the village board passes without some action being justified on the basis of the low tax principle— services are curtailed to avoid a tax raise, purchases of new equipment are postponed in order to avoid expenditures, the trustees complain to each other if street lights are not turned off at sunrise, payrolls are delayed near the end of the fiscal year when funds are short and new taxes have not been collected in order to save interest on a bank loan, state funds and services are accepted and sought "to save the taxpayer's money." It is habitual practice prior to the expenditure of any funds first to investigate whether the object for which the expenditures are being contemplated can be secured without cost by formal request to outside agencies, by informal deals with representatives of outside agencies or from private individuals or groups. Board members display a unanimity of agreement in this most cardinal of principles and apply it as a prior condition to any action except adjournment and accepting the minutes.

The understanding of the successful dominance of the low-tax, low-expenditure principle becomes clearer when placed in the context of the broader interests of businessmen.

Businessmen as a group possess the greatest interest of ownership in the real property of the village. In addition to owning their business establishments, businessmen invest savings in local real property. Almost every businessman owns some residential property and those who have had long and successful careers in business may own as many as five, ten or fifteen homes. Their practice of capital investment in multiple properties provides the link to their adherence to the low-tax, low-expenditure ideology.

As noted, not all members of the board are engaged in retail trade, nor do all possess extensive investments in real property. However, all members of the board adhere to the low-tax ideology. The selection of candidates for public office is based on a prior knowledge of the willingness of the candidate to accept the ideology. In recruiting candidates, all other qualifications for office—incompetence, vulnerability, kinship connections—take a secondary place to this cardinal principle of government. On the village board itself, saving (purchasing secondhand equipment), short-cut measures to prevent expenditures (borrowing equipment and facilities from other agencies and individuals) are virtuous acts. The honored and esteemed member of the board in the eyes of other board members is the one who is quick to see the possibilities of "saving money" or who can think of a way of doing it the "cheap way." Indeed, this is one of the important areas of competition between board members. Hence it happens that even those board members without a direct economic interest voice, sometimes most frequently, the low-tax, low-expenditure ideology. Through these processes the business psychology comes to dominate the philosophy of government of the village board.

MACHINE POLITICS AND THE SELECTION OF OFFICIALS

The effective membership of the local Republican committee consists of three individuals.[2] The chairman of the

[2] Technically the Republican committee is made up of ten elected individuals, two from each of five voting districts. However, this committee is elected merely to comply with party regulations and

Republican committee and the dominating but relatively invisible figure of local politics is Howard Jones, one-time mayor and owner of a feed mill and farm supply business, a farm implement and repair business, a building supplies business, several warehouses and half a dozen homes. In addition to Jones, the committee consists of Sam Lee, town clerk and editor of the local paper, and John Flint, a local lawyer with a local clientele. Flint is legal counsel to the village board and as such sits in attendance at its monthly meetings and possesses the only technical competence available to the board.

It is justifiable to assume that nomination by the Republican committee is tantamount to successful election in the manner of Southern politics. The Democratic party does not offer a slate of candidates for village offices. Hence, the Republican nominating process is crucial. Individuals possessing the qualifications mentioned above are easy to find. It is more difficult to find a qualified person willing to stand for election, not because such persons are not flattered by being considered but rather because they do not want to appear to be eager "to seek public office." The potential candidate is coaxed to run, finally accedes and is elected to office.

The process of nominating candidates is conducted by Jones, Lee and Flint in an approximation of the following manner: Flint, with the assistance of one or two others, draws up a list of three or four possible candidates; he "consults" with Jones, who may make additions or deletions; together they arrange the names in the sequence in which the potential nominees will be approached to be asked to

---

meets as a committee every four years to "instruct" the delegate to the national convention. When local party caucuses are held, newspaper items never carry their names as having been in attendance. A party caucus is usually reported in the newspaper as follows:
". . . The unusual fact about the Republican village caucus this year was that 13 citizens were on hand and no one had to coax or walk the street in search of another villager or two to make the required quorum. . . . Sam Lee acted as chairman of the meeting with Henry Monson acting as secretary. Mr. Lee, R. F. Carpenter and John Flint were selected as a village committee to fill vacancies and make arrangements for the caucus next year.

accept the nomination. Before the committee approaches a potential candidate, the list is shown to one or two more people. The persons whose names are on the list are then approached and one individual finally accepts without knowing how many before him have refused. Some days later Flint, who is politically antagonistic to Lee, tells Lee the name of the person who has accepted the nomination. Lee and Flint then make arrangements for a party caucus, setting and making public the day of the meeting. Lee and Flint and a handful of other individuals whom they have encouraged to attend appear for the caucus on the appointed day, but altogether they do not usually constitute a legally required quorum. Then, as Flint has noted, "Most of the time we have to go out and pick somebody off the street to get a quorum. Sometimes we even have a few Democrats voting in there." In any case, the result is uniformly the same : the party candidate is formally nominated in his absence and in the absence of Jones, who may not know the exact name of the nominee until he reads the newspaper. This nominating process results in the selection of candidates whose social characteristics conform to the requirements for success in village government.

In the past fifteen or twenty years, the years of our knowledge, no nominee, incumbent or new, of the party committee has been opposed by the party caucus. In the past twenty years no Republican candidate has been opposed by a Democratic candidate. Historically, nomination by the Republican caucus is equal to election. Trustees tend to succeed themselves unless they voluntarily retire, resign, move or die.

The election of one trustee occurs every year and the election of the mayor and clerk occurs every three years. Elections are held on the first Tuesday of April between the hours of 12 :00 noon and 4 :00 p.m. (thus excluding from voting those third of the employed individuals who work in surrounding cities) or, as sometimes occurs, between 2 :00 and 6 :00 p.m. and do not coincide with township, state or national elections. Between 15 and 35 individuals out of a potential electorate of 350-450 vote in a village election. In the certainty of a small vote, the board customarily contracts to print only 50 ballots. Village election day makes no dent on the routine affairs of the community. Election results are typically reported in the press as follows:

"In Springdale's village election held Tuesday at the Hose Room, 15 votes were cast.

"The only offices which had to be filled were those of two trustees. Smith and Morris were nominated to succeed themselves. Mr. Smith received a total of 15 votes and Mr. Morris 14."

or

"Slate of Village Officers Voted In as Nominated.

"Perhaps it's due to the fact that people are becoming public-minded, or it may be that good citizens who accept the nomination unopposed for public office are becoming suspicious of sneaky write-in methods; regardless of the reason, 34 villagers went to the polls and voted on Tuesday afternoon. This is in comparison to 13 votes last year. However, no competition or write-ins amounting to anything developed. . . ."

Those who vote are the candidate and those who nominated him and their wives. Lee and Flint make sure that at least 15 people vote. The party maintains a poll watcher who is familiar with the voting habits of those who vote and, should unexpected citizens appear to vote (as indicated in the newspaper clipping above), a party representative, who is on hand, hastily recruits counter-balancing voters. In this manner the inner-machine of the party assures the election of its candidates.[3]

[3] It must not be assumed, however, that the neat and logical operation of the political system as depicted above and explained below occurs through the rational and calculated design of officials and party leaders. Its operation occurs rather as a consequence of dynamics which are beyond the control of any individual or group of individuals. In watching the polls on election day to offset a protest vote, in taking over issues, in controlling the nomination of candidates—in all these actions, political leaders are merely responding to the political context within which they must act. Jones seemingly has some awareness

Public Interests and Political Paralysis

The village board and the Republican committee do not represent all the community views. There exist other groups who would be interested in "desirable" social expenditures, who lament the do-nothing attitude of the village board, and who would be interested in a revision of assessment evaluations. Residents of Back Street, as well as residents of several other streets, constitute an interest group who want paved roads and street lights. More recent migrants from cities (particularly professionals and industrial workers) would like recreational facilities and swimming instruction for their children and a community building as a center for social activities. The village as a whole is interested in snow removal and a garbage and trash removal service. The entire community is interested in better fire protection (replacement of obsolete equipment) and increased water pressure in kitchen spigots. Individual businessmen and home owners have grieved to the board for a reassessment of their property "to bring it in line with other assessments." A large but unorganized group of individuals is interested in bringing industry to the community. No action was taken on any of these measures in the years preceding and during the field work of the study.

These desires for improvement, change and increased expenditures are held by individuals who have no stake in or control over the village board and who are beyond the purview of party politics—they do not vote and only when they have a special cause or a special complaint or request do they attend meetings of the village board. Their efforts to secure the action they desire remain at the level of private complaining or of occasional attendance at a board meeting as individuals who represent themselves or a specialized organi-

---

of these dynamics, but even he is responding to circumstances dictated by his business and his position in the community. Only when the seemingly disparate actions of these leaders are brought into focus and related to each other does the system seem to operate in rational, calculable terms. It would be a mistake to attribute the functionings of the system to the conscious design of those who play the major roles in its operation.

zation with a specialized request. The most frequent complaint of local citizens, including board members themselves, concerns alleged inequities in the assessment structure of taxable property. In the entire history of the community, assessments have not been reviewed and great differences exist in assessments of equivalent properties.

In a specific case where an aggrieved property owner presented his grievances because his property was overassessed, all board members agreed that his grievance was justified. His property was assessed at the same amount or at more than much more valuable properties. The ensuing discussion brought out no more than that there were widespread discrepancies in the tax rolls and that a great many other grievances would be equally justified.

Village assessments are automatically copied from the township tax rolls which have never been reviewed or revised. The village board, however, has the jurisdiction to review and revalue village property, but changes in village assessments would involve recopying township tax rolls since the village assessors do not assess property but merely copy town assessments and for purposes of state subsidies, town and village assessments of village property have to be the same. Moreover, revaluation of one property would set a precedent for the reappraisal of others. On the basis of the time, effort and complexities involved, the matter was dropped, though no formal decision to do this was made.

The paralysis of the board in not being able to cope with this and other problems reflects an underlying paralysis of organized political action in the village at large, except for individual efforts among those groups which desire action. The groups and the individuals who want political action lack the tradition, the specialization and the organization to make their views felt. The complexity of organizing political support; the necessity for historical, legal and technical knowledge in defining an issue clearly; the lack of knowledge of procedure; the lack of time—all these factors lead to inaction and a complaining but dissatisfied acceptance of the "business as usual" ideology of the village board.

The only "politically-minded" organized group in the community is the American Legion. As an enduring organization whose membership has continuity over time, it can and does act as a pressure group. However, the political perspective of the local Legion is narrowly limited to those issues and measures necessary to the accomplishment of its own organizational ends. The Legion is interested in its liquor and gambling (bingo) privileges and in its monopoly over park facilities for baseball and the July 4th carnival. Occasionally it requires the appearance of officials at its public ceremonies and it is interested in the proper maintenance of the town "Honor Roll." The board responds to these interests as if they were demands. Illegal bingo is not prosecuted, the bar is tolerated, all public facilities are monopolized on July 4th and the mayor rides in the lead car of the parade. The Legion accepts an occasional unsolicited cash gift from elected officials. Its organizational ends which require political action are accomplished without overtly engaging in politics.

The Consequences of Political Paralysis

RELIANCE ON EXPERTS

In the village board the dominating and relatively publicly visible figure is the counsel, Flint, who is not an elected member of the board at all. Due to the legal and procedural complexities of conducting the routine business of the village and the necessity of correctly filling and filing the many documents which legalize and support the official actions taken by the board, no action is possible without the assistance of the legal counsel. Moreover, the counsel is the only individual competent to conduct a correspondence with state and other agencies with which the village must do business and he himself insists on following exact legal forms even when only local matters are involved. Meetings of the board do not ordinarily begin until the counsel has arrived.

The relationship between the legal counsel and the board is illustrated in the following protocol:

MONSON started discussing a bill brought to him by Heney, saying that he didn't understand it and would "Let Flint take this and discuss it with him."

MARTIN: "Well, let's get started, then."

FLINT, commenting that there is swearing in to be done tonight, writes at his table while the others watch him: "I'll just fool around with this while you continue."

MONSON reads the minutes.

MARTIN asks for additions or corrections.

FLINT: "Well, I wasn't paying attention. Was there a resolution on the treasurer's report?" Flint feels there should be a separate motion.

MONSON: "No separate resolution."

FLINT: "Well, we could do it tonight. I just think it should be done." (with emphasis)

MORRIS: "Do we have a list of fire appointees? I have a motion that Dickey become a member of the Hose Company."

FLINT: "The chief and the members should be appointed by the board."

MORRIS: "I wonder if we're not a little negligent about that."

FLINT: "Probably they should give us a record every year. From time to time a list comes in, but not regularly."

MORRIS: "I'll see that we get a list this year."

FLINT: "Let's get a motion on the books. A specific time when it would be convenient for them."

MONSON: "Yes. The mayor has to designate the acting mayor. It's a personal appointment. In case he wants to go fishing."

The legal counsel acts and is regarded as a source of information and as an authority not only on legal questions but also on general matters of procedure, precedent and history. When he speaks he is listened to with attention and his suggestions and recommendations are ordinarily accepted without question.

In addition to the board's reliance upon the technical skill of its counsel, it is frequently unable to act without the expert advice of outside experts. When it comes to erecting street signs, for example, the board must deal directly with a sergeant in the state traffic bureau who is familiar with the type of sign required and the regulations about its placement. In matters of youth recreation, the board was advised by a state representative with respect to its legal part in the administration of the program. The reliance of the board on outside experts is seen most clearly, however, in the fact that a large part of its business is conducted by correspondence with state agencies. In this process the village counsel who possesses the necessary skills is the connecting link to the outside agency and it is through him as he acts on the village board that the reliance of the board on experts is demonstrated most clearly.

THE SOCIAL BASIS OF UNANIMITY

The dominating influence of Flint on the board does not deny the possibility of conflict among the members. Beneath the public unanimity of the board, there exist small but important differences of interest between board members. For one, who lives on a street without lights, there exists a potential impulse to secure street lighting in needed places. Another who is superintendent of the fire district is more inclined than the others to spend money on fire equipment. The clerk who owns no business property and is not a voting member of the board would be favorably disposed to a reassessment program. The mayor tends to be more "economy-minded" than some of the trustees. Each participant on the board has a pet interest which serves as a potential basis for conflict. Yet this conflict is never openly apparent and the principle of unanimity of decision is never broken. When board business touches on issues of potential conflict, each board member brings up for subliminal assessment the position of other members on the issue in question—i.e., who would be apt to oppose the measure and with what intensity— and avoids further mention of the topic.

Since the board member has neither skill nor knowledge nor a constituency to support him, he lacks confidence in his own opinion and his own cause. Instead of pushing an idea, he retreats to more familiar territory, the espousal of "economy-mindedness" on which he knows all members agree. When an issue comes up on which the positions of all board members are not known—when some new problem presents itself, for instance—a long process of discussion, during which board members frequently contradict themselves, ensues. This discussion, which appears so strange to the outsider, takes place for the purpose of finding a common ground on which all can agree and in which no opinion stands out. In this way no member irrevocably commits himself on an issue and, hence, does not alienate himself from the other members of the board with whom he must deal from month to month and in his daily living on a "friendly" basis. These dynamics explain the lengthy and poorly directed discussion which occupies the time of the board and provide a partial explanation for the phenomenon of unanimity.

In addition, however, there is always the danger that, should an issue come into the open, conflicting parties will appeal to outside individuals or groups or to the more important figures in the machine. Public sentiment could easily be mobilized around the issues of assessments, street lighting and snow removal. There is the ever-present possibility that an issue can be taken directly to the leaders of the machine since the link between the board and the machine is intimate.

As a consequence of these dynamics, in any situation which suggests that differences of opinion exist, action is postponed or delayed to a subsequent meeting or indefinitely. Between meetings, interested parties are consulted, board members meet and talk informally and some type of "understanding" is reached before the next meeting. If the item at issue is small (where to place a street light), several important individuals in the neighborhood are talked to, and opinion is sounded in other neighborhoods which do not have street lights. If the issue is large (such as a several thousand dollar bank loan, to repair a broken water main—the issue being how good a job is to be done), Howard Jones is consulted directly. In many cases this activity between meetings settles the issue so that it comes up for perfunctory approval at a subsequent meeting; or, if a *modus vivendi* cannot be worked out, nothing further is heard of the issue.

In the ordinary conduct of business in this manner, potential issues and conflicts never become visible at a public level. Undisciplined appeals to outside groups which would threaten the monopoly of power of the controlling group do not occur. The board, especially the trustees who alone possess the voting privilege, openly state that they do not want "to stir up trouble." Since the board members themselves carry responsibility for their actions, they do not take action until the appropriate individuals are consulted and until it is apparent that responsibility is diffused into unanimity. There is the continuous effort to seek the formula by which unanimity can be achieved. Until unanimity is reached, there is a tacit agreement to discuss the proposal and to postpone the decision until the time comes when either by wearing down, time limitations or accident a formula is found. The formula itself takes many forms. Typically it is indefinite postponement. Frequently it is arrived at by "doing what we did last year or ten years ago." Sometimes it is reached by taking "the 'only' legal course open to us according to the law of the state." In no instance is a formula based on a recognition of conflicting interests which require balancing.

DEPENDENCE ON EXTRA-LEGAL BODIES

As a consequence of this structure of decision making, the village board is not usually in a position to act when pressing action is required. When special problems arise which require non-traditional solutions or quick decisions and quick action, extra-legal bodies take over the functions of village government and meet the problem by extra-legal, quasi-legal or private means. Three such problems which have arisen in the recent past may be cited to illustrate the manner in which community action is organized to meet problems requiring special action:

1. Some of the professional families, especially those with young children, desired a recreational program for the community's youth. No such facility existed for children. The State Youth Recreation Commission supports local youth programs by covering 50 percent of costs, provided a legally constituted governing body sponsors the program. Neither the village, town nor school board had ever availed themselves of such funds. A privately organized Youth Recreation Committee was set up, made contact with the State Recreation Commission and learned that one of the local boards must act as sponsor for the program. The chairman of the committee approached each of the boards in turn and received satisfaction from none. Then, through the auspices of this same vigorous chairman, a joint meeting of the town, school and village boards was arranged for the purposes of considering sponsorship of the program. A representative of the State Commission was present to explain legalities and details. The central issue before this joint meeting (each of the boards had already made an initial contribution to the program) was one of the assumption of responsibility and the location of control for the program. The issue was resolved because a private committee had taken the initiative in promoting a program which state law specifically intended should be handled by the village or town board. Moreover, only under pressure and the private committee's willingness to assume administrative responsibility was local government willing to play any part in a program which fell directly within its jurisdiction.

2. The village dam, privately owned by the Jones and Hilton feed mill, no longer serves its original power purpose and has been slowly disintegrating for the past twenty years. On its preservation depend the village swimming

hole and the high-water level necessary for fishing and the beauty of the village itself. A group of professionals and fishermen and property owners along the shores of the stream began to agitate for the preservation of the dam. Jones and Hilton, having no commercial interest in the dam, were not interested in repairing it. The village board refused to place the question on its agenda. Interested individuals then brought the problem of the dam before a business meeting of the Community Club. The Community Club acted quickly, set up a committee and within two years had raised $3,000, and with the permission of Jones and Hilton had repaired the dam over the objection of a sizable body of opinion which felt the dam should not be repaired until the Community Club had acquired the "dam right" and a small plot of surrounding property owned by Jones and Hilton. When the dam was completed and all bills were paid, Jones and Hilton offered to deed the "dam right" and adjoining property over to a "responsible organization" without charge. During the business session of the regular monthly meeting of the Community Club, these facts were reported by Flint along with the comment that the "Community Club was not empowered to own property and therefore could not accept the property. The village would have to do it." Monson, village clerk, announced that the village would accept the deed, "provided adequate provision was made that maintenance remain in the hands of the Community Club." These proposals were embodied in a motion by Flint which was unanimously passed by the members of the club in attendance.

3. In the past seven years, the various committees of the Community Club have concerned themselves with such board functions as the following:

   a. Established a state-supported youth recreation program
   b. Annual testing of swimming water
   c. Repairing and maintaining dam

d. Petitioned the county board of supervisors to repair a road "over which much business comes to Springdale"

e. Called in a representative of the state traffic bureau to explain state traffic policies with respect to Springdale and "complained" to him of inadequate traffic signals and facilities in Springdale

f. Annual setting up of a community Christmas tree

g. Agitated to secure street safety signs for school children

h. Established an industry committee in an effort to attract industry to Springdale

i. Initiated a park development program on property recently deeded to the village

j. Established an annual clean-up day

k. Heard all manner of specific complaints from individuals and organizations on problems related to traffic, road signs, safety, roads, public transportation (bus service), rural mail service, inadequate garbage and snow removal facilities, and so forth

l. Has under consideration the acquisition of a community building.

However, in spite of its extra-legal functioning in the political sphere, the Community Club is not a political body. Political issues are treated as discreet items of business in general meetings without being placed in the context of an overall political program. The functions which the Community Club has co-opted from the village board have been those functions which the board has been eager and willing to give up, those which are regarded as a nuisance or as expensive. The political activities of the Community Club represent political agitation for a specific point or a specific issue or the redress of a specific wrong. Since responsibility is diffused into committees, no central direction is given to an overall political program.

These extra-legal bodies tend to draw into their fold supporters who are not active in village politics. Support for specific issues is usually limited to those with a specialized interest and their interest is sustained only until the specific issue is resolved or crushed. However, if such extra-legal bodies, particularly the Community Club, gather sufficient support in the community as to appear to disturb the routinized equilibria of local politics (the youth program, the dam project, the formation of the Community Club itself), the leaders of both visible and invisible government become interested in the activity and the official governing agency reflects this interest in action. In the background of the dam project lay the interests of Jones, and the final resolution in turning the deed over to the village board publicly reflects a privately reached solution. The invisible government becomes interested in an issue in order to control the activities of extra-legal bodies. The machine may take a direct interest in an issue and openly act as an extra-legal body; it may take over control of other extra-legal bodies for appropriate periods of time; it may influence the organization of extra-legal bodies, as was the case of the Community Club. Hence, it is through these extra-legal temporary groupings and organizations that a certain amount of community action occurs in spite of the fact that village government has abdicated most of its functions.

Political Ceremonies and Political Participation

The pattern of village politics can be summarized in terms of an analysis of the meaning of the political ceremony. The political ceremony consists of the endless and indecisive talk which occurs in formal meetings of the village board. The formal meeting itself is a social ritual in which discussion serves the purpose of avoiding decision making. The postponement and avoidance of decisions has a number of social functions.

The ritual of talking, in the first instance, serves the primary purpose of achieving public unanimity within the board. No board member states his case or argues on issues in irrevocable terms. Rather by continuous exploration of alternatives, blunting of the issues and searching for neutral statements, a point is reached where all the individual perspectives of the board members are merged into one perspective and unanimity is achieved. When such a condition of unanimity is achieved, the issue can be resolved in such a way that no aggrieved board member has need or grounds to appeal to the community at large for support. Hence, no new or outside pressure groups can be brought in to bear on local politics and to threaten the monopoly of power of the village board and its controllers. Unanimity thus makes it difficult for outside groups to find an issue which would threaten the *status quo*.

The same process of endless talk stretching out from meeting to meeting and from year to year means that somehow the issues get lost even when unanimity is not achieved. After indefinite delay in dealing with an issue, the issue itself loses its salience and becomes irrelevant, and no action is required. In such cases unanimity is unnecessary because the issue over which potential conflict might arise has lost its importance with the passage of time.

In other cases the ritual of talk, postponement and unanimity works itself out in such a way that the necessary action gets accomplished without a decision being reached. This occurs in cases involving action relating to the requirements set by higher governmental agencies. In its postponement of decision making, the village board surrenders the legal prerogatives established within the framework of the village charter and state law. In not taking action where it has the option to do so, the village board allows mandatory alternatives to village action to become operative. Hence the state highway commission, the state traffic bureau and other state agencies actually determine village affairs.

In the various alternative cases described above, then, either a minimum of action is taken or only that action which does not threaten the *status quo*. This is understandable in terms of the patterns of political control in the village. The dominant political group is composed of small businessmen and property owners. Avoidance of action on their part represents an avoidance of expenditures and thus, in turn, results in the maintenance of low real-estate taxes.

The avoidance of splits, issues and controversies on the board results in the exclusion from political participation of "outsiders" because the processes of unanimity destroy those issues which might be capitalized upon by dissident groups. Moreover, politics without genuine issues, as a further result, is "dull" (nothing happens) and in terms of open issues there is nothing for which it is worth exercising the ballot. As a result, politics, though discussed incessantly by all, is only an amusing spectacle concerning personalities. Only a handful of individuals vote in village elections, those who have a direct interest—largely village and party officials and their families. Thus, between 15 and 35 voters control village elections and they do so by being interested in them. For other voters, the village board ceremony of continuously talking without accomplishment, while having the effect of producing disgust in those who are interested in political action, has the effect of producing disinterest and apathy among all groups in the community except on those occasions when politics may be viewed as a spectacle—i.e., when a newspaper editorial accuses the trustees of graft when they raise their own salaries. It is a consequence of this apathy that such a small number of voters determines the outcome of an election.

When, in the rare case, an outside interest group (the American Legion, the Community Club or the "professional" group) does actually create an issue and exert pressure which threatens the political monopoly of the political machine, a number of devices are used to prevent such groups from becoming permanent political forces in the community.

The American Legion is literally "bought off" by accepting unsolicited cash gifts from office holders and by being exempted from certain village regulations and enforcement activities relevant to gambling and liquor control. In a more positive manner, the Legion is permitted a monopoly over certain public facilities for certain of its functions (the park for its baseball program; the main road, police officials and the park for its annual carnival). On the occasion of its annual carnival, public officials are expected to and do play a ceremonial function. As long as the Legionnaires receive these exemptions and privileges, they support the local machine. Their active organization of a large number of potential voters represents a threat to the political machine which is forestalled by the grant of these exemptions and privileges. The Legion exercises a form of both positive and negative blackmail over the political machine and deals with it on these terms so long as its privileges and exemptions are granted.

The other interest groups, more transient and temporary in organization than the Legion, cannot be handled so simply. In dealing with them, two devices are available to the village board and the political machine. The first is to postpone and delay decision making until the advocates of new acitvities and expenditures are so "fed-up" that they turn to non-government agencies for support. Thus the Community Club becomes the administrative center where activities which are turned down or avoided by the village board are carried out. The Community Club, a private organization, then, exercises almost all of the activities of government except the minimal non-surrenderable functions of police control, street maintenance, water supply and elections. In exercising these functions, the Community Club uses revenues drawn from contributions, social memberships and money-raising projects rather than taxes to finance its community-wide program.

As a result, then, of surrendering its governmental functions to private organizations, the board keeps taxes low and at the same time allows for pressures for community projects and expenditures to be directed away from itself.

When it is not possible to divert pressures for change and innovation, when extra-legal bodies gain sufficient support for an issue, and when delay and postponement have not resolved the issue, the members of the board and the party machinery feel a threat to their political existence. The advocates of change (usually members of the professional and industrial class who are interested in social improvements) become the bearers of an issue which can arouse the community, bring out community-wide interest in the issue and the elections and, thus, threaten the *status quo*. In such an emergency, and only as a last-resort measure, the village board will consent to act. In acting it takes over the issue advocated by outsiders, and gets the action accomplished with the assistance of the machine. Once this happens the board becomes the sponsor and executor of the program and remains in control of the decisive areas of decision making. The issue as an issue disappears and the opposition to the board dissolves into its previous state of disorganization and is eliminated as a threat. Village government is then able to continue (and acts) as if nothing has happened. By election time there is no issue to dramatize politics and to threaten the control through apathy which the local machine has over elections.

As a further result of these dynamics all opposition groups in the village are, and can only be, organized around a single issue at any one time. All such groups in the past have been temporary and the machine has survived, even though in the process a number of local programs have been accomplished which otherwise might never have happened.

It is in this, perhaps minimal, way that outside interest groups are represented and that to some degree a democratic process is carried out. For, no matter what their own interests may be and no matter how reluctantly they aquiesce, the village hoard and the political machine, in order to maintain political control, must find some method of accommodating these pressures which, if avoided, would result in their loss of control. The reluctant acceptance of these issues and the programs which they entail constitute the foundations of democracy in the rural village.

Chapter 6

The Prosperous Farmers and Town Government

The Organization and Character
of Town Government

THE town board is made up of a supervisor (the chairman of the board), two board members, two police justices, a clerk and a road supervisor. All these officials are elected and, with the exception of the clerk and the road supervisor, all are voting members of the board. The town supervisor is a member of the county board of supervisors and represents the township in an organization which deals with county problems.

The clerk receives a part-time salary of $1,400 a year, keeps minutes of board proceedings, keeps the town financial records, authorizes payments of bills, is the custodian of all town records (births, deaths, marriages, property transfers, assessments), issues all licenses (dogs, hunting, marriage), and serves as the collector of taxes. To conduct the daily routine business of the town, the town maintains an office which is manned by the town clerk.

The position of road supervisor is a full-time position which requires the supervision of four to six employees (road workers) and the overall supervision of town roads and road equipment. Although fire protection is one of the board's important responsibilities, the board is not itself directly concerned with fire-fighting personnel, facilities or equipment. The town board gives financial support to one of the hose companies by providing it with equipment (i.e., "the lower hose company operates the town truck"). Funds which fire insurance companies rebate to rural fire companies in proportion to insurance coverage in the area are made payable to the town board. In addition, the fire companies are integrated into a regional fire district in accordance with state law. The town board makes membership payments to the fire district from funds collected under the fire tax. In fire protection, then, the board merely acts as a financial intermediary in charge of bookkeeping.

Meetings of the town board, like those of the village board, are held at fixed times and places. Contrary to the village board, an air of greater informality prevails (members are addressed by first names and jokes are apt to carry a heavier sexual content). In addition, it occasionally happens that meeting times are changed to accommodate farm members who are otherwise busy, but in no cases do meetings occupy less than two hours of time, no matter how much business there is. Except for these variations, the town board meeting stands as an almost exact copy of the village board meeting. Decisions are delayed until it is apparent that unanimity is possible. A vote is not taken unless it is obvious that all will vote the same. All decisions are the unanimous decisions of the board and all in attendance must indicate approval even though all do not possess the legal qualification to vote on board matters.

Decision making is not only minimized, but all decisions, with the exception of a few small unimportant issues, tend to focus around one area of jurisdiction, the town roads. In meetings observed over a two-year period major board actions consisted of deciding to abandon an unused road, making an out-of-court settlement on a road claim, deciding to buy a new road roller and accepting a state-sponsored road development plan.

Roads, then, and issues and problems connected with roads constitute the central area of decision making on the town board.[1] The actual legal jurisdiction of the board is much

[1] This interest in roads is indicated in the town tax structure and budget. The town imposes three taxes at the following ratio per thousand-dollar evaluation: general tax, $24.40; highway tax, $6.00; fire tax, $1.20. Total revenues from the three sources equal about $75,000. A large portion of the general tax fund, $46,000, automatically

broader than the interest in roads would suggest. The legal jurisdiction of the board includes fire and police protection; licensing; the social welfare of the members of the township; the construction, maintenance and development of new and old roads; and the provision of other services and facilities necessary to the welfare of the township.

However, most of these jurisdictions, either by tradition or by default, have reverted to other agencies of government. Police and welfare functions are performed by the county and state, usually through special administrative arrangements worked out in state bureaus. Licensing of all kinds falls within the administrative scope of the clerk, who performs these functions more as an agent of the state than of town government. The forms and the legal requirements which surround them are derived from state agencies which set procedures and require reports. In this function the clerk is an administrative arm of the state and much of what he does in the daily course of business is not known to the other officials of town government.

Within the known past, no new functions have been undertaken by the board. The chief and only exception to this abdication of functions lies, as we have said, in the area of roads, but this is with respect to certain roads only. Main thoroughfares are the province of the state highway department, which maintains a garage and a road crew in the community. Many of the hard-surface roads fall within the purview of the county road network and their development has been financed out of county funds. The remaining hard-surface roads and a great number of dirt roads, which serve the purpose of connecting the various areas of the township to the arteries of the larger highway system, are the exclusive domain of the town board. Even with these roads, however, the major cost of maintenance and development is carried by

---

reverts to the county according to state equalization formulas. A portion, about half, of the fire tax revenues automatically reverts to the fire district, also according to state equalization formulas. Revenues from the highway tax remain to be spent locally and are supplemented with $27,000 in state aid designated for town roads.

the state highway department, which annually contributes to the local road budget more than twice the amount raised by the local road tax.

In exchange for its road subsidy, the state sets maintenance, construction and equipment standards for town government. A state highway engineer, located in a regional office, serves the double purpose of enforcing state regulations and providing expert advice on the requirements and standards set by law. When the board buys new road equipment, the state engineer gives technical advice and must certify in writing that the equipment fulfills the minimum standards set for such equipment by the state. When a road is rebuilt with state funds, the state engineer sees to it that it is of the proper width, has the proper drainage and a proper thickness of gravel correctly packed. If these requirements are not certified as fulfilled, the town does not receive its road subsidy.

On the other hand the state does not specify *where* roads shall be built. The placement of roads and the decision to improve one road rather than another are an autonomous function of town government. It is within this framework, then, that roads alone constitute the chief business of the board and make up a major portion of its expeditures. It is interesting in this connection that town government is placed in a position where it must deal with relatively large sums of money. For example, the officials of town government must be capable of approving sums as large as $10,000 for a single piece of equipment, and this they are able to do without qualms.

It is a further peculiarity of town government that, although its actual functions pertain exclusively to activities outside the village, the entire township, including voters in the village, votes for the election of its officers. The village voting privilege arises from the fact that the general town tax applies to village property as well as to country property. In consequence, town government is partially supported by village taxpayers who derive no benefit from the activities of town government.

The Social Composition and Psychology
of Board Members

The members of the town board are reelected with almost the same regularity as those of the village board but, as will be noted below, Democrats sometimes win elections and occasionally there is a Democratic upset. The clerk of the board is Sam Lee, who has held this position for the past twenty years and whose father held the same position for thirty years before him. The two police justices tend to be older men, retired farmers or lifelong residents of the township who live either in the village or in the country. The board members are practicing farmers, one of whom is characteristically a traditional farmer and the other in more recent years has been a prosperous Polish farmer. The road supervisor lives outside the village, usually has some knowledge of road construction, has lived there for a long time and does not have a permanent or full-time job (small chicken farmer, manager of a rural postal station, etc.). As will be explained below, the road supervisor may be either a Republican or a Democrat.

Traditionally the town supervisor has been a farmer and a Republican who is active in village affairs. For fifteen years prior to 1949 he was a prosperous farmer, Melbin, who had become prosperous during the decade of the Forties. Due to differences over party policies on the county board of supervisors, Melbin was not nominated by the local party to succeed himself in 1949. Instead, a popular local entrepreneur was nominated and defeated by a Democratic candidate, Richard Calvin, who has remained in office to the present time. Calvin is a part-time appliance dealer who lives just outside the incorporated limits of the village.

The composition of the board at any time represents an ostensible balance between village and country members, the country members being drawn from different sections of the township. However, Lee, Calvin and one police justice, while considered "village representatives," have strong connections with farm people and must profess or have some basis for implying a psychological identification with township affairs and farmers—i.e., having grown up on a farm, having many farm friends, being a retired farmer. A candidate for supervisor must ordinarily have extensions into both the village and the country. If he is a farmer, he is usually active in many village affairs, which also means that he lives relatively close to the village. If he is a businessman, he usually has a farm clientele and belongs to such farm organizations as the Grange. Psychologically the town supervisor must bridge, at least symbolically, the village-country difference.

The town board, like the village board, is oriented to keeping taxes down. The records show that at one time or another every member of the board has subscribed to the "keep taxes down" rhetoric. The candidate for town supervisor, whether Democrat or Republican, cannot be elected unless he is known as a "low tax man." However, the psychological atmosphere in which this rhetoric is voiced differs from that of the village board.

Combined town tax rates in relation to the village rate run in the ratio of ten to one. The town budget, including state road subsidies, comes close to $100,000 and, even though a large percentage of this is allocated to fixed costs (automatically turned over to the county and the fire district according to fixed formulas), the board members must nevertheless approve what is regarded as a high tax rate and must approve a budget which runs into "six figures." More specifically, in terms of "free decisions," the board must annually approve expenditures of close to $25,000 for roads. Although the low tax ideology is central to the board, it must face up to its fixed commitments and to the necessity of roads.

Roads are of course highly visible to those who use them. If their condition is poor, if they have not been graded or graveled for a long time or if the maintenance crew has not been seen working on them "since the spring thaw," the road supervisor and the board are held directly responsible. It is this fact more than any other which determines the psychological atmosphere of the town board. The immediate and visible consequences of poor road conditions make the board capable of approving what are regarded as a high tax rate and expenditures of large sums of money.

In addition, however, this circumstance in combination with the abdication of other functions and the low tax attitude leads to a psychological acceptance of *roads as the only jurisdiction* of town government. The acceptance of this limitation of jurisdiction is a primary qualification for membership on the board. Within this psychological atmosphere, however, the board must take due account of the existence of a village constituency which derives no benefits from the board's actions. Village property owners pay the town general tax and constitute an important and easily mobilized electorate in township elections. It is at this point that the low-expenditure ideology becomes partly understandable and that the connecting link between village and town government is provided by the invisible government of the community.

Personalities Embodying Farmer-Business Conflicts; The Invisible Government

As we have noted, the major figures in the Republican party, that is, the effective Republican committee, are John Flint, Sam Lee and Howard Jones. Flint is the legal counsel to the *village* board and, in his capacity as a member of the party, this board is his jurisdiction. He initiates the nomination proceedings for village elections and intimately guides the proceedings of the board itself. Flint, however, is not important in township politics. He does not attend town board meetings in either an official or unofficial capacity. He is not known to be intimate with any members of the town board and in township elections his activities are limited to getting out the village vote. Although he may privately voice dissatisfaction with the state of town government, his effective political reference group is the village, and his participation in town politics would be a direct challenge to Sam Lee.

Sam Lee is the link between the town board and the effective Republican committee. As clerk of the board since the death of his father twenty years ago, Lee has an intimate knowledge of the affairs of the town, and is the only man in town who knows the fiscal setup of town government. The public records of town government have been in the Lee family for fifty years and in many cases the system of record keeping and the whereabouts of the records themselves are known only to Lee.

Lee is also the owner and editor of the local weekly newspaper, the *Springdale Press*, which he inherited from his father along with the clerkship of the board. Until recently when, for reasons of health, he sold out his interests in the newspaper, the office and meeting place of the town board and the repository of its records have been the front office and editorial room of the print shop. The daily business of the board as conducted by its clerk was transacted across the business counter of the newspaper, and board meetings took place in an atmosphere of printer's ink. The minutes which Lee kept as clerk of the board became the basis of a news item in the next issue of the newspaper. The town board office is now located in the abandoned railroad station and Lee continues with a more tangential interest in the newspaper; he holds the mortgage on the establishment and works "by the hour" for the new editor.

On several occasions in the past, Flint as a member of the Republican committee has sought to nominate an alternative candidate for the position of town clerk. In each case Lee has successfully foiled the attempt by threatening to run for town supervisor if he should not be nominated for the clerkship. Except for one or two occasions, the Democrats do not back a candidate for the clerkship. Lee has been able to maintain his position as town clerk by his personal friendliness, by being critical of Flint, by being the champion of underdog causes (particularly in the village), and by his outspoken editorial views in the *Springdale Press*. Traditionally, Lee has assumed the position of attacker of the village board—editorials on village board members as money grabbers when they raised their own pay, agitation for board action or snow removal—while simultaneously he has carried out some of the major functions of the village board as president of the Community Club and chairman of the committee on the dam. In his capacity as chairman of the committee on the dam, he was largely responsible for raising the $3,000 necessary to preserving the dam. In the village he is known as a critic of a village government which does nothing, and as a man who accomplishes desirable social projects.

As editor and town clerk he has "social contacts" with a wide range of rural residents. The newspaper carries a social column for each of the rural areas ("Mrs. Smith and her daughter, Velma, went to Rockland on a shopping trip last Thursday," "Mr. and Mrs. Jones of Smithfield were the weekend guests of Mr. and Mrs. Rodney Alexander," "Peter Kloski has a new Farmall tractor"), a segment of the paper which serves as a communicator of important social facts for the rural readership. As town clerk he issues birth, marriage and death certificates; dog, hunting and fishing licenses; and records all property assessments. As a result of this dual position his contacts with the public extend throughout the township and, due to his "friendly, helpful and talkative" manner, he is on personal terms with a great many people. Over a period of twenty years he has developed a wide arc of independent supporters.

Lee is assured of the personal loyalty of sufficient number of individuals to be elected to any position on the town board. However, his supporters are not organized and are not independent of other leaders of the invisible government. Moreover, by his simultaneous association with the invisible government of the township and by his attacks on village government, there are pockets of resentment against him in the township (particularly in the poor road areas) and in the village. Hence, he has not been able to set himself up as an independent force in local politics, and continues his close identification with the Republican committee.

Lee has supported his position on the Republican committee by the political uses to which he has put his paper in state elections. Candidates for the state legislature and for the national congress approach Lee directly for the support of his newspaper. In concrete terms this means carrying the picture of the candidate and a front-page news story on the virtues of his character and accomplishments. When these candidates visit the community, they do so under the auspices of Lee, who introduces them to friends and newcomers and to all those who transact business with him in his capacity as editor and clerk. This link between Lee and county and state candidates at election time, and the potential power and prestige by association which is implied by such connections, supports his position in local political circles.

In addition, however, as clerk of the board Lee is the supervisor of township elections. He sees to it that ballots are printed and distributed to each of the five voting districts in the township. He does these chores personally and in doing them comes in contact with those who officiate at the polls in each of the districts. He has known these people for a long time and has had a voice in their selection. It is through them that he gauges political sentiment in each of the districts and is kept informed of voting trends on election day. In this capacity he serves a positively useful purpose for the party committee and simultaneously supports his own position within it.

As a result of these circumstances Lee is a force, but not an independent one, in township politics and in the Republican committee. The opposition both within and outside the committee has not been able to dislodge him. For lack of an independent and coherent organization of his own, he must express himself politically through the Republican committee. He does this through a relationship with Howard Jones, who invisibly connects both the visible and invisible governments of the village and town—in the village through Flint and in the town through Lee. The invisible government has its key in the person of Jones.

Jones, a name familiar to the community for a hundred years, is the second son of a man who made the name important as a cattle dealer in the preceding generation. Howard Jones entered the feed business in 1918 in partnership with an older man, Richard Hilton, who now plays only a minor part in the business and community. Since 1918 the business has expanded to include building supplies, farm implements, machinery repairs, lumber, hardware and an extensive delivery service. The business employs six to eight workers and a bookkeeper. Local competition consists of a Grange League Federation outlet which does one-tenth the business of Jones and Hilton, and which has no local connection to the Grange.

The line of supplies merchandized by the firm and the repair and feed grinding services which it offers are sufficiently broad to meet the needs of village and rural non-farm residents as well as farmers. A large proportion of home repair and construction materials business and a great proportion of the available farm business is handled by the firm. A substantial portion of the business is conducted on short-term credit, and perhaps 5 to 10 percent is conducted on long-term credit. No interest is charged on extended credits. Cash payments within thirty days receive a 1 percent discount. During the 1920's and particularly during the 1930's the firm "carried" a substantial number of farmers who are successful today, especially the Polish farmers who now uniformly state that Howard Jones was "the only man who trusted us when we first came." The firm carries mortgages on a number of farms and is known to have foreclosed only once (on an outsider).

The business is located in the village and is a focal point for farmers who come to the village. Any farmer who does business with the firm makes a trip to the "mill" at least every week or two. On a rainy day there is a congestion of traffic around the mill and the farmer regards his visit as much a social as a business occasion. He wants to talk and to meet friends. He wants to know how other farmers are doing, "how much young heifers are bringing," whether grains are "going up or down," and he wants to discuss milk prices, farming practices and new types of machinery. At the mill he has an opportunity to do this with other farmers and with the proprietors.

Jones has an intimate knowledge of the affairs of the

farmers who are his customers. He knows what their indebtedness is, what their long-range expansion plans are, what their seasonal needs are and what their family life is like (i.e., whether the wife is a helpmate, which sons are interested in farming, what "quality" people they are).

It is generally acknowledged and has been demonstrated that Jones is capable of securing a great many farm signatures on petitions. He is in close contact with one or two outstanding farmers in each of the main farm neighborhoods and it is through these farmers that he circulates petitions and information. When it is necessary to have a farm representation at a public hearing in the county seat or at a town board meeting, Jones is capable of assuring that representation. It is said that "he can have fifty farmers in the village inside of a half-hour, rain or shine." In important elections he takes an active part in getting out the farm vote. In purely local elections, unless there is a "contest," his activities are not publicly visible.

As a result of his extensive and peculiar relationships with the farmers of the township, Jones is a power in town government. He expresses this power both positively and negatively through Lee. Lee, who plays a major role in the nomination of township candidates, must consult with Jones before Republican party nominations become official. In village government the position analogous to Lee's is held by Flint, and these two men as individuals embody the village-rural clash of interest. Aside from immediate personality differences between the two, Lee attacks the village board as penny pinchers (while alternatingly attacking them as "money grabbers"), as poor businessmen and for dereliction of duty. While engaging in such attacks, Lee in his private activities carries out some of the functions of village government and, hence, his attack cannot be construed as an attack on the village at large.

Flint and others on the village board focus their attack on Lee on the cost of town government (inefficiency of the clerk, poor administration) to a village constituency which derives no benefit from town government. This attack, however, is veiled since an attack on town government can easily be construed by farmers as an effort to reduce expenditures on roads, the most immediate and visible consequence of the existence of town government. Farmers, who are viewed in the popular mind as providing the main economic base of the town, are the one group in the town whom no one consciously offends. Ironically, as will be noted below, it is these farmers who prevent the town board from making expenditures on village activities since they can see no direct benefit to themselves from town investments in the village. In this sense, then, Lee and Flint stand as symbols of the village-rural conflict.

Jones stands as a higher power in this conflict. He too, in a personal and political way, is involved in the conflict. He has economic and property interests in the village and for fifteen years up to 1949 was its mayor. In village affairs, as the most successful businessman in town, he accepts the ideology of the village board. Due to his peculiar position, however, he has personal and political extensions into the township. Good roads are important to the conduct of his business and farmers are his most important customers. In a very real way Jones's position embodies all the elements of the conflict and this fact places him in a dual position. The manner in which he resolves this conflict with respect to his own position in local politics provides the basis for understanding how a balance is maintained within the invisible government.

Jones practices a knife-edge aloofness from the conflict between Lee and Flint and all that it represents. Neither Flint nor Lee takes his conflicts to Jones for resolution. Hence it is a mutually respected traditional practice to avoid a "showdown battle," and the effective Republican committee maintains its coherence and control within the framework of these differences. The independent strength which Jones has among farmers, not to mention his personal wealth and prestige, enhances his position in relation to Lee, who also has strength among farmers; because of this, Lee is satisfied to be regularly renominated to the clerkship while tacitly agreeing not to upset the balance of forces in the invisible government.

As a result of this intricate constellation of relationships, Jones is the controlling figure in both village and town government. However, due to the village-rural conflict and his own dual position in relation to it, he must remain publicly anonymous and exercise control invisibly. He cannot appear to commit himself overwhelmingly in the village-rural conflict or he would become identified with one side and lose the support and control of the other. The effective Republican committee would be split. It is in this sense that Jones is the invisible government over the village and town, and it is his relationship with prosperous farmers which makes it possible for the board to act on the issue of roads.

The Dominance of Prosperous Farmers

Prosperous farmers have tended to dominate town government less by occupying its formal positions than by acting (successfully) as a pressure group. It is possible that they could fill the positions of one or both board members and even of town supervisor since, if they indicated an interest or a desire, they could easily secure the nomination. In practice, however, prosperous farmers have no desire to occupy their time with the regular official meetings of the board. These meetings are dull, lengthy and require a type of activity which is alien to the productive "get-things-done" attitude of the prosperous farmer. Melbin became town supervisor while he was still a struggling hill farmer and kept the position even after he became prosperous because he had larger political ambitions. The Polish member, Kinserna, holds the position less as a prosperous farmer than as a Pole who sees it as an avenue to social acceptance in a dominantly "American" environment. When prosperous farmers happen to be on the board they seem to be there for reasons other than openly influencing board policies in favor of the group they represent.

Prosperous farmers are interested in good roads as an

adjunct to their business operations and because a good road fronting their property enhances the value of that property. As a consequence of this specialized interest, they become interested in town government only on those occasions when road policies are under consideration. These occasions are rare, once in a year or two and sometimes not for five years. In the intervening years their roads are maintained on a seasonal basis to their satisfaction or, if not, they approach the town supervisor personally "to see that something is done to get my road graded and oiled."

When road policies are under consideration before the board, prosperous farmers organize delegations to attend such meetings for the purpose of exerting pressure to influence decisions. This was done in 1951 when the board was considering a state-supported ten-year road development plan for rural townships. State legislation provided for the state to bear 75 percent of the program's cost and stipulated that local boards hold public hearings on the plan. Springdale's town board held such a hearing which was attended by about 100 people. After this hearing, the board decided, but not in a decisive way, not to participate in the program. The farmers "heard" that the board was ready to jettison the plan and at the next meeting of the board four prosperous farmers along with the state highway engineer came "to make sure this program is adopted." At this meeting the board reversed its decision under the pressure of the prosperous farmers. The first question in the protocol below is by Stevens, the road superintendent, and is directed at Lashly, the state engineer:

"Stevens asks what about construction of bridges, etc., the law has no provisions for that sort of thing. Lashly brushes this off, says his candid opinion is that the town should adopt the program. Fridel announces that we (sweep of hand indicating Best, Burdin and Havland, all prosperous farmers) are here to make sure this program is adopted. Fridel adds, 'I understood that the town board was opposed to going in on the program.' (Woodhouse, Calvin, Elson, board members, weakly say, 'No, no.') Fridel continues, 'This is the first town board meeting I've ever attended.' Elson says if he likes it he should come more often. Fridel says he doesn't want to butt in but this sort of thing (roads) is in his line. Calvin says Fridel misunderstands—this is a public meeting—they like to hear all sides. (All this in a very friendly fashion.) There is much joking about widening roads—who will pay for fences that have to be set back. Lashly says if roads are being improved people are pretty cooperative. Then Lashly says that if the town is going to get into the program they will have to have a resolution. Calvin asks, 'What do you fellows want to do about it—do you want to go in?' Elson says, 'Don't see why not.' Woodhouse says that the picture has changed completely since the meeting in the school, and adds that Butts, the state representative at the public hearing held at the school, had said that the road project had to be continuous over ten years, but now he knows it can be spread around and he is all for it. Then followed a discussion on whose road would be fixed first under the program—danger of favoritism. Best, contributing for the first time, said, 'No problem here—we're a peaceable bunch.' Lashly asks, 'How are you going to satisfy people whose roads won't be built till 1958?' "

With this and only this action, since there is no other public record on acceptance of the plan, the board entered the ten-year road plan which shows that in spite of its low-tax, low-expenditure ideology the board can be forced into programs which are costly, if it is urged to do so by the prosperous farmers.

In matters other than roads the prosperous farmers leave the board to its various ceremonialisms and do not interfere. But it is precisely on the issue of roads that the nexus between Howard Jones and the farmers, especially prosperous ones, finds its meaning. Farmers need good roads for their daily deliveries of milk and the value of farm property is related to the quality of the road on which it is located. At this point the business and political interests of Jones coincide with those of the farmers. These farmers are his customers and their roads are travelled by his delivery trucks. However, as the protocol above suggests, not all roads can be fixed equally well or at the same time. The prosperous farmers make sure that their roads get preferential treatment. Jones, however, cannot identify himself too closely with one segment of farmers since they are all his customers; for this reason, even though he is in favor of road expenditures, he does not play a visible part in promoting them. His interests are expressed through the prosperous farmers in this as well as other political activities already mentioned. Hence he is able to continue as the main force in the invisible government of the town as well as of the village even when these governments exclude large segments of the population which are important to him in his business.

THE EXCLUDED GROUPS

Prosperous farmers represent only a portion of the constituency of the town board. One third of its constituency is made up of residents of the village; another third is composed of rural-dwelling industrial workers and shack people; the last third is composed of prosperous farmers and traditional farmers.[2] The village constituency has little or no interest in township affairs except with respect to the tax rate, which at worst is grumblingly accepted along with the low tax rhetoric. The only two groups who are psychologically located in township affairs are the traditional farmers and the prosperous farmers. The industrial workers are scattered and isolated and if they are active are oriented to village activ-

[2] Three small settlements (Clinton, Pelham and Hendy's Hollow) located on the periphery of the township have their psychological locus in communities in adjoining townships. This group comprises about one-fourth of the voting population but takes no part in village or township activities. However, they constitute an important segment of the voting population and are considered in this context below.

ities. The shack people have psychologically abdicated from the community and, in their lack of illusions caused by their psychology of resentment and lack of vested interests, are aware of the various public screens of politics. Their resentment results only in private and unorganized mutterings and complaints, since their time and attention is absorbed with too many other private matters concerned with daily living and pleasures.

The traditional farmers are a minority of the farm community, representing about a third of all the farmers. Since they are a small group who by the standards of prosperous farmers are not successful and since they are apt to represent lowly assessed property, they do not constitute a force in town government. Their lack of success tends to disqualify them from having a political voice even though several may be board members. In matters of road maintenance their voice, when heard, carries no weight. The road superintendent who may come from this group is a symbolic figurehead with no voice in determining which roads are to be maintained and improved. At best he is able to do an occasional favor (a free load of gravel, clearing a driveway) for a traditional farmer who may be a personal friend. With this exception, the traditional farmers as a group do not benefit from township government.

The ceremony of selecting nominees from both the village and the country and from different geographical areas of the country gives the illusion of representation for all groups. The Polish group is represented on the board by a prosperous Polish farmer who serves the ceremonial function of being a representative of the Polish group at the same time that roads in the Polish areas are among the worst in the township. The political biases of the board are revealed in the condition of specific roads and in the location of good roads. These biases reflect those forces in the community, the prosperous farmers, who can make the board act. However, the excluded groups are not always willing to tolerate the results of road decisions and because of this the board and the invisible government must cope periodically with their accumulated resentments.

Roads and the Election Process

THE MEANING OF ROADS

Since farmers and grain merchants depend on roads as an adjunct of their business, it is understandable that all politics in both visible and invisible government centers on the issue of roads. As noted, the type and condition of roads reflect on property values and furthermore on the general esteem in which a man is held in the community. To live on a rutted, one-lane, dead-end, dirt road in and of itself makes a man an object of derision. In addition to this, road conditions partly determine the rate of depreciation ("wear and tear") of those vehicles which travel on them. In an area where most back roads have a gravel surface, this consideration is important in terms of rate of replacement of cars and trucks. In these circumstances it is apparent why the road supervisor holds only a nominal position and why decisions on roads are made by other agencies of government.

The village is not dependent on the town for its roads since the state takes responsibility for main thoroughfares. Therefore the exclusion of the village in town road policies makes little practical difference except at the symbolic level, where it constitutes a slap in the face to the dignity of village government.

The shack people do not expect good roads since they are fully aware that they are beyond the pale when it comes to influencing such decisions; furthermore, by regarding the official government as "the crooks on top," they exclude themselves from an attempt to participate.

The industrial workers are politically unorganized and do not own important property. Although they are in reality important to the local business economy, the public image holds them to be economically dispensable. The rural nonfarm population which commutes to work to the nearby industrial centers is, of course, as dependent upon roads as the farmers. When road issues arise, they will follow the lead of any group which has a gripe and is willing to express it.

Accidents of geography as well as affluence are important in the dynamics of politics. An industrial worker who lives on the same road with a number of prosperous farmers will be well off and, likewise, prosperous farmers living on roads with a number of traditional farmers, shack people and industrial workers will not be well off.

Almost all groups, then, including the excluded ones, have a central interest in roads. In view of limitations on road funds—available resources are not sufficient to repair and maintain all roads equally well—resentments develop and accumulate. When there is a sufficient accumulation of these resentments, the routinized equilibria of the election process in town government is upset.

POLITICAL PARTIES AND THE ELECTION PROCESS

Although the town board is just as inactive as the village board except when prodded to action on roads, the voting in town elections is proportionally much greater in relation to the total potential electorate than is the case in village elections. Out of a town electorate of 1,600-1,700 as many as 500-700 actually vote in a typical election.

Township elections are held every two years on odd-numbered years and consequently never coincide with national or state elections except in special instances for the purpose of filling unexpired terms. County elections are also held on even-numbered years and village elections, which occur on odd-numbered years are held in April, eight months before town elections. Township elections, with the exception of the inclusion of an occasional county or state ballot for one or two offices, are a town affair.

Traditionally the position of road supervisor has rotated between a Republican and a Democrat at six- to eight-year intervals. It is part of the folklore of local politics that the road supervisor receives fewer and fewer votes in each election as he makes more and more enemies during the period of his incumbency. His daily actions in the maintenance of roads are highly visible and even though he has no voice in road policies, over a period of years he "offends" sufficient voters to be "thrown out of office." He is the major scapegoat of town politics and is the victim of town board road policies. Yet once in office, he never resigns and hence is replaced by the opposition party candidate who takes office and begins the cycle over again.

The greater voting interest in township elections is partly accounted for by the fact that the position of road supervisor is usually an issue, and partly by the fact that both the Democratic and Republican parties nominate a slate of candidates for town positions. Since there is typically no intra-party opposition within the Republican party, the only party which has a primary, the primary election is a formality which receives little or no public notice. The caucus of each party selects its slate of candidates and waits for the final election.

Historically the selection of a slate of Democratic candidates has been of ritual significance only. Within the memory of living politicians, the Democratic party has always failed to elect even a single candidate to a voting position on the board.

The weakness of the Democratic party organization is indicated by the following exchange taken from a town board meeting:

> "Lee read a letter from Robert Cassidy of Rockford, the Democratic county committeeman—appointing two Democratic poll-watchers—'election inspectors' for District 3—Canterville—the two mentioned are Burke and Merle. Calvin (chairman of the town Democratic Committee) asked who did that for the Democrats before. Lee rather tolerantly explained that '*we*' always see to it that there are two Democrats. These two have been doing it for some time but he (Cassidy) just got around to writing us."

Moreover, the Democratic poll-watchers are present at few if any elections, including those for national offices. The party organization, which consists of two or three individuals, has existed primarily to be in a position to designate a Democrat to the position of postmaster. For this reason the fiction of a party organization and the nomination of candidates for township positions have been continued. But the party is so weak that it is usually unable to offer a full slate of candidates, i.e., willing candidates cannot be found. Typically, at a minimum, a supervisor, one councilman and a road supervisor are nominated and defeated. The continued nomination of candidates for these positions is to a certain extent accounted for by the fact that they frequently receive one-quarter to one-third of the votes cast and that a road supervisor is occasionally elected. Those who vote for the Democratic candidates represent (1) a relatively steady protest vote against the road policies of the town board, particularly their consistent failure to repair certain roads and (2) a protest vote of settlements located on the periphery of the township whose members have no voice in township affairs and in Republican party politics. This relatively steady protest vote has acted to force the Democratic committee to nominate candidates even when the committee itself would find it simpler not to and would prefer not to. The traditional function of the Democratic party is to profit from resentments on road issues.

Up to 1949 the voting members of the town board have all been Republicans, renominated as a formality until they have resigned and reelected every two years over Democratic candidates. The town clerk, with his large independent following, has typically been unopposed. From 500 to 700 voters have reelected the Republican candidates by 5 to 1 margins. With the exception of the town supervisor, this has continued to the present. In 1949 the Republicans lost the position of town supervisor to a Democrat and from that time until 1953 the invisible government was threatened by a loss of control. The reaction of invisible government to this threat reveals the organizational dynamics of invisible government and the mechanisms of political warfare in the rural township.

ROADS AND THE DISENFRANCHISED: A CRUCIAL CASE

As pointed out, the Democratic party on regular occasions wins the seat of road supervisor. However, in political terms this is a ceremony since basic road decisions are made by the board, which is Republican-dominated. However, the road issue is so decisive that, at times, in combination with other circumstances, it can overcome the Republican habit.

In 1949 a Democratic town supervisor (Calvin) was put in office by a vote of 661 to 562 in an election which drew more voters in a town contest than any in the memory of living politicians. It was an election in which the town clerk was unopposed. On pressure from the county committee, the previous Republican incumbent, Melbin, was not renominated by the local committee. On the county board Melbin had opposed the investment of a large sum of money on a new cow barn for the county fair grounds. His refusal to support this action led to his failure to be renominated. The popular businessman nominated in his place and defeated was in part the victim of local resentment against the highhanded action of the county committee in local affairs. However, this election was the occasion of several special county and statewide contests. The high number of voters is accounted for by the fact of these contests. Typically state and national elections bring a total vote of between 80-90 percent of the electorate, or about 1,400 voters. The relatively smaller number of voters in this election can be attributed to the special state contests for which sufficient local enthusiasm could not be aroused. Although state Republican nominees carried the township by a 10 to 2 margin, the Democratic supervisor was elected by a 6 to 5 margin. A sufficient number of protest Republican votes had been cast to defeat the Republican party nominee for town supervisor.

The Republican committee of the town and those who are invisibly associated with it are responsible to higher party organizations for getting the vote out in important elections. In concrete terms this means newspaper publicity, word-of-mouth reminders and, most important, the organization of car-pools on election day to bring voters to the polls. In such elections Jones, Flint, Lee and their lesser neighborhood "captains" are seen bringing carloads of voters to the polls.

Many of those they brought out on this occasion contributed to the defeat of their own candidate.

As a result of Calvin's election, Springdale politicians became the butt of jokes among county politicians. Springdale, the Republican stronghold, was represented on the county board of supervisors by a Democrat, the only Democrat on the county board. Local politicians predicted dire consequences for Springdale—Springdale would have no voice in county affairs, county services would be curtailed. Indeed, the projected hard-topping of an important county road in the township was delayed. Beneath the public fanfare, however, local politicians were not too concerned. Calvin quickly proved himself to be a "low tax man" and the controlling group of Republicans began calling him "the stingiest town supervisor Springdale ever had."

Two years later public interest in the township election ran high. The invisible government of the town had become highly visible and the electorate eagerly viewed the spectacle. Without question, the Republican party was "out to get Calvin." To oppose him they nominated Russel White, a lifelong resident of Springdale in his late sixties, president and major owner of the locally owned telephone company. In keeping with custom, neither candidate engaged in any formal campaigning—no speeches, no special visiting, a single advertisement in the newspaper. On election day the voters were brought or came to the polls in greater numbers than usual. Calvin, the only Democratic nominee besides road supervisor, was elected by a vote of 464 to 417 in an election which otherwise ran a customary course.

The Republican committee had erred in its selection of a candidate, had not yet "found a suitable candidate to present to the public." In addition to the usual protest vote, the voters had voted *against* White, the owner and supervisor of the telephone company, rather than *for* White, the candidate for town supervisor. Local telephones are of the older magneto, crank type. Many rural subscribers are on party lines with ten or twelve other subscribers. Moreover, the state public service commission had recently granted a raise in telephone rates. Hence, although White was well known, he was known in an unfavorable context. Calvin remained as supervisor for two more years, and the hard-topping of the county road was still delayed.

In the ensuing two years, James West, a traditional farmer with a family name going back 100 years in Springdale history and generally accorded little respect—in fact laughed at ("five acres of potatoes and 500 gladiola bulbs")—organized the residents along his road and led them in a road protest to the town board. In his protest, West was given little satisfaction by the town board. In 1952 he attended four successive meetings and in one instance appeared with a contingent of supporters. Excerpts from the records of the first and last meetings indicate his relationship with the board:

CALVIN called the meeting to order, saying, "Mr. West has something to say to us." West was sitting at the back of the office, and stood up to talk. He started to talk in a loud, somewhat nervous manner, addressing himself to Stevens. "Stevens, Bill Lashly [the state engineer] says that bridge by my place won't cost $1,000 to fix. He says it won't even cost $100. All you need is four railroad ties. The only thing is high water might loosen them."

STEVENS (Stevens and the other board members adopted a half-soothing, half-humorous tone in talking to West, as though soothing a fractious child. In spite of West's occasional anger, they didn't respond in kind, apparently feeling quite securely in command of the situation): "West, we can't do that. What would happen in high water or in case of an ice flow? Besides you can't get good ties off this branch line. They're all rotten."

KINSERNA agrees that the ties are no good.

WEST: "What's to be done?" (He sounds angry.)

STEVENS: "Well, I don't know. In the first place you were out" (meaning West's bridge is not on the list for repair under the ten-year road plan).

WEST: "Who excluded us?"

STEVENS starts to explain that the branch line gets cast-off ties from the main line and when the branch line discards ties, they are useless.

WEST: "Just a minute! Who excluded us?"

STEVENS: "Nobody a-purpose."

KINSERNA agrees with Stevens.

ELSON: "Did Lashly name a pacific (sic) bridge?"

WEST ignores Elson. (He appears to be hard of hearing, asked for repetition several times.) "Something's got to be done. More people go to my farm than any farm in Dane county."

ELSON: "You say you got the most important farm in the county? Maybe we ought to tell the assessor about that."

WEST: "I didn't say that. A lot of people come there, though. I have a business." (Elson mutters that "we all have business.")

STEVENS says that ice would be blocked up if the bridge is cribbed and that the bridge is pretty good, he recently put a 12-ton grader over it.

WEST (angry again): "Who is telling the truth? If Bill Lashly is a liar, I'd like to know about it. He's a friend of mine. I lost sale of 600 bushels of potatoes, because a truck wouldn't go across that bridge."

LEE: "Andy's mules wouldn't go across the lower bridge during the 4th of July parade, Jimmy. (This sally is considered successful, judging by the smiles of various board members.)

CALVIN: "Didn't those people have anything smaller they could pick up the potatoes with?"

WEST: (calmer): "I don't know. It was a P&C outfit. They had a big ten-wheeler and they wouldn't come across that bridge with it to pick up the sacks."

WOODHOUSE: "I remember when that bridge had an abutment in the middle. I guess you wouldn't remember that, Jimmy."

STEVENS: "Ask Lashly where he gets his ties."

ELSON: "How many ties did he say you needed?"

WEST: "Four."

ELSON: "You can't do it."

WEST (seems angry again) : "Bill Lashly says you can. He's a University graduate and an engineer. He says put four ties upright under the middle."

WOODHOUSE : "I don't think that would do, Jimmy. I thought you meant cribbing."

ELSON : "So did I."

STEVENS : "No permanent support, water would wash it right away. That's a gravel bed there. You know what water does to gravel."

WEST : "Very interesting. Bill Lashly says one thing and you say another. Who's lying? He says there are lots of bridges fixed like that all over the county."

CALVIN : "You'd better look at some of the bridges Lashly meant, and decide how that would work."

WEST makes one last stand, asking if they hadn't planned to put black top on some of the roads (an expensive procedure compared to his request for four ties). He seems to think Lashly told him they were going to. They deny it. West leaves, saying thanks.

[At the fourth meeting he attended, West went unnoticed by the Board for a period of two hours. Then finally, as the board is still considering other business. . . .]

LEE and CALVIN start talking together, but they are cut off by a murmur among the three men in the back. Suddenly, West strides out, muttering so that everyone can hear : "What the hell's the use of being here if you don't get recognized?" He slams the door : there is an embarrassed silence.

WOODHOUSE : "Well, put that in your pipe and smoke it."

STEVENS (surprised) : "I suppose he wanted us to ask *his* advice."

The board heard no more from West for almost a year when he announced his candidacy for town supervisor on the Republican ticket. Without seeking party support, he secured sufficient signatures on nominating petitions to insure himself a place on the primary ballot as a Republican candidate. The party nominated Melbin, the man who had been town supervisor for twelve years up to 1949. The Republican party was to have one of its first hotly contested primaries. During the summer of 1953, West, a bachelor who lives with his sister in a state of almost total isolation from social and community affairs, began a vigorous campaign. For a period of three months prior to the primary West and his sister were seen making social-political calls to the homes of some 300-500 voters. This political technique represented an unprecedented innovation in Springdale politics. Moreover, he anchored his campaign on the issues of "poor roads" and "throw the rotten clique out."

The coming primary was noted in the press five days prior to the election in a news item which by its length broke with all tradition in the coverage of a local primary. The opposing candidates were described by Lee as follows:

Primaries To Be Held Tuesday, September 15

"In the town of Springdale, one of the very few contests throughout the county will be staged. This contest is for the very important office—head of the local town government, the office of supervisor.

"James West, an agriculturist, drew first position on the ballot. He is a graduate of the university, a native of Springdale and has been engaged in the growing of potatoes and other farm products for a number of years. He also grows thousands of gladioli each season. He has been working very hard in his effort to receive the Republican nomination and has called at practically every home in the township.

"Melbin, his opponent, whose name will be second on the ballot, is also well known and has had plenty of political experience. He is also a native of Springdale and for twelve years represented this township on the board of supervisors. Four years ago he decided to retire from the office and declined to run again. Besides his political life, he has been active in many community and farm organizations."

On the following Tuesday the voters elected West to head the Republican ticket as town supervisor. West received 258 votes and Melbin 225. The voting by election districts shows that Melbin received almost 200 of his votes from village voters. West had a mandate from the rural residents to turn the rascals out. The Springdale press reported the event in part as follows:

"West To Head Republican Ticket

"What proved to be one of the largest primary elections in the town of Springdale was held on Tuesday when a closely contested election was won by James C. West.

"A total of 483 Republican voters used the privilege of their franchise to nominate West to head their ticket for the office of supervisor in the coming November election.

"Mr. West conducted a campaign in which he called on nearly all households in the town. His campaign proved most successful because of the fact that he defeated a well-known farmer and a former supervisor, Melbin, who had a record of doing a good job as supervisor and also active in all community functions."

Six months earlier the Democratic incumbent, Calvin, had indicated that he would not run again. At the time of the Republican primary, the Democratic caucus had not yet nominated its candidate. In the time between the Republican primary and the Democratic caucus, Calvin was urged to change his mind by the Republican committee and was renominated by the Democrats—i.e., by himself.

Political campaigning was conducted on an unprecedented scale. West continued his house-to-house calls and repeated calls on people he had seen earlier. The local Republican committee refused to vote him the traditional $50 given to support the party's nominee for supervisor. West appealed to the county committee and received another refusal. He conducted his campaign on his own resources and in the early morning of the day of the election distributed typewritten handbills on the doorstep "of every house in the village."

Meanwhile the Republican committee gave official support to *neither* candidate. However, the members of the committee as individuals gave their unofficial support to Calvin. It became common public knowledge that "the powers that be" wanted West defeated. West became the object of negative gossip—he would double road taxes, his own road would be the only one fixed, "he'll make Springdale the laughing-stock of the county." The clerk of the county board of Supervisors, an important Republican in county politics, signed a paid advertisement in the local paper testifying to Calvin's diligence as a member of the county board. Calvin, whom the Republicans had opposed in two previous elections, was now given their active support at both the township and county levels. On election day the Republican party organization brought out the voters to vote for Calvin, the Democrat.

On election day 566 votes for Calvin as against 520 for West were cast to reelect the incumbent. Out of a total of 1,117 votes,[3] 751 were cast in the village districts[4] where Calvin received his greatest majority. The Republican party had turned out the village vote while the country protest vote was given to West on the road issue.

Calvin, who had been more unacceptable as a Democrat than as an supervisor in the preceding years, had become a better choice as a "low-tax, low-expenditure man" than an unpredictable and uncontrolled, though Republican, West. The size of West's support showed the extent of a dissenting vote against the controlling group and showed equally the effectiveness of the controlling group's organization and ability to get out a vote along desired lines. The election made it possible for the board to settle scores with West and his neighbors, whose punishment took the form of little or no maintenance for their road. With this exception, town government could continue its customary policies as if nothing had happened. The disaffected and dissatisfied country groups were left without a champion for their cause, and the road issue, except for mutterings, was closed for two more years or until such time as accumulated resentments would be organized by another political novice outside the invisible government.

[3] 33 voters cast blank ballots.
[4] In town elections the village voting districts include part of the surrounding countryside so that more than the 300-400 village voters are tallied in the village districts.

Discipline by County and State Machines

The selection of Republican nominees for township offices takes place in the Republican caucus but, as with village nominations, preliminary screening is done by the party committee with Flint, in this case, playing a minor role. In the township Lee and Jones are joined in their activities as political stage managers by Mr. Young. Young is a lawyer, a former county judge, legal counsel on a fee basis to the town board, has a law practice in the county seat and devotes himself to politics. He is the Springdale member of the county Republican committee and a high-order Mason who holds office in the statewide Masonic organization. Young plays no part in village affairs; his detachment from the village is symbolically illustrated by his daily departure to the county seat.

It is in his position as a county committeeman that Young is of interest to a discussion of township politics. The town board is linked to the county board of supervisors through the town supervisor. The county committee is interested in the composition of the county board of supervisors; they like to have only Republicans. Young's purview on the county committee is Springdale township and it is on this basis that local committee nominees must be screened by him. The action to depose Melbin in 1949 because of his rift with the county board of supervisors and the action to support Calvin, the Democrat, over West in 1953 were communicated to the town from the county seat through Young.

As a county committeeman and Mason, Young's influence reaches into county and state political affairs. On this basis he has access to higher authorities in the county, region and state. He has personal associations with state legislators and congressmen who represent Springdale. He sits at the speakers' table with a senator running for reelection to the U.S. Senate. These associations with higher authorities and important politicians give him prestige and power in the town. Hence, his "grass roots" political position is based on his higher position and in this respect he is different from both

Lee and Jones. He is less well known to the population at
large in the township than they are and, although he is
consulted far less frequently than Lee or Jones, he is always
consulted on issues of great importance. To a certain extent
Flint is in competition with Young since, as a lawyer and
local committeeman, he has formal and informal connections
at the county level. But since Flint's domain is a village
government which has no extensions or ramifications beyond itself, he carries little weight in the county committee
with which he does his best to maintain cooperative relationships.

Young's direct access to the county committee gives him
a virtual veto power in the selection of Republican township
candidates, particularly in the selection of the town supervisor. Party dominance in the county is maintained by in-
suring party dominance in the county board of supervisors.
Hence, county committeemen, Young in Springdale, directly
intervene in the selection of the party nominee for town
supervisor.

The only other occasions on which Young operates in
township politics is in the nomination and election of a state
assemblyman who represents the county. It is his function
to support the county committee's nominee for the state
assembly by discouraging local individuals from running in
the primary, or, if necessary by encouraging a local person
to run if county strategy requires a split vote along certain
lines to insure the nomination of the favored nominee. Any
politician in the township who wants to run for a county
office or the state assembly or senate will, as a matter of
course, consult with Young before doing so. If it is several
months before the primary, Young may not be in a position
to make a positive recommendation—"The county picture
has not yet become clear." When the "picture" becomes clear
it may be necessary to have a Springdale candidate for a
certain office in order to draw votes from an independent
Republican in a nearby area who will run regardless of the
county committee. Another aspirant will be absolutely discouraged in order to achieve the opposite. In a county with

two competing cities, the smaller one being the county seat, such decisions may be delayed until the last moment. When this happens pre-primary politics may become very intensive and no candidate will know his status with the party committee until the last moment because the picture "takes a long time in clearing."

If the county situation remains unstable—i.e., a large number of potential candidates remain—until shortly before the primary, the state party machinery enters the picture and forces the elimination of some candidates without appearing to do so in a highhanded way. State headquarters may also enter the picture if it is necessary to prevent a certain candidate from gaining the nomination or, in extreme cases, to purge an incumbent. The ways in which the state may intervene in the pre-primary process in the town and county vary with specific situations and specific aspirants. Whatever is the policy in any specific case will affect Young's policy at the level of township politics since the continuance of his position in the town depends upon his acting in a way which is consonant with state party policy as it is transmitted through the county Republican committee.

The county committee responds favorably to state party policy on such personnel matters because the higher party levels make all patronage decisions. State patronage consists not only of jobs but also of state contributions to the budget of the county board of supervisors. Under Republican state administrations the relationship between the rural county and the state is based upon a continuous exchange of favorable subsidy policies in return for not only Republican success at the polls but the success of specific Republicans who can be counted upon to be cooperative in the state legislature and in county affairs.

State legislation may directly simplify the processes of Republican control at the township level without reference to the County board of supervisors. The ten-year road plan, mentioned before, was a measure intended to relieve the "road pressure" on town governments. However, the low-expenditure ideology is so binding on local officials that they were psychologically incapable of making the connection between this policy and their own political survival. Acceptance of the road policy had to be pushed through by the prosperous farmers and the state engineer. At this point the state processes of control can be unwittingly sabotaged by local officials who see all politics in local terms and in terms of local personalities and all of whom, outside of Young, are guided by a blind suspicion of state government.

Chapter 7

The Clash of Class Interests
in School Politics

Organization and Character
of the School Board

THE INSTITUTIONAL SETTING. The school board is composed of five elected board members, each elected for a five-year term on successive years. The board itself elects one of its members as chairman. In addition to these board members, who alone possess the voting privilege, an appointed clerk, an appointed legal counsel, and the principal and district superintendent (who are *ex-officio* members) attend the board meetings. Meetings are held monthly except during the summer months when school is recessed.

The geographical boundaries of the centralized school district approximately coincide with the legal boundaries of the township. The school is located in the village and has an attendance of approximately 600 students in grades 1 through 12 from all sections of the township.

A budget of a quarter of a million dollars makes the school the major "industry" of the village, a major purchaser of goods and services and the source of a substantial section of purchasing power. Every family with school-age children has a daily contact with it for nine and one-half months of the year. School buses cover the township roads twice a day. Most of the major social, cultural and athletic events of the community take place within its halls.

In contrast to the village and town boards, the school board is faced with making important decisions on issues which have far-reaching consequences in the community at large. Politically it is the area in which most community issues, interest, activities and discussion are present. The decisions of the school board focus on the following problems:

1. The budget, specifically as related to school buses, expanded curriculum and expanded plant facilities, which together determine the school tax rate.

2. The proportioning of the agricultural curriculum as against college preparatory and industrial and business crafts curricula.

3. Appointments and reappointments of teachers, and granting tenure.

4. The appointment of janitors, bus drivers and motor repairmen.

5. School food and supply purchases.

All these are crucial issues in the community and decisions made in connection with them have extensions into many other sectors of community life. The reappointment of a teacher determines his continued residence in the community. School buying affects the volume of local business. Curricula offerings determine the type of education children receive.

The decisions of the school board are highly visible in their consequences to the entire community, not alone through the direct contact which adults have with school affairs, but particularly through reports they receive directly from their children. The consequences of decisions of the school board are almost as visible as the actions of the teacher in the classroom. This situation makes it difficult for the board to maintain secrecy with respect to its decisions, and results in greater efforts at concealment. The greater efforts to conceal result in a more strict adherence to the principle of unanimity of decision.

The school board, like the other governing boards, reaches its decisions through a process of discussion which results in an inchoately arrived-at unanimous decision in which no vote, or only a perfunctory one, is taken. Agreement becomes apparent to all present or dissenting opinion silences itself and the final vote is recorded as unanimous. In the ordinary routine meeting (all meetings are open to the public but not attended) business is conducted on this basis with little apparent friction or difference of opinion. When it appears that differences exist and that several sides must be heard or when a major item of new business is to be discussed, the board adjourns to executive session from which the public is excluded.

CONCEALMENT AND CRISIS

Any one of the problem areas mentioned above can easily become the focal point around which a public crisis can develop, and no year passes without the occurrence of a crisis. Because of this susceptibility it becomes central to the psychology of the members of the board to attempt to minimize or avoid crises, and this leads to further demands for unanimity and concealment. Research protocols reveal this process in a major crisis which developed in connection with the dismissal of a principal. The reasons for the dismissal of the principal were not given to the public. The P.T.A., which supported the principal, invited the board to attend a P.T.A. meeting to explain the reasons for the dismissal. Two hundred citizens attended the meeting, which, to insure impartiality, was chaired by a minister from another town. After three hours of wrangling, no answer was given to the central question of *why* the principal was dismissed. The meeting was reported as follows:

"The main question asked by three or four people was, 'What were the specific reasons for Marsh's dismissal?' The board refused to answer this question. The following was the sequence of events:

1. Rev. Vicker read the question stated somewhat differently from four to five papers. He said he would not read the questioner's names although all the questions were signed.
2. The board members just sat staring ahead.
3. Rev. Vicker repeated the question and asked if anyone wanted to speak about the question. He turned facing the board.
4. Holden (chairman of the board) stood up, faced the

audience. He said that the board was elected to decide about school matters and they thought that it was for the best interests of the school that Marsh's contract not be renewed. Holden said he would need to have the names of the questioners so he would know better how to answer the question. Vicker then got the approval of Mrs. Regner for reading these names and read the names, E. F. Rotter and Furness. There may have been one or two more names read but the practice of reading names was not continued throughout the meeting.

5. Rev. Vicker repeated the question and said he felt it had not been answered. He understood that the board didn't want to but that they should be explicit about their decision not to answer or should answer the question. (He was applauded by the audience.)

6. After what seemed to be a long pause Holden said he didn't feel that this was the proper body to receive the answer to the question, that the matter concerned the whole school district and that if and when the board decided to give its reasons for Marsh's dismissal the board would call its own meeting.

7. Vicker: 'Then you're not going to answer the question now?'

8. Holden: 'That's right.'

9. Vicker then went on to the next question."

Three days later the board at a special open meeting of its own, attended by 250 individuals, still refused to answer any specific questions in connection with the dismissal and remained unanimous in their agreement not to divulge any information, in spite of the fact that one member of the board was known to be opposed to the dismissal. Once the action had been taken and intense interest and pressure had been aroused, the iron laws of unanimity and concealment remained intact even in the face of the opposition of the member.

Due to the high visibility of the consequences of decisions, to the *necessity* of making decisions in order to keep a large institution going and to efforts to conceal the locus of decisions from a highly interested public, the school board and school policies become the focal point of public crisis. Almost every major decision of the board carries within it the seed of crisis. In the past five years these crises, half of which have resulted in mass protest meetings, have centered on the following issues: a school construction program, a businessmen's protest against the school administration for permitting "socialism in the school," the dismissal of the principal and the dismissals of popular teachers. Yet, in spite of these crises, the decisions of the board stand and the social composition of the board remains the same from year to year.

Selection and Social Composition of Board Members

Elections of board members take place at the annual school board meeting which is usually attended by 30-90 individuals, depending upon the intensity of previous crises. Candidates must be nominated by a petition containing at least 25 signatures. Typically one candidate is nominated in this manner and is elected to office by a near unanimous vote of all those present at the meeting. Candidates may not be nominated from the floor, but there are usually one or two write-in votes. Those who attend the annual meeting vary from year to year but in any one year the majority of those in attendance are made up of relatives and friends of the nominee. The board hires a clerk, a counsel and a principal who then attend board meetings. The superintendent of schools is appointed by outside agencies.[1]

[1] The position of district superintendent of schools in rural areas is a hangover from the days of pre-centralization, which in Springdale occurred in 1937. He then acted to coordinate and maintain standards for all one-room schoolhouses in the district, an area comprising a large part of the county. Centralization and consolidation have reduced his duties to "form filling and administrative detail." The principal, by virtue of his close and daily contact with school affairs, has necessarily taken over a large part of his functions and duties. Hence superintendents are generally unfamiliar and unacquainted with the problems of any one central school and have no voice in policy as it is made and executed day-by-day. Since superintendents are powerless except as members of the board, where they do not possess necessary

The central fact of the social composition of the school board is the dominance of rural over village interests. The board is always made up of 4 rural members and 1 village member. Historically this dominance stems from informal political agreements made at the time of centralization in 1937. In an effort to insure passage of the centralization referendum, which was opposed by rural interests, village interests at that time "agreed" to a school board composed of 4 members from the old rural districts and 1 from the old village district. This agreement has been respected up to the present time.

The rural members have traditionally been "respectable" prosperous farmers who have been residents of the township for all or most of their lives. The fifth member has always fulfilled the requirement of residence in the village, but this has not in itself insured a representation of village interests. Prior to centralization, the village district was dominated by "retired farmers." For twenty continuous years prior to centralization, Hilton, a partner in the Jones and Hilton firm, sat as a member of the board. After centralization, Hilton continued to sit as the village representative of the new centralized board. When Hilton retired from the board, he was replaced by Ralph Jones, son of Howard Jones and junior partner in the firm of Jones and Hilton. It is reasonable to affirm that the village position on the school board has traditionally been held by the Jones and Hilton feed mill. The interests represented on the school board are overwhelmingly rural and, moreover, are the interests of the prosperous farmers.

---

and sufficient information they are generally regarded as incompetent. The president of the school board, sitting in the same room with the superintendent at the public meeting of the board mentioned in the text above, referred to Springdale's superintendent in the following manner: "As noted earlier, Holden had stated that the school superintendent was of no value to the board—'He was as much value to the board as three wheels are to a bicycle.' Then Holden was interrupted by Vicker for making personal comments. Holden said that Anderson (school superintendent) was present and could speak for himself. This was not quite so, as no one was allowed to speak from the audience."

The school principal is always a non-resident outside expert. The clerk of the board is usually a white-collar worker who is capable of acting as scribe and record keeper. Although for a long period of time, the clerk's job was held by a man who was also accountant for the Jones and Hilton firm, the position is not crucial and has been held at various times by whoever "can be coaxed into accepting it." The legal counsel since centralization has been Flint, whose connections, as noted previously, are to the village board and the Republican committee.

The Republican committee as such plays no legal function in school affairs. At this point politics are separated from education. Political parties do not support school board candidates and do not formally meet to nominate them.

The most invisible act of local politics is the process of selecting nominees for school board membership. The public becomes aware that the processes are completed with the appearance of a small note in the *Springdale Press* which states:

"Annual School District Meeting July 8

"The annual meeting of the inhabitants of Springdale Central School, District No. 1, will be held next Tuesday evening in the school auditorium.

"The only nomination for the office of trustee for a term of five years, filed with the school clerk, was that of Henry Hanks. The person elected will succeed B. D. Toth. Any citizen has the same privilege of writing in the name as he has always enjoyed before. . . ."

Behind these outward appearances, the members of the board, the legal counsel and, without doubt, Howard Jones have selected the nominee and have secured his acceptance of the nomination. An individual who is not a member of the invisible government is secured to carry out the public act of circulating the petition until 25 signatures have been obtained. The petition is then filed with the clerk of the board, whereupon the nominating process has been legalized. Since petition forms must be secured from the clerk and returned to him, it is easy to know of the existence of opposition candidates but, in reality, this problem never arises. The formal election of the nominee is typically reported in the press as follows:

"Henry Hanks Elected School Trustee

"About 90 persons were present at what was later termed a very dull school meeting on Tuesday evening at the Central School.

"Only one name appeared on the ballot for trustee for a term of five years to succeed B. D. Toth, whose term expired. Henry Hanks had presented to the clerk of the board a petition with over 25 signers and, therefore, was a candidate. He received the majority of the votes cast with a few scattered names being written in for various persons in the community. He was declared elected and the meeting adjourned."

In this manner the board perpetuates itself and the dominance of prosperous farmers.

This process of selection and the rural dominance which it sustains have connections of a special character to invisible government. Flint expresses his influence on school policy exclusively as counsel. Lee, whose influence is expressed through the party organization, is excluded from school politics. Indeed, he frequently acts as the antagonist of the board when issues are raised to the public level. The antagonisms between Lee and Flint result partly from this difference of influence in forming school policy. Lee's exclusion permits him from time to time to lead attacks on the board.

Even though school politics is not a part of party politics, Howard Jones is not excluded from school affairs since his firm has one of its partners sitting on the board. In addition, however, Jones is a close personal friend of Holden, the president of the board and a prosperous farmer. Holden came to the community twenty-five years ago with little capital and has since become successful in large part because of the Jones and Hilton credit policies which supported him in his early years as a struggling farmer. Through this network of processes and relationships Howard Jones plays a central part in school policy.

The Consequences of Rural Dominance

Rural dominance has its consequences in the overall administration and character of the school. Although farmers represent only one-third of the population, a heavy emphasis in the school curriculum is placed on home economics and agricultural training. Between 1945 and 1951, 21 out of a total of 57 male graduates took the agricultural course, yet only 4 of the 21 were engaged in farming in 1951. The major opportunities for the school's graduates lie in industry, business and college. The business course, a relatively recent addition taught by one person, consists of business accounting and secretarial training; its inclusion in the curriculum represents a concession to businessmen. The industrial arts program consists of a mechanics course which is geared to tractor and automobile repairs. No provision is made for industrial training to qualify students for employment in industry, where the large majority seek jobs. As a consequence most graduates take unskilled jobs since regional industries do not hire them as apprentices. The college preparatory course, the other major offering, meets minimum state requirements and on the whole qualifies students for admission to state teacher's colleges, where three or four go each year. Agricultural training is overemphasized and perpetuates a tradition of what has largely become useless training.

The school bus service, which represents an annual budget item of $25,000 and a capital investment of $100,000, is provided for rural children only. The dozen jobs connected with operating this transportation system constitute the major political plums which the board has to offer and these jobs, except for two or three, are given to farmers.

The appointment of teachers has far-reaching consequences not only for education but also for the social composition of the community. Preference is shown for native daughters who return to the community from college. Three or four teachers are the wives of farmers, and several more represent village families. The great proportion of teachers, however, must be hired from the "outside," which usually means the importation of 30-35 families into the village; the school chooses these carefully. One of the primary criteria used in selecting teachers is their social origin—whether they were "reared" in a city or in the country. The applicant who comes from a farm or a small town is uniformly appointed if a choice between two candidates is available; by and large the staff is composed of teachers who have a rural background. Through such processes of teacher selection an attempt is made to perpetuate the rural tradition and to minimize innovative tendencies which might run counter to it.

The business conditions of the community can be affected by school purchasing policies, particularly by purchases of food for the cafeteria. Traditionally the school board has supported local groceries by purchasing food supplies equally from all five groceries on a rotating weekly basis. It once offended local merchants during a major construction program by not following a policy of local buying. This can happen because local prices are not competitive and because state construction requirements set minimum standards and prices.

Businessmen are the only group in the community who take a direct and organized interest in school policy. Since the board is controlled by rural interests, the relations between businessmen and the school board constitute an important segment of school politics.

Rural Dominance and the Businessmen

Business interests and farm interests coincide in the low-tax, low-expenditure ideology and at this level a *modus-vivendi* in school policy exists between the two sets of interests. Beyond this, business interests, because they are narrow, are accommodated easily by the board in the interests of local "peace and harmony." When it is necessary for the businessmen to make their voices heard, they express themselves through the business bureau. They are generally interested in two things: the maintenance of law and order for the protection of property, and the effects of school policy on the level of local business.

In concrete terms the maintenance of law and order means receiving cooperation from the school to insure an orderly and disciplined adolescent population on the village streets. The central school accounts for the daily concentration of 500-600 children who represent a daily threat to the "peace and order" of the village. By virtue of the school bus service a large percentage of these children safely by-pass the village on their way to and from school. The major problem is the noon hour, which in response to business interest is taken up with a program of movies and other forms of organized recreation. That this interest is respected by school policy is shown by the following excerpt from the school principal's newspaper column:

"Noon Hour Program

"We are scheduling a noon-hour program that will give all children some good healthy activity of their own choosing during their free time. We do this for two reasons: *the first, to keep them under supervision to cover our legal liability and our moral obligation to you*; the second, to develop their leadership ability and their skills in organization and activity.

"This program will include such things as intramural sports, publishing a school paper, publishing a school annual, Future Farmers of America, Future Homemakers of America, other clubs and hobby activities. If at any time your child needs to go to town for you to do some shopping he will be able to get a pass from the office to do so. These passes will be issued during the noon hour or a scheduled recess period. We wish you would help us impress him with the fact that he needs the pass, though. Our ideal is to be able to account for the whereabouts of every child at every minute of the day. His cooperation will protect his privilege and negate the need for overly stringent regulations."

Where school policy affects local business, however, conflicts arise and businessmen bring pressure to bear on the school administration in an effort to protect their business. Since members of the school board are prosperous farmers they tend to think in terms of buying where it is cheapest. In their personal affairs they are accustomed to mail-order purchases, to shopping around and to hunting for bargains. They are psychologically capable of bypassing village tradesmen when it is to their economic advantage. They bring this attitude with them to the board of education and hence it happens that the largest part of school expenditures are made with outside firms. This is a source of constant irritation to the businessmen and it leads to resentment against those who administrate the board's policies: the principal and his assistants. Since the businessmen are powerless to change the board's purchasing policies, their resentments must find expression in other channels. The classic businessmen's issue rests on the sales competition of student money-raising enterprises, which are supervised by the administration rather than by the school board.

On one occasion this issue of sales competition was broadly debated in the business bureau as one of "socialism in the school." High-school seniors were raising money for an annual trip to Washington, D.C., by selling ice cream to each other. Lee, attacking the school as a threat to business interests, wrote an editorial entitled "Socialism in the School"; following this, the matter was brought up for official consideration at a meeting of the business bureau. The school principal and his assistant attended the meeting reported as follows:

"Stating the Problem

"Martin called for any new business. There was a long pause. Finally someone asked Lee if there wasn't something he wanted to bring up. Thus prodded, Lee said he had stated his position in his paper and that several other people who were here at this meeting had agreed with him. Without naming anyone, he asked them if they wanted to

air their complaints now. There was another very long pause. Nobody moved to speak, and it appeared that Lee would be left 'out on a limb,' as he had implied in his editorial. Martin finally asked if there was any further discussion. Marsh, the school principal, now jumped in. He stated that Lee was wrong about two things: the school did not sell cigarettes to teachers, and it sold no bulk, package ice cream. He added that the kids made only about $8 a week on their ice-cream concession.

"Drawing the battle lines

"Quincy, the restaurant keeper, now found his tongue. He said that the guy who drives the truck told him that he delivers enough ice cream at the school for them all to swim in. He added, with feeling, that his business has been going to pot since the kids started selling ice cream. Marsh reported that they had ice cream in the school cafeteria, too, as part of the regular school lunch, and that the total deliveries to the school averaged only 30 to 40 gallons a week. All agreed that the kids should have ice cream with their lunch. Quincy insisted that his business was hurt, and hurt bad, and that he was a taxpayer and they couldn't tolerate this sort of thing. In a larger town, perhaps it was O.K., but Springdale is too small. He used to get all the kids' business on athletic nights, but now his place is deserted. He referred to Paltrey, the candy store owner, and said that his business was being wrecked, too; but that he was afraid to speak up. Davis, the principal, now joined in Marsh's support. He stated that the kids sold ice cream as part of their drive to raise money for the senior trip to Washington, that these sales were only one of many things they did to raise the needed money (about $1,700 is needed), that earning their own money in this way was a valuable educational experience in the ways of capitalism (they knew they would have to sell a lot of ice cream, candy, and popcorn to break even, and knew that they could lose money if anything went wrong), that the ice cream they sold was only a small proportion of that con-

sumed in the community, that the kids would enjoy their trip more if they had to work for it themselves, that next year many of them would be in uniform in Korea, and that it would be unpatriotic to deny them this trip. Davis did not seem to gain any support, but his arguments had some effect. All agreed that the kids ought to have their trip to Washington, and most were apparently surprised to hear how much it would cost. There followed some discussion of whether alternative means could be found to get the money.

"Digressions

"Cortland, a grocery owner, now attempted to enlarge the issue. 'Why are we so concerned about ice cream and popcorn?" he asked. 'Why don't we talk about the more important things? A lot of money was spent when the new school wing was put up: why wasn't this money spent locally? Why doesn't the school buy its food supplies, its furnishings, its light bulbs, etc., etc., from local businessmen?' Emerson, the hardware dealer, indicated that he had sold some supplies to the school. He added that if other businesses were less successful here, perhaps they had better look to their own business practices. He said one reason that people didn't shop locally was that the stores were closed a good deal of the time. Go to Rockford on a Wednesday, he said, and you will see half the people of Springdale there. This brought out some discussion about why people can't plan their shopping to buy ahead (for the Wednesday afternoon closing just as they do for Sunday.) There seemed to be a good deal of dissatisfaction with the local business practices. Someone told Quincy that one reason he was losing money was that his place was closed half the time. Quincy reported that he was always open. This was generally denied about the room, and Quincy covered by saying that business was so poor he couldn't afford to stay open in the evenings anymore. Davis jumped in to say that that was one reason the kids had to provide their own ice cream. Davis added that Quincy and some

others had got the kids sore by their outspoken attacks on the high school. It appeared now that a definite element of boycott might be present; the kids were getting revenge on Quincy by staying away deliberately, and buying all their ice cream within the school. The discussion drifted back to the matter of closings, and someone suggested that the stores ought to get together and stagger their closing hours, so that one grocery store would always be open. Nothing came of this proposal. Someone else pointed out that another reason Quincy was failing was that every other store in town now carried ice cream too; his former monopoly was broken. Quincy repeated his attack on the school, and said he knew for a fact that they did sell bulk ice cream to teachers. Marsh flatly denied this, said it was strictly against the rules, and if anyone was violating them he wanted to know who. Quincy asserted that he had seen a teacher go down the main street with a large package of ice cream, from the school. Marsh now backtracked and said, yes, there had been one instance. Teachers could buy the small cartons at the cafeteria, just like everyone else, and for the same price. This teacher was having a party, and ordered a large number, to take home. She had been allowed to do this, but when the matter came to the principal's attention, he said that hereafter no take-home orders would be filled. At this point, Marsh, to recover lost ground, retreated to his office and returned with the ice-cream vouchers, which he read to the group—weekly purchases ranged from about $12 to about $45.

"Back to the main theme

"The discussion was now drifting back to the school problem again. Davis attempted to pacify the group by saying that, if they had had any idea in advance that so much fuss would be raised he would not have let the kids go into the business without talking it over with the business people first. But he quickly switched to aggression by adding that it could all have been worked out peacefully if the disturbed merchants had come to him to talk it over, instead of spreading a lot of stories behind his back. The first he knew about all this, he claimed, was when he read it in the newspaper."

The protest was effective and ice-cream sales along with a junior class popcorn-vending venture were terminated by the administration. This, in turn, aroused the resentment of farm families whose children's trip to Washington, D.C., was at stake. The school board, however, remained aloof from the issue, thus permitting the administration to absorb the resentment and guaranteeing the continuation of rural dominance on the board in exchange for a minor concession to business interests at the cost of the administration's program.

All other groups in the community who may be said to have special interests in school policy are given no direct or indirect political representation except as they express themselves in the P.T.A., discussed below. These include the professionals, industrial workers, traditional farmers, shack people and the marginal middle class, all of whom fall beyond the purview of educational politics.

The Principal as an Alien Expert

THE ROLE OF THE PRINCIPAL

The role of the principal represents a unique and unusual factor in local politics. He expresses himself politically through his specialized interests in education. Although his primary interest is in education, he must deal with and through political forces to accomplish his ends. His position is the focal point around which a large segment of politics takes place and his ability to evade, bypass and manipulate invisible government determines his success as a principal and the continuance of his appointment. The dismissed principal alluded to earlier, Marsh, was unsuccessful in this task and in spite of a large unorganized body of supporting opinion lost out to the forces desiring his removal. The case of his successor, Peabody, incumbent since 1951, epitomizes the process and reality of the principal's political role.

Peabody, a man in his mid-thirties, and his wife live in a "self-imposed" isolation from the rest of the community, including the community of teachers. His private as well as his social life is almost unknown to the community. All of his contacts with the community result from his position as principal, a position to which he devotes almost all his time and energy and which he fills with a high degree of technical competence.

The school principal, always known as "The Professor," is central to the life of the community, but he is known to it almost exclusively through his professional activities and for this reason he can be treated as a public figure only as the community knows him in the following of his capacities: (1) Through school children who see him in his day-to-day role as the authority of the school. (2) Through his activities in the P.T.A. and its various committees in which he takes an active interest. (3) As the author of a weekly column in the newspaper on school policy and affairs. (4) As an ex-officio, non-voting member of the school board. In each of these capacities his central interest is in promoting education for the community. Together these activities constitute his job, make him the personal embodiment of education and draw him into the political scene as a central figure.

THE PRINCIPAL AND THE PUBLIC

Through his newspaper column and daily supervision of the school, the principal has mechanisms for distributing information and an image of himself to the public. At this level Peabody has established a reputation for being a good disciplinarian, a trait highly valued by the community, but not a harsh disciplinarian (he recommended dismissal of a teacher regarded as too harsh). He has raised the standards of classroom work (more homework for students), but has not increased the number of failures (everyone's child is still getting educated). He has supported a modern approach to sex education, but not in a radical manner (abrupt dismissal of a teacher who discussed sex in a classroom not connected with hygiene.) In his newspaper column he discusses a great variety of school facts and problems, such as school board meetings, teachers meetings, the budget, curriculum problems, and occasionally he suggests methods for improving the school. The following excerpts taken from the principal's newspaper column suggest the care he takes not to offend any one segment of the community, and indicate the plane on which he deals with the public.

"AFTER FOUR O'CLOCK

BY

Alvin Peabody, Principal

"The other day a friend of ours came to us with a question. (We would like to underscore the point that anyone who comes directly to us with questions, doubts, or complaints is our best friend.) Anyway, this person was wondering just what the school program would be like now that there was a new principal. He had started worrying because of all the attention that was being given to the agricultural advisory committee—we think that perhaps he had gotten the impression that the school was going to emphasize agriculture to the exclusion of other things.

"We gave our best forthright answer to that friend by saying that we believe a school should offer a broad enough program to meet the needs of as many youngsters as possible. The only limitation being the ability of the community to finance such a program—we just can't go 'hog wild' with expensive ideas that are bigger than the size of our pocketbook. . . .

"Ever since we started teaching, we have been plagued with a question—'Do rural children need a different kind of education from that provided for urban children?' After more than a decade of working with youngsters, there are many aspects of that question that still go unanswered. However, we have begun to articulate some of the differences between rural and urban children. These differences should have some bearing on the nature of the educational program in the rural central school, just how much of a bearing could be the subject of extensive study by more capable educators than we presume to be.

"When we start to evaluate rural living and its influences on growing children, we are naturally prejudiced in favor of it. Our many pleasant memories of a childhood on the farm color our thinking to the point where we have little sympathy with urban living. . . .

"We have a new course underway at school—perhaps some of you who have youngsters in the junior or senior class have heard some of it. High-school boys and girls have many problems in their adjustment to adult life. They need help with these problems but are loathe to discuss them with a counselor or have not identified them well enough to put them in the form of questions. We hope that through this new class they will find an outlet for discussing common problems in group discussion, but without the need to identify any problem as being that of any one individual.

"We might call this class by a high-sounding name such as psychology or mental health, but because it is scheduled as a part of the health education program, we are calling it just plain 'health.' The best way we can describe what will be covered is to say that we hope to help each student to equip himself with some knowledge of the science of getting along with other people. . . ."

THE PRINCIPAL AND THE PARENT-TEACHER ASSOCIATION

While the newspaper column appeals to local pride and prejudice, the principal's actions in the P.T.A. are oriented to introducing his educational philosophy and other innovations to a specialized segment of the community which is interested in education as such. The P.T.A. membership is composed of the teachers, wives of professional and industrial workers and the wives of a handful of prosperous farmers. The attending membership, excluding the teachers, adds up to 30-40 persons who are interested in P.T.A. activities because they have school-age children. Their interest in the school, moreover, is apt to be most intense at those points where school problems impinge directly on their child's grade; the membership's interests tend to be atomized. More than this, however, the group as a whole is not organized on an independent basis; they meet under the auspices of the school and revert to congeries of atomized individuals outside of meetings. One of the reasons for this is that historically the local P.T.A. has never been well organized or active. Peabody has taken a direct interest in organizing P.T.A. activities and plays a decisive role in its affairs.

Through a step-by-step progression in the course of his administration, Peabody has introduced a variety of modern educational practices and methods to the P.T.A. Health (sex) education, a new reading program for the elementary grades (reading "readiness"), new curriculum additions (driver training, vocational education), new plant expansion plans— all such innovations are first introduced in the P.T.A. Through his control over teachers and his requirement that they attend P.T.A. meetings (on alternating years a teacher is president of the P.T.A.), and due to his ability to secure special speakers and programs, the principal plays a dominating and controlling role in this organization. He uses his dominant position for the purpose of gaining acceptance for his educational programs. However, at no point in this procedure does it appear that the P.T.A. has been forced to accept the principal's ideas. For, through the process of committees and agendas, it appears publicly that P.T.A. members themselves, when making their reports, have originated the ideas which have been given them by the principal. Through the complexities of this procedure, the P.T.A. voices the policies of the principal and, in turn, the principal uses the P.T.A. as an informal political instrument against those interests in the village and town which oppose his program. While doing this however, he is careful to restrain the P.T.A. if it gets overly ambitious. He is careful, moreover, to report in his column P.T.A. activities as P.T.A. activities and not as his own policies.

The P.T.A., however, is most important in concrete policy matters as these are brought before the board of education.

Here the P.T.A. does not act directly, but rather acts through the principal. At this point the function of the P.T.A. is to create the issues and define the problems necessary to carrying out the educational policies of the principal. The principal mediates between the P.T.A. and the school board and presents the P.T.A. educational program to the board as the program of a pressure group.

In his relations with the P.T.A. the principal is able to pre-test his ideas before a segment of the community which is interested in education and which represents groups otherwise not heard. When it appears that the P.T.A. is ready to support his views, a resolution is passed for presentation to the board. Since the principal prepares the agenda for board meetings, the resolution is assured a hearing.

At times the principal must restrain the enthusiasms of the P.T.A. Since he is generally aware of the thinking of the board members, he knows in advance what constitutes a reasonable request and what measures will arouse antagonism and be rejected. When he cannot kill "unreasonable" P.T.A. requests within the P.T.A.—a rare circumstance—the P.T.A. officers themselves present the issue to the board. Thus the principal dissociates himself from unpopular causes and does not jeopardize his relations with the board. In some circumstances he kills or dissociates himself from ideas which he himself first introduced to the P.T.A., a fact which leads to the development of resentments against him within the P.T.A.

However, through the operation of such intricate processes, Peabody has succeeded in instituting a number of his ideas: hiring a professional cafeteria manager to replace a local person and introducing several new courses. More significant, through these processes he has managed to create an independent group of lay advisors. These lay advisors are organized into committees (school expansion committee, agricultural advisory committee, vocational advisory committee) which are composed of *individuals* who do not otherwise participate in school affairs. Each committee contains a mixture of farmers, businessmen, professionals, and industrial workers, while Peabody is an ex-officio member of each committee and coordinates their combined activities. What is interesting about the lay advisory committees is that they do not involve any new *groups* in school affairs: they extend and broaden the base of participation of those groups already involved in P.T.A. affairs. Moreover, by mixing-up members of different classes on each committee, the principal seems deliberately to be atomizing the classes. He handles these committees in the same manner as he handles the P.T.A., the committees report to the school board and also to the P.T.A. and hence have the effect of giving the voice of the P.T.A. a broader base. Thus the principal involves a broader segment of the community in his program and brings himself to the school board with public support for his program.

THE PRINCIPAL AND THE BOARD OF EDUCATION

The principal comes to the board meeting as a technical expert and as the administrator of board policies. As the day-to-day administrator of policy and as an expert, he enjoys a tactical advantage over the board members who are concerned with education only once a month. He has a thoroughgoing knowledge of state legal and administrative requirements and he understands the problems of school curricula and daily administration in detail. While the principal possesses the powers of the expert in relation to amateurs, the amateurs, in this case, control the budget and are responsible for hiring the expert. It is in this context that the relations between the principal and the board are worked out. This relationship, as reported by an observer of board meetings, may be described as follows:

> First, there are the minor problems of administrative detail which Peabody presents at school board meetings. In most cases he has already reached a solution to the problem and action has been taken. He may be doing this merely to keep the board informed on such matters. There is the possibility that he wants the board to be aware of the fact that he is handling these things efficiently.

Secondly, there are problems of a strictly professional nature which Peabody feels quite capable of solving and which he is, in fact, quite capable of handling. He, nevertheless, presents these problems to the board for their "advice," since he is "new here and not acquainted with past policy." Invariably, the board responds in a specific way when these problems are presented. Holden and Tafe quickly draw the line, indicating that such problems are the business of Peabody and that they choose to rely on his judgment and discretion. Ralph Jones is more inclined to want to air these matters. He apparently feels better-equipped to discuss professional matters. But, nine times out of ten, Peabody has solved the problem and made a decision previous to the meeting and is well armed with supportive material to back his stand. His strategy is approximately as follows:

1. Become aware of all the facts of the case.
2. On the basis of these facts, paying special attention to the reactions of the significant people involved, reach a decision.
3. Formulate a definite plan of action based on the decision, implementing every step of the action in detail.
4. Come to the board meeting fully prepared with the detailed solution of the problem and then present the problem as though you just realized the problem existed and "could the board help you with some advice since you are new and inexperienced in Springdale and they are familiar with the precedent."
5. Let the board knock it about for a while while you sit back and size up their individual stands on the issue.
6. Present the facts and the carefully worked out solution, countering every argument with a better one, being, of course, very tactful.
7. Wait for Jones to make the motion that your plan be adopted.

Thirdly, there are problems which involve mostly matters which are of direct concern to the board because they involve finances or public relations between the school and the community. Here again, Peabody ascertains as many of the facts in advance as is possible. He decides for himself what course of action he would prefer. But here the board stands firm on its right to decide the course of action. In this general area Peabody uses his influence and whatever methods of persuasion he knows in order to gain his own ends, but he is extremely careful to do it in a subtle way. He does not run headlong into the board, because he is aware that they want and need some area in which they can feel that they know better than him. For example, when Peabody proposed the buying of the P.A. system with the surplus money from the budget, he was met with abrupt and almost reprimanding resistance from all the board members.

The board respects Peabody and his knowledge of his profession. They feel that their own actions are constantly under his scrutiny and are careful not to go out on a limb with respect to educational practices and principles. But where they have the edge, where they hold the purse-strings, they try to exercise their power.

On the whole, Peabody seems to have taken much of the power from the board. They are ambivalent about this. They are pleased, on one hand, to have a principal to whom they can turn over an immense amount of responsibility with complete confidence. But at the same time they don't want to lose the upper hand in the bargain. Holden has foreseen this and fears it. The others have sensed it to a lesser degree. The board cannot attack the very thing in Peabody that has put him in the position he is in now, so they will keep trying in other ways to keep him in check."

It is in and through the school board, in this manner, that the principal as an expert has an opportunity to achieve his educational program. As an expert his powers are based on administrative and manipulative skills and these skills must be coordinated with the political philosophy of the school board. Hence, the principal is able to institute most easily

those elements of his program which coincide with the sentiments of the school board as he finds it or as he is able to
change it. The board and Peabody have discontinued cafeteria
food purchases from local groceries and instead now make
these purchases more efficiently and at less cost through
wholesalers. Both the principal and the board were psychologically capable of alienating local businessmen in this way.
The addition of a professional cafeteria manager was justified
on the basis of greater efficiency and cost savings "in the long
run." The principal can, however, receive no concessions for
his teaching staff. Teachers are expected to work "full time,"
to be on call at all times and generally to devote themselves
to the school and its activities while leading exemplary lives
in the community. The principal defers to the board in its
expectations of teachers and, in consequence, he is disliked
by the teachers since they have no spokesman to represent
their interests on the board of education. When it comes to
such complex issues as school expansion and curriculum
changes, the principal restructures the position of the board
in relation to the community. The lay advisory committees
are an effort to create an independent organization which will
give the principal's position public support. In addition, he
has for the first time in Springdale history succeeded in
placing a rural non-farm resident on the board. Through this
process of joining with the board while at the same time
altering its composition and its position in the community,
the principal promotes his educational program.

THE INTERNAL CONTRADICTIONS OF THE PRINCIPAL'S ROLE

In these terms, then, the school principal is an alien
expert who knows the ways and laws of the world and who
uses this knowledge to shape the community as it bears on
him and his ends, which are necessarily in the selfish interests of education. However, in dealing with the various segments of the community with which he comes in direct
contact, he must recognize differences of power. He must
recognize the interests of the farmers, professionals, industrial
workers, party politics, the generalized desire for low taxes,

and he must give each of these elements their due weight in his educational calculations. To the extent that he makes an accurate assessment of local power relations and acts on this assessment he has a chance, at least in the short run, to succeed with his program.

While giving due weight to these various interests he must at the same time try not to alienate any one of them. As a result he publicly tends to try to agree with everyone and his public statements are of sufficient generality as to be satisfactory to almost all groups. However, when pressed, he agrees most, in terms of his rhetoric, with the rural interests since this is the dominant group within and through whom he must work.

This he must do even though his underlying educational program is against a lopsided, farm-dominated school system. Vocational training, college preparation, a guidance program and modern methods are central to his educational philosophy. But in order to accomplish his program, he must constantly make concessions to the dominant interests behind school policy and attempt to implement his program through more indirect and subtle means. As a consequence of this, it frequently happens that he is forced to dissociate himself from his own ideas in the P.T.A. and to take public positions which are inconsistent with his long-range program.

However, in making these concessions, and sometimes being overly subtle in his approach, he alienates the village by being overly affirmative to the town interests, even though his ideas correspond to village interests—a fact which only few recognize. After one year of Peabody's incumbency, Flint recognized this sufficiently to resign his position as legal counsel to the board in the sure knowledge that "The school's in good hands now. They don't need me around anymore." But others, who are not in a position to observe the principal's acts at close range and who must form their opinions from his public statements, begin to form into nuclei of opposition.

In addition, it remains as a fact that the political maneuverings of the principal are resented by those groups before and against whom he displays his knowledge and technique. He remains an alien expert who cannot conceal the rationality of his calculations and operations. At this point, particularly with respect to budgetary considerations, the school board acts as a watchdog agency and always jealously guards this prerogative. Moreover, the board is always in a position to create an issue which will lead to the removal or resignation of the principal. One member of invisible government, in agreement with the principal's educational policy, has remarked that "He's a little too inhuman—has never got into anything in the town. He's good for Springdale until he gets things straightened out. Then we'll have to get rid of him." But this cannot be done as easily now as in the past. Recent state laws designed to protect the security of teachers now include an automatic tenure provision upon completion of five years of continuous teaching in the school. Thus the principal's position is supported by state law. The board's position in relation to the principal, particularly in view of Peabody's ability to prevent organized opposition to himself, has been considerably weakened. In fact, for the first time in the history of the community, the principal is a permanent part of local politics until he elects to resign or is forced to resign in response to extra-legal pressures.

Chapter 8

Reciprocal Political Relations Between Springdale
and Mass Society

*Institutional Linkages to State
and National Politics*

THE one area of politics absent from the preceding description
is the relationship between local politics and state and national
politics. Local politics at each of the levels described takes
place within the framework of larger forces. The three points
at which local politics are linked to the broader political
scene are the state subsidy, state and national elections and
national agricultural policies.

LOCAL POLITICS AND THE STATE SUBSIDY

The effects of state aid are openly apparent insofar as the
granting of aid is conditioned upon the regulations and requirements which define how and under what circumstances
it shall be spent by the local agency. As has been noted, the
state subsidy is crucial in defining the tasks of village and
town government. State educational policies also play an
important part in the centralized school. Department of education syllabi, state regents examinations and state salary
schedules for teachers provide the framework within which
the local board of education and the administration must
adapt itself.

More important than administrative requirements, however, is the fact of the existence and volume of the subsidy.
Although village and town governments receive a large proportion of their operating budgets from state agencies, it is in
educational aid that the key to local and state politics is found.

In Springdale, which in 1953 had a school budget of
$248,000, local school taxes yielded $42,000. Except for
$5,000 received as tuition and transportation payments from

out-of-district students and as payments from the federal government in support of the rural school lunch program, the remainder of the budget, approximately $200,000, is made up of direct state aid. From the political point of view, this means that less of politics is apparent than would otherwise be the case.

The political factor in state educational aid appears at two different levels in local politics. On the one hand it affects local assessments and tax rates; on the other, in combination with subsidies to village and town government, it serves as a direct link to state politics.

Of the four types of state educational aid, three apply exclusively to rural areas. "Attendance aid" which applies to all public schools in the state regardless of location is calculated on a flat rate of $220 per pupil for the elementary grades and $274 per pupil in grades 7-12 (assuming full attendance in both cases) *less a local millage deduction per $1,000 of full valuation of taxable local real estate.* The local community makes up the remainder of the flat rate in proportion to the full valuation of its local taxable real estate. In areas where real-estate assessments are low, a greater percentage of the educational burden is carried by the state.

It is in the state attendance aid formula that the rationale for local assessment policies is found. In Springdale assessed valuations run in the proportion of one-fifth to one-twentieth of salable value, and within at least the last fifty years no attempt has been made by village or town government to reassess property valuations. Instead of increasing revenues by increasing assessments, revenues are increased by increasing tax rates. Between 1941 and 1952 the school tax rate was increased from 5.36 mills to 21.05 mills, while the local cost per pupil increased from $28.00 to $76.54. In these same years the assessed valuation per pupil dropped from $5,225 to $3,636 while state aid costs per pupil increased from $179.14 to $326.34. Hence a partial explanation of otherwise incomprehensible local assessment policies is provided by state attendance aid formulas. These arrangements make it possible to increase school revenues without disturbing the structure of local assessments as they relate to village and town government and without bringing into public view the inequities in assessments of various local properties. The same rationale which underlies state attendance aid formulas also underlies the aid formulas to village and town government. However, at this level the rationale is implemented by the use of equalization formulas. Discrepancies between total assessed valuation and total "real" valuation between townships within a county are equalized by formula. The formula assigns a total valuation to taxable property within the township irrespective of local assessment levels. State aid is then paid as a percentage of total valuation determined by the equalization formula. In short, for aid purposes to village and town governments, the state makes its own assessments. There is, hence, no interference with local assessment practices and policies and there is no interference with the advantages which accrue to the rural centralized school from state subsidization policies with reference to education.

The other three types of state educational aid refer exclusively to rural areas. An automatic 12 percent increase is added to central school districts after the basic attendance aid formula has been computed. This is a specific differential allowed for the purpose of financing education in rural areas. Additionally, rural central schools and rural union free schools receive a special "transportation aid." This aid is computed on the basis of the cost of operating a school bus on a per-pupil, seat-mile basis. Aid computation is made on the basis of pupil seat miles travelled times the rate granted (by the state), less a one mill tax on property valuation. Springdale received $20,000 of transportation aid. Lastly, rural schools receive aid in the construction of school buildings. Local quotas are computed on the basis of building costs, pupil enrollment and local ability to pay. Seventy percent of the cost of Springdale's 1949 school expansion program was covered by this type of aid.

Eighty percent, or $200,000, of the school budget exclusive of building aid is derived from these various forms of aid.

Village government collects approximately $11,000 in real estate and water taxes while it receives approximately $5,000 in direct cash aid from the state plus direct state investments in local facilities such as roads, which do not appear in the village budget. In the general fund of town government, approximately $11,000 out of $13,000 is accounted for by direct state aid. For town highway purposes approximately $8,000 represents local revenue while the state contributes $27,000 in direct cash aid. For $2,000 raised in local fire taxes which the town remits to the fire district, town government receives a fire-protection system which is largely supported by the state at other levels. These state aid funds are administered and expended (allowing for state requirements) by local officials on the various governing boards.

The county in which Springdale is located receives roughly $20.00 in state aid for every $1.00 which it pays in taxes of all kinds. State aid is raised by taxes levied on a statewide basis. Among others these include income, corporation, gasoline and luxury taxes. Inheritance taxes are specifically earmarked for educational purposes. Ninety-five percent of the taxes from which aid is derived is levied in the metropolitan urban centers of the state. The degree of freedom given to local politics by virtue of these state aid programs is achieved by the dominance of essentially up-state New York rural Republicans over essentially Democratic urban areas, particularly metropolitan New York City.

The financial freedom given to local politics and government by the dominance of up-state Republicanism over urban Democratic centers is a universally recognized phenomenon in the community. Lee in his newspaper is one of the chief publicists of the concrete rewards which accrue to the community from statewide Republican control. Community experts, the principal, the lawyer, and outside experts from the land grant college repeatedly point out the favorable position of the community which results from state aid policies. At this point the knowledge of this favorable treatment by the state ties in with the rural dwellers' morally superior and victorious attitude over urban life, and it makes the expression of resentments against urban life all the more psychologically necessary.

Favorable state aid balances are only one of a number of ways in which the rural community is given preferential treatment. Special concessions are made to farmers in the statewide distribution of roads, in special registration rates for farm vehicles, in the absence of taxes on tractors and other farm implements, etc. The land grant college extension program is specifically geared to the needs of the rural community. State conservation policies (construction of ponds) tie in with farmers' land improvement programs. Weed and pest control campaigns are direct services performed by state agencies. Farmer's livestock losses due to dogs are reimbursed from special funds made up of dog license fees collected throughout the state. These and many other little favors demonstrate to the rural dweller his privileged position in state policy.

It is at this level that the importance of a large vote in state elections becomes apparent and that an explanation is given to the increased political activity and interest in state elections which is nowhere as apparent in local elections. In addition, it is at this point that the role of formal local political unanimity under the Republicans, allowing for clique deviations and personal enmities, has an exchange value in state politics, and that the link between local politics and state politics is provided.

LOCAL POLITICS AND STATE AND NATIONAL ELECTIONS

Local elections are separated from state and national elections by iron rules of procedure and custom. State and national elections never regularly coincide with village and town elections. During state and national elections polling places are open from 1:00 p.m. to 10:00 p.m., in contrast to village elections (when they are open for four hours) and town elections (when they are open six to seven hours), in both of the latter cases during daylight hours only. In contrast to village and town elections, state and national elections always coincide.

In these broader elections, all emphasis is placed on stimulating interest. Politics and candidates become an open subject of discussion on the street corners, in business establishments and over the open countryside. The party machinery is greased and oiled even in its most remote extensions in the surrounding hills. Delegations are organized to attend political rallies held at the county seat.

It is at this point, and only this point, that women are called in for political activity. The women's Republican club is always reactivated and refurbished at election time. The primary function of the club, which is composed of the wives of Young, Flint, Jones, Hilton and others, is to insure a large registration of voters and to stimulate their interest in voting.

It is a peculiarity of state election regulations that personal registration is not required of rural voters. In non-personal registration areas a voter is considered registered if he voted in the previous election: by voting he reaffirms his registration. If he has not voted in a previous election, election inspectors send him a postal card which, if signed and returned, constitutes registration. A person may, if he chooses, register his name personally during open registration days or he may register with party workers who call at his door. Newcomers, youths who have just turned twenty-one and people who have moved from one voting district in the township to another are systematically canvassed by party workers. This system of registration, along with the efforts of party workers, results in an almost total registration of all qualified voters. In mid-October the press reports registration results as follows:

"1,613 People Registered in Springdale Last Saturday for November Election"

". . . In Springdale, where the board copies from the previous year's book and the inspectors and party leaders endeavor to register all, there was a total enrollment of 1,613.

"Saturday will be the last registration day when the election inspectors will sit at the five various districts and add any names not already accounted for. The polls will be open from 1 p.m. to 10 p.m. Again the press urges all newcomers or people moving the past year, from one district to another, to go to their new polling place and make sure you are registered. If you are not registered, you cannot vote on election day and remember . . . a good keen contest is coming up. It isn't a privilege to vote; it's a duty."

In the combined state and national election of 1952, 1,613 were eligible to vote. Out of that number, more than 1,450 actually got to the polls to vote. In a vote which except for its size was regarded as typical, all Republican candidates defeated their Democratic rivals by margins of six to one. The press reported the election results as follows:

Largest Vote in Springdale's History Recorded Tuesday

"Springdale, no different from former years, just more so, was joined by the nation in recording a landslide victory for General Eisenhower in Tuesday's election.

"It was evident from the minute the polls opened that something different was taking place. The vote was heavy and voters were standing in line at nine o'clock in the two village polling places to vote.

"Naturally, the sweeping victory for Gen. Ike in this county was also accompanied by a victory for all national, state and county officials.

"The vote by office in Springdale:

President		*Justice Supreme Court*	
Eisenhower	1204	Anderson, R.	1160
Stevenson	260	Eaton, D.	251
U.S. Senator		*State Senator*	
Ives, R.	1194	Republican	1403
Cashmore, D.	237	No opponent	

Member of Assembly

Republican	1090
Democrat	343

The apathy of village elections and the relative apathy of town elections, except in very special circumstances, stand in sharp contrast to voting interest in state and national elections. Moreover, as noted in the press comment above, Republican landslides are confidently expected in these elections.

However, the lumping together of state and national elections hides a significant difference in meaning between these elections at the level of local politics. To a large extent the political extensions of local politics end at the state level.

To be sure, the district congressman and the U.S. Senator are known by Lee, Flint, Jones and Young, but this is by virtue of their need for local support, and contacts between these local political figures and national officeholders are limited to election times. At election time the district Congressional representative is conducted through the village by Lee. Otherwise the local party committee attends political rallies at the county seat and Young has his picture taken while standing beside an important personage—these are the limits of local extensions to national politics.

Procedures for nominating candidates for national offices include at the most only the county Republican chairman, and even he has little voice in nominations beyond the selection of the Congressional representative whose constituency in this case includes four counties. Senatorial and Presidential nominations, of course, are made at higher levels and through different processes which exclude politicians in Springdale.

For local politics, as we have noted, the state election is a bread-and-butter proposition. The color and interest which is given to state elections by national figures helps to bring out the vote for state candidates who receive the same vote. This tends to hide the fact that the political calculus of local politicians is oriented to state politics. In off-year elections for the U.S. Senate or House of Representatives, local voting enthusiasms and political activity are low. A Democratic candidate for Senator has the best chance of winning when there is not also a gubernatorial contest. The increased political activity at the local level in state elections represents an exchange of rural votes for favorable state Republican policies with reference to rural areas.

Due to the dominance of the small businessmen and because of the mechanics of elections, the village is always Republican. At times the farmers can and do vote Democratic and they are always capable of voting against the village interests. They do this in part because they are inclined to vote in accordance with their pocketbooks and because they resent even the petty pretensions of the village and its past history of social and political dominance. At the same time, the "radicalism" of the farmers in Springdale almost always returns to the norm of Republicanism. This is because farm *leaders* are village businessmen. If the village business politician, who is also the farm leader, is to maintain his position as a Republican leader in local government, he must bring out a Republican vote in state and national elections even when there are tensions between his farm constituency and state and national party policies. The success of the Republican party in state and national elections can be attributed to the facts of (1) rural resentments against Democratic cities, (2) the success of the state aid formulas in directing urban funds to rural areas (3) the personal effectiveness of Jones as a leader and (4) the absence of farm leadership deriving from farmers themselves, which in itself is accounted for by the fact that farming is a twelve to eighteen hour a day job that makes it difficult for farmers to see each other often.

FEDERAL AGRICULTURAL POLICY AND LOCAL POLITICS

The only area of national politics which reaches into Springdale and into which local political forces express themselves directly is agricultural policy and administration. The central agricultural issues in the community are connected to the problems of farm prices, farm price supports and parity prices. These political problems are relevant only to the agricultural segment of the community and, as a consequence, the local political machinery (visible and invisible) as such is not concerned directly with these issues.

However, this lack of concern on the part of the local political machinery does not mean that the issue is neglected but rather, again, additional and separate quasi-legal and private bodies and machinery are added to local politics. In this case these quasi-legal and private bodies address themselves explicitly and almost exclusively to the single problem of farm pricing mechanisms.

These bodies are the Farm Bureau and the various milk producers' associations such as the Dairymen's League and the New York Cooperative Milk Producers' Association. They deal with milk pricing problems in different ways and on several planes. The Farm Bureau itself, at least on the local level, is primarily concerned with farmers' education and political action. The county agent is a representative of the state land grant college and the Department of Agriculture, and serves as the technical advisor to the leadership and membership of the local Farm Bureau. The county agent is the only formal link between the Department of Agriculture and the farmer. In his capacity as "advisor" to the Farm Bureau, he has above him a board of directors composed of county farmers who technically hire him and to whom he is responsible.

The various milk producers' associations are usually composed of regional committees, a central state organization and, in some cases, a national headquarters with offices in Washington, D.C. Only two Springdale farmers (Fridel and Albert Hanks) hold positions in these organizations, both at the regional level, one in the Dairymen's League and one in a cooperative producers' association.

In terms of issues relevant to agricultural politics, each of these organizations, the Farm Bureau and the producers' association, has a single specialized area of interest.

The Farm Bureau is interested in farm prices, supports and parity formulas insofar as these are determined by Congressional action and within the Department of Agriculture. Locally this means having a representation of articulate local farmers attend regional Congressional committee hearings and regional Department of Agriculture hearings. These hearings are held on such agricultural issues as the butter and cheese price support programs, fertilizer programs or farm credit policies. Producers' associations are interested in the price of milk, as such. The price of milk is determined by the milk price administrator of the New York milk shed area with offices in New York City. The determination of the exact price of milk is based on a fixed formula of which the chief variables are total production in the milk shed area, the fluid use/non-fluid use ratio of total production and the distance of the producer from the metropolitan New York City fluid consumption market. The formula, known as the milk price order, specifies exact but different prices for milk according to its consumption use. The greatest price is received for milk consumed as a fresh fluid, lesser prices are received for milk consumed as ice cream, cheese, dry milk, etc. If a farmer is a qualified participating member of the milk shed (i.e., is certified to have his milk shipped to the New York City market) he receives the formula price for his milk irrespective of the use to which his milk is eventually put. The milk price order guarantees all producers the same price. The producer's return for his milk varies from month to month and year to year according to changes in fluid milk consumption, milk production and the changing ratio of fluid to non-fluid uses of milk. Milk price variations do not occur outside the framework of the formula unless the milk price order itself is changed.

The milk price order can be changed only by petitioning the Department of Agriculture, the administrating agency of the federal milk price order. Producers' associations through their legal counsels submit petitions to the department for such changes in the formula which will increase the producer's return on his milk. Processors and distributors may also submit such petitions. The Department of Agriculture may accept or reject any such petitions. When it accepts such a petition, it conducts hearings throughout the milk shed area and hears the "arguments" of producers, processors and distributors on the proposed change in the milk price order. When the hearings are completed the Department of Agriculture may either approve or disapprove the proposed change. If the change is approved by the department, it must be put to a vote of all farmers who are participating members of the milk shed. The farmer may vote either "yes" or "no." If he votes not to accept the change, the milk price order is no longer valid, no longer binding on the participating members. This means there is no longer a milk price order for the milk price administrator to administrate and an end to the controlled marketing of milk. In other words, unless the farmer votes "yes" he is voting for a free milk market of the variety he remembers from the early 1930's. Farmers' participation in the determination of milk prices is, in short, reduced to a ritual.

This is not to say that farmer participation in milk price fixing is not essential. His participation is essential at the level where these issues are considered by hearings of Congressional and administrative committees. At such hearings it is necessary and desirable to hear testimony from "actual" farmers and to have a large body of farmers in attendance while the hearings are being conducted.

It is at this level that farm policy issues connect national and local politics. Delegations of local farmers must be mobilized to attend hearings. Farmers are mobilized by four different sets of interconnected interests. The county agent, usually the first to have knowledge of impending hearings, distributes this knowledge to his contacts throughout the county. Simultaneously, local officers in the producers' associations (Fridel and Hanks) learn of the hearing from above and, perhaps, also, from the county agent. Howard Jones, whose interests are in farm prosperity, is informed by both sources and is called upon to assist in mobilizing the local delegation, a request which he accepts as an opportunity enabling him to identify with farmers' interests as well as his own.

Aside from Fridel and Hanks, who play no part in either visible or invisible local government, Jones is the only local political figure who participates in politics at this national level. The psychological jurisdictions of Lee, Flint and Young stop short of this level, while all others, excepting Jones, are politically important only for special farm issues which have no carryover value to local political affairs. In fact Fridel, who has a state-wide reputation for his activities in the Dairymen's League, is deliberately excluded from local clique politics, which he has been attempting to enter for ten years. When he informally announced his candidacy for the state assembly on the Republican ticket, he was advised by the Republican county committee not to run.

Due to these arrangements in agricultural politics, the voice of local agricultural interests is the voice of the prosperous farmers. The county agent, with his interests in innovation, efficiency, modernization and rational businesslike farming, is psychologically oriented to the rational prosperous farmer. The very life style and farming methods of the traditional farmer leave the program of the county agent without any appeal. Fridel and Hanks are prosperous rational farmers. Jones deals with and through prosperous farmers and is oriented to their interests. Moreover, this group disdains traditional farming methods and those who practice them and has, in short, no respect for the evident lack of success of traditional farmers. As a result of such processes, the traditional segment of the farming community is left out of even the narrow range of political activity which focuses on farm issues.

Effective Political Jurisdictions
of Local Leaders

The preceding discussion presents a highly complex, intricate and particularistic picture of rural politics. It suggests that no simple or general theory of politics is sufficient to exhaust the concrete and detailed data which make up the political life of Springdale. Theories of politics which are based on "class" and interest groups, for example, point to vital facts in the political process, but they are, at best, preliminary steps in the process of understanding the detailed dynamics of the political situation. The political process is based on a complex integration of economic, social (class and interest groups), psychological, legal and administrative facts. These processes are linked together by an intricate structure of leadership and by the techniques of "domination" directed by political leaders at their potential and actual as well as their imagined political constituencies.

In each of the political subdivisions studied there is a dominant political class. That is, in each case one major social and economic segment within the jurisdictional boundaries of the political unit has succeeded in monopolizing the legal apparatus of the government, and has used such monopolies to express its interests. The word "interests," however, is too narrow a term. Because of the frequent lack of issues and the character of the groups themselves, it would be more correct to state that the dominant group brings to the government apparatus which it controls a psychological tone which reflects the character of that leadership group.

THE PSYCHOLOGICAL TONE OF VILLAGE,
TOWN AND SCHOOL GOVERNMENT

The Village. In the village the businessmen are the dominant group. The professionals, the industrial workers, the shack people and the lower middle-class groups are to all intents and purposes disenfranchised except in terms of temporary issues. In dominating village government, the businessmen give to it a character of niggardliness which reflects their scarcity psychology and their interest in low taxes. In following the path of the dominant political group, local government is forced to surrender its potential political powers to the agencies of state government which, because they have funds at their disposal, are able to fulfill functions which might otherwise be fulfilled by village government. However, in the long run, this results in a shifting of the tax load and tax jurisdiction from local to state government. This result is, in one sense, regarded as favorable to the village, since it means that income from taxes collected in urban areas can be spent in rural areas through state agencies and by grants-in-aid.

The same surrender of jurisdiction operates within purely

local affairs. Here, however, it reflects the attempts of business-controlled government to maintain control while resisting the temporary and sporadic but continuous pressures of other groups to introduce issues which reflect their needs and aspirations.

The professional group, the industrial workers and some marginal middle-class groups are not motivated either by desires for mobility or by demands for economy in government. Rather, their disenchantment with the American Dream had led them into the pursuit of stylized leisure and consumption and, in some cases, almost compulsive social activities. In politics, this means agitation for community improvement in terms of community activities, youth programs, extended community services and the other amenities of a later and more sophisticated age. In part the agitation for such programs is in itself a social activity which is meaningful in its own terms. However, all such activities cost money, mean increased taxes and are, from the point of view of the leaders of village government, wasteful and improvident.

The leaders of village government meet such demands by discussion, by cogitation and by delay. They exhaust the impatience of the enthusiastic amateurs until the latter find it more expedient to undertake the activities through community organizations and through private action. Political leaders act only when pressures appear to be so great as to threaten their hold on political offices. They then act to steal the issue and to control the administration of the proposed project. Other groups, such as the Legion, which represent a continuous threat to the power monopoly, are "bought off" by minimal concessions, including exemption from local laws and law enforcement.

The techniques of control include, then, the ritual of discussion, delay and postponement as well as the surrender, through these means, of governmental functions to other groups and agencies. In addition, they include the technique of unanimity which itself is achieved through discussion, delay and postponement. In political terms unanimity means there are no short and clear public divisions within the ruling bodies which would require outsiders to take an active part in the internal aspects of government. Talking and unanimity kill active public interest and restrict the villager's interest in politics to those occasions when it is a spectacle, at which time he participates only as part of an audience. Since active political interest is deadened, only a relatively few citizens vote and control elections.

The fact that business control rests upon a dull but unanimous political façade means, further, that when decisions are to be made, they are made behind the scenes by the highly visible "invisible" government, the local bosses. The political decisions of the bosses are decisive. They select candidates, follow all details of community life and take an active interest in community affairs. By the nature of their political and non-political positions (respectively an editor, a lawyer and a successful businessman who underwrites farmers) they are in continuous contact with a great many people and arrange all the political details of the community. They are, hence, in a position which provides an opportunity for the continuous exercise of political concentration. Their semi-professional involvement in political affairs guarantees them victory over the political amateurs who operate only in terms of individual issues.

None of the bosses of village government is himself an elected policy-making official. In his younger days Jones served as mayor. Flint serves as an appointed legal counsel and Lee's connection to the town board is as clerk. However, although they are not policy-making officials, they select elected officials. Their criteria of selection appear to be dependability, vulnerability and amenability to control. The policy-making officials of the board are neither competent nor original. They are, in general, economically vulnerable, so that either the token payments they receive as board members or the contacts and position they, hence, enjoy are socially and economically important to them. Only an individual who is strongly predisposed to support the low-tax, low-expenditure policy is selected without being otherwise vulnerable. The mediocrity of the board thus assures control by invisible government, guarantees the low-tax philosophy and discourages active interest in village politics by outsiders.

The Township. As in the village, a dominant group monopolizes the power of the town board. To all intents and purposes the village, the traditional farmers, the shack people, the workers and the middle class are disenfranchised. The town board reflects the interests and the psychological atmosphere of the prosperous farmers. Although prosperous farmers do not occupy official positions, they make their views felt as a pressure group. In this sense the town board is surrounded by a more buoyant and confident air which is generated by the success of the prosperous farmers, even though they too are interested in tax reductions. The tone given to town government by prosperous farmers contrasts with the village government not only in its air of triumph but also in terms of the rivalry against the village which it supports. The storekeepers and businessmen of the village have been on the economic decline since the turn of the century. The prosperous farmers are parvenues who have arrived only since the late Thirties and especially since the war and postwar prosperity years. They particularly enjoy their success in comparison to the village businessmen, on whom they look down as penny pinchers and small-time operators. In turn, they are resented by the business group, who see them as profligate in their spending, investments and borrowing and as not appreciating the value of the dollar.

Given this social rivalry, the town board as an expression of the interests of prosperous farmers is inclined to oppose the village board regardless of issues, and vice versa. So that while both groups are low-tax advocates, the social and political rivalries of the two groups in non-political spheres transcend their political similarities.

The major issue in town politics, in the light of an abdication of functions similar to that of the village board, is roads. The amount of money spent on construction and improvement of roads and the location of roads is the major political plum and interest of the town board.

In the juggling of road matters it is perhaps natural that

the prosperous farmers should come out ahead. However, since roads are a vital necessity to all groups, particularly to rural groups, road maintenance and construction become a public issue upon which opposition can be based. Every decision concerned with the location and improvement of roads alienates some element of the rural community. When sufficient alienation accumulates, there are political repercussions. The Democratic party in this iron-bound Republican area exists primarily to capitalize on these defections. Of course the Democratic party exists to collect patronage from the state and federal governments, but beyond this, the position of road supervisor is the only office to which a Democrat is normally able to be elected.

In other positions the Republicans as a matter of course win the elections. Only when traditional farmers and workers become aroused over the issues of roads does a Democrat become elected. It is interesting to note that in issues involving conflicts between party loyalty and the low-tax philosophy, the Republican machine is more likely to support the low-tax man, even when he is a Democrat, than a high-tax traditional farmer on the Republican ticket.

The School Board. The school district is the most interesting segment of local government because it is at this level that all aspects and pressures of all phases of community life are expressed in politics. This is due to the high social visibility of the school, its economic importance, the importance attached to education and the fact that the school district embraces the jurisdictions of both the village and town governments.

The prosperous farmers dominate the school board. This is true not only because of the economic ascendancy of prosperous farmers but also because the major figure in invisible government, Howard Jones, while ostensibly representing the village, actually orients his policies to the prosperous farmers since it is to them that his economic fortunes are tied.

As a consequence of this dominance, a number of facts are explained. The curriculum of the central school reflects the needs of the farmers, though these are not the needs of the

student body. The low-expenditure policy of the board reflects the interests of the farmers, but it is not alien to the
interests of village businessmen. At the same time, the board
tends not to respond to the interests of businessmen in its
purchasing policies, and the administration with the tacit
support of the board sponsors competitive student businessmen. Indeed, it would appear that the prosperous farmers
enjoy using school policy to tease and taunt the village businessmen for their penuriousness.

The village professional and industrial groups, who are
activity- rather than tax-conscious, are a continuous pressure
group in school affairs. Their pressuring continuously taxes
the board's ingenuity for improving the stalling and delaying
techniques of administration. The pressuring activities of
these groups is kept alive by the professional interest of the
school principal, who is concerned with modernizing and
improving school facilities.

He has so far succeeded in not arousing an overwhelming
opposition by using the techniques of avoiding open conflicts
with the dominant group, by using other groups to sponsor
his proposals and by never allowing himself to be placed
in a position where he must openly discuss and confront
issues. To the farm interests he is a farm man. He thus
manages to keep his position while working out a long-range
program which is contrary to the one he is publicly forced to
support. However, because of the contradictions in the appearances he is forced to take, he confounds would-be supporters as well as enemies. This is partly the result of the
fact that he is forced to work alone and underground in an
environment which places a negative premium on the open
expression of his purposes.

In spite of the handicaps he works under, the principal
represents a major force in remolding the community. He
can influence the community partly because he is a technical
expert confronting amateurs and partly because he has behind
him the techniques, the knowledge and the access to a great
number of the technical and legal resources of the society at
large. Moreover, the educational trends he attempts to intro-

duce into the community are strongly supported in the society at large and in the state educational and financial sources that sponsor and underwrite community education. Finally, the principal's program appeals to groups in the community which are emergent. His program, to a large extent, depends on the support he gets from non-farm and non-business groups. Using these groups as a lever, he places strong pressures on the expenditure and educational policies of invisible government.

The school district, as the crucial area of local politics, is best understood in terms of its financing. It is financed primarily by grants-in-aid from the state. The sources of state educational aid are derived from metropolitan areas rather than from local taxes. Thus the school symbolizes and expresses up-state rural Republican dominance over industrial and commercial urban areas, particularly New York City.

The Republican monopoly of governmental agencies in the community must, thus, be understood in these terms. These administrative and financial considerations go hand in hand with rural sentiments of resentment which arise from dependence on the great metropolitan centers in other affairs.

POLITICAL LEADERS AS MIRRORS FOR THEIR CONSTITUENCIES

The previous discussion has turned again and again in passing to a recurrent group of political leaders who express and symbolize the dynamics of the political community. They not only point up the boundaries of the actual jurisdictions of political units but also indicate the significant linkages and combinations within local government and the relationships between local government and the political agencies of the wider society. These political figures are Flint, Lee, Jones, Peabody and Young. Flint, Lee and Jones make up the effective Republican committee.

Flint, a relatively new man of fifteen years residence in the village, is legal counsel to the village board and focuses his interests in village politics. He is the lawyer for many of the village businessmen as well as their chief political arranger and spokesman. He bases his activities on technical mastery of the details of handling the legal relations of the village to the state administration and in this capacity he is indispensable. This indispensability he has acquired by assiduous devotion to village affairs. Moreover, he has assumed on his own time and frequently at his own expense many of the onerous administrative details of village government. His occupation as a lawyer frees him from the fixed time limitations which are characteristic of most other employed persons in the village. He is thus free to circulate about the village, to handle the numerous details of his self-selected position and to keep in constant touch with his less mobile associates. Hence, his activities blanket the whole village. He canvasses local businessmen in selecting candidates and is always available for meetings and discussions connected with community organizations of all types. At election time he watches the polls and is able to determine the outcome of an election by knowing the predisposition of those who avail themselves of the opportunity to vote. For Flint, then, there is no secret ballot in village elections. If the wrong people vote from the point of view of the Republican committee, Flint makes sure that other voters are secured whose votes will insure a Republican victory. He is primarily important at the village level, but because of his experience in dealing with the state administration he has some weight at the state level. He is not influential at the town or county levels.

His lack of influence at the town level is partly due to his conflict with Lee. Lee is oriented to town government, where he serves as town clerk. His activities as editor and his friendly personality make him a well-liked fellow, especially to the farmers. In village affairs he is regarded as a troublemaker who agitates for new activities and criticizes the "deadness" of village government. This latter activity represents less an attack on village business control from the viewpoint of alienated villagers than the heckling of the village by prosperous farmers. In addition, it expresses some of the resentment he directs at Flint, who on the basis of technical ability has gained prerogatives previously held by Lee.

Lee does not have a secure *organizational* base in community politics. Rather it is his genial and likeable personality and his capacity for taking on thankless, boring tasks that gives him his position. Again, the lack of a temporal work routine frees him from fixed time limitations and makes him available for the kind of social and political circulation necessary to the maintenance of his position.

The conflict between Flint and Lee is kept from becoming a serious matter by Jones. Jones is the cement that keeps the invisible government together. In the village he is preeminent because of his family heritage and the success of his business. He is dominant in the town because of the type and history of his business, which together were crucial in setting up a number of farmers who are now prosperous. He is personally well liked by the dominant farm group which follows his leadership. He is neither a striking nor controversial figure and few people see anything in him which they can dislike. The nature of his business keeps him in constant touch with farmers whose problems, plans, assets and families he knows. He is consulted both as a businessman and as an individual by a large segment of the farm population. He tends to circulate more through the township than the village, but on the whole people are inclined to want to see him, and they do so at his place of business, where he is willing to talk at any time.

From this position Jones is able to wield influence in all aspects of local government. No official can be nominated to the village, town or school boards without his approval. As the third man on the effective Republican committee he serves with Lee, who is oriented to town affairs, and Flint, who is oriented to village affairs. In spite of his dual position as a village businessman oriented to the prosperous farmers, Jones leans in the direction of the farmers. This emphasis is expressed through the action of his son on the school board who as a village representative represents, in effect, the customers of the Jones and Hilton firm. In effect, then, the village is not represented on the school board.

Jones is also one of the few men in local politics who has a direct and active interest and influence in national and state politics. But it is important to note that his interest and influence in state and national politics are not connected with his activities as a political boss in local politics. As a farm implement and feed dealer he is interested in the welfare of the farmers. Since agricultural policies and prosperity are affected by state and national farm policies, Jones is often asked to represent farmers and farm organizations before higher government groups, to serve as a member of farm delegations and to be a representative of farm causes.

Such activities strengthen Jones's position in local politics, but he does not use the channels of the Republican party as his means of influencing policy at a state and national level. Instead, he uses farm pressure groups.

The dual and contradictory roles which Jones assumes by virtue of being both a businessman and a farm representative in the village and the township are expressed in the amorphousness of his political profile. He is a pleasant person and, while wielding tremendous power, never appears to assert himself. Lee and Flint, who have much less authority, are much more assertive and outspoken in the exhibition of their political convictions. In withdrawing from the appearance of being involved in political controversy, Jones is forced to act out the role of the political schizophrenic, a role which is characteristic of the basic conflict between the two major leadership classes, the businessmen and the farmers.

Young, who is a member of the county Republican committee, is the connecting link between local government and state politics. While living in Springdale, he works in the county seat at Rockford. He does not participate in the social life of the village, but rather orients almost all of his activities to county affairs. However, his activity in county affairs is not as one of the many men striving to influence local issues in a particular direction on the basis of internal issues in the county; rather, his function is to keep the machine intact and able to deliver the vote in state and national elections. As a part of this task, he is responsible for adjudicating intra-party strife and for selecting desirable party candidates for the primary.

The basis of his strength, then, is not the local support he possesses but the external position he occupies. He is the gate-keeper in Springdale for the county and state party organizations, and all local politicians must deal with him.

As an "agent" for the state machine his major function is to organize the party to get out the vote for statewide elections. He does not do this in a conspicuous way, nor does he have to, since the normal party processes are activated as a matter of habit at election times. He enters the election process only on those occasions when special measures are required to stimulate the voters for state-wide elections. It is at this point that he occupies a peculiar position with respect to the local machine. The local machine, as previously indicated, functions most effectively in elections in which there is little interest and in which there is a relatively light vote. When interest is increased and when a higher per-centage of voters participate in elections, a greater percentage of the alienated groups and areas in the township vote. This endangers the local machine in off-year state-wide elections and can, at times, result in Democratic victories in local elections.

The necessity for a large Republican vote in the township represents the attempt of the Republican party to offset Democratic majorities in the urban and metropolitan areas. In supporting such a program, the upstate township guarantees for itself a higher proportion of state funds than could be expected on the basis of either tax contributions or a Democratic state administration.

The last figure in local politics, the principal, cannot be considered a politician in the same sense as the others. His interests in politics flow from his interests in developing a model school system. His political interest is part of his professional ethic. In involving himself in government, he finds himself opposed to the low-cost, low-tax philosophy of the dominant groups in invisible government. Because of his "administrative" finesse, however, this is not a direct and publicly visible issue. However, to achieve his program, the principal is forced to activate segments of the community which are not otherwise active in politics. In doing so, without being fully aware of the full implications of his actions, he makes the most direct attack on the local political system. He threatens it by bringing into active politics new and different political forces: the professionals, the industrial workers and several Polish farmers who are interested in education. By the consequences of his actions, he challenges the monopolies of power held by businessmen in the village and prosperous farmers in the township. These have been the traditional bases of politics in Springdale.

LOCAL LEADERSHIP AND NATIONAL POLITICS

State politics for the local community have been described as an exchange of local votes for state aid, and the organization of the state machine as it impinges on local politics has been shaped by this fact. The very same exchange has been bolstered at the psychological level by local resentments of urban and metropolitan culture which overshadow the rural community in so many other ways. The resentment of urban areas is greater than the resentments which are aroused by and expressed at the dominance by the state Republican machine.

At the state level all other issues are subsumed under the issues of rural and urban dominance in all its fiscal, political and psychological dimensions. Issues apart from this are almost absent.

At the level of national politics, the local machine is important only in terms of the mechanics of getting out the vote. At the level of policy formation, it is the local "non-political"—i.e., non-party—apparatus that is decisive. The Farm Bureau, the Grange and the producers' cooperatives are continuously and seriously concerned with national and state substantive policies. They, not the party, are the pressure groups. They, not the party, inform their publics of the vital issues, gather consensus and attempt to communicate with the policy-makers in government. Their interest is continuous while the party apparatus deals in votes, not issues, and is operative at this level only at election times. It is perhaps the most significant description of the role of the local machine in national politics that, when the leader of local invisible government wishes to influence important policy, he does so as a representative of a special interest group instead of as a representative of the party. In terms of national political issues, then, the local party organization is to all intents and purposes non-political.

IV

The Reconciliation of Symbolic Appearances and Institutional Realities

Chapter 9

───────────◄◉►───────────

Religion and the Affirmation of the Present

The Place of the Church in Community Life

CHURCH-GOING is of major importance in the social life of Springdale simply because it constitutes so great a part of the publicly visible community activity. Church activities involve relatively large groups of people and occur in conspicuous places at fixed times. A large part of the attention of the community is captured by activities centered in the churches.

The major portion of church activity occurs in four Protestant churches located in the village. The churches and the number of participants in each are:

1. *Baptist.* 135[1] local members, of whom between 70 and 100 attend church regularly and participate in other church activities.

2. *Episcopal.* 100 active and inactive[2] communicants. Between 30 and 50 attend regularly and take part in other related activities.

3. *Congregational.* 100 members, of whom 30-50 participate.

4. *Methodist.* 250 members, about half of whom participate.[3]

[1] The official total membership of this as well as other churches is about 25 percent higher than the figures given here. This results from the practice of retaining names on membership rolls after people have moved from the community.

[2] Those who have not taken communion for one or more years. They are still members of the church, but not in good standing.

[3] In addition to the village churches, there are seven others (two Methodist, two Baptist, one Episcopal, one Seventh Day Adventist and one Catholic), all located in rural parts of the township. The Seventh Day Adventists are situated on the fringe of the community and appeal to a small regional membership which includes few Springdalers. The Catholic church, also located on the geographical fringe, was built by and serves about 20-30 local Polish families. Catholic activities are physically and psychologically segregated from the life

Sunday morning in Springdale is a time of exclusive devotion to religious pursuits, to the exclusion of all other public affairs. Each church, surrounded by cars, becomes a focal point of activity and no other organized activity exists to compete with the specifically religious. The Sunday service and schools, however, by no means exhaust the range of church activities.

Altogether, church-related activities constitute approximately 50 percent of all organized social activities in the community. Each church sponsors a broad range of activities and supports a number of auxiliary organizations. These vary slightly from church to church but, on the whole, with the exception of the Baptists, the pattern of activities of any one church is relatively indistinguishable from any other. Characteristically there are a board of trustees or deacons, a ladies aid, a missionary society, a men's society, youth groups and a choir. All such organizations conduct their own social programs, a fact which again multiplies the number of church-connected activities. Under auxiliary auspices fall the church supper, the ice-cream social, the bake sale, the rummage sale, the men's supper, the hay rides and the picnics. The Baptists explicitly reject such social and money-raising activities—for them there are no suppers, no bake sales and no ice-cream socials. The church for them is an exclusively religious fellowship and money is collected by the direct means of tithing and contributions; women's activities are organized

---

of the community, whose religious tone is given by Protestantism. Non-Polish Catholics attend churches in other communities. In this sense the Catholics are socially invisible.

The other country churches are officially or informally linked to their village counterparts. They represent a 19th century phase of rural religious decentralization and are now supported by small congregations and do not retain a minister. One exception should be noted: of the two Baptist churches, only one is affiliated to the village church. The other is a schismatic group which absorbs elements hostile to the aggressive theology of the minister in the village.

The village churches are made up of persons from all parts of the township and include the bulk of the church-goers. The membership figures given do not include the rural affiliates and this study deals only with the village churches.

in a missionary society, youth activities in bible classes and men's fellowship in a tither's association. As an added layer, evangelistic speakers are almost a weekly feature of the Baptist church program.

The range of activities centered in the churches and the extensiveness of the programs offered by the auxiliaries, then, are sufficiently broad to attract people to the church and to appeal to a variety of interests.

The churches are an important part of the life of the whole community because of the public nature of their activities. Most of their social activities are open to anyone who cares to attend. In practice, however, the public social activities of one church—a supper or ice-cream social, for example— are attended only by members of that and other churches. Irrespective of which church is sponsor, the clientele for these activities is much the same. It is for this reason that the churches cooperate with each other to divide the available dates on the social calender—i.e., Methodists have a Harvest Supper while Congregationalists have the July Fourth Dinner; no two churches have bake sales or rummage sales at the same time, etc.

In consequence, although the churches organize the major portion of the public life of the community, their activities involve only the 300-400 persons who are interested in church activities. This, of course, is only a small portion of the 1,700 adults involved in the life of the community. Nevertheless, the multiplication of the activities of these 400 people, by participation in numerous church programs and social activities, is so great as to give the appearance of dominating the whole of the public life of the entire community.

Class and Church Membership

All of the class groups are not equally involved in church activities and church memberships are not distributed along class lines. The basic core of memberships in all churches is drawn from various segments of the middle and marginal middle classes. All of the churches claim the membership of at least one of the old aristocratic families. The professionals, with the exception of most teachers (who are Catholics and attend church in another community), are perhaps the most thoroughly involved in church life.

Only a small percentage of industrial workers, who are otherwise similar to the professionals in style of living, are church-involved. Prosperous farmers provide the core membership of the Methodist church and are scattered throughout other churches. Businessmen's participation depends on whether they think active participation in one church will have a negative effect on their business chances. About half are active members of churches, equally divided among all denominations.

In Springdale church membership is largely determined by considerations other than class. Kinship, marriage and family tradition all play a part in explaining the mixed class composition of the congregations. Children, with few exceptions, adopt the church of their parents. However, affiliation by kinship does not assure family continuity in a given church. In the Protestant churches, unless the husband is without a church, the wife upon marriage affiliates with the church of her spouse and any children who are products of this mating do likewise. Siblings and first cousins who all trace their descent to a common maternal grandfather can belong to different churches. Except for the Baptist church, where marriage tends to be endogamous, marriage tends to cut across church lines relatively freely. Beyond the nuclear family, kinship groups are not identified with a particular church.

Characteristically, church membership is determined by the husband's church preferences and these preferences are determined by family tradition. New migrants to a community generally enter a local church according to their prior predispositions. These factors of tradition and custom rather than class or theology account for the mixed social and economic composition of the congregations.

Only one class is decisively and completely uncommitted to church life, the shack people. They neither attend church nor participate in the various activities that surround the churches. The traditional farmers are the only other class grouping that stands apart from the religious sphere of community life. Their traditional family church affiliations are to country churches which have fallen into disuse and they have not been willing to shift their membership to a village church. They do not participate because of their incapacity to adjust to the 20th century trend to centralized churches.

Although there is preponderantly a mixture of class and church membership, there are a few points at which class and church meet. The membership of the Baptist church consists largely of members of the marginal middle class, but this does not mean that all members of this class are church participants. Although all churches include a few prosperous farmers, the majority of these farmers are Methodists. The historic 19th century appeal of Wesleyanism to farmers is reflected in the social composition of the contemporary church. The Congregational church commands the greatest percentage of the professional class, but does not monopolize this group. There are no professionals in the Baptist church. Outside of these tendencies, no one church is exclusively monopolized by any one class group.

Church Leadership

LAY LEADERSHIP

The lay leadership of Protestant churches concerns itself with church government, fund raising and auxiliary organizations. The professional ministerial leadership is concerned with the specifically religious but, of course, is not excluded from lay leadership problems.

The lay leadership necessary to planning and executing the programs of auxiliary organizations is largely provided by the professional and industrial segments of the middle class. All choir directors, Sunday School superintendents and teachers stem from these groups. This is also true of lay administrative assistants—unpaid clerical workers, mimeograph machine operators, etc. Youth leaders and officers and workers in men's and women's organizations tend predominantly to come from this group. There are, of course exceptions to this pattern: farmers do occasionally hold office in church organizations but on the whole they are less successful simply because they do not have time; women's church organizations more frequently tend to recruit leadership on a broader class basis, but this results from the fact that women simply participate in church life more than do men. The same groups perform the organizational and executive functions in the churches in the same sense that they do in almost any secular social activities. These are the groups with an interest in social activities and with time to devote to them.

At the level of church government and fund raising, another level of lay leadership is invoked. Trustees, deacons and vestrymen are frequently persons who play no other part in church activities, including Sunday morning attendance. This is partly explained by the different function which they serve in the church. Church government is concerned with administrative policy, finances and, in those cases where it is a prerogative of the local church, with hiring and firing the minister. In the Baptist and Congregational churches the trustees are the supreme authorities in hiring the minister and fixing his salary, and the minister is accountable for his activities to them. In the Episcopal and Methodist churches the minister is appointed by higher authorities, but even here the trustees are crucial since they as well as the minister have access to the higher authorities; the trustees are in a position to make appeals to higher authorities for the removal of undesirable ministers. Such policy matters represent a different order of leadership since, in the end, church policy determines the specific character of the church.

In a roll call of lay policy leaders one finds many of the same names that are found in our discussion of political institutions. Howard Jones and William Holden (president of the school board) stand out as leaders of the Methodist church. The key figures in the Congregational church are Flint (who several years ago replaced Young in this capacity), Melbin (the unsuccessful party candidate for supervisor), Monson (a village trustee and relative of Howard

Jones), Hanks (one of the leaders in agricultural politics) and Grainger (the 4-H agent). Calvin is one of the leading lay figures in the Baptist church and Hilton and Fridel (leader in agricultural politics) stand out in the Episcopal church. In both of the latter cases, however, there is less overlap between religious and political leadership; in the Episcopal church because it has a mission status and practically no autonomous local decision making powers, and in the Baptist church, since a sharp distinction is drawn between sacred and secular activities, political behavior does not materially improve one's chances for salvation.

The other lay governing officials of the churches have the one characteristic in common of being prominent in some way. These include successful businessmen, an occasional retired professional with a long successful career in the community and several older men who fall into the old aristocratic class. This segment of the church governing leadership, when it participates in the organized public life of the community at all, does so only in annual church meetings and fund-raising campaigns. Their leadership consists of lending the prestige of their name to the church in return for a position of only symbolic significance.

THE ROLE OF THE MINISTER IN CHURCH AND COMMUNITY

In the religious and organizational spheres, the minister mediates between the local church and the religious life of the outside world. In his capacity as a minister of a church, he faces a congregation which to him is a given entity, though to a certain extent he can influence its size and composition. As a professional who deals with other professionals in his denomination, he has intimate contacts with regional, state and national denominational organizations. In terms of his own background—his training, his religious impulses and the friendships he has built up in the course of his career— these outside connections are as meaningful or perhaps more meaningful to him than his local ties. Neither his congregation nor the community regards him as a permanent resident. He may remain in the community one year or five years or, in exceptional circumstances, perhaps even ten, but in no instances in Springdale has he remained a lifetime. There has been a turnover of all ministers in the ten years prior to the end of this study and two of the churches have had as many as three in this period of time. It is apparent that though the minister lives and acts within the community, his stable referent group lies elsewhere.

These facts affect the minister's position in his own church. The fact that the Baptists and Congregationalists, in contrast to the Methodists and Episcopalians, possess the power to select and hire their own minister is unimportant to the dynamics of the minister's position in his own church. Under either system the minister has received a large body of training and has developed values which he brings to the community with him and which may or may not be acceptable to his congregation. The great diversity of Protestant practice from community to community even within the same denomination is a truism among ministers. What was acceptable to a minister's previous congregation may not be acceptable to his new one. What the young seminary student has learned in the course of his theological studies in an Eastern seminary is apt to strike a note of discord when voiced in a rural community.

In addition to this background, he constantly receives church publications—magazines, abstracts and pamphlets—attends church conferences and is continuously exposed to resolutions of conferences and policy statements of national and international bodies. Because of his own background and his professional interests, he is inclined to give weight to these things, or at least pay attention to them, whether or not he personally accepts their contents.

As a consequence of these combined factors, even if he does not wholly accept larger church policy, the minister's own views do not always coincide with those of his congregation. The Congregational and Episcopalian ministers both hold views which are not publicly acceptable to their congregations or to the community. In keeping with the positions of national denominational organizations, both accept doctrines of social and economic welfare, racial equality, industrial democracy, liberal politics and United Nations internationalism—all of which are doctrines alien to the dominant tone of Springdale. The Baptist and Methodist ministers are not concerned with such worldly affairs, but each in his way also represents alien ideas. Ten years ago the Baptist minister brought to Springdale a radical evangelistic fundamentalism previously unrepresented in the town. Two years ago a new Methodist minister upset both his congregation and the community with a strict, almost fanatical approach against the ordinary "sins"—smoking, drinking and card playing—which are so much a part of the everyday fabric of community life.

In the Protestant churches, whether a minister can impose his views on his congregation depends on the nature of the congregation, his personality and his skill in dealing with the congregation. Different ministers have different degrees of success, but a good share of the church program and character is given by the minister's previous experience, theological seminaries and outside church organizations. The character of the church does not wholly originate in the community.

This does not mean, however, that all the social and religious policies of the larger church organizations are reflected back into the community through the minister or that the minister's personal views, especially when they are at variance with established community belief, are automatically reflected in community life. The minister is in the peculiar position of having to play down those views which are inappropriate to the public values of the community. To a large extent he is unable to express what he personally believes, except for accepted, uncontroversial dogma. The Episcopal and Congregational ministers do not publicly express their views on social policy even though these views carry the imprimatur of higher church officials. The new Methodist minister quickly learned to play down his public condemnation of sin. The Baptist minister learned to restrict his evangelizing of fundamentalism to his own congregation. To different degrees for different ministers, the congregations and the community socialize the minister to local values. Of all the ministers, the Baptist has most successfully imposed his views on his congregation. In ten years he has separated his church from the Northern Baptist Convention and shifted it to a position even more fundamentalistic than the Southern Convention. Where a minister attempts to impose his views, whatever their source, the composition of his congregation will be altered in proportion to the intensity with which he pursues his own purpose.

What is interesting, however, in connection with the policies of national church organizations, is that ecumenicalism, the great contemporary movement to unify the Protestant churches, receives practically no *public* expression in Springdale. For the past twenty years, since its beginnings in 1937 and with the organization of the World Council of Churches in 1948 and the Evanston meeting in 1954, the upper echelons of church leadership have been overwhelmingly concerned with the World Council in its mission to achieve Protestant unity. Church publications have literally been flooded with information and analyses of its meetings and pronouncements. The only medium through which these events penetrate to the local churches are the Sunday School texts, themselves edited and published by national organizations and distributed to the local churches. The World Council (one could just as well take the National Council) not only makes pronouncements on inter-church policy, it also covers the broad social questions of the day. The section in the Evanston report on "Our Oneness in Christ and Our Disunity as Churches" is complemented by sections on "The Responsible Society in a World Perspective" and "International Affairs." It would be quite unthinkable for any minister in Springdale to direct public attention to even such a diluted statement as found in section III, paragraph 20 of the Evanston report: "The concrete issues in all countries concern the newly evolving forms of economic organization, and the relative roles of the state, organized groups and private enterprise."

Although the minister must stay largely within the bounds of local social belief and practice, some of the most important *programs* of the local church emanate from the outside. These programs, though they tend to be of long-standing tradition, receive constant transfusions from the outside. All missionary activities—old clothes and book collections, mission Sunday, the adopted missionary, support of a specific mission church in Uganda or the Pacific—are direct responses to upper level organizational direction.

The executive secretary of the state building commission, the state superintendent of churches or the bishop provide the "push" for church renovation programs, and supply a trained organizer familiar with the ways of the small community to organize fund-raising campaigns. State and regional conventions, summer retreats and Bible camps are attended by the leading laity and provide a direct linkage between the local church and supra-local organizations. Outside of these traditional processes, which vary in extent from church to church, the minister exercises a censorship function over what is admitted into the religious life of the community.

MINISTERIAL LIMITATIONS ON EXTERNAL INFLUENCES

When one looks beyond the traditionally accepted programs, the upper levels of the church world are by and large isolated from the world of the community. The basis of this isolation in a particular church depends on the attitude of the minister to supra-church policy. The following describes the policy of each minister.

1. The Baptist minister, a decisive, positive-minded person with highly personal theological convictions, has disaffiliated his church from all larger church organizations. He sees his mission as one of building a new Christian church by transforming the religious life of the community from the bottom up. His church is isolated because he rejects supra-church policy and organizations whose programs are aimed at the local church.

2. The Methodist minister rejects supra-church policy because he himself, with the exception of his notions of sin, largely accepts community values. He accepts and acts within

the community status system and caters to the dominant social characteristics of church activities. Ecumenicalism, Oxnamism and religious interpretations of social issues are shielded from the congregation.

3. The Episcopalian minister, a young man trained in one of the liberal Eastern seminaries, accepts supra-church policies. He regards pastoral work as a branch of psychiatry, respects the authority of the church hierarchy, concerns himself with industrial working conditions and holds positive attitudes toward unionism, social and economic equality and racial tolerance. He knows, however, that he cannot express these values in the community: "One thing you have to do when you come to a small town parish is win their confidence: you have to act like them. We learn that much sociology, anyhow."

4. The Congregational minister accepts larger church policy and occasionally expresses it in opposition to the local community and important segments of his church. In the pulpit he has mentioned the "working class," the "business class," the "commercialization of the church and the absence of spiritual life" in the community, though usually this is done indirectly and by innuendo.

When we speak of a minister opposing local values, it does not mean that the community he faces is a monolithic body. There are also, of course, conflicts within the local community. The minister accepts, selects and rejects what is meaningful to him from among those aspects of church policy over which there is conflict and presents this to a heterogeneous congregation and community. He will and does get different responses from different groups. The middle-class groups which place a high value on community unity, cooperation and social participation form a strong opposition to the Baptist minister. People like Sam Lee, who are active participants in the social life of the community, drop their membership in the Baptist church; others attend the schismatic Baptist church which flourishes on the basis of opposition to fundamentalism. The Congregational minister "sticks his nose" in political and economic issues "where his nose has no right to be" and alienates the business and political leaders, including some in his congregation who then form an opposition to him within his own church. In general, community leaders and organizational participators who like to give the community the appearance of social unanimity resent his public excursions into areas of conflict. The "hell and damnation" of the Baptist and Methodist ministers alienates the enlightened professionals and practically all of the college-educated; just as the "Catholic appearance" of the Episcopalian minister arouses the hostility of members of churches which lack formal ritual and hierarchic administration. But even beyond all this, church policy as reflected through the minister is frequently less important than the personal behavior and personality of the minister.

THE MINISTER AS A PERSON

The minister is one of the most socially visible participants in the life of the community. Like the school principal, he has a social identity for a large number of people which is more clearly defined than that of some of the leading political figures. Because of the public character of his activities and simply because of his associations with the religious, he stands out. People take an interest in his public behavior and in his private life and judge him on the basis of his personality and how he "fits" into the life of the community. A large part of his activities do not occur in religious contexts. He and his wife's comportment in non-religious as well as religious contexts is closely watched, and is evaluated on the basis of local standards. To a large extent his success in the community is determined by the personal equation, almost irrespective of his religious beliefs.

Because he is a man of God, the minister is expected to act in an exemplary fashion. Yet what is considered exemplary behavior is defined differently by different groups and, moreover, the minister exists as a person as well as a role. Hence, his personal behavior is usually subject to severe criticism by the following criteria:

1. The minister must be able to "get along with people" by being a "good fellow" and by being non-controversial and non-political. It is paradoxical that the Baptist minister, who represents the most controversial religious views, is also regarded personally as one of the best ministers in town. In his day-to-day relations with people he is friendly, personable, "says hello to everybody" and never discusses religion or politics. People in violent disagreement with his theology cannot dislike him and, in fact, many accept him and excuse his theology because they like him personally. No other minister receives such a wide area of personal acceptance. The Episcopalian minister tends to be more formal in personal relations or, when he attempts informality, it is apt to be regarded as awkward and condescending; he is not "of the people." The Methodist minister has been known to take personal issue with people who smoke or drink, to try to change their personal habits; hence people are critical of him because they are uncomfortable in his presence. The Congregational minister is apt to verbalize issues which everyone is aware of but have tacitly agreed not to mention. By violating middle-class conventions of public etiquette, he becomes known as a cantankerous troublemaker.

2. In general the minister is more severely criticized for the *length* of his sermon than its contents.

3. If a minister's wife does not associate on a broad basis she is considered snobbish. If she is not a "helpmate" in her husband's work (participation in ladies' groups, as Sunday School teacher, fund raiser) she is resented for not contributing to the welfare of the church. On the other hand, she must not give the appearance of trying to "run the church."

4. If the minister is not a good organizer (ability to keep activities moving, ideas for programs, a deep interest in church finances) he is a poor minister. No allowances are made for lack of administrative ability.

5. Severest criticism is leveled against the "intellectual" minister: "He's a brilliant man, but what this church needs is a good organizer," "It's all right to talk about all those high-blown ideas, but people just don't want to sit through

a dull sermon." Moreover, the intellectual minister is not a good pastoral man in a community where every church member expects routine ministerial visitations and special visitations in time of illness and family crisis.

The minister's comportment in any one or all of these areas may override in importance all theological and policy considerations to such an extent that religion gets lost in issues of his personality and behavior.

Inter-Church Relationships: Ecumenicalism

Ecumenicalism is one of the most important aspects of external church policy which has an effect on the religious life of the community. Ecumenical policies of larger church bodies are designed to find their expression in local inter-church affairs. All Protestant supra-church bodies, with the exception of some segments of the Baptist church, support the ecumenical movement, the statement of which is best given in section 1, "Our Oneness in Christ and Our Disunity as Churches," of the Second Assembly of the World Council of Churches:

> "We ask each other whether we do not sin when we deny the sole lordship of Christ over the Church by claiming the vineyard for our own, by possessing our 'Church' for ourselves, by regarding our theology, order, history, nationality, etc., as our own 'valued treasures,' thus involving ourselves more and more in the separation of sin. The point at which we are unable to renounce the things which divide us, because we believe that obedience to God himself compels us to stand fast—this is the point at which we come together to ask for mercy and light. So that what we believe to be our faithfulness must bring us together at the foot of the cross. . . . By planting the cross of Christ in the midst of our divisions we believe he will overrule all their sin and make them serve his purpose of unity."

> "Concretely, this means that when churches, in their actual historical situations, reach a point of readiness and a time of decision, then their witnessing may require

obedience unto death. They may then have to be prepared to offer up some of their accustomed, inherited forms of life in unity with other churches without complete certainty as to all that will emerge from the step of faith." "In thanking God joyfully for the actual oneness he has given us in the World Council of Churches, we must try to understand the theological implications of this ecumenical fact and to implement it in the concrete relations of neighbor churches. With the Lund Conference on Faith and Order, we ask the churches, "Whether they should not act together in all matters except those in which deep differences of conviction compel them to act separately."[4]

At the local level ecumenicalism is expressed in the following programs:

1. Joint religious services on special occasions such as Christmas, Easter or the dedication of a church renovation program.

2. Joint summer Bible classes (Baptist participation not always certain).

3. A community choir made up of members of different church choirs and organized partly under the auspices of the Community Club.

4. Joint sponsorship of "Go to Church Week."

5. Joint sponsorship to support the American Legion "Back to God" movement.

6. The ministerial council, composed of the four ministers and designed to consider problems of mutual interest, serves as the center which stimulates all ecumenical programs.

While all churches, including the Baptist, which is theologically anti-ecumenicalist, participate in inter-church cooperation, ecumenicalism as practiced conceals a variety of problems. Ecumenicalism, as indicated in the official statement given above, is in conflict with the essential expansive and missionary nature of each individual church.

[4] Reprinted in entirety in *The Christian Century,* Sept. 22, 1954, pp. 1135-57.

One of the major problems is "allocation of shares" (the clergy's term) of the market for each church's congregation. Each church fears the loss of its jurisdictional rights over its membership and lay leadership. The merging of church activities in cooperative programs has the effect of drawing members away from the church and of centering their religious activities in an alien church. The loss of exclusive domain over members and their activities constitutes a threat to the identity and integrity of the church, which the membership and particularly the minister is committed to preserve: for the minister because his work is judged by his superiors largely in terms of the size and vigor of his congregation, and, for the parishioners because they constitute a social set within which they feel most comfortable. Hence, in the midst of ecumenicalism, the various churches act to preserve their differences.

This is done by publicly cooperating in inter-church activities while privately disparaging each other's ministers and churches. The Episcopalians and Congregationalists laugh at the "hell fire and damnation" sermons of the Baptist and Methodist ministers, while the latter express their indignation at the low state of morals in the former. The Episcopalians are horrified by the individualistic state of Congregational and Baptist theology while being criticized in turn by the latter for their undemocratic church hierarchy. Mutual criticisms and attacks are made on ministers, theology, organizational structure—on almost anything—but are always expressed privately among the in-group and, hence, serve the purpose of minimizing the impact of publicly practiced ecumenicalism.

At another level the preservation of church integrity and differences leads to a special form of local *sub-rosa* ecumenicalism which permits the public appearance of cordial inter-church relations while preserving all differences between the churches:

1. *The Ritualization of Ecumenical Practice.* Rules governing behavior in inter-church gatherings are such that no

church is given unequal psychological or social access to the members of another church. In union services the ministers of all churches play a part and the assignments of parts are equally rationed over a period of time between the ministers and the churches. Sermons to joint congregations are non-sectarian in content; emphasis is placed on areas where a prior unanimity of agreement exists. In inter-church meetings of lay leaders and ministers, each group arrives, sits and leaves together in a body—a symbolic act of the separateness of each church, particularly when it is realized that persons who are friends in other social contexts duly observe this ritual. Thus to a large extent ecumenical practice brings people together in a physical sense only.

2. *Informal and Tacit Agreements.* Tacit anti-poaching agreements exist which have the effect of law without the sanctions of law. A minister limits his pastoral work to his own congregation. More than this, the fear of being accused of proselytizing, of competing for souls, is so great that a minister has practically nothing but formal social contacts outside the membership of his own congregation. Under such agreements, adolescent experimentation in religion becomes a problem. A minister advises children whose parents belong to another church to stay with his parents' church—and he is apt to inform his colleagues when such cases occur. Such arrangements call a moratorium on competition for those already committed to a church.

New members of the community are allocated to churches according to fixed and rigid rules of assignment. If a new-comer has had a previous affiliation with a denomination represented in Springdale, the minister of that denomination has an "exclusive" on him—other ministers will report such cases to him. Another set of agreements exists for newcomers who have belonged to denominations not represented in Springdale. Episcopalians are given an exclusive on Catholics and Lutherans; Nazarene and Church of Christ members are turned over to the Baptists; Presbyterians are allocated to either the Methodists or the Episcopalians, depending on the character of their previous church.

This type of informal horse trading, however, is not without its problems. In the first place, there is no agency empowered to impose sanctions on infractions. Secondly, the informal tacit nature of the agreements leaves room for differences of opinion in interpretation. While the agreements exist, they do not wholly solve the problem of regulating competition. They merely civilize it.

Nonetheless, pseudo-ecumenicalism forces the minister to employ other means of competition for membership. His job performance as a minister is most easily judged by the community, his congregation and his superiors by the simple indices of attendance and membership figures and the size of his annual budget. In spite of the fact that total church membership is fairly constant, a church is viewed as not being dynamic unless it shows a continuous increase in these indices; attendance figures for the previous week and the matching Sunday of the previous year are posted weekly for all to see, and church budgets are published regularly. It is in this context that, in spite of agreements, expansionist tendencies are expressed. These lead to violations of agreements, creative misinterpretations of agreements and other forms of competition:

1. It occasionally happens, particularly among relative newcomers, that a family changes its church affiliation. Although the family has been assigned to a church, the family's other social activities are not rigidly fixed. A competing minister, especially if he feels this family is religiously misplaced, may cultivate them socially sufficiently to cause a change in church affiliation. Several such cases exist. They represent pending jurisdictional disputes.

2. The exclusive control over membership which agreements prescribe is creatively circumvented by making laymen responsible for their infraction. Instead of engaging in proselytizing himself, the minister acts through a member of his congregation. He asks the parishioner to try to bring some inactive member of another church to his church. At a more indirect and diluted level each minister always emphasizes that his church program is open to everyone; from the pulpit

he encourages his congregation to "bring your friends and neighbors" and reminds them that the missionary responsibility lies with the individual member.

3. Competition among churches is openly expressed by the technique of offering non-religious or non-sectarian programs which will attract outsiders. To different degrees the churches offer public socials, movies, visiting missionaries or transient evangelists and advertize such events on a community-wide basis. The success of any one church leads to resentment and stimulates similar programs in other churches.

The largest number of competitive programs is aimed at high-school students. Each church has youth groups, schools and social programs designed specifically for them. There is general public approval for such programs since no alternative "secular" social activities are available to the youth outside the school—no movies, no dance hall, no youth clubs. The churches fill a social vacuum. Filling this vacuum provides the churches with a socially acceptable competitive arena so long as no one church succeeds more than others. A child may later join a church with which his first contacts were purely social. Participation in church social programs does not clearly fall within the scope of anti-poaching agreements and, hence, become a major technique for compromising the regulation of competition.

Inter-church competition can remain in relatively private layers of life so long as no one church out-competes the others—i.e., publicly dramatizes itself and attracts new people. The Baptist church, while cooperating in ecumenical and *sub-rosa* ecumenical practice, makes aggressive appeals to members of other churches. It alone has a regular program of outside evangelistic speakers and it emphasizes an extensive youth program. These activities fall outside the network of *sub-rosa* ecumenicalism. The success of the Baptists leads to resentments on the part of other church leaders and to complaints by other groups in the community. Hence though the Baptist church cooperates in almost all ecumenical programs, it is accused of being non-cooperative and non-community minded, of proselytizing.

GENUINE BUT UNSUCCESSFUL ECUMENICITY: A CRUCIAL CASE

A crucial case in genuine but not fully completed ecumenicalism occurred between 1943 and 1950 in relation to the Episcopalian and Congregational churches. During the war years neither church could support a minister and, in fact, for a number of years before that the Congregationalists had only a part-time minister and the Episcopalians had none. Both church buildings had had no repairs for forty or fifty years and the Episcopalian church had been practically abandoned. Because they were self-supporting churches in a community hard hit by the depression, the financial and membership situations of both had seriously deteriorated; there was literally no Episcopalian church since there were no active communicants and no budget.

In 1942, at a time when the Congregationalists had no minister, the diocese reestablished the Episcopalian church as a mission; a minister and a budget allocated from diocese funds were sent into the community and the title to the church building, as is usual in such cases, reverted to the diocese. The first service was attended by seven people, but within a short period of time, under the vigorous leadership of the new minister, Bryce, the church had a membership of fifty adults and a fully developed church program, including schools and socials. The success of Bryce was considered phenomenal even by the oldest members of the community.

Bryce soon came to be regarded as an exceptional minister and as a remarkable member of the community. He was a deeply religious man who was selfless and never obviously did anything to further himself or his own cause. Because he set a personal example of high character and of almost total devotion to his work, everyone came to like him and, in fact, never in his career in Springdale did he develop any public enemies. In his personal relationships he was friendly to everyone ("even went in the saloon with his white collar to talk to the drunks") and, what is more, was willing to help "anyone in trouble without trying to make them an Episcopalian." Thus he helped people to get jobs, assisted in adoptions, made contacts with welfare agencies, arranged transportation so people could get their children to Sunday School and the like. While doing all these things he built up the Episcopalian congregation by visiting all people who were known at one time to have been Episcopalians and by visiting Catholics known not to be attending any church. His pastoral activities were extensive and intimately intensive, but never overbearing: "he understood people."

After Bryce had been in the community for a while and had become well known, the Congregationalists invited him to conduct their Sunday morning service. Bryce had made it known to several Congregationalists that he would be willing to do this, but he never participated in arranging the invitation except to give his assurances that he would conduct a Congregational service. Although he was ecumenically minded, he apparently felt that merger was either too drastic a step or not possible.

In spite of some misgivings and opposition, the Congregationalists appointed Bryce as minister under an arrangement whereby he would preach a Congregational service every Sunday in addition to his Episcopalian service in his own church. The opposition was not based on Bryce as a person but rather on the theological and organizational effect that his pastorate would have on the church. It was felt that he would naturally spend more time with his own church and thus weaken the Congregational church; and it was thought that Episcopalianism would inevitably creep into the Congregational service. However, in the face of economic difficulties the arrangement to have Bryce as a minister was accepted by the Congregationalists.

The initial fears turned out to be baseless. When Bryce preached in the Congregational church, he eliminated all Episcopalian symbols: he did not wear his garb, there were no altar boys, Congregational hymnals and prayers were used and sacraments were never mentioned. In his pastoral work with Congregationalists he wore a business suit and emphasized a social and psychiatric approach. After several months the arrangement was changed so that Bryce preached for one consecutive month in one church and the following month in the other church, in each case observing the service of the church he was in. On alternate months if a Congregationalist wanted to attend church, he had to attend an Episcopalian service and vice versa for the Episcopalians. This system existed for almost seven years without exhausting Bryce's patience.

Different members of each congregation responded quite differently to these arrangements. On the whole the Episcopalians voiced few objections, although a few attended only their own service. About 15 out of 40 Congregationalists attended only their own service. There were some pressures for merger in both churches. These pressures were based on the class character and psychology of the congregations; both churches contained a number of professionals who were friends or who knew each other socially outside of church contexts. For them, merger posed neither an organizational nor a theological problem, and they were willing to place the future fate of both churches in their faith in Bryce.

However, as soon as it became apparent that a "merger movement" was underway—that is, that some people were beginning to discuss it—a strong opposition developed within the Congregationalist church. The opposition consisted of people who had been life members and, in some cases, of persons whose fathers before them had been life members or descendants of founders of the church. It also consisted of the lay leadership which at this time consisted essentially of one man, Young. Young was chairman of the board of directors, handled all church finances, paid the minister and frequently personally made up church deficits—so much of the church organization was embodied in his person that "no one had any idea of what was going on." The prospects of merger were anathema to those with historical identifications and intimate organizational connections to the church; they saw the destruction of a Congregationalist tradition established by the community's founding fathers, the disappearance of an important historical site and the loss of a symbol of genuine—i.e., non-"Catholic"—Protestantism. They felt that they would be absorbed and dissolved by a predominantly Episcopalian congregation that was expanding while their own church was not. Theological issues based on the incompatibility of Congregationalism and Episcopalianism were important, significantly, for this, the older generation in contrast to the younger professionals who were more concerned with social consequences. That is to say, for the older generation theology still retained some of its 19th century meanings.

After some bitterness and acrimony, the opposition to merger succeeded. Young managed to raise the money necessary to hire a new Congregational minister and in 1950 Bryce's services were discontinued. Only two public monuments remained as evidence of the ecumenical ruins: (1) one Congregational family made a permanent shift to Episcopalianism and has been a prime missionary target for the Congregationalists ever since and (2) due to either prior agreement or to successful counteropposition, Young released his sway over the church to Flint. For Flint, who had then been in the community only ten years, this meant consolidating his position in the village at the expense of Young, whose interests in the church were largely extracurricular since his political referent group is at the county level; for Young, it meant making a concession, after winning the argument, to preserve the church for his lifetime, at least.

This failure of ecumenicalism can be attributed to three major factors: (1) the individuals opposed to merger, the older and more established group, felt they would get lost as the number of Episcopalians grew while the number of Congregationalists declined because no new members were added; (2) the opposition leaders were powerful and respected men in the community at large beyond the church and because of this could hold sway over the well-intentioned ecumenicalists; (3) the rising economic prosperity in the mid and late Forties in Springdale permitted the Congregationalists to tax themselves at rates sufficient to hire their own full-time minister.

The near merger was possible in the first instance, however, only because of the financial difficulties of both churches which arose out of the depression. It is unlikely that anyone would have considered merger if both churches had been solvent, as they are at present. Secondly, even at its peak, this case of ecumenicalism was possible and successful only by playing down all theological differences and issues so much that Bryce to all intents and purpose was a part-time Congregationalist, a role which he realized that as a local minister he had to act out in order to achieve *any* ecumenicalism. Lastly, the temporary merger was possible because of the similarities in the social composition of the congregations: the presence of socially like-minded professionals in both groups who were relative newcomers to the community and not bound by tradition. What is interesting about this case, however, is that although it illustrates inter-church competition, it is primarily concerned with those who are already church members. Competition for the unchurched reveals yet another plane of church life in the community.

Church Competition and the Unchurched

The competition for church membership is geared only to newcomers and the already churched, those who have a church affiliation. The bulk of the population which is not church-going is not the object of missionary work. The thousand individuals who are not members of a church, excluding a small number who go to church in other communities, are made up of two distinct groups:

1. Those who have been approached by one or more ministers and have consistently resisted; these are people who outwardly give the impression of being good prospects, but who turn out not to be. They become known as intransigents by all the ministers, none of whom attempt any longer to involve them in church activities.

2. Those who are simply known to be non-church-going people: the immoral, the irresponsible, those without self-respect, the "unreliable." Proselytizing activities are never aimed at this group; church programs are not designed to appeal to them and ministers never visit them.

In the face of inter-church competition for membership, this absence of missionary effort requires explanation.

Psychologically, for the first group, it means that the effort required to gain these persons as new members is so great that the ministers feel they do not have the time or the persuasive skills necessary to "sell" them religion and active church participation. For the second group, the explanation lies in the fact that the ministers and their laymen are often simply unaware of the existence of the traditionally unchurched. They either do not see the unchurched or they have no desire to pollute the church membership with socially undesirable types. This attitude results in an almost total neglect of local missionary opportunities.

While the mission opportunity on the local scene goes unseen, each church carries on an extensive missionary program for non-Christians in remote places. Collections of mission funds, clothing, books, missionary speakers and the adoption of a distant mission church make up an important part of the churches' programs. The community of the damned still exists, but it is not noticed in one's immediate environment.

In spite of inter-church competition and in spite of *sub-rosa* ecumenicalism, formal ecumenicalism is still celebrated by a number of church programs which have at least symbolical significance. The ministerial council exists, the joint summer Bible classes meet and the community choir sings from time to time. This means that at the public level, in any case, the relations among the churches are carried on in a civilized manner.

The Place of Theology in Ecumenicalism

The tensions and problems raised by ecumenicalism and by the similarities in the social programs of the churches are partially solved by differences in theology. The previous discussion which has focused on church programs has emphasized the similarities in the activities of the different churches. Theology, as used, emphasizes the differences and helps to preserve the jurisdictional boundaries between the churches.

On theological grounds no minister completely commits himself to ecumenicalism, keeping, as it were, a theological ace in the hole to prevent the ecumenical absorption of his own church. The Episcopal minister refuses to participate in any joint activity of a sacramental nature; the sacraments signalize the identity of Episcopalianism. The Methodists and Baptists decline participation in any joint activity which implies an historical attitude to the Bible and to Christ; their badge of distinction is the apocalyptic Biblical literature, *Revelation, Ezekiel* and *Daniel.* The Baptists, in addition, distinguish themselves by the adult baptism. The Congregationalists and Baptists refuse participation in any activity which acknowledges a worldly hierarchy of religious officials; for them the church is and can only be the living Church of Christ in which each man has a direct, unmediated tie to God.

Such theological differences play an important part in maintaining the identity of each church. For the membership they provide a way of justifying their commitment to a given church: "I wouldn't want to be a member of a church that had a bishop." "If you look at *Revelation,* you can see this is an apostate age." "In our church you have a definite book of prayers." "What I like about my church is that the minister can't tell me what to do." For the minister they represent sales points that competitors cannot meet: only the Baptists can offer baptism by full immersion; the Episcopalian minister alone administers sacraments in church and home; if you are a Congregationalist you have the liberty of conscience and belief—no one tells you what to believe; when you are an Episcopalian, you know there is a strong organization of like-minded behind you; the Baptists give you the truth of the Bible, the only undeviating truth, the word of the Lord. All ministers emphasize the theological points that distinguish their doctrine from the others and highlight these differences as the badge of their church. Theology itself, then, becomes an organizational device for holding and recruiting members and, as such, it becomes a branch of administration.

However, it must be recognized, in order not to give a distorted perspective, that no matter what other activities occur at say a social or organizational level, theology, no matter how imperfectly practiced, is a central part of the framework of rhetoric and discussion surrounding church-centered activities. Of course, this is neither new nor startling. When contradictions in alternatives are available, all parties to a discussion can phrase their position in at least bad theological terms. Thus a church supper is no different from any other supper in any other context except that (a) it is sponsored by the church and takes place in a church building, (b) church-like words are used, (c) a distinctly religious atmosphere prevails: conversation is subdued and behavior is formal and restrained.

But theology in the past has had other meanings, has signified more than a rhetoric. It has defined an attitude to life and to God. It has defined specifically religious attitudes and values. It has placed a premium on certain psychological states and feelings as being desirable and exalted and has created frameworks within which ethical and moral codes are meaningful in other spheres of life. From a social-psychological point of view, it has provided the theoretical foundations for sets of perspectives which for a particular theology can be defined as "the religious."

The Baptists and Theology

Theology, in the above sense, is important for only one group in the community, the Baptists, who in Springdale form an exclusive religious community of their own. In the Baptist doctrine the church is conceived as a living church—"a company of believers in Jesus Christ, linked with him in baptism and associated for worship, work and fellowship." The official position of the Baptist church in relation to the rest of the community is derived from this definition of the living church. In practice it means that the church is a "fellowship of people based on a fellowship of faith, it is a fellowship separated from the larger community, it is a community in itself." A Baptist is a person who "is called out of the secular community into the church" and his "primary loyalty is to the fellowship of Christ." The organization of the church community takes its cue from the new testament and attempts to make itself a model of the Early Christian Church. Within these terms the Baptists have become a "spiritual community" within an alien secular society to which they refuse to accommodate.

The contemporary world is regarded as apostate; Baptists remove themselves from it, not wishing to have anything to do with it. The religious way, while unsuccessful in this world, provides salvation for those who duly prepare themselves in the present. To the Baptist the emotional religious experiences of conversion to the way of Christ, of being publicly saved and of adult baptism by total immersion are the central personal experiences of life that give him a sense of pride, distinction and self-esteem, whatever his worldly position. The combined consequences of this orientation lead to a theological abnegation of this world wherever possible under the conditions of modern living.

In this theology, accommodation is replaced by evangelization, but for "practical" reasons (of *sub-rosa* ecumenicalism), the missionary attitude is reduced to "neighborliness." Stemming from this attitude, the Baptists have become a social enclave within the secular community, while the doctrine provides the justification for controlling the religious and social actions of its members in relation to specific issues as they arise in the community.

The doctrine requires Baptists to abstain from all community functions except the political and educational. Voting, holding political office, teaching and belonging to the P.T.A. are permitted on grounds that this is the only way to keep civil government out of the church and to keep education directed to inculcating the virtues of "obedience and respect for authority." The esteemed Baptist boycotts all other forms of community activity. Since the conception of the "Baptist community" is linked with the pietistic morality of Baptist theology, members are prohibited from all participation not directed to "fellowship and pressing business." This prohibition specifically excludes association for entertainment, secret lodges, idle sociability and gossip. Organizations which condone drinking, dancing or recreation are prohibited. Organized charity drives are boycotted on grounds that they are not administered and controlled entirely by Christians (in the Baptist sense of the term). In special instances the minister and deacons of the church have explicitly permitted participation in certain community affairs where it is felt the ends of the activity are in consonance with Baptist doctrine.

No other church assumes such a monastic attitude toward the community. The Congregational church, whose organizational structure is patterned on the living church of the New Testament, adapts itself to the changing circumstances of secular life and encourages secular action within the secular framework. Episcopalians and Methodists freely engage in community affairs and feel their engagement remains consistent with religious belief. For these groups no sharp line distinguishes sacred from secular activity. By its exclusiveness and by the moral and ethical imperialism of its members, the Baptist church stands out as a peculiar group in the life of the community. By his theology and his social isolation from the secular, the Baptist appears to others to be "queer"—non-cooperative, unsociable, fervently religious.

The distinctive feature of Baptist religious practice is that it is not ordinary—i.e., it is removed from the non-religious. It is "peculiar" in the sense that the religious attitude and perspective are distinct from the non-religious.

The Place of Religion in Community Life

The characteristics of other religions in Springdale do not have this Baptist quality of peculiarity. They are ordinary —i.e., similar to the regular activities of people acting in public social activities. The religious halo for these people is one that surrounds activities which in their intrinsic qualities are not religious, i.e., not peculiar.

Church life, then, is an added layer of social activity which merely thickens the public life of the four hundred people who participate. Since all persons in the community do not participate equally, it is not a mere replication of the total behavior of the community. It is characteristic only of that portion which is the most social and most external in its activities. Church activities afford an opportunity whereby these social activities can find expression in additional ways. Church activity, then, lends quality and depth to the external and social aspects of the public life of the community. The multiplication of church activities and the duplication of church programs give the community the appearance of greater domination by these public social activities than is actually the case when one views the total population of the town. But since these other groups do not participate, the activities of the church participants magnify the appearances of one segment of the community almost to the point where all others are obliterated from the public view.

Chapter 10

Community Integration through Leadership

Generalized Leadership

IN the final analysis religion serves to accentuate and emphasize the public values of the community and to surround those values with a framework of church activity which further accentuates participation in and commitment to those values. This, however, is accomplished only for the lives of those individuals who are religiously active. In a similar way, secular leadership gives coherence to the institutional framework of the community as a whole. The interlocking, duplication and overlapping of leadership roles tend to channel community policy into relatively few hands, and it results, at the level of the personalities of the leaders, in some degree of community coordination. That is, a wide range of community activities are coordinated simply because a small number of individuals are engaged in a wide range of leadership positions.

The extent to which this coordination is effective, however, is an interesting question which is open to exploration on the basis of our data. Moreover, the roles of leaders and would-be leaders that are not coordinated is also an important part of the leadership process since the activity represented by these roles may help to account for innovation, diversity and change.

Four of Springdale's leaders have appeared and reappeared in almost all contexts in our previous discussion. These leaders are Jones, Lee, Flint and Young. Jones is the farm feed and mill operator, Lee the editor of the paper and town clerk, Flint the lawyer and legal counsel to organizations, and Young the county committeeman and high-order Mason. When one reviews the organized public life of the community from the perspective of leadership, it is quickly apparent that this small number of individuals occupies a great many of the available positions. In fact, one encounters the same faces over and over again in almost every community context. This is as true for the political, educational and religious spheres already described as it is true for other community activities. Whenever an important community matter is considered in the community club, the presence of Jones is inevitable. It was Flint who wrote the articles of organization and incorporation of the Community Club and Lee has served as its president, as well as holding innumerable committee chairmanships. Flint, Lee and Jones have each had a turn at serving as president of the businessmen's bureau and have also occupied chairmanships of its more important committees—school, industry and ethics. Flint is a member of the board of directors of the local library and from time to time is chairman of a charitable drive. Lee has been fire chief and an active participant in the fire-fighting companies for many years. One or more of these men sits on the board of directors of almost every organization in town, from the cemetery association to the telephone company. Young is more specialized, but equally crucial. His specialization lies in his connections with outside agencies. His interests as a formal political link to the county involves him in all local activities that have any external implications, so that while he is less apt to hold formal community positions, he is informally brought into all activities that overlap with the outside world.

The extent to which such overlapping of leadership constitutes domination, the extent to which some areas of community life are free from the influence of this central leadership group and the extent to which different leadership groups appear to dominate in different institutional spheres—all these are separate problems subject to special analysis. However, looking only at the summation of such leadership roles, we can gain another view of the structure of the public life of the community.

PRIMARY AND SECONDARY LEADERSHIP ROLES

Not all of the positions which the dominant leaders hold are equally important. Some can almost be called honorary positions which an individual gains by being dominant in other positions. When Lee is elected to the presidency of the Community Club and when Flint is made president of the business bureau, they are being given a form of social recognition for their community work in general. A nominating committee decides that "it is about time Lee is made president because of everything he's done." In this sense such positions are honorary and are thrust upon "generalized leaders," even though their occupancy involves work and even though it may be flattering to receive such recognition.

While a given leader may occupy a great many positions, not all positions are of equal importance to him. The occupancy of some serve simply as legitimations for the occupancy of still other positions. Being a church member and a lay church leader establishes prestige and an identification with an institution whose purposes are held to be materially disinterested. All of the generalized leaders maintain church affiliations. Moreover, they carry this identification further by giving financial and verbal support to almost any religious activity. Similarly, they occupy positions in charitable money-raising drives and community projects designed to "benefit the whole community." As individuals they feel they must occupy these positions not because of the positions themselves but because of other dominant positions: Flint's church and charitable activities support his party and village board positions, Lee's community work and fire-fighting activities support his town board position.

It can be said that of the numerous positions an individual may occupy some are master positions in the sense that they account for the dominance of a public personality. The other positions—the honorary and the legitimizing and the unwanted positions—are mere reflections of the master positions. The secondary positions are meaningful because they support and sustain the positions of generalized leadership.

In order to understand the leadership dynamics of the community, it is always important to locate and distinguish one type of leadership position from the other.[1]

THE DYNAMICS OF SECONDARY LEADERSHIP ROLES

The qualifications for leadership in a given sphere are to a certain extent based on an individual's being situated in a special set of circumstances so that it is strategically possible for him to be available, prepared and, perhaps, indispensable for a number of different positions. Moreover, once an individual has acquired the halo of being a public leader, he is drawn into additional positions just because he is known as a leader.

Men like Lee, Flint, Jones and Young, simply on the basis of past experience, are walking libraries of community history, of similar organizational problems encountered in the past and of other people's capabilities and personal problems. They are experts on legal procedures and policy matters and have an experiential basis of judgment in such matters; and they are recognized by others as having such attributes. They are in a position to put specific issues, policies and conflicts in the broad framework of the total community and its past and, because of this, lesser individuals will not or are not able to act without them. As a result of these processes, leadership accumulates leadership even when the individual does not desire the position of leadership. Flint, particularly because of his knowledge of legal forms, is constantly called upon to serve in advisory capacities in a great variety of organizations. He is called in as a consultant, for example, by almost all the committees of the Community Club, by the fire companies and by the library association, and he accepts all such calls either by attending the meeting or by conferring with committee and organizational heads. Although he complains about these demands on his time, he is forced to accept

[1] Floyd Hunter, *Community Power Structure: A Study of Decision Makers*, University of North Carolina Press, Chapel Hill, N.C., 1953, and H. H. Gerth and C. Wright Mills, *Character and Social Structure*, Harcourt Brace and Co., N.Y., 1953.

such secondary duties, even when they are not desired, in order to sustain and follow through on what he regards as his primary positions. He tries to resist such demands on his time and frequently publicly complains about being over-burdened and overworked, but invariably he accedes "because I know nobody else will do the job—there aren't enough leaders in this town."

Thus it happens that the general leader is called into consultations and discussions in which he is not *primarily* interested. Were he to refuse such demands over a period of time, he would not possess the knowledge of community affairs necessary to the leadership positions which he regards as important, especially the various governing boards and the Republican committee.

Community leaders, regardless of their reluctance to extend their leadership into secondary positions, are forced to submit to pressures to become involved in unwanted and alien activities because, if they do not accept such secondary positions, they are likely to be thought of as selfish power grabbers who want only to take and not to give. Hence, there is always the risk of losing power in the primary spheres if they refuse to extend themselves into secondary spheres. Seen from their own perspective, however, this is not a coldly and rationally derived calculus. It is important to note that these community leaders believe in social participation and public service as a basic form of self-legitimation; though they may complain of overwork and burdensome responsibility, these are also statements of ˙self-justification which reveal the psychological importance of the activity for the self-image.

However, this overwhelming occupancy of so many important positions by so few men places stresses on other potential leadership groups. People who aspire to generalized leadership or people who are interested in leadership in only one area find access to preferred positions blocked by generalized leaders who are frequently not primarily interested in holding the positions to which the potential leadership aspires. In any specialized organization—the church, the

Community Club—there are always those known as the grumblers who complain about the monopolization of positions by the few. This is equally true in politics, where people like West and Fridei aspire to gain leadership positions but in their attempts come face to face with an impenetrable resistance not so much because the generalized leaders are unwilling to accept new personnel but rather because such unsolicited aspirants represent a threat to the closed superstructure of power. Such aspirants reveal the existence of stresses which are continuously present in the community's system of leadership.

SUPPORTING LEADERSHIP POSITIONS

The multiplication of leadership roles by a relatively small number of unspecialized leaders has a further consequence. Simply because these top leaders are involved in such a wide and continuous range of activities—literally day and night— the amount of time they can give to any one activity is necessarily limited. That is, they are not in a position to do leg work, administration and other forms of detailed work. Their leadership tends to involve the intangibles of consultation, policy discussions, advising and the informal bringing together of information and data based on all their "positions" as all of their background bears on a particular situation. This is simply to say, for example, that Flint in his role as village counsel or Lee in his role as town clerk is able to coordinate in his own person all facts and factors in the total life of the community which bear on the particular problem being considered. At any one time Flint is the only man who is in a position to coordinate the decisions of the Community Club and the village board. Indeed in the combination of Flint, Lee, Jones and Young one could gain almost a complete picture of the major activities, plans, personnel and decisions that make up the life of the community at any given moment.

In order for such a leadership complex to operate, a secondary type of role complex exists which supports and sustains and makes possible the efficient leadership of top leaders. These are the roles of the workers, the doers and the executors. When decisions are made, when top leaders have decided upon a course of action, they call upon others to do the actual work: they themselves are concerned only with checking work as it is done, and are continuously involved in a succession of other policy matters in other spheres of community life. For them leadership is a continuous shifting between receiving reports on actions relevant to past decisions and making new decisions which result again in receiving new reports. Below the top layer of leadership there exists a varied assortment of people upon whom generalized leaders can rely to carry out programs. These consist of professionals, particularly teachers, young wives of industrial workers who are willing to spend part of their day in organizational activities, a few industrial workers and a host of people with specialized interests in sports, education, culture, community betterment and so forth. In other instances they may be people (particularly women) who are simply known to have time and an interest in getting out and doing something. Each community leader knows who these people are and to a certain extent each has his own private constituency of workers whom he can call upon when necessary.

If, for example, Lee is put in charge of a Community Club fund-raising project—a dance and Mardi Gras—he has to get committee chairmen for tickets, program, refreshments, music, arrangements, publicity and entertainment. He knows exactly who is competent and who has had previous experience in each of these fields and, moreover, he can get these persons to accept the positions. When Flint is made the chairman of the Boy Scout drive, he knows beforehand whom he can select as neighborhood captains. In either case the chairman simply has a few meetings with the workers—laying out the campaign—and then receives individual progress reports from committee chairmen or captains.

This second group of technical leaders enlarges and magnifies the number of individuals that constitute the leadership corps of the town. They are selected and recruited on a number of bases. Each of the aspirants to such indispensable but secondary positions is assessed and scrutinized in his various capacities as he performs a successive number of technical tasks. On the basis of past performance, an image of him as an organizational personality arises in the "leadership mind" and in the "public mind." Once this image forms and crystallizes, he wears it as a public definition and as a yoke for the rest of his life in the community. The secondary leader becomes typed as a good canvasser, as a secretary, as a reliable chairman of a committtee in youth affairs or as a good president of an organization. For any specific individual this image constitutes the assessment of his leadership potential, so that Hinkle is viewed as a good secretary and Spaar as a good publicity man and whenever a good secretary or publicity chairman is needed, Hinkle and Spaar immediately come to mind, irrespective of the issues or the sphere of activity involved.

Formal Leadership and Organizational Power

There is no clear relationship between technical or secondary positions in formal "offices" or chairs and the actual control of policy within the community. The highest political leaders in the community, for example, may have no formal political positions, though they may have a position in a church. Jones and Young hold no political office and Flint is only the appointed clerk of the village board. Similarly, many of those who are simply technical implementers and who make no major policy decisions may occupy what appear to be the top official positions. The mayor, for example, and frequently the president of the Community Club are persons who have no voice in the determination of community affairs. There is, hence, no way to decipher the relationship between position and power except by detailed ideographic examination of the lines of decision making and policy formulation.

Specialized Leadership Roles

The appearance that power is monolithic, even within the limitations noted above, would be false if we did not consider the community's specialized leadership roles. There are a great many leaders who are interested in and oriented to only one institutional sphere. In a sense, for such leaders, the interest in leadership flows from an interest in that sphere rather than from an interest in leadership itself. For instance, the interest may be purely occupational; a given occupational position qualifies an individual for a position as a leader for roles surrounding and appropriate to that occupation. Leadership stops at the limits or at the boundary of the impact of the occupation. Teachers and ministers both fall within this category.

RELIGIOUS LEADERSHIP

A minister's job is a public role. He deals with a great many people and he deals with them on public occasions. In an important sphere of a relatively large segment of community life he is a preeminent expert, so that at least formally he is consulted in all matters pertaining to religion. As pointed out previously, however, the role of the minister is highly restricted to the organizational and social aspects of religion in the narrow sense of the word. That is, the community leadership restricts his leadership activities because religion, taken in the broadest theological sense, has implications for all aspects of community life; theoretically religion affects all aspects of the private life of individuals as well as the community at large. To carry out the precepts of theology would result in domination of all aspects of community life by religion and the ministers. This, as we have shown, is not the case. Historically this problem has been recognized throughout American history. Delimiting the leadership role of the minister and depleting the content of religion is a way of preserving the balance between religious and secular leadership. In politics, for instance, in each of the churches, political leaders are important members of the congregation, but they do not use the church as an instrument for the control of the town. In fact, political leaders are not interested in *religious* prestige and only infrequently enhance their works with the religious halo. Frequently, too, they are not primarily interested in the religious positions which they hold, but rather hold them because they have been asked and were not able to refuse. But since they hold religious positions, they *do* use these positions to circumscribe and limit the role of the minister and the role of religion in the community. This is because there is at all levels of leadership a recognition that religion is potentially all-embracing. Hence, it can be said that the greatest enemies of the ministers are the church boards and the lay bodies which are staffed by the community's political leaders.

THE BAPTISTS AS A TEST CASE

The one community group that takes religion seriously and attempts to make a way of life of religion finds itself totally at odds with civil society. The Baptist's theological and practical solution to this conflict is to withdraw from civil society. As we have noted in the discussion of religion, the Baptists exercise a strict control over the civil participation permitted its membership. Participation in politics and education is permitted for the negative purpose of preventing these spheres from encroaching on the religious.

The recognition that religion, in this sense of the word, is at odds with civil society is illustrated in Lee's relationship to the Baptist church. When the Baptist program took a fundamentalistic turn under the leadership of the new minister, Lee could no longer maintain both his religious participation and his secular activities in community projects. In being forced to make a choice, he left the church, thereby indicating his scale of values and demonstrating the conflict. Prior to this conflict Lee had occupied a position in the Baptist church similar to Flint's position in the Congregational church and Jones's position in the Methodist church.

During the period of this study Lee sold his newspaper to an outsider who was also a loyal Baptist. The character of the newspaper quickly changed from religious neutralism to fervent partisanship, i.e., top priority was given to religious news, weekly prayers, religious editorials. The conflict between religious and secular life which had lain dormant under Lee's policy of strict separation became an open issue which threatened both the newspaper's circulation and the precarious equilibrium which prevails between political and religious leaders. In fact, several of the generalized leaders, when asked what they considered the community's major problem, named the Baptists: "This town won't be set right until we do something about the Baptists," "When things are running along smoothly the Baptists always stir up trouble." The "Baptist problem" is all the more real for the generalized leaders because they do not have one of their number installed in any of its lay leadership positions. Hence they can neither coordinate nor control Baptist activities in relation to their other activities, and so the Baptists become unpredictable and, thus, resented.

To complete the picture, although the town supervisor, Calvin, is a Baptist (and the only one who holds any formally important position in the community), he severely limits his political activities to the formal occasion of the public meeting, and either is not admitted or refuses to participate at the informal level of politics. Thus as an individual he is able to resolve the potential conflict between his religious and secular activities by scrupulously avoiding any situation which would force him to intervene in religious affairs for secular purposes.

OTHER SPECIALIZED LEADERSHIP ROLES

The chief characteristic of all other specialized leaders—the school principal, the 4-H agent and the teachers—is their vulnerability. They are hired experts and as such they can be replaced and are replaceable. But the institutional positions of the school principal and the 4-H agent are important in the town in that they can theoretically be influential in the determination of policy. In their respective spheres their voice is important in budgetary allocations and personnel policies so that what they do is of importance to large segments of the town. Moreover, their positions in the community, like those of the ministers, are supported to some degree by their relationship to outside institutions: the 4-H agent to the land grant college and the principal to schools of education and the state department of education.

Because their positions are important and because they are technical experts with specialized knowledge, they, along with the ministers, tend to be closely watched. All three—minister, principal and 4-H agent—are in identical positions in that they come face to face with one or more of the faces of the general leaders. Flint and the younger Jones watch the school. The lay leadership of each of the churches except the Baptist includes a general leader. The 4-H agent is more difficult to watch because many of his activities carry him throughout the county and his board of trustees is county-wide in scope so that he is not organizationally or institutionally completely located in Springdale. The job of watching him locally, then, is apt to fall on any one of the general leaders, depending on the 4-H agent's activities at any given time. His activities in the Community Club are scrutinized by Lee and Flint while his work in the countryside is watched indirectly by Jones through his rural contacts.

This watchdog function always seems to be present. The watchdog is there not so much because the general leaders are deliberately scrutinizing the specialized leaders but rather because the positions of the latter are important and generalized leaders watch everything of importance. Hence, it happens by unconscious design that the specialized leaders are severely restricted in their activities. If they attempt to do something that is potentially upsetting, counterpressures are brought to bear on them. Jones as a farm leader can organize pressures on the 4-H agent's superiors in the agricultural college and on his county board of trustees. Jones, Flint and Lee, until the latter left the Baptist church, can go above the organizational head of the ministers. In school politics, Jones and Flint operating in concert can appeal to the state's regional educational supervisor and can informally approach professors in schools of education who are personally and professionally important to the principal. These processes tend to assure that the roles of religious, educational and 4-H leaders do not overbalance community life, and that the individuals who are the technical leaders of these agencies do not infringe on the general community and the general leaders of the community.

TEACHERS AS TECHNICAL LEADERS

Teachers are a special case because they tend not to be permanent members of the community and because their individual positions are so clearly vulnerable. These differences in their position mean that they do not receive the care and attention that more formidable characters like the principal or ministers receive. Aside from their actual classroom work they exist, in large part, as a replacement pool for spare talent as it is needed for various organizational jobs.

As a group, teachers are expected to play a part in community organizations and to respond willingly when asked to take on some worthwhile community activity—acting in plays, chairing committees, soliciting, conducting discussions and so forth. Of course all teachers do not respond as desired. Different teachers take different positions in the extent to which they will allow their talents to be used in non-occupational activities. Some respond positively to the expectations placed on them and act out the role of being public servants in all phases of their life in the town. They can be counted upon to carry out secondary leadership positions without questioning policies or policy makers. They form an important core of the active "doers" and are conspicuous in organized public life. Others resent the role assigned to them, complain of demands on their time and constantly attempt to minimize their participation to perfunctory attendance at monthly P.T.A. meetings. Others see themselves as being used "by the powers that be," gripe in private and either refuse to participate or do so only under duress. Any of these alternatives is possible simply because there are a great many teachers and no single one occupies a position sufficiently conspicuous to bring him to the attention of the community leaders. At the job level, however, the character of their response to expectations affects their career possibilities within the local school.

ETHNIC LEADERSHIP

One last type of specialized leadership role is based on the ethnic factor arising from the presence of the Polish group. The Poles exist as a social and ethnic enclave within what is a predominantly "American" community. Their separate social, organizational and religious life sets them outside the mainstream of community affairs. An additional factor contributing to their social isolation is the fact that the Poles are a physically dispersed group. In spite of this, however, they constitute an important element, and because of this they have to be taken into account by the leadership group which concerns itself with all aspects of community life; recognition must be given to the numerical and economic importance of the Poles. The general leadership solves this problem by recognizing and selecting an amenable Pole, Kinserna, to act as an intermediary between the community and the Polish group. When it is necessary to get out the Polish vote, when it is necessary to solicit the Poles for charitable drives or when it is necessary to sound out opinion on a road issue, the contact with the Poles is almost always through Kinserna. Kinserna himself is flattered by this attention from members of a group whom he considers his social superiors, a fact which makes him relatively easy to control. Within his own group he is accepted both because he is socially acceptable to the dominant out-group and also because he is economically the most successful Pole among the Poles, who measure success primarily by economic criteria. Kinserna is the one socially visible Pole in the community. His visibility is enhanced by his political position as a member of the town board. To the Poles he is valued as being "recognized" by the "Americans" and to the Americans he is one of the few recognized Poles. The particular character of this connecting link makes it possible to get the Poles to accept measures and policies which are disadvantageous to them and which do not reflect their numerical and economic importance in the community; roads in Polish areas are among the poorest in the town. The Poles are stronger than they realize but, due to these dynamics, they do not realize their strength and, hence, they can be controlled relatively easily without their realizing the character of the political bargain they accept.

SPECIALIZED LEADERSHIP AND SOCIAL CHANGE

Although the organizational powers of specialized leaders are limited, power takes many forms in addition to the organizational. As noted previously, the power and influence of specialized leaders is very great in effecting diffused styles of life, patterns of taste and consumption, agriculture, religion and education—all of the higher levels of values—but it does not effectively penetrate the channels of organizational control and policy making. *It is for this reason that the more diffused collective life of the town has a different dynamic than does its organized life. For this reason the town can change in its external appearances, in its demographic composition, in its cultural content and in the whole nature of its public life and character without experiencing any change in the individuals and groups who exercise organizational and political control.*

But, in addition, there are definite processes which account for changes in the importance of generalized leaders in the community. Unlike more diffuse changes which result from the activities of specialized leaders, those changes which affect the character of social classes always affect the character of life and the image of it which general leaders mirror. Thus the recent rise to dominance of farmers colors the community's self-image, though this is only in degree. At the political level this is expressed in the predominance of farm-oriented leaders in all important aspects of the organized life of the community. The relative decline in the social and political influence of businessmen in the last forty years goes hand in hand with the increasing influence of farmers and the social, but not organizational, influence of the consumption-minded middle class: all this leads to a reshaping of the community's character. Although the psychological characteristics of the businessmen are still present, they do not dominate community life except in the purely political segments of village

politics as expressed by Flint. The psychological characteristics of the farmers have percolated through almost all
aspects of the public life. The farmer's importance is seen in
purest form in the general symbolization of the community as
an agricultural community, the equation of the town with the
farmers and their interests and the belief that the prosperity
of the town rests on the prosperity of the prosperous farmers.
At the interpersonal level this is reflected in the willingness
of all groups to talk to the farmer in his language and on his
terms even when this is alien to one's own language and life
circumstances.

Class and Leadership

THE BUSINESSMEN

A number of small businessmen occupy formal leadership
positions, but it is precisely they who are not the real leaders.
Yet it is remarkable that in politics, at least at the village
level, the political perspective of the small businessman is
the dominant one. The gap between their lack of actual
leadership while holding formal political positions and the
dominance of their perspective in village politics is bridged by
the political brokers. Flint and Jones are the primary brokers
for the businessmen, though it is Flint who is most exclusively oriented to the business community.

From the standpoint of the leadership process it is important to consider the special characteristics of the political
broker. What precisely is his function? To what extent is he
an errand boy and to what extent does he impose his leadership? How does he respond to various types of tensions and
pressures?

Economically Flint is dependent on the businessmen since
they constitute an important part of his legal clientele and
since he receives fees from public funds which they administrate, but this does not mean that he is an errand boy. For
any specific issue the businessmen do not actually know what
they want or how to get it. They *do* know, in a general way,
what kind of end result would be satisfactory. It is Flint who
has to tell them what is desirable from their point of view in
specific situations. Moreover, he definitely and indispensably

is the only person who can tell them what are the most efficient techniques for reaching their goals. When the railroad announced a plan to eliminate its Springdale service it was Flint who coordinated their views, convinced them that the issue pertained to them and provided them with the technical know-how for organizing and conducting their defense before the Public Service Commission.

What is more, Flint talks more to the individual businessmen than they talk to each other, so that at any given time he has more information about them than they have of each other. He knows more what they think as a group than any one of them. He sees issues and events from a perspective which includes all the individual perspectives of the businessmen, while each businessman has a perspective which arises from the peculiarities of his own position. This means that Flint more than any single businessman is in a position to create a favorable atmosphere for one or another side of an issue. He can give a businessman ideas which the businessman otherwise would not have had and, by knowing beforehand what each individual businessman thinks, he can compromise the conflicting views of different businessmen before they individually know that they have differences of opinion. In this way he creates an *atmosphere* by creating a business viewpoint on an issue where without him such a viewpoint might not come into being.

This, of course, does not mean that the broker possesses unlimited power. The major limit on his power as a broker is that he cannot be obviously and demonstrably wrong in a way that the error can be definitely attributed to him. That is, the ultimate check on his power and leadership is the possibility of not being able to cover up his mistakes. It must be remembered that his power and leadership is largely informal and hence rests simply in the confidence of the conferring group.

However, the business group is only one of the reference groups that Flint faces. The other referent group that he faces is, as it were, a referent group of one, namely, Jones, who is the gatekeeper to almost all upper levels of politics. Jones, himself a businessman but an economic giant among midgets, is much more than a businessman. Because of his peculiar position, as we have noted, he faces all groups in the community. But, as we have also noted, Jones does not deal directly with the businessmen, but rather deals with them through Flint. This is necessary for him because he cannot afford to be identified with any one faction in the town. It is for this reason that Flint is placed in the position wherein he has "to clear it with Jones."

The test case in political dominance arises when Flint is placed in such a position that his interests as a representative of the business group are at odds with the interests of Jones as a representative of other groups. Such conflicts ordinarily revolve around the town tax rate or some indirect expression of the tax rate such as an appropriation for roads or road equipment. The question is: How does Flint resolve the conflict? First, he attempts to mediate the two sets of interests and to placate both—to assure the businessmen that a proposed new road will improve business and to encourage attempts to build the road without a noticeable tax increase. But when conflicts cannot be resolved at this level, Flint must defer to Jones and, what is more, he must justify his action to the businessmen. This is not always difficult since the businessmen recognize the dominance of the other interests represented by Jones.

THE PROSPEROUS FARMERS

Lee operates at almost the same level with reference to the farmers, but in this case both Lee and Jones face the farmers directly. Both meet them personally, but they do not necessarily compete with each other. Lee deals with the farmers as a political figure who makes political contacts. The farmers identify him as a political figure and his concerns are the immediate and direct issues in the politics of the town board.

Jones, the dominant political figure in the community, does not have to discuss politics with the farmers. His relations with the farmers and their relations with him take place in what appear to be non-political contexts. He circulates among farmers both in his place of business and in visits to farmers' homes on occasions which are quite natural to the conduct of his business and to his personal likes and dislikes. Since he occupies no political office, no one has any direct excuse to approach him on purely political terms except Flint, Lee and Young. This means that he does not have to discuss politics publicly at the level of immediate issues and procedural conflicts. Yet, through his "non-political" contacts and discussions and from reports from others, he continuously "knows" and understands the big political picture for the entire area. There is thus no occasion for him to be publicly political except to those others who are openly identified with the public process of politics. This has numerous consequences.

Everyone in the community knows that Jones is the most powerful man in town and that he is the political boss, but only a few can deal with him directly as a political boss. His personality reinforces his unapproachability. He is a shy, quiet, unassuming man who never appears to stand out in public situations. This role of political unapproachability and "open public anonymity" has the following political consequences:

1. There are almost no occasions on which he is forced to play a public political role (to "stick out his public neck") in conflicts between the various interests he represents. His subordinates are forced to fight publicly among themselves, and when the issue is resolved in favor of one group, he has never been openly involved even though the resolution of the conflict could not occur without his private intervention. Only on the rare occasion when his machine is directly threatened by outsiders like West will he show his hand publicly. An open public gesture on his part is a formidable act and is understood by all as a *caveat*. Jones acts publicly only when his own political existence is threatened.

2. In instances where unanimity is achieved by all parties to a conflict or where there is no conflict, Jones identifies himself with the unanimity and publicly takes his stand. He avoids a public stand on any divisive issues.

3. Due to these factors, Jones appears to have very little shape or form to most segments of the population. Groups who wish to influence policy or share power recognize that Jones is the major blockage, but, because of the very shapelessness of his political profile and his apparent abstinence from politics, he is not even accessible for public attack. Since he cannot be explicitly linked with politics, it is impossible to organize opposition against him—there is nothing explicit that can be opposed—and it is futile to attack his subordinates because they do not have the power.

4. As a further consequence of the formlessness of his political sway, it is not easy to place limits on the extent of his power. It is not even possible for an opposition group to estimate and assess the extent and limits of his power and knowledge within his private sphere of operations. For this reason it is just as easy for groups who would be inclined to oppose Jones to overestimate his authority as to underestimate it. All groups and individuals overestimate his authority, but by this very fact they increase his power, since they act on the basis of their estimation.

Different groups and individuals respond differently to the structure of Springdale's politics. Most groups who are interested in politics simply accept the fact of Jones's authority without attempting to measure it. They rather attempt to work within it by attempting to influence Flint and Lee. Neighborhood groups in rural areas approach Lee when they are interested in road improvements. In all matters pertaining to the village it is almost automatic for people to see Flint.

The Political Innovator

The only group which attempts to measure Jones's authority is the "community improvement" group, composed largely of the professional segment of the middle class. This is not a permanent political group, but rather a loose temporary grouping whose personnel changes with changes in issues. Different individuals from within this class organize temporarily around issues in which they have a highly specific interest—the youth recreation program, the swimming hole. The leadership for such temporary interest groupings is not formalized, but, again, varies to a certain extent according to issues.

To the extent that there is any one person who is most frequently involved in community improvement activities, it is Jack Grainger, the 4-H agent. Grainger's work is mainly concerned with organizing 4-H groups, setting up programs and recruiting leadership for youth groups. His professional work is highly specialized, but he comes in contact with a great many persons, particularly farm families. He has a reputation for being interested in civic affairs and he belongs to a great many organizations in both the county seat and in Springdale. It is in Springdale, because of residence, that his civic interests find their highest expression.

Grainger has a professional interest in community improvement which is based on his specialized interests as a 4-H worker and a personal interest in civic affairs which stems from his occupational ideology of community improvement. For this reason he can be used as a typical example of the independent political innovator. However, he is not a political innovator in all his positions. He holds many official leadership positions which are occupationally routinized and by their routinization are limited and do not involve innovation. It is as an innovator in non-occupational contexts in Springdale that Grainger stands as a symbol for the "community improvement" group. Grainger's position in influencing community affairs is somewhat limited by the facts that his 4-H role involves (1) work with young people in such a way that he is expected to avoid controversy (this makes it difficult for people who usually deal with him at his job level to deal with him at the level of politics) and (2) being an employee of those with whom he engages in political controversy. However, in spite of these limitations on his freedom of maneuver, his professional ideology of community improvement is so strongly internalized that he pursues it even when it gets him into trouble. Community improvement is so important to him—so much a part of what he is—that his activities sometimes transcend his good sense and actually threaten his occupational position. It is for these reasons that he always appears to be engaging in quixotic adventures. His career in community activities adds up to a curious mixture of successes and defeats. He was one of the first to accept and promote the youth recreation program which was finally accepted by the established political agencies after considerable dispute and, then, taken over by them. He was instrumental in establishing the Community Club, but when it was finally established he was no longer a central figure in its organizational structure. However, he has also agitated for a number of programs—a community center, adolescent social activities, youth participation in the Community Club—which have been consistently resisted. Since he is involved in a great many community activities, he is frequently in a position as a committee chairman or director which gives him an opportunity to influence nominations and appointments. In this capacity he frequently recommends names that are undesirable or unknown to the generalized leaders. He does this because he feels the leadership base of the community is too narrow and, in doing so, he frequently upsets the overall plans of men like Lee or Flint. Such efforts to implement the extension of community leadership make him unpredictable and dangerous, and lead to failure in some instances where failure would not be necessary.

In attempting to organize interest in and political support for the programs he is interested in, he competes in the village with Flint on a political basis and with Lee in the area of his non-political village activities. It thus happens that when Grainger has an idea for a project or a program it is invariably criticized as unworkable or unnecessary by both Lee and Flint, and as soon as one of his ideas seems to be gaining acceptance, he is pushed into the background. However, Grainger is not always willing to let himself be pushed aside because, for one reason, acceptance of his ideas in the community contributes to his occupational prestige in the eyes of his superiors, in the agricultural college. Therefore he is interested, by virtue of his own organizational position, in getting credit where he feels it is due, a fact which intensifies and makes public the competitive character of the relationship he has with Lee and Flint.

However, both Flint and Lee, as we have noted, work within well-defined limits: their activities are coordinated by Jones and differences between them are adjudicated by Jones. The difference in Grainger's position, in addition to the fact that he operates as a political amateur, is that he has only those sets of limits placed on his activities which he imposes on himself, and, furthermore, he has to impose these self-limits without possessing a knowledge of the "big picture" provided to Flint and Lee by Jones. Therefore, he learns his limits only by stumbling into mistakes, overextending himself and experiencing the rejection of his ideas, proposals, programs and organized protests. In spite of this, he never stops trying even though he never increases the personal effectiveness of his political activities. That is, his political experiences do not accumulate into a permanent leadership position; every venture is a separate venture in which he has to prove himself all over again. Simply because he does not stop trying, he is different from all of the others in the circle of amateurs who concern themselves with community improvement.

In the past, all of the other amateurs have tended, when experiencing defeat, to retreat to apathy and to withdraw from the public scene insofar as controversial issues are concerned. Numerous relics of such past defeats exist in the community, and there are also many others who after experiencing defeat have left the community. It is for these reasons that the personnel in the community improvement group is constantly changing. The impulses to community improvement are continuous, but the resistances are also continuous.

Jones, however, is not a vindictive man. In being victorious in community conflicts, he does not later punish his opponents. Rather, the opposition is always allowed to enter the area of permitted social leadership at the technical and work levels.

The biographies of almost all newcomers to the community, particularly professionals who are interested in changing the town, run a typical course "from doing something about this town" to contributing to constructive community activities. With the exception of the old aristocratic families who largely serve only in ceremonial functions, this exhausts the groups who provide leadership for the community at any significant level. However, individual members of all the classes, except the shack people, can become workers in the organized social activities of the community:

1. *Traditional farmers* may hold ceremonial positions in the Grange and may serve on various work committees in the· churches or the Grange.

2. *Prosperous farmers* may hold higher ceremonial positions in the Grange and the Masons, may occupy some of the higher lay positions in the churches and occasionally serve on committees in the Community Club, or, as in one case, can be its president. When prosperous farmers do not occupy higher positions it is not because they cannot but rather because they are reluctant and feel they do not have time.

3. *The businessmen* carry on the routine program of the business bureau—plan the dinner meetings, secure the speakers and chair the committees concerned with business ethics and outside competition. Some assist in church canvasses and others help on Community Club projects and programs; they may be on a program committee or they may act in plays. Some of their wives are in the ladies' aids and book clubs.

4. *Professionals* and *skilled workers* carry the major burden of the work load in the churches, the Community Club, the P.T.A., the Masons, the library and the dramatic and choral activities.

5. The *marginal middle class*, particularly the aspiring investors and hard-working consumers, carry out the projects and programs of the American Legion and also occupy its higher positions. They also almost exclusively staff and man the positions and activities of the volunteer fire companies.

The description of such positions and the classes that fill them tell something about the nature of the organizations, but it tells very little about the dynamics of the community. Primarily, this is because at the very point where important decisions affecting the structure of the community are made, the real decision makers occupy no important formal positions which are relevant to the decision. The decision makers may occupy positions which are only a *reflection* of the informal positions they hold, and which are not the positions which announce the decisions.

Leadership and Social Change

Decision making in the community is not a specialized function. The decisive leaders of the community do not occupy any specialized positions and are not limited in their decision making to decisions which affect only one sphere of the life of the community. Rather the same individuals, some of whom occupy no formal positions, are involved in making decisions which affect all aspects of the community. They shift their focus of attention from sphere to sphere as decisions in one particular sphere affect different aspects of the community in different ways.

As a permanent "policy" (although policy is too calculating an expression since they are simply following the logic of their attempt to maintain control) they attempt to limit the areas in which specialized leaders can exercise authority and influence the community. They attempt to restrict the activities of all specialized expert groups except the political expert, that is, themselves. It must be remembered, however, that this attempt to control is with respect to local affairs only. They attempt to retain control within the local community at the same time that the local community is changing and is influenced by the outside world. In spite of the complexities of the problems of local control, these amount to almost nothing in comparison to the changes the community is undergoing with reference to and as a product of the outside world. In a sense, then, the opposition to the local leadership does not consist of dissident groups within the community but rather the whole trend of mass society which impinges on the local arena. In his attempts to deal with such larger trends in modern society, the hard-boiled realistic politician takes on as his adversary the major currents of change in modern society that affect the small town. Seen in this light, the political realists become genuine romanticists, and so it appears that it is precisely such romanticism which seems to keep the local society functioning regardless of the stresses and strains under which it operates.

However, one must not overlook the fact that their control in the local community is exercised from the standpoint of a number of real political bases. They draw their support from all the dominant groups in the town. From one point of view, then, it is not their own narrow class interest that they express, though this is not always as clear in the case of Jones, but even he goes much beyond his own immediate class interests in his political concerns. To a certain extent, then, politics and the direction of community affairs have an autonomy of their own. Perhaps this is simply because those who are concerned with politics become submerged in the aesthetics and the sheer rhythm of politics.

But even when they are not directly concerned with their own class interests, the political managers must take into account the class interests of the significant economic groups that impinge upon politics and they must weigh and balance the interests of these groups. They must develop programs which are combinations and compromises that reflect the weight, the interests, the activity and the intensity of feeling of these groups. In a sense the political managers, then, are actors who play to a passive audience and who, after all their histrionics, depend on their ability to please and entertain groups which frequently appear to be only observers. The players aim all their acting at the audience and the audience acts only to approve or reject. Only in extreme situations is the audience seen as the instigator in the interchange between player and audience, but if one follows the plays performed and the manner in which they are played, one can see the relationship between the player and the audience.

However, to account for changes in the play and in the acting, it is always necessary to account for changes in the composition of that part of the audience which has the interest and the price of a ticket. At some points the audience changes to the point where certain actors lack the ability and the skills to please it, and these are the crucial points in the history of the town. The dynamics of the town which change the composition and character of the political audience thus, while hidden, are decisive in determining the scene, the cast and the play.

Chapter 11

───────◆───────

Personality and the Minimization
of Personal Conflicts

LEADERSHIP provides a way in which the major areas of community activity are given a semblance of order and integration, an order and integration that extend into the major institutional areas of community life. While integration thus exists at the institutional level, there is always the possibility that it does not reach down into the personal lives of the community members. In order for community integration to exist it must in some way be achieved in terms of the psychological make-up of individuals. This is not a simple problem, since we have noted that Springdalers live in a world of rich and complicated values that are often determined by both the local and external societies and their major institutions. Regardless of the conflicts between the public values incorporated by the individual and the institutional framework in which he must act, the Springdaler must necessarily somehow resolve the problems of day-to-day living; he must work, marry, have children and find some way of coming to terms with himself and his neighbors. Adhering to publicly stated values while at the same time facing the necessity of acting in immediate situations places a strain on the psychological make-up of the person.

The Social-Psychological Dilemmas of Rural Life

Conflicts between values and institutions can be expressed in four major dilemmas which confront the members of the community. These dilemmas, which are central to small-town life but which are not equally apparent and applicable to all individuals and classes, are as follows:

1. The small-town resident assumes the role of the warm, friendly, sociable, helpful good neighbor and friend. However,

the forms of social competition and the struggle for individual success cause each man to examine his neighbors' pocketbook, to estimate his own gains and losses in relation to theirs, to devalue his neighbors' successes, so that by comparison he does not stand in invidious contrast, and to emphasize his own virtues in order the better to absorb his own defeats. In the light of these contrasting behavior complexes, the individual has the psychological problem of resolving the self-image of the warm community member with the image of himself as a relatively successful member of the community in its various forms of social and economic competition.

2. The goal of success as a major value and meaning in life stands in contrast to the inaccessibility of the means to achieving success. The institutional means to achieving success are limited and are not equally available to all groups. The life career represents a succession of adjustments of success aspirations to immediate realities.

3. The illusion of democratic control over his own affairs given by the formal structure of government stands in sharp contrast to the actual basis of local politics which is controlled by external agencies. Even if the individual is in the favored group within village, town or school politics—that is, an active participant in the decision making process—his personal activity accounts less for his success than the collective activity of his group. The dynamics of political victory result more from the operation of the system than from the activities of the individual. This, of course, holds only for the more favored groups which control the informal government. Other groups have little or no basis for making a link between the illusion of democratic control and the reality of small-town political dependency. The bulk of the local shopkeepers and farmers have a "reality link" to politics only on the issues of low taxes or roads. Most of the professionals, the old aristocrats, workers, traditional farmers and all of the shack people stand entirely outside the decision making process.

4. The belief and illusion of local independence and self-determination prevent a recognition of the central place of national and state institutions in local affairs. The reality of

outside institutional dominance to which the town must respond is given only subliminal, pragmatic recognition. The community simply adjusts to mechanisms which are seen only dimly and rarely understood. Even the successful are successful primarily in accommodating to these factors rather than in initiating independent action.

At certain levels, all of these problems are not abstract and distant from the ordinary person. The farmer is aware of his economic dependence when he buys farm machinery and when he markets his products. Fluctuations in the price system and shortages of consumer goods in war and peace tend to highlight this dependency nexus in concrete fashion for almost everyone. The factory worker is in daily contact with the forces of modern industrial society. Local political and educational leaders are constantly reminded of connections to state and federal agencies through the various systems of financial grants-in-aid to the community. The life experience of everyone includes, as part of his social knowledge, ascents and descents in the class position of individuals, personal failures and aborted ambitions. There is at one level of conversation a resigned acceptance of a democratic malaise—"What good is one vote from one small town?" Hence, these problems in relatively concrete and specific terms represent real problems for specific individuals. But the contradiction between the illusions and the realities of small-town existence are a contradiction at only one level of perception since the things perceived are seen from a point of view which obscures and confuses the issues in conflict.

At another level, the problems involved are problems of simple action, since the "real world" in its totality represents a set of resistances to the personal goals, plans and aspirations of men and their illusions and to the basis around which they organize their experiences and personalities. In a sense, then, these contradictions and dilemmas in different degrees and to different persons represent personal crises at the most intimate and private level. Yet the community appears to function in what appears to be an integrated manner. The psychological techniques of adjustment to these problems take on a variety of forms.

Solutions to the Social-Psychological Dilemmas

IDEOSYNCRATIC MODES OF ADJUSTMENT

Initially it must be noted that a certain number of individuals find their "solution" in pathological behavior disorders. The social life of Springdale claims its toll of alcoholics, sexual perverts, social isolates and other forms of ill-defined disorders. These types, which remain relatively socially hidden and protected from the public view, number only 20 to 30 individuals. Their presence is highlighted and they become publicly visible only in exceptional circumstances connected with acts of violence and "sex scandals." Those who make up the group of social isolates, however, are neither seen nor heard and live their daily existence outside the mainstream of community life. How it is possible for two specific individuals, who may be technically classified as insane, to exist is a mystery to the other residents of the community. The psychological response of the pathologically disabled is based on an incapacity to deal with the problem.

Aside from sheer incapacity to deal with the problem, there are certain socially stylized ways of finding release from the psychological tensions. For some individuals a pattern of avoidance based on a withdrawal from the life of the community can provide a basis for adjustment. Some individuals pursue ideosyncratic hobbies or other forms of highly private activities; others make a fetish of pets; one is totally engaged in the collection and collation of the performance records of twenty years of athletic heroes; another builds innumerable birdhouses which he stores in a shed.

It is characteristic of some members of the old aristocracy to withdraw for years into the private sanctuary of the home, during which time they may be seen by only a handful of other people. As a class, the aristocrats withdraw from the affairs of the community and live in a private world made up of their own vanishing set.

Other groups organize their life around an autonomous ritualization of a given set of activities. Elements in the marginal middle class exhibit this by their fetishistic emulation of middle-class virtues. Life is organized on a perpetually unsuccessful attempt to become a farmer or a businessman, or attempts to achieve respectability are expressed in compulsive expressions of cleanliness, neatness and morality. However, the forms of withdrawal and ritualization present no problem with respect to definitions of individual normality as held by the community at large.

COMMUNITY DEFINITIONS OF NORMALITY

Normality in a community setting has two aspects. The first, the simple concept of insanity or lunacy, requires no explanation. The second, described above as ideosyncratic modes of adjustment, is more complex. In this case, if the "abnormal" is predictable and not immediately threatening to others, it becomes part of the normal setting. The abnormal is a secondary consideration in social situations and the individual dealing with the abnormal calculates for it and takes it into account in the same way that he must necessarily take any significant factor into account as a setting for his actions. In this context the abnormality is neither more or less important nor more or less striking than any number of other factors. It is accepted, and in that sense it is normal. When it is necessary to deal with such abnormal personalities as part of one's own normal actions, it is convenient to define the abnormality as quaint, colorful, humorous or as merely another variety of human diversity, in order thereby to permit the normal flow of action. For the abnormal person in such situations this represents social acceptance of his behavior, and his behavior can continue to be regarded as normal by himself so long as it does not threaten the plans and activities of the normal. In still other instances the abnormal can be regarded as normal by the simple technique of not recognizing what for the psychiatrist would appear to be pathological. In this category, for example, would fall the small-town response to symbolic homosexuality, fetishisms, compulsive collecting and extreme forms of self-imposed social isolation. In terms of local perceptions and definitions such behavior is either not seen or, if seen, is socially acceptable. The ideosyncratics have abandoned or ritualized their place within the social world and by doing so have also abandoned any attempt to compete socially and economically. This does not mean, however, for those whose abnormality is visible, that they are condemned for failing to fulfill the dominant norms of the public ideology since the public statement of the positive segments of the ideology is sufficiently broad to accommodate them. In public evaluations they either fulfill the image of the easy-going, uncompetitive community member and good neighbor or the image of industriousness and constructive work. In either case a basis is provided for social acceptability which, in turn, leads to a publicly acceptable self-image irrespective of the private tensions which may accompany such psychological responses to the dilemmas of small-town life.

CLASS DEVIANCY

The public self-image of the community is not held by all groups. Socially standardized deviance is permitted for one major sub-group, the shack people, even though this deviance is not approved in the dominant public ideology. The shack people openly and defiantly reject the whole fabric of the public life and live a private code of pleasure, relaxation or debauchery. Some of them in extreme reaction to the public ideology openly resist, criticize and attack it; one can assume that the playing out of this role is done with extreme consequences for the individual's psychological balance and may in some cases lead to personality disorganization. With others, on the other hand, the code of the shack is a secure position which can be supported without tension. Since they reject the dominant ideology as irrelevant to their situation and do not feel compelled to attack it, the mainstream of community values lies outside the scope of their perception. Shack life, then, involves the gratification of immediate wants and desires, irregular work habits and the organization of personal affairs around private codes. Shack dwellers do not accept pressures to conformity and scale down their aspirations to a point within the reach of personal attainment. By virtue of their rejection of the public ideology, the shack people, when they are noticed at all, become the focus of a scorn and derision such that as individuals they stand for the concrete embodiment of all that is bad and base in life.

The professional classes, at the other extreme, recognize, though by no means explicitly, the limitations which they face within their own position. They too attempt to resolve their personal conflicts by loosening the economic requirements upon themselves, which amounts to a voluntary reduction of their work load, and when necessary by seeking psychiatric help.

Even though one does not expect the psychiatrist to appear on the rural scene, he exists for and is available to those who want his services; but recourse to such measures remains a fairly closely held secret. However, the professional classes assume that a person does not have to be insane or pathologically disturbed to seek a psychiatrist. Some professionals are aware of their alienation from the dominant values of the public ideology and, partly as a consequence of this alienation, become social "crusaders" who try to reshape the public life of the town by focussing an extreme emphasis on social and cultural reforms and on activities which serve as a substitute for work. They follow this course of action even though this brings down resentment on them by those whom they regard as the less educated and more backward and frequently more successful farmers and businessmen.

THE "STRAIN TO NORMALITY"

Even when those various types of "adjustive" response are taken into account, there remain large segments of the population for whom they are inaccessible or inadequate. The various forms of social release may be inadequate for several reasons. The individual may lack the intellectual background to recognize his problem, or he may not permit himself to engage in deviant behavior because it would involve a loss in prestige. For the person who is preeminently concerned with respectability and for whom the normal channels for the expression of deviancy are closed, there exist other breaking points at other thresholds of personality disorganization which, when they occur, take more dramatic forms and are apt to occur suddenly. For still others the act of acting out normalcy becomes a positive value in and of itself. These "normal" types can tolerate the deviancy of others who do not constitute an immediate threat to them so long as they are able to put them in a joking situation and, hence, discount them. However, for these persons, who strive for normalcy, other psychological mechanisms prevent the disorganization of their activity and personality.

Major Modes of Adjustment

THE REPRESSION OF INCONVENIENT FACTS

One of the major modes of adjustment for the individual is to fail to see the problem at an *explicit, conscious,* level and to repress from consciousness all those negative elements which intrude into personal activities and images. This does not mean, however, that the individual is unaware of the existence of the problems.

At the level of *action* (as opposed to the level of consciousness) all the factors which make for the recognition of the problems are present in the actions of the individual even though there is never any need or occasion to discuss them. The farmer's actions in relation to the structure of farm prices imply an acute sensitivity to the larger institutional forces of the mass society. He recognizes his dependence upon market conditions by adjusting his daily farm operation to current market trends. The businessman deals with wholesalers and nationally organized distributors in making up the greatest portion of his inventory and sees through these actions the dependence of his business upon the mass producers who advertise his goods and stipulate their prices. Industrial workers engaged in the production of specialized automotive and computing machine parts are forced to recognize some of the basic facts of modern industrial organization

—its centralization, its interdependence and the relationship between production and employment schedules and decisions made in remote places. Public officials and the leaders of invisible government imply by their political actions a sharp awareness of the dependency of the town on outside political agencies; when possible they always look for a way to finance local projects with state funds. Indeed because of the experience of war, depression, unemployment and an uncertain dairy products market, almost the entire community is sensitized to the underlying forces which create the chasm between objective realities and socially stylized illusions.

In some circumstances the members of the small community will even discuss these conditions of reality at an explicit level, but usually this occurs only when the relevance of reality is made in impersonalized terms and without reference to any specific individual, unless it be to a personal enemy or at the level of very confidential gossip. Farmers who discuss the practical aspects of farm operations do so in the context of federal supports and subsidies and in relation to current price and credit structures as they are regulated by federal agencies and as they change with changes in administrations. Businessmen talk about outside competition, particularly supermarkets and the newer type of large-scale hard-goods retail outlets, and the consequences for them of federal "easy credit" and "cheap money policies." The reality of the small-town circumstance is clearly verbalized in the business affairs of community organizations. Members of the American Legion realize and publicly admit their powerlessness as a group in the determination of national policy— "the politicians in Washington take care of that." Town and village officials as well as school board members refer to state policy and state fiscal aid in all of their meetings almost as a matter of habit without ever fully realizing the extent of Springdale's administrative and financial dependency on state government.

All these explicit mentions of community dependence are made in the context of highly specific detailed cases. No generalization sums up these detailed statements, so that individuals are not explicitly aware of the total amount of their dependence. Particularizations prevent the realization of the total impression.

The technique of particularization is one of the most pervasive ways of avoiding reality. It operates to make possible not only the failure to recognize dependence but also the avoidance of the realities of social class and inequalities. The Springdaler is able to maintain his equalitarian ideology because he avoids generalizing about class differences. The attributes of class are seen only in terms of the particular behavior of particular persons. Thus a new purchase is talked about only in terms of the individual who makes it, rather than the class style of the purchase. There are, of course, several exceptions. The half dozen aristocratic families are recognized as a class; that is, they are seen as a collection of families who have socially desirable characteristics such as being "old families," having authentically acquired heirlooms and appearing not to be strivers. The members of the book clubs, on the other hand, are almost recognized as a class— they are at least recognized as a clique. Their glaring violation of the norms of equality forces some perception of their existence even though it leads to negative appraisals. In all other cases, however, class phenomena are dissolved into particularizations and "all other cases" involves the major activities of the major groups in the community.

The extent of the community's social, economic and political dependence is frequently made explicit by outside experts who remind the community of its helplessness as a way of exploiting fears for their own ends. The school principal reminds the school board that action which it contemplates taking can be done only at the risk of losing state aid. The milk price administrator reminds farmers that the alternative to rejecting the milk price order is no milk price order at all and a return to marketing chaos. The state road commissioner informs the village board that the new state highway must either pass over main street or bypass the village entirely. At this level, those who are involved accept the reality, but respond by resenting the agents and institutions of mass society. The act of resentment by itself, however, seems to be a psychologically insufficient response. To absorb the shock, other modes of response are available. Springdalers ridicule and joke about the outside experts, behind their backs. The inalterable decision which represents a victory for the outside world may be accepted without any further talk or mention being made of it, as if in denial of its existence. A defeat is turned to victory or is twisted in a way to make it appear to be an advantage for the community either by forgetting the central (and lost) issue or by emphasizing peripheral and pseudo issues; thus the subsidy or the state-supported road is always a victory over urban life.

Only in specialized instances is there an approximation to a conscious and explicit verbalization of the individual's objective relation to reality. Recognition is given to only parts of the reality and in a way which is not personally damaging. On the one hand an individual may highlight his own success by attributing the failure of others to the objective reality of social forces. This occurs particularly among industrial workers. For them in their work it is easy to see those aspects of the dynamics of modern society which favor the person who sees it. Those who are employed in secure industries easily see the objective reality when they contrast themselves with other local workers whose jobs are dependent upon the seasonal fluctuations of the physically remote automotive industry. Similar processes occur among farmers and businessmen who can and do attribute farm and business failures to declining prices, overproduction and inadequate profit margins. The recognition of some societal forces enables the individual to exculpate himself from personal blame by attaching the blame to impersonal forces over which he has no control. While his analysis may be correct in general form, it frequently does not account for the failure of the specific individual in situations where others do not fail.

In situations of extreme personal crisis the individual may verbalize the underlying conditions of his crisis in complete form, especially if his relationship to the informant is that of the stranger. Frustrated hopes, ambitions, and aspirations as well as blockages to opportunity, self-expression and social acceptance are apt to be revealed to the investigator. The loss of a job, a business failure, overcapitalization in a period of declining farm prices, the sudden realization that promotion is not possible, failure to secure tenure, the threat of foreclosure, the realization of hopeless indebtedness, the rerouted highway which bypasses the individual's place of business, the sudden knowledge that one has been the object of adverse gossip by friends, the gnawing awareness that one is excluded from preferred groups, the contact with outsiders who in contrast with oneself appear to be leading exciting lives—anything which places the individual in a situation highlighting his own desperate circumstance tends to raise private fears and anxieties to the public level. Only in such circumstances does the observer realize that these fears and anxieties, which imply at least a subliminal recognition of a negative reality, were present all the time even though the individual in his ordinary daily routine of activities may neither have thought nor talked about them. It is only through such cases that the observer has evidence that there are high degrees of generally unverbalized recognitions of the dilemmas. In ordinary circumstances these inconvenient facts are repressed.

The field worker, like the therapist, frequently comes in contact with more of the intimate and private than other members of the community. In the absence of the therapeutic situation of the interview, individuals do not openly express their anxieties and, in the absence of the field worker who is a stranger, demonstrate an ability to live through these crises without revealing the presence of anxiety in public. As a result the public life is always more "normal" than the private. Since this is the case, any individual who wants to participate in the public life is forced to repress his private anxieties in order to be able to express the public image which is created by similar expressions on the part of others.

With the exception of extreme crisis situations, then, the individual's recognition of the problem is not defined so sharply as to pose unsolvable personal problems which might lead him to the pathological forms of adjustment mentioned earlier. Other psychologically adjustive mechanisms also contribute to the basic pattern of adjustment by avoidance.

THE FALSIFICATION OF MEMORY AND THE SUBSTITUTION OF GOALS

The sharpness of the conflict between illusion and reality is avoided, it appears, by the unconscious altering and falsification of memories. It is a relatively easy matter to reconstruct life histories both by interviewing individuals concerning their own past and by interviewing different individuals in different age groups.

The age of youth is one of aspirations and illusions expressed in their highest and most ambitious form. The ambitions of some of the high-school youth to become scientists, executives, military officers, big league baseball players or farm operators stagger the imagination of even the successful. The limitations imposed on such ambitions by aptitude and intelligence tests at this stage are easily ignored, since parents tend to encourage ambitiousness. Even those least endowed and those with least opportunity, who appear to their elders to lack all ambition, seem rather to merely take for granted in some vague way the inevitability of success. In the stage of a few years beyond high school one still finds would-be actors, businessmen, writers, big name musicians and so forth.

By middle age or even by the age of thirty or thirty-five the youthful illusions are no longer apparent. The would-be scientist is a radio repairman, the executive is a bookkeeper, the artist is a sign painter and the actor takes a part in local drama. The professional man who in his youth imagined fame is now satisfied with a routine, drab practice. The ex-valedictorian, as a way of self-assurance, talks about his brightness in high-school days. For still others whole periods of the past seem to be completely cut off.

The realization of lack of fulfillment of aspiration and ambition might pose an unsolvable personal problem if the falsification of memory did not occur, and if the hopes and ambitions of a past decade or two remained salient in the present perspective. But the individual, as he passes through time, does not live in spans of decades or years. Rather, he lives in terms of seasons, days and hours and the focus of his attention is turned to immediate pressures, pleasures and events. Through a slow and gradual process of altering hopes and aspirations in phase with the reality situation at any given moment, the youthful illusions disappear with time. As they are in process of disappearing, other thoughts of a more concrete and specific nature occupy the individual's attention, and new goals are unconsciously substituted for those that are being abandoned. Hence, simply by thinking of other things, the individual does not come face-to-face with himself as he was and with what he wanted to be ten, twenty or thirty years ago. As a consequence, his present self, instead of entertaining the youthful dream of a 500-acre farm, entertains the plan to buy a home freezer by the fall; and perhaps the immediate gratification of the home freezer at a conscious level gives him the satisfaction that the 500-acre farm might have given to the other self of his youth. In times of crisis or in the therapeutic interview the individual frequently recalls past self-images and aspirations. Personal crisis can be accompanied by self-pity and self-depreciation and in these circumstances a person is apt consciously to berate himself for his failure to achieve—a life is verbally reenacted against the standard of the youthful ambition. By collapsing time, the person comes face to face with what he is and what he hoped to be and to have. Such cases illustrate that the abandoned aspirations are never quite forgotten. They are rather repressed and at the unconscious level constitute a constant irritant which must be continuously repressed, but which in critical instances breaks through and threatens the individual's immediate adjustment.

THE SURRENDER OF ILLUSIONS

Sociologists and social psychologists have placed great emphasis upon the conflict between levels of aspiration and levels of achievement, between institutionalized goals and institutionalized means, between the largeness of personal goals and the poverty of institutional means. However, our observations in Springdale would suggest that they fail to recognize the almost infinite capacity of individual social elasticity and adaptability in dealing with immediate situations in such a way as to avoid or suppress what appears to the observer to be an obvious contradiction and a potential basis for intense personal conflict.

To be sure, not all people are equally able to come to terms with their immediate situation and reconstitute their memories. Different individuals and classes have different points and thresholds of surrender in their life cycle.

1. In a manner of speaking, the shack people surrender their illusions before birth; the process of socialization in Springdale's shack culture does not include an internalization of any high aspirations. This, of course, can apply only to those who are born and raised in the shack. There are also those who descend to the shack and surrender their aspirations within their own lifetime. The fact that this can happen at odd times and in unexpected places serves as a phantom that haunts all other groups. When this type is publicly mentioned at all, he is despised because he is a living reminder of what could happen to oneself. This knowledge, because it is personally dangerous, is repressed and with it goes the repression of the knowledge and recognition of the very existence of the shack people. This becomes a dynamic accounting for the social invisibility of the shack people and the appearance of community integration.

2. Most workers, skilled as well as unskilled, are individuals who in their youth entertained higher aspirations than those achieved. For them their lack of opportunity to go to college or to acquire a technical skill, along with their acceptance of their first job in unskilled labor shortly after graduating from high school—all this at the age of twenty—lead to a surrender of their illusions in the relatively short period of a few years.

3. The old aristocrats and the traditional farmers, each in their own way, retain their relatively specialized illusions

in the face of the present and live exclusively in a falsified past which serves as a basis for giving meaning to their existence in their privately defined present. Their lives are organized around a present conception of the values and virtues of the life of the "good old days." Genealogical fetishisms, tombstone research, and compulsive affirmations of outmoded tastes are the behavioral reflections of private worlds. These forms of behavior are not only accepted but also emulated by other groups; the aristocrats are emulated by the professional group, which lacks local antecedents, and the traditional farmers are envied by the prosperous farmers who are caught up in the dynamics of mass society. "Upper class," then, stands as a positive symbol for other groups and to this extent is legitimized.

4. The shopkeepers attempt to maintain illusions which are based on a conception of a world which no longer exists. The days of individual opportunity in the expanding frontier and the days prior to the automobile and mass merchandizing on which their present conceptions are based stand as an historical mockery to their failure to surrender. The shopkeepers find a partial escape by their ability to complain openly about their circumstances.

5. The prosperous farmers, up to the age of forty at least, live in the future and not at all in the past. Those who successfully survived the depression experienced a revitalization of their aspirations in the war and postwar years. Those who started in the late depression or early war years have not experienced the process of even temporary disillusionment. For them the opportunity of the frontier still exists. These farmers live in terms of future goals which still seem possible of fulfillment, and live in the present only in terms of immediate plans and daily and seasonal demands. Hence they exhibit a psychology of buoyancy and optimism. They are in a position to be able to claim that they have accomplished something and to give the appearance of self-satisfaction which to others appears as stridency and condescension.

6. The fee professionals, trained and educated outside the town, make their decision to surrender when they make their

decision to migrate to and establish their practice in Springdale. What they had hoped for was to achieve a professional monopoly in a place where competition was not too great— "to be a big fish in a little pond." The teacher or other salaried professional publicly signalizes his act of surrender by buying a house in Springdale; he is no longer interested in moving to the preferred city school system, or up the organizational hierarchy, and he accepts the fate of slow promotions and small increments in pay characteristic of country school organizations. At this stage the town recognizes his surrender by beginning to treat him as an insider subject to all the forms of local competition.

For some professionals the decision to migrate to the town is based on a romantic image of the rural community; disenchantment comes later with firsthand experience. Some of these disenchanted leave as soon as the experience of rural life has had an impact, a fact attested to by the high rate of turnover among them. Others attempt to face disillusionment brazenly by acting, especially to their urban friends, as if no disenchantment existed; only the virtues of rural life are emphasized. And some, of course, scale down their expectations of small-town life and live affirmatively within it.

The economic reality of mobility ceilings cannot fail to be recognized by the professionals. Social mobility and activity then act as a substitute for economic mobility and activity and provide the area in which personal conflict finds its highest expression.

These processes, as they occur in the various classes, are more than a social-psychological phenomenon. They are a personal and individual phenomenon for every person who confronts illusion with reality within his own life span. When the transition from aspiration to achievement takes place, it coincides with changes in patterns of work, leisure, identification, consumption and, in fact, in almost every aspect of living. When the farmer who rents his farm realizes that there is little hope for farm ownership, he stops devoting all his energies to productive work. He may begin to buy luxury machinery and to beautify his home. He begins to sleep later in the morning and he begins to take fishing trips, or he gives up the idea of a farm completely and seeks employment in industry. In some instances the realization is so crushing that he allows himself to be reduced to the shack culture. There are instances of businessmen who, having reached the uppermost limits of business success in Springdale, have sold out "in the prime of life" and have since lived on savings within a framework of minimum consumption. An industrial worker who for five years willingly accepted factory discipline, remained loyal to the company and was a model worker, after realizing that his attempt to become a foreman would be unsuccessful, now bitterly complains of his bosses and factory work in general. In another parallel case, the individual after years of steady, sober work is now an unreliable worker and well on the path to alcoholism.

In some cases, particularly among farmers, a man who ten years ago was penniless and without illusions is now a highly successful farm operator. For such individuals the once tarnished illusions take on a new reality and reinforce the public image of the public ideology.

However, these processes are also more than personal ideosyncratic events in the life of the town. When a sufficient number of people surrender their hopes and aspirations in a given direction, the psychological and social character of the town is reconstituted and it is at this point that the linkage between social and economic forces and the personal fate of individuals take on a social character. Hence, the social and economic fate of the class of businessmen has been relatively standardized in a given direction over the past thirty years; their individual psychological responses (a scarcity perspective) have followed in the wake of the changing dimensions of the mass society. The class of farmers who have achieved success within the past fifteen years originally stemmed from various segments of the industrial and shack classes. In their transition to the class of prosperous farmer, their psychological character and perspective has changed in the direction of expansiveness. Today they comprise an important segment of the prosperous farmers and in their contemporary actions are easily differentiated from the actions of the groups from which they originated.

MUTUAL REINFORCEMENT OF THE PUBLIC IDEOLOGY

But, due to the social character of systems of illusions, these dynamic processes in character occur relatively slowly. There is silent recognition among members of the community that facts and ideas which are disturbing to the accepted system of illusions are not to be verbalized except, perhaps, as we have noted, in connection with one's enemies. Instead, the social mores of the small town at every opportunity demand that only those facts and ideas which support the dreamwork of everyday life are to be verbalized and selected out for emphasis and repetition. People note other people's successes, comment on them with public congratulations and expect similar recognition for themselves. Mutual complimenting is a standard form of public intercourse while failures and defeats, though known to all, are not given public expression. In this process each individual reinforces the illusions of the other. Only at the intimate level of gossip are discussions of failure tolerated.

In terms of unconscious interpersonal technique, this requires that a particular individual have a fairly sensitive knowledge of the illusions held by another person and, in interacting with him, he must act and respond to the illusion as a reality. On the other hand, one does not support a person who has completely lost his illusions. This is a *faux pas* and an insult and contrary to all forms of interpersonal etiquette; in such cases the relationship is carried on on the basis of formal greetings and inconsequential small talk—the weather, hunting or baseball scores. What is thus involved is a series of graded levels of conversation and conversational content between individuals at different levels of adherence to illusions of success. The code of the proper conversational level is as proper as the code of formalities among the Japanese.

The social learning necessary to know what conversational tone to take with other individuals is elaborately involved and constitutes the etiquette of public conversation. In his first contacts with the community the outside observer quickly learns the habit of avoiding direct discussions of reality after he meets with negative or blank responses to his own *faux pas* in this area. The observer's adjustment to community life consists in large part of learning these codes of conversational etiquette. In the small town, at least at a subliminal level, people are recognized and evaluated on the basis of their likemindedness with respect to the publicly stated social dream.

AVOIDANCE OF PUBLIC STATEMENTS OF DISENCHANTMENT AND THE EXCLUSION OF THE DISENCHANTED

The public nature of the facts of mutual support are clearly demonstrated by differences in level of discussion depending upon size and composition of group. In personal conversations with intimate friends, expressions of disenchantment are likely to be heard quite frequently. As the group becomes larger and less intimate, the public ideology becomes a more prominent and forceful focus of attention. Individuals who express disenchantment in private conversations are less likely to speak in larger groups, or, if they do, they change their tone. But, even more than this, those individuals and groups who have publicly expressed disenchantment find it difficult both to participate in and to accept the type of rhetoric and exhortation characteristic of public life. As a consequence, the disenchanted withdraw from the public life of the community and, hence, by default leave the field of public and particularly organizational life open to the exponents of the world of illusion. It is for this reason that the public life is dominated by the system of illusion even though many persons do not in an inner way hold to its tenets.

Moreover, public meetings serve as ceremonial occasions at which all of the illusions enunciated reflect the public ideology. In light of the tenacity with which the exponents of the public ideology cling to it, it becomes understandable why it is possible to hear day after day and week after week what to an outsider appears to be an endless repetition of high-sounding cliches and sentimental rhetoric. The dominant, publicly repeated ideology proclaims Springdale to be "a wholesome friendly place, the best place to bring up children, and made up of ordinary people, just folks, trying to make their community a better place to live. Nobody here has to worry about having friends, all you have to do is be friendly yourself. No problems are too big for Springdale, it's the outsiders that cause all the trouble. People here have a lot of community spirit, you can always get people to take part, but usually the busiest people are the most reliable. One thing about Springdale, nobody is excluded, this is a democratic town. Anybody who tries to run things gets pushed down, but fast. If you join clubs you can learn things and have a lot of fun too. Everybody was invited and fun was had by all." These and other expressions, reported in Chapter 2, at a verbal level, conceal the basic dynamics of the town.

THE EXTERNALIZATION OF THE SELF

All of the above forms of avoidance occur only at the verbal and symbolic levels. Adjustment at this level would be inadequate if other forms of action which make possible other forms of involvement and commitment were not available to the exponents of the public ideology. The greatest dangers to a system of illusions which is threatened by an uncompromising reality are introspection and thought. That is, the individual cannot scrutinize himself to the point where he sees facts which would threaten the position he is in and over which he has little control. For, in seeing such facts, in confronting the reality beneath his illusions, in juxtaposing earlier aspirations against the achievement of age, he would find it difficult and painful to follow through on the path which he must take in his present situation to survive in that situation. Hence, he must falsify these facts in order to live in the present. In order to succeed in avoiding the reality of the situation, he must give a major portion of the life span to developing forms and techniques of self-avoidance. However, it is not too difficult to find these techniques and the techniques themselves are not too inconsistent with the public statement of the ideology.

Work as Self-Avoidance. The major technique of self-avoidance is work. The farmer and the businessman drive themselves in their work almost to the point of exhaustion. It would be a mistake to assume that sheer economic advantage even under an economic ideology could produce the fabulous work efforts and activities of these groups. The farmer is always occupied with his plans, his chores or his field work and in this process of activity he always has something external to himself to think about. In the morning, even before eating, he immediately goes to his chores, which he performs in a state of half-sleep. By the time he is awake and aware of himself he already finds himself integrated into a routine of activities which absorb his thoughts. His day represents a continuous succession of activities and tasks. While engaged in the execution of any given task his mind is preoccupied with laying plans for succeeding activities. And so through the hours, the days and the seasons alternatives to self-preoccupation are constantly available. The objects of thought are relatively immediate, practical and mundane things.

Similarly, the businessman applies himself to a great number of diversified activities which provide him with innumerable small jobs which are never finished. He shifts from waiting on a customer, to restocking his shelves, to checking his inventories, to sweeping the floor and so on and on. Such activity partly serves the purpose of enabling a person not to come to terms with himself.

The problem is much more difficult for the industrial worker, whose work on the moving line ties him to a given spot in an activity which is not too personally involving. It is difficult to know what occupies his thoughts during his working hours, but his inability to cope with introspection and self-reflection is indicated by the intensity with which he pursues work outside of the job. His home is a place not just for living but, more important, requires maintenance and constant improvement. Painting, landscaping, gardening, the addition of a new garage, the insulation of the attic—all these and other projects with the passing of seasons make continuous demands for his attention. His automobile is regarded with affection, almost like an intimate companion, and treated with the utmost care. The amount of time given to polishing, maintaining, tinkering with and talking about cars staggers the imagination. One cannot assume even with the capital investment represented in a home and car that these activities can be explained as reflecting economic interests. To an important degree they represent extensions of the personality and have the psychological meaning of making externalization possible by providing meaningful opportunities for a continuous outer involvement.

Sociability and Passivity as Self-Externalization. Productive work is only one of a number of ways of accomplishing the same purpose. Social activities in community organizations and in informal social groups, where emphasis is placed upon the constant exchange of personalities, social forms and "small talk," can be involving for all but the schizoid personalities. Springdale offers a multitude of opportunities for involvement in socially engaging activities. The innumerable committees, organizational meetings, card parties and canvasses are available for those who are not otherwise involved. The continuous emphasis on social and organizational activities by the professional groups can be accounted for not only in terms of their rejection of economic mobility but also as a substitute therapy for the externalization of personality by work. In both instances the form of the therapy is consonant with the ideology.

Religious activities such as suppers, choirs and fund raising involve a great deal of physical and social effort and support the process of continuous externalization. Conversely, the "spiritual" content of a religious doctrine potentially involves the application of purely religious and ethical messages to the life of the individual. The religious can theoretically force introspection and self-awareness by raising the question of how the quality of life is related to God and doctrines. This, however, is a form of introspection and awareness that would threaten the defense of daily living in the community. In order to avoid such confrontation of the self, the purely religious aspects of religion are avoided and deemphasized while the social and administrative aspects are accentuated; in this way religion contributes to the life of the community and facilitates personal adjustment. This applies to all religious groups in the community except the Baptists. For them religion means a repudiation of the content of community values, but the same psychological techniques used by other groups are used by them with reference to the Baptist community.

The Baptist church is filled with activities whose appearance are less secular, but which have the same objective and external character to which the Baptist can submit. The exaltation of the Baptist's private life in the feeling of salvation enables him to justify his rejection of community values. Moreover, in terms of Baptist fundamentalism, the dilemmas of modern society are not viewed as important; hence, the psychological feeling of salvation is raised to a level which can preclude almost all mundane matters. The importance that the Baptist attaches to theology and the emotion of achieved states of grace can exist only against the background of a feeling of relief from the imminence of the world.

For those who can not or will not participate in the public life of the town there are always the media of mass culture, though these are potentially dangerous because not all forms of private recreation are amenable to the same needs. One can, for example, buy a book by a serious author which, if read, could turn a personality into itself. Reading is an intimate, solitary experience which, if accompanied by thought, can lead an individual into self-reflection and to a consideration of the meaning of his existence in relation to the outer world. But there is little evidence that these processes occur in Springdale. Reading tends to be regarded as a technique of self-improvement, a form of recreation; it can become a part of routine habitual behavior, as, for example, reading the daily newspaper at a given hour in a given chair. Practical books on the techniques of living, do-it-yourself manuals and correspondence course textbooks form the bulk of the literary diet. Fortunately, in addition, since inexpensive books are easily available, the purveyors of the mass media have taken every precaution, it seems, to allow the individual to escape from his immediate situation into worlds of violence, sex, sadism, humor and romanticism.

Sports represent a halfway mark between work and social and passive participation, all of which place a high premium on the otherness and externality of activity. In Springdale training in athletic interests and proficiency begins at an early age. The young adult in the modern age has a legacy of physical skills to fall back on if and when psychological conditions require it. Active sports like baseball play an important part in the years of robust youth. They furthermore constitute an important outlet for the occupationally dissatisfied, the underemployed, and for those for whom other activities are not sufficiently absorbing. Physical skill and effort exhaust the body and prevent meditative self-examination.

Automatization of Personality. In those cases where some form of personality externalization is not present and when at the same time all forms of introspectiveness and self-insight are absent, what is left of the personality is the dulled, autonomic, ritualization of behavior where inner control is exercised to such an extent that no disturbing interferences are allowed to enter into thought. The individual adheres to a fixed and repetitive daily, weekly and seasonal routine in which no one day, week or year exhibits any significant deviation from any other. The chief instruments of discipline are the clock, the calendar and the weather which are used as significant signs in guiding the individual from one activity to the next so that thought, even at the level of making elementary choices, can be eliminated. Personal and social life becomes barren, and the personal mechanics and daily routine of living become the end-all of existence. All types of activities whose operation is based upon an objective, external, automatic rhythm to which an individual can bend himself serve the function of enabling him to lose himself in an objective ceremony. Thus an individual avoids dealing with himself except insofar as he does so through the instrument of an external mechanism. The individual can avoid physical isolation and the threat of loneliness which it implies by engaging in the quasi-automatic ritual of social agencies. The rituals of religious practice and their fixed time and place of occurrence, the procedural rituals of formal meetings and the ceremonialisms of parades, spectatorship and the public festivities of holiday occasions—all link the automatic individual to the automatic segments of public life. But more than this, other activities which are not intrinsically rituals are ritualized in order to permit such individuals to function publicly. It is at this point that inoffensive stylized humor, standardized greetings which are given the appearance of intimacy by the cheerfulness with which they are spoken and the sheer volume of talk devoted to the weather and jokes gain meaning as public extensions of private lives organized around external rituals. In these types of adjustment, loss of self becomes the price one pays for attempting to maintain one's equilibrium in an alien world. This aspect of self-externalization is present in the social activities surrounding all classes and institutions; it is almost totally characteristic of the ritualistic segment of the marginal middle class.

Generalized Anxiety. Social and self-understanding is not, however, an easy solution to these problems. There are individuals in Springdale who possess these qualities, but their life in the community involves other types of problems. First, although they may have an understanding of what are the dilemmas in the community, understanding is not a solution to the dilemmas, and so they are left in the position of either trying to determine what to do or of not knowing what to do. As a consequence of the difficulty of finding a solution, they are disturbed about their situation and tend to have free floating anxieties. In addition, they are disturbed because they cannot communicate their insight and perception of the problem to other members of the community because such insight and perception are a threat to the illusions of the externally oriented segments of the population. There are some who, under these circumstances, have sufficient inner strength to be tolerant, kind and understanding. They contain, absorb and live with their own perceptions and insights even though this is at a great cost to themselves. There are a few who are in personal and intimate contact with each other. This is true of one minister and one teacher who both seem to understand the problems facing the community. In their public role neither is permitted an open expression of their understanding since such expression would involve them in conflict and would hurt others. The minister, then, is forced to provide a social religion to the public while he practices a religion for himself which he believes to be consistent with Christianity. The school teacher does occasionally verbalize his understanding. However, his ideas are regarded as so strange and so unrelated to the practical activities of life in the community that he is regarded as a harmless and humorous oddity, and this is a role that he consciously has come to play. He survives in the community by not threatening anyone, but his survival is based on the fact that no one wants to understand him. In finding each other and in gaining a basis for communication, the condition of which is a recognition of reality, such persons create a private world which sustains a detachment, in some sense, from the dominant illusions of the community.

The various patterns of externalization all have one trait in common; *they occur in a continuous sequence in which no single activity or event is likely to resolve the problem for a specific individual for any length of time.* The activities of externalization must continuously be repeated and reinforced with little surcease. This is why illness, retirement and other unusual circumstances which make for prospects of "time on your hands" are dreaded and why social activities are organized to prevent social isolation on such occasions. The organized "visitations" of the ill and the "sunshine" committees of almost all organizations help to keep the bedridden and the incapacitated involved. Retirement from active work, particularly among farmers and businessmen, tends not to occur. Instead, progression into old age is merely marked by a reduction in work load in consonance with the reduction in physical ability. However, old age and retirement among people who are forced to retire at a fixed age creates problems since alternative work patterns are difficult to develop in the advanced ages, and it is for this group that the community does not provide easily available substitute patterns of involvement. It is interesting that the break in continuous activity for this group has in recent years found its resolution in migration to the cities of Florida which hold out the promise of a program of activities for the retired. But, to complete the picture, those who for one reason or another must remain in the town make a successful adjustment by resurrecting and living within an earlier period of their lives. Numerous examples exist among the aged: the man who for all practical purposes of conversation and thought lives in the decade of the Twenties; the woman who talks of living acquaintances, not seen for ten or fifteen years, as she remembers them when last seen; the old-timers who seek each other out to talk of the town as it was forty years ago; and, of course, senility has it normal rate of occurrence. In such cases life is arrested at a point which is consonant with the individual's retreat and withdrawal. This form of resolution is a frequent occurrence which is treated with a sympathetic tolerance by the rest of the community, so that the illusions around which such lives are organized are not challenged.

Social Structure and the Psychology of Adjustment

The emphasis on the continuous nature of work and other socially therapeutic activities indicates that the basic problems confronting the community are unresolved. The dilemmas arising from the contrast between illusion and reality, between idea and experience, are as continuously present as are the means for exorcizing them. This means that all forms of stability in the community are temporary. Minor and violent shifts in the dimensions of community life are always possible, though they may occur after long years of apparent stability during which illusion has been accepted as "reality" and has not been challenged by reality as experienced. If a sudden, negative and disastrous shift in the outside situation occurs, the defense mechanisms of the affected members of the community may not be able to accommodate to the strains placed upon the personality. A single event such as a collapse of farm prices or an inflationary trend could challenge a whole class of individuals whose life organization is based on similar illusions. But, since change for those who live through it and perceive it appears to occur slowly, new and unrecognized forms of personal illusion and institutional resolution of personal problems are an ever-recurrent possibility. For this reason bizarre forms of personality disorganization can occur in unexpected ways and at odd times in unexpected quarters. And for this reason, furthermore, the prediction of future events lies outside the scope of simple projection of present trends.

In the meantime the individual in the community must continue to live out his daily life. The various forms of illusion and defense enable him to make the most of his situation in a world over which he has relatively little control. These very same forms of illusion and defense enable him to perform his life in a useful and productive way and, to a certain extent, to live a full and not wholly unenjoyable life. They enable the individual to get along with his friends and neighbors, to be more often than not considerate and helpful. And for those who must bear the burden of uncontrolled events, they constitute the mechanisms by which the person can attempt to gain some of his own goals in a community where the attainment of individual goals is not always consonant with the goals held by others.

The psychological processes are doubly important in terms of the "objective problems" faced by the community. Objectively, the community members live in a world which they do not control. They come to this world, however, with a belief in their ability to shape their own destinies. In fact, in almost every sphere of their lives they find their inherited beliefs and traditions at odds with their institutions and social environment.

But the people of Springdale are unwilling to recognize the defeat of their values, their personal impotence in the face of larger events and any failure in their way of life. By techniques of self-avoidance and self-deception, they strive to avoid facing issues which, if recognized, would threaten the total fabric of their personal and social existence. Instead of facing the issues, they make compromises and modify their behavior in some cases, and reaffirm their traditional patterns in other cases. They do this, however, without any overt conscious recognition of the basic problems.

Because they do not recognize their defeat, they are not defeated. The compromises, the self-deception and the self-avoidance are mechanisms which work; for, in operating on the basis of contradictory, illogical and conflicting assumptions, they are able to cope in their day-to-day lives with their immediate problems in a way that permits some degree of satisfaction, recognition and achievement. There are many ways in which one could note that Springdalers do not achieve the optimum material and psychological rewards for their strivings, but such achievement does not appear to lie within the framework of their social structure. Life, then, consists in making an adjustment that is as satisfactory as possible within a world which is not often tractable to basic wishes and desires.

V

The Findings, Methods, Theory and
Implications of a Community Study

Chapter 12

—◁◉▷—

A Theory of the Contemporary
American Community

The Key Problems and Findings in Springdale

SINCE working on *Small Town in Mass Society* ten years ago
we have been preoccupied with assessing the meaning of the small
town in relationship to the evolution of American society, to its
historic past, its present, its implications for the future of American society, and its significance for newly emerging life styles in
the society as a whole. This has involved a review of other sociological, literary and journalistic studies of which there have
been an abundant number in recent times on the rural, suburban, urban and university communities. Just as journalistic
and literary studies of the suburb abound so also do studies of
university towns which have received a large share of "scientific" attention because they are easily accessible to the university professor and because they fascinate him in the light of his
own particular existence.

In reviewing this literature and in working with it in detail
with our graduate students at the City University of New York
and the New School for Social Research, we have inevitably
used our own field work and our own study as a point of departure. The central questions and problems we raised for the
data we gathered in Springdale and interpreted in our book
have served us as a paradigm or outline for assessing the place
of the community in American society. Before going to this
broader topic, let us review the problems and findings of the
Springdale study.

The central problem which evoked our study of Springdale
was discovery of the relationship between Springdale and the
larger society. In our initial contacts with the community, we
had found that even those local accomplishments of which the
people were so proud were the result of operations of the large-

scale, impersonal machinery of outside organizations whose policies in most cases were not even addressed to Springdale as a particular place but to Springdale as one of hundreds of similar towns which fell in a given category. Thus land–grant college programs, milk-pricing decisions and telephone company policies applied to all towns like Springdale; but Springdalers, of course, did not see these larger realities. Springdale could only respond to these outside forces, but quite often took its own response to be a sign that the town was being original and creative. When we first noticed that these processes of initiation and response were at work, we undertook a survey of all major cultural and institutional areas in the community for the purpose of isolating those aspects of the life and organization of the community which were intrinsic to it and those which were the products of the surrounding society.

Despite our attempt to find original and indigenous sources of the community's culture and values, we were unable to find any. Instead we found external sources and origins for everything that the community cherished as being most genuinely representative of its own spirit. Moreover, we found that the community harbored genuine resentments against the urban centers and institutions which by the process of invidious comparison devalued by their very pervasiveness all that the community was, stood for and believed in. The most original and creative elements in the community were these resentments and the attempts which the town made in collusion with other rural, upstate blocs (in legislative and lobbying activities), through gerrymandering and delays in legislative reapportionments, to encumber urban areas especially New York City, with financial demands and political favoritism. In some measure the town succeeded in these efforts and such successes were especially enjoyed in the community.

As we pursued this line of analysis, we became aware of the fact that the community did not respond as a unit to the external institutions and forces that determined its internal structure and culture. There were significant differences in the way different segments of the community responded to different parts of the outside society. In some cases like that of the expanding dairy farmers, the outside society (via favorable dairy marketing policies) provided opportunities for growth to Springdale dairy farmers. In other cases like that of the centralization of merchandizing practices, the competition from the outside society (supermarkets in the county seat) caused local institutions (small businesses) to shrivel and decay. It was through such differential rates of growth and decline that the very character of the community itself was transformed.

The uneven rates of assimilation of external elements into the community resulted in considerable variety and differentiation in the community's culture, life styles and institutional structure. For example, almost every period of American cultural history was actively represented by some segment of the community—ideologies of grass-roots Jacksonian democratic populism existed in combination with idealistic, anticorporate, muckrakerism in the style of Lincoln Steffens, and on top of this one could find the latest forms and substances of sophisticated, college-bred, urban, upper-middle class life styles. In between these forms, the town still sang songs that went backwards through the decades of the '40's, '30's, '20's and World War I. It was as if the town at the point in time when we studied it was a summation of the archeology of American history. In a word, the culture of the town was stratified in terms of various periods of American history as well as in its selective adaptation to contemporary institutions.

There are two ideas in *Small Town in Mass Society* that we think are innovations and that are especially relevant to a formulation of a theory of the American community. The first concerns the attempts of Springdalers to deal with the effects of the penetration of their community by new ideas, cultural forms and life styles which appear to be alien to the older ideas and life styles which have become part of their way of life. The second idea concerns the significance of the new cultural forms and life styles themselves.

Springdale's older traditions are part of the ideals of Jacksonian democracy which properly belong to the tradition of the frontier, of democratic populism and the ideology of economic growth and expansiveness. This nineteenth century complex of values still had considerable vitality in Springdale when we studied it. Springdalers believed in a democratic society that provides equal representation for all, equal opportunity for mobility based on individual effort and skill and upon friendliness, neighborliness and mutual aid. However, we found that all of these values are at odds with the institutional realities of the community. If he were to look, the Springdaler would have found that:

1. Almost all aspects of his town were controlled by external forces over which he had little control; the idea of democratic self-determination had no basis in fact.

2. Even within the town, political life was controlled by a small clique of party professionals whose desire was to keep real estate taxes down even though this policy was contrary to the wishes and aspirations of the educated middle class. Instead of being expansive and investment oriented, the town fathers were stingy and anal.

3. The avenues for opportunity, growth and expansiveness within the town were severely limited. The Rotarian optimism of the Better Business Bureau had a hollow and false ring. Economic growth was limited to the prosperous farmers while small businessmen increasingly became franchise operators. Personal growth and opportunity for most people could only be achieved by leaving the town. For those in the younger generation who remained, inheritance of wealth, status and position was the major basis of social and self-definition.

4. Social inequalities (inherited and economic) and sharp competitiveness within the community were in conflict with the cooperative, friendly, warm self-image of the inhabitants and of the town.

The dilemmas and contradictions that are a consequence of these differences between reality and belief resulted in complicated patterns of social and personal self-deception which permitted Springdalers to retain their system of belief while at the same time allowing them to act within the framework of those social realities which denied the tenability of their beliefs. What we saw in Springdale was an elaborate but routinely accepted set of social defenses that made it possible for Springdalers to live with their situation. The genius of these defenses was that it allowed for an accommodation between older traditions and beliefs and the newer institutional forms.

The second idea that we regard as increasingly important was the new life styles that were being introduced into the community at the time we did the study. This was our "discovery" of the emergence of the new middle class. This new middle class was composed primarily of college educated professionals and white collar and managerial workers. These people often deliberately, but sometimes involuntarily, underemployed themselves, and instead of seeking a meaningful existence in economic mobility and relentless work, addressed their lives to the achievement of stylized consumption, cultural and prestigious social and recreational activity and to efforts to be sophisticated, smart and urbane. All of these traits stood in contrast to the rural vulgarity, the materialism, the unrelenting work and the lowbrow leisure of the traditional populist values and of contemporary mass media.

Springdale's new middle classes, small in size though they were, engaged in the process of importing sophisticated cultural life styles from urban society and from the nearby state-Ivy university. By doing this, they were engaged in a process of revolutionizing the life styles of the community. Even though they were an avant-garde minority in social and cultural affairs and even though they were active in social organizations and clubs, they were effectively excluded from political control of the town. In politics they participated only as technicians and as voters in activities controlled by business leaders and farm spokesmen who were interested in holding the line on real estate taxes.

Springdale as a Microcosm in the Macrocosm

We have argued that Springdale imported and retained as its "own" elements from all historical and many cultural epochs in American society. We can infer that the same processes described for Springdale occurred and are occurring at various levels and localities in American society at large. We wish to show how the major themes expressed in the life of Springdale are representative of larger themes characteristic of American life as a whole. The dominant culture and life styles so remarkably preserved in Springdale were representative of almost all of the American past. They were so well preserved because of the attempt of the residents of the town to maintain a familiar way of life and a traditional ideology in the face of a society that devalues that way of life. The living characteristics of Springdale were part of the characteristics of the late frontier, of nineteenth-century industrial and commercial culture and of a belief in agrarian democracy and independence. The supporting ideology for this past was a simple, optimistic materialism which Mencken in the 1920's called Yahooism, boosterism, Rotarianism and the ideology of the *boobus Americanus*. Sinclair Lewis etched the personality and culture of Main Street America in acid and unrelentingly barbed terms. Sherwood Anderson and Edward Arlington Robinson described the period and its ideologies in somewhat more sympathetic and tender but not essentially different terms. Despite these negative descriptions, the essential characteristics of traditional frontier democracy, apart from its naïve and "uncultured" materialism, did involve a genuine development of local democracy, equalitarianism, friendliness, economic aggressiveness, mobility, expansiveness and opportunity consciousness. Springdalers who upheld these values were correct in their insistence that their traditional values embody the central values of the American past in both its best and its most characteristic senses.

However, the changes in American society that have put Springdale on the defensive are changes that have occurred during the past one hundred years, while the ideology of Springdale is based on the period from 1810 to 1860. Institutional changes that negate the ideology are based on developments that began during and after the Civil War and continue to operate up to the present. Industrialization has led to opportunities in the urban centers while the population of the rural community and rural society has been increasingly depleted.

Governmental, business, religious and educational super-bureaucracies far distant from the rural town formulate policies to which the rural world can respond only with resentment. The urban proletariat has replaced the rural majority only in turn to be replaced in numerical primacy by the new middle classes and by service workers who are not primary producers. The "family farm" though it still exists is now a big business industrialized in its operations and administratively organized; but for the most part farming is now corporately organized. While decreasing in number, the units of production have greatly increased in size. Throughout the country the rural countryside and old farm houses have been invaded by the commuting industrial, white collar and professional classes. The older rural predominance is a thing of the past, a fact that is gradually being reluctantly acknowledged by the acceptance of reapportionment legislation.

Factors in the Emergence of New Middle-Class Life Styles

After the Civil War, America was inundated with a flood of immigrants primarily from Eastern, Southern and Southeastern Europe. Escaping from poverty caused by overpopulation due to rising birth rates, by shrinkage in the size of agricultural holdings and by slow growth in the industrial sector, these immigrants saw in America undreamed of opportunities which either did not exist in their own countries or were denied to them. In responding to the opportunities that America offered, the immigrant affirmed the validity of and gave added impetus to the economic optimism and expansiveness that characterized an expanding frontier and later an expanding industrial society. In being converts to the American way, the immigrants supported and deepened the American dream. They became the true Americans, especially as third and older generations of Americans lost their naïve enthusiasms because of a lack of success in American society or because if successful, they emulated European rather than American models of upper- and upper-middle class life. For example, in Springdale it was Polish and Finnish immigrants and their children who in their escape from urban factory work and coal mining revived Springdale's agriculture in the twenties and thirties. The older generation of Americans had given up or accepted defeat due to the prolonged agricultural depression that continued from the early twenties to the late thirties. Springdale's older industrial and business classes that had emerged during the post-Civil War industrial expansion were already defunct. Those of their descendants who remained in the town were a declining aristocracy which lived off claims for status that were no longer recognized by the newer groups. In the case of one illustrious family whose name figures prominently in the historical annals at the turn of the century, the remaining descendants included an aged and destitute dowager who was supported by her middle-aged sons, the eldest of whom had a moderately successful military career, and the youngest of whom was for the most part unemployed and would have been considered "shack" if he had not had his name. The fortunes of this family spanned four generations between the Civil War and 1950. Where once they had been immigrants, they were now being replaced in income power and status by a newer set of immigrants who, in fact, saw opportunities where the older Americans did not see them.

When immigration ended in 1924, a major support for the continuous revitalization of the American dream was cut off. The end of immigration forced American society to live off its own capacity to renew its spirit from its own resources. As we shall see, American society has failed in this respect, but its failure has been masked because it usually takes at least three generations to produce either a gentleman or a total outcast. The second generation of the Eastern and South European immigration now makes up a large part of the middle class and the lower-middle working and service classes. The third generation since the closing of mass immigration is just now entering into maturity.

Throughout American history, *successful* immigrants of the third generation have tended to adopt sophisticated culture and/ or the degenerate life styles that are reminiscent of a European aristocracy. These third-generation life styles are opposed to the simple, direct, naïve, democratic, optimistic and vulgar materialism of popular democracy. These life styles are alien to the dominant tradition, just as that of the career military officer in the above example is a contravention of traditional values. Those in the third generation who are unsuccessful, the failures, either regress to an acceptance of a lower-class way of life or to the degeneracy of a backwoods "Appalachian," "Swamp Yankee" culture, whether in the city or in the country. If the third generation is not wholly degenerate or skid-row, it desperately hangs on to tatters of past respectability by means of hoarding, penuriousness and a defensive worship of the American past, even though such worship of the past in America is un-American. Springdale showed that the pre- and post-Civil War American traditions gave way in the face of immigrant Americanism. At present the United States faces a problematic future with respect to the third generation of the last stage of immigration.

In the same sense that the end of immigration has weakened the American dream, the urbanization of American society and the decline in the proportion of the population engaged in agriculture as compared to those engaged in secondary industries and business has resulted in a shift away from frontier democracy. The vast waves of immigration into the United States were paralleled by an equally significant internal migration from the country to the cities. The sons and daughters of American farmers sought not only the economic opportunities of urban life but also its excitement, its glamour and its offer of escape from country bondage. For the first generation rural-born urbanite, the city was the frontier which offered hope, a sense of adventure and optimism, and an opportunity for mobility. But just as in the case of the foreign born immigrant, the opportunities in the city were more salient to the first and second generation of rural migrants. The successful urbanite takes urbanism for granted and not only adjusts to new styles of urban sophistication but helps to invent wholly new forms of urban living which are not rooted in the American tradition. Failure in any urban generation produces the functional equivalents of Appalachian culture, the ghetto of outcasts. The city produces, in addition, unique patterns of bohemian, artistic, intellectual, homosexual, beat, hippie, criminal and other "deviant communities" simply because in the size and anonymity of the metropolis, individuals who would be isolated or noticeable in a smaller community can come together and form communities of deviants without being particularly noticed. The urban area thus creates centers from which life styles that have been historically deviant or nonexistent can be created, thickened, reinforced and disseminated. In this latter respect, urbanism, as an established aspect of American society, not only provides for the weakening of the frontier tradition, but creates new and varied life styles which are alien to and replace the relatively more simple frontier tradition.

The creation of these new styles, it must be noted, is directly related to the nature and conditions of the American economy. Changes in the structure of American industry, in the amount and quality of government, and in the growth of new service, leisure, educational and other institutions have produced a new class of white collar workers, officials, managers and professionals. The majority of these are employees whose working hours are limited by the nature of their jobs and by wages and hours legislation. This new class has more leisure available simply because the opportunity to exploit oneself through overwork is not as easy as it was when self-employment in agriculture, small business, or in handicrafts were the characteristic forms of employment. Changes in the methods, styles, and uses of leisure are thus a central aspect in the emergence of new life styles in American society. The availability of leisure is a function of newer forms of work patterns.

The simple, naïve optimism of the frontier and earlier industrial capitalism, as Lynd, Warner and Hunter have pointed out, was shattered by the Depression. In the thirties this naïve optimism became replaced by a defensive optimism in which the credo of the frontier and economic liberalism began to look backward rather than, as in the original frontier spirit, forward. But the defensiveness of the thirties was replaced in the fifties and sixties by a premature optimism celebrated by American intellectuals who glorified a new economic expansiveness, based not on the expansion of the frontier or of primary industry, but upon the expansion of the consumption and service sectors of society, including the expansion of education, government, foundations, science and military institutions.

This newer optimism of the fifties and sixties was radically different from the optimism of earlier periods because it accepted a managed, bureaucratic, mass consumption and mass leisure society, whose leaders, rather than being self-made men who operated within the framework of a laissez-faire society, were business managers and government bureaucrats aided by university trained scientific and managerial intellectuals.

The last major factor which influenced the production of new life styles is to be found in the mass education of soldiers during World War II and under the G.I. Bill of Rights, and in the subsequent trend toward mass higher education that these educational experiments spurred. Under wartime education, the G.I. Bill of Rights and the later mass education of millions of youth, a significant portion of this group, which was to become the new middle class, was given a preview of its own future life styles as presented to them during their collegiate years by the university and by the college professor.

Millions of American students who rejected the parochialism and the immigrant status of their fathers as un-American thought they found a true Americanism in the university, though in fact the immigrant and rural traditions were more characteristically American. Until the 1930's American university professors tended to be drawn from old stock, who had already made the transition to the American version of the genteel life. Art, literature, poetry, music, scholarship, book learning and the cultural pursuits were rejected by the populist and frontier traditions, and prevailed largely on the Eastern seaboard where the passage of generations had made these aristocratic European pursuits respectable.

The next generation of professors, our present one, came mainly from the first generation of G.I. Bill students who assimilated their version of Americanism from professors of old American stock.

While still on the campus these students were provided with a total way of life that included classroom study, social life, student politics and culture. The contrast between this life and their past life in immigrant or rural American households only reaffirmed the desire already inculcated in them by their parents to slough off the ethnic and rural traditions which even their parents regarded with a degree of embarrassment. While on campus these students were socialized only to the possibility of a different way of life. It was after graduation when these, by now, millions of college students entered the suburbs and the new, managerial, bureaucratic, professional and service occupations that the new life styles and new culture became crystallized.

Again these classes experienced enforced opportunities for leisure if not in the first years of their careers, by the time of early middle age, though the age of enforced leisure seems to be getting younger and younger. The structure of work in large-scale enterprises and bureaucracies causes the new middle class to find alternative means for using its time. It is at this point that the new middle class reinvokes an interest in its collegiate experiences with culture, sports and social life. While in college these experiences may not have been particularly salient: the courses in music or art appreciation and tennis or badminton were thought to be pleasant but somehow luxurious when considered in relation to earning a degree in order to get a job. It was only later that this collegiate exposure to culture and recreational pursuits took on special meanings and became a reservoir upon which to draw in order to fabricate a life style to replace the ethnic and rural provincial traditions.

As a result, the new middle classes become culture consumers. They are interested in art, music, literature, plays, books, psychology, anthropology and even popular sociology. They are self-consciously interested in good taste, modern design and decorating. They have become interested in what previously were upper-class sports: tennis, squash, golf, boating. Horseback riding in the middle class is in the Eastern tradition of genteel leisure rather than the Western tradition of matter-of-fact work. The country club, the community center and, ironically, the church have been major centers for an active, sophisticated, cultured social life.

Almost all other dimensions of the middle-class life style have undergone revision. In sexual codes, there has been an increasing liberation from the Puritanism of the American Protestant past. In part, this is due to the decline of the ideologically supported image of hell and damnation under the increasing influence of secularism and science; even the last holdouts, the Baptist and Methodist churches, have moderated their earlier positions on sexual codes. Also, one cannot discount the impact of the notion of sexual freedom based upon Freudian psychology and upon cultural relativism which have exposed several generations to the sexual life of savages and the inner fantasies and secret behavior of prudish Victorians. The idea of sexual liberation and sophistication is also a result, in part, of exposure to European models of sophistication especially as conveyed earlier by the Waughs, Huxley and Noel Coward, and later by French, Italian and Swedish images of *la dolce vita*. Finally, one cannot discount the importance of the simple fact of increased leisure time in permitting greater exploration and development in this area.

Religiously, this new middle class has abandoned all that the Bible-belt once stood for and has transformed the earlier forms of ethnic catholicism into modern forms of American "churchgoing" and sometimes social action directed by priestly leadership which itself sometimes expresses the new middle-class values by demanding a break with age-old celibacy rules. Fundamentalism is regarded as gauche and all middle-class churches of whatever faith place a high premium on tone, style, architectural sophistication and intellectualized religion.

Politically the new middle class is infinitely more liberal than were the middle classes of the pre-1930's. However, these new liberals are not always active in national politics and are interested in local politics in quite special ways. They do not vote according to the older traditional patterns of Republican and Democratic bloc voting at any level—urban, state or regional.

If they are sons of farmers or businessmen in the North and the East, members of this class are more likely to vote Democratic than did their parents. If they are sons of immigrants who lived in urban Democratic ghettos, they are more likely to vote

Republican in the suburbs. If they moved to the far West, there is no predictable pattern between how they vote and how their parents voted. If they are in Southern cities, they begin to find it easier to vote Republican.

In short, the new middle classes are developing a perspective of their own that focuses on an interest in a liberal, cultured, sophisticated way of life that is often independent of the traditional identification between voting and position in the economic structure.

The impact of the new classes on politics has made itself felt strongly with respect to political style. The older frontier style of politics involved personal warmth, "cornball" localism, vulgarity, and lowbrow anti-intellectualism. In the past, highly sophisticated, intellectual, cultivated and broad-minded political leaders have had to pretend they were rustic boobs in order to retain their popularity with local constituencies. In urban politics, the ethnic politician was forced to retain his accent and his hyphenated Americanism, and he was forced to prove that he had not outgrown his ghetto roots. Neither of these older American styles appeal to the new middle classes.

The new middle classes have become devotees of literate, articulate, cultured, sophisticated and vital "patrician-like" politicians. Representatives of the style most congenial to them are people like Adlai Stevenson, Averell Harriman, John and Robert Kennedy, John Lindsay, Nelson Rockefeller, Eugene McCarthy and Charles Percy. These men are cast not as "lords" of the masses as was the case with F.D.R. but rather as the distillations of new middle-class aspirations and styles. The middle class and its particular expectations have become sufficiently recognizable to call forth a leadership style willing to cater to it. Of course this has not become a dominant style, but rather one that exists in proportion to the quantitative importance of the middle class. Recent examples of successful political leaders who show that the older styles continue to exist along with the newer one are presidents Johnson, Truman and Eisenhower, and mayors La Guardia, Wagner and Daley. For the new middle classes these older styles are regarded as uncouth, crude and at times vulgar. Thus, for example, much if not most of the reaction against Johnson in the new middle class stems from his populist, Texan-frontier, uncultivated style. By the same token much of his support is based upon the consonance of his populist style with the personal styles of his constituencies. Eastern sophisticated middle-class style "liberalism" wherever it is expressed in urban America is at odds with the older layers of frontier populism in the smaller towns and in the segments of urban populations which, though they live in cities, are still populist in mentality. A large part of politics in the United States is a reflection of one or the other of these orientations to political styles. The "educated" middle class would like to conceal its politics of identification with symbols by finding *issues* that express its identification, but just as for the populists, issues are frequently less important to them than political symbols that allow them to identify with an image of dignified, educated, reasonableness which is all the more compelling if it is linked to "Ivy-collegianism."

In local politics, especially in the suburbs, the new middle classes have been intensely interested in municipal services, in education and school affairs, in the P.T.A. and, as a summation of all this, in the school budget. For them the idea of quality education has had the highest value and they have shown little respect for traditional tax rates.

In their attitudes of irreverence toward the tax rate, which in America has been a sacred cow, the new middle class has made a major break with the tradition of local politics in the United States. In middle-class communities the major and most emotional political issue is the size of the school budget. This issue is probably the major political issue in American society insofar as it involves more participation, more activity and more personal involvement than any other issue, including foreign policy and, at the moment, 1967, the war in Vietnam. While the middle-class demonstrations against American foreign policy and the war in Vietnam appear, because of the visibility of public protest, to be a central preoccupation, this is misleading. For the middle classes the school issue is much more important, but because this issue is fought at a local level and because it is a *local* issue for thousands of different and decentralized jurisdictions, it is rarely seen as so central an issue as the more obvious political protests against national policy. Because of its local particularity, the impact on the public consciousness of this issue is hardly perceived. A mass demonstration on the Pentagon has the quality of a national drama, but such dramas occur at infrequent intervals. The new middle class lives with the school issue through the lives of its children and this is a process that commands their attention on a daily and weekly basis. While the new middle class may be capable of extreme expressions of moral indignation against national political policies, its material commitments are to the education of its children and to helping them avoid the draft. It is perhaps unfair to reduce middle-class politics to the issue of parental interests in children without offering more demonstrably conclusive evidence. When President Johnson proposed in 1966 that the draft be conducted on a lottery basis, all candidates irrespective of class having an equal chance of being selected, it was the middle class that appeared to have the greatest objections to this procedure. The issue of the lottery-draft was quietly dropped, but it served as a reminder to the middle class that its sons have been protected (by attending the university) from the risks of war. When presented with an issue either of education or the draft that affects its children, the middle class responds not in terms of higher moral values but in terms of self-interest.

In describing this new middle class as we have above, we have described in somewhat more detail the same middle class whose emergence in Springdale we recorded. When we first noticed this class in Springdale, we were not fully aware of what we had encountered though we realized that it was a unique feature of the life of Springdale. Our awareness of what we saw at that time was heightened by the work of other sociologists and social analysts such as Seeley, Merton, Spectorsky, Mills, Dahl, Whyte and Riesman who, in their work, were responding to aspects of the same phenomenon. In the late forties and early fifties a number of different observers responded to the same reality and each saw his discovery in terms of the problem that concerned him.

When we studied Springdale we saw this new middle class in the process of expressing these new life styles in a small town.

At that time this class was unable to impose its "style" on the organizational and political life of the town. The middle class we observed was aggressive and defensive, never sure that it belonged in Springdale but unable to leave it because it had no other place to go. What we saw at that time was the avantgarde of that class, but it was so weak as to be hardly noticeable. However, in retrospect the weakness of that middle class was a simple function of the fact that Springdale was removed from the urban centers of the United States. It rather represented earlier stages of American history which remained viable to the residents of the town because they were more committed to the past than to the future. Springdale represented an earlier stage in American society and was not in the mainstream of American history except for a tiny middle class that had then begun to appear in the town. At that time Springdale had just barely begun to register what was a dominant fact of American life.

The Middle-Class Revolution in American Society

From our experience in Springdale as it was amplified by the works of other students of the middle class, it became clear that a revolution in American social structure and life styles had taken place. In comparing our own work with that of Mills, Seeley, Whyte and Riesman, it is clear that the middle-class revolution has occurred at unequal rates in different communities. A community like Springdale at the time we studied it was further removed from the middle-class revolution than other communities like the new suburbs of New York, Cleveland, Milwaukee, St. Louis and so on. The rate of penetration of the new middle-class style varies according to place and size of town. With time, the middle-class revolution has spread and penetrated into more and more communities, eventually touching even the most remote hamlets. By now the new middle class and its styles have been felt in all communities in the country irrespective of size. However, this revolution has not been felt at equal rates and equal levels of intensity in all communities. The differences in rates and intensities account for many of the different types of communities that now exist in the

United States. In general terms we would specify four types of communities in which the middle-class revolution has expressed itself.

THE SMALL RURAL TOWN

Springdale at the time we studied it represented a traditional American community in which the middle-class revolution was working itself out. The new middle classes were *not* influential in a political sense, but were influential in their participation in social organizations and in their "way of life" which transmitted new styles to the community. They were in the process of revolutionizing the traditional habits of the town. The more remote a town from the centers of influence, the more removed it will be from the middle-class revolution. No doubt there are communities in *all* parts of the country which still manage to resist the dominance of the new middle-class life and intellectual styles. However, it would appear that the small town in the long run will be absorbed into the middle-class culture. Springdale at the time we studied it was already a backwash. Those communities that are still like it now represent the last link in America to the nineteenth century and its values.

THE UNIVERSITY TOWN

In those American university towns which do not have industries, the new middle classes are personified by the college professor, college administrators and by other professionals who are attracted to the town as a place of residence because of the cultural tone given to the town by the university. Frequently the university town is dominated by a middle-class life style which is an academic variant of the new middle-class life style in general. This life style exhibits an emphasis on cultural consumption of the performing arts as provided by university sponsored music, drama and art shows *and* an active political interest which reveals a parochial and sometimes self-righteous liberalism. In national affairs segments of this group have been leaders in civil rights and peace politics, and other more substantial segments of this same community have been politically involved as experts, consultants and propagandists for the White House and government agencies with respect to foreign, military and domestic policies. In local politics the university middle class has a greater unity of interest which focuses on schools and public services and in its support of these activities has broken from the traditional virtues of parsimony in government and the low-tax ideology characteristic of small businessmen in small communities. These unique features are given a special emphasis to the extent that the university middle classes are self-conscious of their alienation from the ethos of their surrounding region; they stand out and are resented by other segments of the new middle classes. They wear their liberalism as a badge, but they cannot take their way of life for granted.

In some university towns, academicians acting as an interest group have succeeded in gaining control of the machinery of local government. They have done this either directly by taking control of a local party apparatus, by making political alliances with other like-minded groups or by serving as "technical consultants" in solving the specialized problems of government such as municipal finance, assessment policy, zoning and so on. Wherever this shift in political control has occurred, it has had revolutionary effects on the political life of the communities involved, for it has resulted in the defeat of business leaders who traditionally have controlled local government in smaller communities. In larger and medium-sized cities where the university is only one of a number of interest groups, university members have had occasion to make alliances with ethnic and labor leaders and have shared and traded power with them. This has occurred quite frequently in traditionally Republican communities which have now become intermittently Democratic.

The size of the town in which a university is located is the critical factor in determining the capacity of professorial liberalism to place its stamp on the public political life of the community.

THE SUBURBAN COMMUNITY

A similar revolution in middle-class styles has taken place in the suburbs of the great metropolises of America. The people who live in these bedroom communities are the managerial, professional, technical and administrative staffs of the great private and governmental agencies whose offices are located in the central city. In fact the growth of the suburbs and the new middle class has been proportionate to the growth in size of large-scale enterprises since the end of World War II. Hence, the commuter has become a major factor in American life. Large-scale commuting has also introduced new features into the living styles of the middle class. For regardless of the respectability they are constrained to demonstrate while at their work site, in their home communities they are "free" to develop life styles that play on a variety of themes and variations. The local themes around which these life styles have been built are:

1. The pursuit of socially organized high culture and leisure activities which are focused around a church or temple. Though the activities are not religious in character, the church provides the setting and legitimating tone for forms of sophistication that would have been alien to the ethnic church or to earlier Protestantism.

2. The organization of life around sports and a social life centered in the country club. Golf, dancing, fishing, tennis, bridge, boating, travel, swimming are organized into a way of life that emphasizes physical fitness, activity, fresh air and sunshine.

3. The development of refined interests and tastes in cultural activities which are organized in associations, groups, leagues and clubs devoted to the pursuit of art, drama, music and other cultural projects. Activity takes the form of attending concerts, lectures, exhibitions, classes, holding memberships in book and art clubs and participation as performers, artists, promoters, organizers and supporters of the arts.

4. The pursuit of a life of gaiety and wit, modern living and the fun morality. Life is active, informal, sophisticated and broadly tolerant of modern moral and ethical codes. In this group cultural tastes run to folk dancing and singing, the cocktail and costume party and the discothèque.

These styles mix in different ways in different suburbs, but in some cases whole suburbs will be known for a single, predominant style. However, in spite of such differences in emphasis, these communities exhibit characteristic traits. A large amount of formal and informal group activity focuses on the schools, the P.T.A. and class mothers and on debate, discussion, opposition and support of the school budget. Specific issues arise which are part of the school budget: special courses, teacher salary schedules, technical facilities and so on. Local political groups are organized and exist for one school board election because the issues involved do not parallel any other political issues. After the election such groups disband only to be re-organized frequently along different lines for the next election. During the phase of overt school politics in these communities a substantial portion of the community's attention will be absorbed by the school conflict. Newspaper advertisements are published in support of or opposition to the budget or the bond issue. These are written, financed and published by voluntary committees which also print and distribute handbills, petitions and bulk mailings. Letters to the editor comprise a serious form of public debate. Public meetings, rump caucuses and especially the meetings of the school board are scenes of oral debates, personal animus and expressions of political passions. For short periods of time before and during the election of school board members and/or the vote on the budget or bond issue, these debates become the central focus of the public life of much of suburbia. Talk continues for a short while after the election. In some cases permanent personal animosities develop which lead to avoidance relationships that are retained for a long time. If a defeat is particularly humiliating, the loser may consider leaving the community. If the issue is particularly intense and lines are sharply drawn, the children in school may be drawn into the conflict and their relationships with teachers and administrators may be affected. If teachers become involved, their involvement can affect their job status in the school. Short of sex, school issues touch most deeply the passions of suburbia.

Second in importance to school-oriented politics are civic improvement groups which have an interest in reforming and modernizing the community; critical issues include street lighting, sanitation, sidewalk paving, stop signs, safety at intersections, architectural uniformity, preservation of historical monuments, library improvement, zoning and community planning. In more recent times the suburbs have been confronted with the suburbanite Negro who wishes to join the suburban community. This is a newer issue which has been added to the others and at times has involved as much passion for the whites as the school question.

The groups which make up suburbia react differently to the issues mentioned above. The newer middle classes and the recent arrivals in the suburbs are likely to support all issues aimed at improving the community. They care less about the tax rate and display a willingness to have the best services, the best facilities and a cultured environment. On the other hand, the older groups who lived in the suburbs before the influx of the newer middle classes are more apt to oppose the innovations. For them it may or may not be a question of taxes. If the older residents are locals who lived in what was previously a small town that became a suburb during the expansion since World War II, taxes are likely to be the issue because these older groups do not have urban sources of income; their income is apt to be derived locally, from industry or from small business, and is less apt to reflect recent inflationary trends. If the older residents are suburbanites from an earlier period, as, for example, prior to World War II, they are apt to be derived from different ethnic stock and are apt to be more secure and established in their style of life. Their sources of income are not only urban derived but they include some rentiers. In this case taxes are not the issue. The issue is rather one of resenting the newer ethnic and arriviste aspirants whose exuberance and hunger for culture is alien to community tradition. They also resent the boisterousness, the energy and the ceaseless activity of the new arrivals who appear to be pushing their way into organizations and institutions which were regarded as being securely held. The older strata of suburbanites had been accustomed to running the community and resent the new challengers. The new middle classes represent a style that upsets their stable ways of life.

Conflicts such as these are typical of the suburban way of

life and its culture. How these conflicts are resolved is not predictable. Some suburbs, for example the working-class suburbs, were created from scratch and do not exhibit these characteristics. Other suburbs are still dominated by the older middle classes and exhibit a quality of stability and tradition that may be the envy of the newer suburbs as well as a model for emulation. These older suburbs can only survive in their accustomed style if their inhabitants sustain their urban sources of income, but inevitably because of age and death they will be replaced by representatives of the newer styles. In some suburbs, the newer middle class has been completely successful in imposing its style on the suburb and have taken over the political as well as the social institutions in the community. In still other cases, the issue still hangs in balance with no clear and decisive resolution in favor of either the new or the old. In such cases opposing factions sometimes win and sometimes lose. What appears to be a victory may be only a temporary one because the losers had not sufficiently mobilized their forces at the time of their defeat. The suburban political drama takes a very large variety of forms.

The decisive factor in determining victory or defeat for the new middle classes in the suburbs appears to be based on the percentage of the total population that they constitute. When the new middle classes are a sizable minority, they color the whole life of the town but they do not occupy the major institutional positions. When they are a small minority, they live out their life styles in social enclaves and barely impose their tone on the town, dominating nothing. When their number grows to a size sufficient to give them a feeling that they are unjustly unrecognized and deprived by official institutions, they are apt to make a bid to control the community. No one has yet measured what proportion is necessary for the new middle class to achieve dominance. However, at some point in the continuing conflict between older tradition and new middle-class aspirations a struggle for the control of the public life of the town ensues. When the new middle class becomes dominant, it succeeds in imposing its style on other segments of the community. For the past twenty years the new middle class has for the most part succeeded in asserting its style in hundreds of American suburbs.

THE NEW URBAN MIDDLE CLASS

The same kinds of life styles and public issues characteristic of the suburbs occur in greatly magnified forms within the metropolis. Certain sectors of the city become the residential centers of the new urban middle classes—silk stocking districts. These are areas in which high rent housing and housing developments are concentrated. In New York City, for example, this would include Peter Cooper and Stuyvesant Town, the old (west) Greenwich Village and Washington Square, the upper west side, the east sixties, Brooklyn Heights and recently Park Slope. In each of these areas, a major proportion of the population are college educated professionals, managers, technically trained bureaucrats and employed intellectuals. Being closer to the heart of things, they regard themselves as more sophisticated, avant-garde and au courant than are their suburban counterparts who have opted for home ownership and a nonurban environment for their children. In fact, many suburbanites had resided in these urban middle-class enclaves prior to their children's having reached school age at which point they moved to the suburbs to avoid the complexities and expense of urban family living.

Within the new urban, middle-class enclaves all of the variations in suburban life styles are exhibited as in suburbia, except that they are expressed with greater intensity, variety, and modern sophistication. For example, the urban "swinger" has a style that can be expressed more completely if the devotee lives in Manhattan than if he attempts the style while living in the suburbs. To some extent the residential location of the urban segment of the middle class is determined by the age of children. The urban middle class is most apt to be quite young (with preschool children) or middle-aged (with college-enrolled children). The suburbanites tend to have school-age children younger than college age. Other observers have noted that there is considerable physical mobility between the suburbs and the preferred cliff dwelling areas of the metropolis. Place of residence is thus not the critical factor in defining the new middle class.

However, members of the new urban middle class have introduced one major innovation into the middle class life style. A substantial number of them have entered politics as ideological and/or party activists. In their case, however, they have abandoned the ethnic and bossism political style to which their immigrant parents were frequently committed. Instead they have entered reform politics and have helped to create an image of reform politics as cultured, clean and civilized. Thus reform politics has been responsible for creating a new type of urban political hero whose image is based on cleanness as opposed to bossist corruption. Robert Wagner, the Yale man who was mayor of New York City and was dubbed an old-time boss by the reformers, was followed by John Lindsay, another Yale man, who "came up smelling clean." In New York City the reform political club membership almost coincides with the membership of the alumni associations of City College of New York, Fordham and New York universities. The politics of the urban middle class are liberal and focus on political honesty, integrity, anti-bossism and a commitment to high municipal expenditures for improvements of a cultural, educational and humanitarian nature. Under reform leadership the City supports "happenings," park improvements, cultural events and tries to make it a "fun city" as opposed to La Guardia who limited his style to honest, efficient administration and to chasing fire engines and reading comics over the radio during a newspaper strike (which would now be regarded as "campy" by part of the less political urban middle class). The political problem of the urban middle class is that as soon as a reform politician is elected to office he is forced to make compromises with the older ethnic bosses and populist politicians in the national, state or city administrations. As soon as he makes these compromises the reform middle class becomes disenchanted and begins to look for new reform candidates, and the original reform candidate is likely to lose the support of his idealistic and liberal constituency. If the elected reform politician does not make these compromises, he finds it almost impossible to function as an urban politician in gaining support for his programs and his district. For the urban middle class, narrow class interest in the traditional ethnic and lower-class sense of the term is of less interest than are liberal and cultured orientations and the ideology of political purity. Political life for the politically oriented segments of the urban middle class is thus a continuous succession of defeats which are never accepted as final defeats because there is always the hope that reform will ultimately win. In the meantime, this middle class can sustain a sense of high-mindedness, reform and purity while not substantially altering the total pattern of urban politics. Our analysis, of course, does not by itself help us to comprehend the older ghetto or the newer race politics of the metropolis. In part, however, the new radical and racial leadership is drawn from disaffected, college-trained, minority youth. On the urban political scene the middle class has not and is not likely to become sufficiently powerful to dominate urban politics.

The Future of the Middle Class and Its Life Styles

In the previous discussion we have attempted to define the new life styles of the new middle classes. We have indicated the nature of these life styles at their most typical centers. We have further indicated that these life styles have become diffused throughout our nation's population and are triumphing over older styles as their bearers become a larger proportion of the population of an area. Due to changes in the educational and occupational structure of our society, which make America a more and more middle-class society, we can expect these life styles to permeate all areas of our society. In the short or long run even the life styles of the rural community will be affected. We would, of course, expect them to penetrate middle-size communities, depending, again, on the proximity to centers of diffusion. We noted that even in Springdale the new middle class had already made a significant impact as early as 1955. At the other extreme, while the urban middle class has emerged as a distinctive phenomenon and has made an impact on urban society, it is less clear what its chances for future predominance are.

Insofar as urban areas are centers for diffusion of these life styles they have an importance that goes far beyond their dominance in an immediate urban location. Knowing the centers from which diffusion takes place and the rates of diffusion are important in predicting the future. In general the East and West Coast metropolises are the centers from which the diffusion takes place. In some respects the West Coast has been more inventive and more modern in its cultural development than the East. This claim to cultural leadership by the West is one that is resented by the cultural and other leaders of the East Coast (a few years ago this contest was fought in terms of population statistics, but now that California clearly has a larger population than New York the basis on which superiority is to be judged has shifted to other grounds). While the East and West Coast metropolises advance their claims against each other, the metropolises in the Midwest, particularly Chicago, strive hard to advance their own claims. However, they appear to be trying to advance their own claims primarily by self-consciously trying not to be impressed by either coast. So far Chicago and the Middle Western urban metropolises have not been able to challenge the inventiveness and cultural sophistication of either of the coasts. Their claims have for the most part been unheard except by themselves.

However, within each of these dominant geographic areas, these giant metropolises have been the center for the development of new cultural and life-style themes, particularly in their suburban, exurban, bohemian and silk stocking neighborhoods. The concentration in depth of these life styles varies by region and by city size. In New York, Boston, San Francisco and Los Angeles, the avant-garde middle class reaches its highest expression of "modernity" and sophistication. Places like Chicago are still once removed from the "creative centers." St. Louis, Dallas, Milwaukee, Cleveland, New Orleans and other cities somewhat more distant from the center exhibit a striving, aggressive, somewhat provincial pretentiousness that rings hollow in the face of the "truly authentic" East and West Coast culture. The rural community and the small town which are most intellectually and culturally distant from the urban centers are farthest removed no matter how physically proximate they may be to the center of urban culture.

The university town regardless of its size is always a sub-center for these new styles because the university citizenry has direct access to them insofar as the styles themselves are products of the university. The university thus becomes a transmission belt to the rest of the immediate vicinity surrounding it irrespective of the density of population in the region. While the East and West coasts set styles at a national level, each university town plays a similar role for a more restricted audience.

However, all areas including rural ones are not far removed from the centers of cultural innovation. The mass media, especially television, the film (particularly foreign ones) and magazines (especially *Life* and *Look*) disseminate these new life styles almost instantaneously to all sectors of the society, including the deep South, the Maine mountains, the Ozark Hills and rural Appalachia. Under the mass-media system, no area is more remote than another. However, the success of this cultural transmission depends a great deal on the receptivity of the population in the middle-sized cities and in the rural areas to this new cultural exposure and the new life styles.

There are two groups that are most receptive and hence most critical as points of penetration for the introduction of the new life styles in the rural areas:

1. The college educated new middle classes in the 25 to 45 age group who live in tension with the populist culture of their communities. This group feels restricted and hemmed in by traditional small-town values which it escapes from by identifying with external sophisticated styles. This group orients itself to the nearby university and the higher culture as it is transmitted by the mass media.

2. Teen-age youth, especially the children of middle-class parents, who are dissatisfied with the provinciality and narrowness of small-town life look to the mass media for styles of rebellion against what they regard to be the complacency, the hypocrisy and dullness of their elders, particularly their parents. Thus it is these young people who are the first in their communities to become aware of the new styles and to adopt them

as a form of self-assertion; consequently, they are responsible for introducing them into the town and to their elders. The parents sometimes adopt the styles directly from their children: the mini-skirt would be a case in point as would be the introduction of longer hair styles and beards for men. When these young people go to college they discover more personal and authentic forms and sources of rebellion and more accessible targets in the form of the university administration, the bureaucracy and repressive professors.

To the extent that the remotest areas are thus penetrated we can predict that the revolution from populist, frontier culture is in the process of being disseminated throughout the nation, even in the South, the West and the "upstate" and "downstate" regions of all parts of the country. No doubt such communities are less penetrated than those with multiple forms of access, but the penetration is quite deep and is likely to continue. It may take twenty-five to fifty years before such penetration is completed. But the fact of the penetration, its intensity and its quality pose a number of problems.

The depopulation of the rural community is by no means complete. The intensification of large-scale capital investment in agriculture will continue to drive owners of what were formerly known as family-sized farms out of farming. Many of these farmers and particularly their children will seek work and opportunity in the city. But in "rural" areas, employed managers and technicians, many with university training, will become increasingly numerous and important not only in agriculture, but as officials in local branches of national and regional businesses which are increasingly being located in formerly rural areas. So too as Federal agencies penetrate more deeply and intensively, rural employment will include government officials, hospital technicians and nurses, military personnel, inspectors and investigators, and specialized educational and welfare personnel. Through these personnel channels, the residues of university training and culture will incessantly permeate the rural community with the urban middle-class styles.

Rural youth will continue as in the past to leave the rural community as the city and the university become more compelling magnets. While in the past the rural community has had an over-aged population because of the youthful migration, this tendency is now being corrected by the development of specialized communities for the aged which, with the help of Federal aid, depopulate the rural community of some of its aged residents. The desirability of Florida, California and the Southwest as places for retirement communities has corrected somewhat the age distribution in small towns. This population redistribution will help to weaken the commitment of the rural town to its past traditions and will make it more accessible to modern forms of culture.

After all of these changes have taken place, what remains is the probability of a continuous and enduring battle between the proponents of populist culture and the bearers of the new urban life styles, for wherever the latter group reaches sufficient size it challenges the older, traditional group for leadership. In the threat to its leadership the older group sees that it not only faces the loss of community leadership and higher real estate taxes but also the defeat of its entire way of life. This way of life though on the decline has long historical roots. It is identified with grass-roots democracy, with Americanism and with all the virtues of the American past. For those committed to the past and its values, this decline will be hard to digest.

The danger for the United States is that the hostility, defensiveness, and counteraggressiveness engendered by the immanence of defeat, will become the basis for a backlash against the full sweep forward of American history as it develops in the present and the future. Populism gone sour could become the source of an antidemocratic, quasi-totalitarian reaction which in spite of its origins in an earlier democratic ideology could turn against the new cultural styles evolving in our society. There is thus the risk that in resisting these new life styles populist democracy may become the basis for new social movements which could subvert the foundations of the present by holding to romanticized images of the past. An organized nativistic movement based partly on a xenophobic isolationism could shelter under its cover not only defensive populists but a variety of other groups whose resentments are less crystallized but which could find a focus in some form of nativism.

We have indicated that the new life styles are not based on un-American ideas but rather have evolved out of fundamental organizational, economic, educational, and demographic changes in American society. These changes represent fundamental and perhaps irreversible trends in the very structure of American society. Whether one likes the direction of these trends or not, they cannot be wished away, abolished by law or reversed by going back to the past without doing violence to the emergent society. The older populist classes will have to learn to accept defeat gracefully. The newer middle classes, for their part, will have to learn to accept success without exacting vengeance for real or imaginary defeats which occurred in the period prior to its victory. A direct confrontation based on these opposing orientations will have to be avoided if the United States hopes to cope with its other problems.

Chapter 13

———————————<◈>———————————

Methods of Community Research

PARTICIPANT OBSERVATION AND THE COLLECTION AND INTERPRETATION OF DATA*

THE PRACTICAL and technical problems as well as many of the advantages and disadvantages of participant observation as a data-gathering technique have been well stated.[1] We propose to discuss some of the effects on data of the social position of the participant observer. The role of the participant observer and the images which respondents hold of him are central to the definition of his social position; together these two factors shape the circumstances under which he works and the type of data he will be able to collect.

In a broad sense the social position of the observer determines *what* he is likely to see. The way in which he sees and interprets his data will be largely conditioned by his theoretical precon-

* Reprinted, with permission of the University of Chicago Press, from the *American Journal of Sociology*, Vol. 60, No. 4 (January 1955), pp. 355-60.

[1] See especially the following: Florence R. Kluckhohn, "The Participant Observer Technique in Small Communities," *American Journal of Sociology*, XLVI (November, 1940), 331-43; William F. Whyte, *Street Corner Society* (Chicago: University of Chicago Press, 1943), Preface, pp. v-x, and also his "Observational Field-Work Methods" in Marie Jahoda, Morton Deutsch, and Stuart W. Cook (eds.), *Research Methods in the Social Sciences* (New York: Dryden Press, 1951), II, 393-514; Marie Jahoda *et al.*, "Data Collection: Observational Methods," *ibid.*, Vol. I, chap. v; Benjamin D. Paul, "Interview Techniques and Field Relations," in A. L. Kroeber *et al.* (eds.), *Anthropology Today: An Encyclopedic Inventory* (Chicago: University of Chicago Press, 1953), pp. 430-51; and Edward C. Devereux, "Functions, Advantages and Limitations of Semi-controlled Observation" (Ithaca, N.Y.: Staff Files, "Cornell Studies in Social Growth," Department of Child Development and Family Relationships, Cornell University, 1953).

ceptions, but this is a separate problem with which we will not be concerned.[2] What an observer will see will depend largely on his particular position in a network of relationships. To the extent that this is the case, this discussion of relatively well-known but frequently unstated observations is not purely academic. The task assumes the necessity of less concern with methodological refinements for handling data after they are collected and more concern with establishing canons of validity and the need, too, for a better balance between the standardization of field techniques and the establishment of standards for the evaluation of field data according to their source and the collector.

Broader Relevance of Participant Observation

As a technique, participant observation is central to all the social sciences. It has been singled out and treated as a rather specialized field approach with peculiar problems of its own, but this has obscured the extent to which the various social sciences depend upon it. Participant observation enables the research worker to secure his data within the mediums, symbols, and experiential worlds which have meaning to his respondents. Its intent is to prevent imposing alien meanings upon the actions of the subjects. Anthropologists dealing with cultures other than their own have consciously recognized and utilized the technique as a matter of necessity. Experimental psychologists who try their own instruments out on themselves as well as psychiatrists who undergo analysis are practicing a form of participant observation for much the same purpose as the anthropologist.

The sociologist who limits his work to his own society is constantly exploiting his personal background of experience as a basis of knowledge. In making up structured interviews, he draws on his knowledge of meanings gained from participation in the social order he is studying. He can be assured of a modicum of successful communication only because he is dealing in

[2] Oscar Lewis has devoted considerable attention to this problem. See especially his *Life in a Mexican Village: Tepoztlan Restudied* (Springfield: University of Illinois Press, 1951) and "Controls and Experiments in Field Work," in Kroeber *et al.* (eds.), *Anthropology Today*, pp. 452-75.

the same language and symbolic system as his respondents. Those who have worked with structured techniques in non-Western societies and languages will attest to the difficulty encountered in adjusting their meanings to the common meanings of the society investigated, a fact which highlights the extent to which the sociologist is a participant observer in almost all his work.[3]

In view of this widespread dependence upon participant observation as a source of data and as a basis for giving them meaning, a discussion of the factors which condition data obtained by this method is warranted.

Our source of immediate experience is the Springdale community of Upstate New York.[4] Experience as a participant observer in one's own culture sets the major problems of this technique into clearer focus. The objectification and self-analysis of the role of the participant observer in one's own society has the advantage that communication is in the same language and symbolic system.

Formation of Respondent Images of the Participant Observer

Whether the field worker is totally, partially, or not at all disguised, the respondent forms an image of him and uses that image as a basis of response. Without such an image the relationship between the field worker and the respondent, by definition does not exist.

The essential thing in any field situation is the assumption of some position in a structure of relationships. The position is assumed not only by various types of participant observers but

[3] F. C. Bartlett's "Psychological Methods and Anthropological Problems," *Africa*, X (October, 1937), 401-19, illustrates this problem.

[4] This work was conducted under the sponsorship of the Department of Child Development and Family Relationships in the New York State College of Home Economics at Cornell University. It is part of a larger project entitled "Cornell Studies in Social Growth" and represents an outgrowth of a study in the determinants of constructive social behavior in the person, the family, and the community. The research program is supported in part by grants from the National Institute of Mental Health, United States Public Health Service, and the Committee on the Early Identification of Talent of the Social Science Research Council with the aid of funds granted to the Council by the John and Mary R. Markle Foundation.

by all interviewers. The undisguised interviewer establishes his personal identity or the identity of the organization he works for and, hence, makes himself and the questions he asks plausible to his respondent. In disguised interviewing, including that of the totally disguised participant observer, a plausible role is no less important even though it may be more complex and more vaguely defined; but the first concern remains the assumption of a credible role. Likewise the totally disguised social scientist, even as genuine participant, is always located in a given network of relationships.

Every research project is in a position partly to influence image formation by the way it identifies itself. However, these self-definitions are always dependent on verbalizations, and, at best, the influence they have is minimal unless supported overtly by the research worker. Field workers are well aware that the public is likely not to accept their statements at face value; gossip and talk between potential respondents when a research program first enters the field attests to this fact. This talk places the research worker in the context of the values, standards, and expectations of the population being studied, and its effect is to establish the identity of the field worker in the eyes of the public.

There is tremendous variation from field situation to field situation in the assignment of identity to the field worker. In the usual anthropological field situation he is identified as a trader, missionary, district officer, or foreign spy—any role with which the native population has had previous contact and experience. In time these ascriptions can and do change so that the anthropologist, for example, may even gain an identity within a kinship structure:

> He was assigned on the basis of residence to an appropriate Kwoma lineage and, by equation with a given generation, was called "younger brother" or "father" or "elder uncle," depending on the particular "kinsman" who addressed him. Having found a place for Whiting in the kingship, the Kwoma could orient their social behavior accordingly.[5]

[5] Benjamin D. Paul in Kroeber *et al.* (eds.), *Anthropology Today*, p. 434.

In every case the field worker is fitted into a plausible role by the population he is studying and within a context meaningful to them. There seem to be no cases where field workers have not found a basis upon which subjects could react toward them. This is true even in the face of tremendous language barriers. Moreover, the necessary images and the basis for reaction which they provide are not only always found, but they are demanded by the mere fact of the research worker's intrusion into the life of his subjects. Even when a field worker is ejected, the image and meaningful context exists.

Social Role of the Participant Observer

Once he is placed in a meaningful context, the social position of the researcher is assured. His approach to the social structure is subsequently conditioned by his position.

Obviously the ascription and the assumption of a plausible role are not the equivalent of placing the participant observer in th experimental world of his subjects. Indeed, this impossibility is not his objective. For to achieve the experience of the subject, along with the baggage of perceptions that goes along with it, is to deny a chance for objectivity. Instead, an observer usually prefers to keep his identity vague; he avoids committing his allegiance—in short, his personality—to segments of the society. This is true even when he studies specialized segments of mass societies and organizations. In this case the observer may deliberately antagonize management, for example, in order to gain the confidence of the union or segments of it. However, within the union he has further to choose between competing factions, competing leaders, or leadership-membership cleavages. The anthropologist integrated into a kinship system or class faces the same problem. Eventually, no matter the size of the group he is studying, the observer is forced to face the problem of divided interests. He is "asked" to answer the question, "Who do you speak for?" and it is an answer to this question which, in the interests of research, he avoids.

Consequently, the observer remains marginal to the society or organization or segments of them which he studies. By his conscious action he stands between the major social divisions, not necessarily above them, but surely apart from them. Occupationally concerned with the objectification of action and events, he attempts to transcend all the local cleavages and discords. In avoiding commitments to political issues, he plays the role of political eunuch. He is socially marginal to the extent that he measures his society as a noninvolved outsider and avoids committing his loyalties and allegiances to segments of it. This is not hypocrisy but rather, as Howe has noted of Stendhal, it is living a ruse.[6] Being both a participant and an observer is "the strategy of having one's cake and eating it too": "Deceiving the society to study it and wooing the society to live in it." His position is always ambivalent, and this ambivalence shapes the character of the data he secures and the manner of securing them.

The Participant Observer's Data

All the information which the participant observer secures is conditioned by the meaningful context into which he is placed and by his own perspective as shaped by his being socially marginal. Together these circumstances greatly affect the kind of data he can get and the kind of experience he can have. The meaningful context into which he is placed by the public provides the latter with their basis for response, and his marginality specifies the order of experience possible for him.

To the extent that the observer's data are conditioned by the basis upon which subjects respond to him, the anthropologist studying another culture has one important advantage. He can justifiably maintain an attitude of naïveté and on this basis exploit his situation as a stranger to the fullest possible extent. Indeed, it is relatively easy to breach local customs and standards and still maintain a tenable research position in the society. This naïve attitude cannot be assumed in working in his own culture, for the simple reason that the respondent cannot accept it as plausible. In fact, the difficulty of securing data may be increased by the "ethnocentrism" of some respondents who

[6] Irving Howe, "Stendhal: The Politics of Survival," in William Phillips and Philip Rahv (eds.), *The Avon Book of Modern Writing* (New York: Avon Publishing Co., 1953), pp. 60-61.

assume that their own experiences are similar to those of others. Yet with the increased complexity, specialization and pluralization of roles in American society, the social science observer is likely to have had no direct contact at all with whole ranges of experience. With the exception of his professional world (and partly because of his professionalization), he is something of a stranger in his own society without being in a position to exploit his innocence. He has the disadvantage of living in a society in which his experience is limited, while, at the same time, he is regarded as a knowledgeable member of all segments of it.

If the participant observer seeks genuine experiences, unqualifiedly immersing and committing himself in the group he is studying, it may become impossible for him to objectify his own experiences for research purposes; in committing his loyalites he develops vested interests which will inevitably enter into his observations. Anthropologists who have "gone native" are cases in point; some of them stop publishing material entirely.[7] And all anthropologists have learned to make appropriate compensation in data interpreted by missionaries, traders, and government officials, no matter how excellent the material may be.

In practice, the solution to the dilemma of genuine versus spurious experiences is to make use of individuals who are socially marginal in the society being studied. In almost any society in this postcolonial and specialized age, the observer is likely to find persons with a penchant for seeing themselves objectively in relation to their society, such as the traveled Pacific Islander and the small-town "intellectual." But they differ from the social scientist in one important respect: a portion of their experience, no matter how much it is subsequently objectified, has been gained within the society under study. When the social scientist studies a society, he characteristically makes his first contacts with these marginal persons, and they will vary according to his interests and the identity he claims for himself. Even when the observer tries to avoid the marginal individuals, he is nevertheless sought out by them. This is not unfortunate, for these types are a bridge, perhaps the most important one, to the meanings of the society. It is they who provide him with his first in-

[7] Paul, in *Anthropology Today*, p. 435, names Frank Cushing as one.

sights into the workings of the society. The sociologist studying his own society is, to varying degrees according to the relation between his background of experience and his object of study, his own bridge. Without such a bridge, without at least an interpreter or one lone native who can utter a word or two in another language, the observer would have no basis for approaching his data. The social marginality of the participant observer's role with all the limitations it imposes provides a basis for communication and, hence, ultimately, for understanding.

Field Tactics and Data Evaluation

When the participant observer sets out to collect his data, he is faced with two types of problems: the tactical problem of maneuver in the field and the evaluation of the data. The two problems are related in that the data to be evaluated are conditioned by the field tactics. The discussion of them will be limited to selected problems central to the technique of participant observation: the tactical problem of conformity or nonconformity, the observer's experience as related to the imputation of meaning and the formulation of categories, and the significance of participant observation to the study of social change.

Conformity or nonconformity to local standards and styles of living when engaging in field research is a relevant issue only in so far as the choice affects the research. Conformity is always conformity to specified standards and implies nonconformity to other possible standards. Almost all societies or groups in the contemporary world present alternative forms of behavior based on differing internal standards. Consequently it is hardly possible to conform to the standards of an entire society, and, hence, to follow a general policy of conformity is to follow no policy at all. Any policy which is designed to guide the field worker's actions must be based on a deliberate judgment as to which sources of information must be used to secure data. In the adopting of standards necessary to keep these sources open, other sources are likely to be alienated and closed off, or data from them may be distorted.

Moreover, conscious conformity to any standards, at best, is "artificial," for the participant observer does not commit himself to the point of genuine partisan action. In the interests of objectivity this is necessarily the case. In failing to make genuine commitments, he reveals his socially marginal position and the outside standards upon which he acts. In these terms the old argument posed by Radin, who said, "For any anthropologist to imagine that anything can be gained by 'going native' is a delusion and a snare," and by Goldenweiser, who said of sharing the lives of the natives and participating in their culture, "The more successful an anthropologist is in doing this, the better foundation he has laid for his future work,"[8] is no argument at all. The decision to assume standards and values or the degree to which participation is required is best made on the basis of the data to be collected and not on the basis of *standard* field practice.

The related tactical problem of conscious identification with groups, causes, or issues can be treated similarly. Complete and total neutrality is extremely difficult, if not impossible, to assume even where research considerations seem to demand it. By virtue of his research, no matter how transitory and irrespective of the exact dimensions of his marginal position, the investigator must react to the actions of his respondents. Neutrality even to the point of total silence is a form of reaction and not only will be considered as such by all parties to the conflict but also implies a specific attitude toward the issue— being above it, outside it, more important than it, not interested in it. Whatever meanings respondents attach to neutrality will, henceforth, be used as a further basis for response. This is true even when respondents demand an opinion or approval in structured interview situations. Failure to make a commitment can create resentment, hostility, and antagonism just as easily as taking a stand. In both cases, but each in its own way, relationships will be altered and, hence, data will be affected.

The data secured by the participant observer, except in so far as he reports personal experiences, cannot be independent of his subjects' ability and willingness to report. He is obliged to impute meaning to both their verbal and their nonverbal actions. His

[8] Both quoted in Paul, *ibid.*, p. 438.

own experiences, though genuine, are at best vicarious approximations of those of his respondents; he never completely enters their world, and, by definition, if he did, he would assume the values, premises, and standards of his subjects and thereby lose his usefulness to research except as another subject. If the action observed is purely physical—the daily, routine physical movements of an individual, for example—the observer-interpreter cannot understand its meaning unless he communicates with the person involved in the action and gains insight into its meaning for the actor. Of course, studying within the meanings of his own society gives the observer a background of standardized meanings on which to draw. One knows that a man walking down the street at a certain time every morning is probably going to work. But the action of Raymond in *One Boy's Day*[9] was observed precisely because it was not known. In more complicated action in a segment of society in which the observer does not have experience, he gains it vicariously by talking with others and in that way secures almost all his data.

The respondent, on the other hand, is not necessarily able to verbalize his experiences, and, as attested to by psychoanalysis, it is quite probable that he will not understand their meaning. The greater the social distance between the observer and the observed, the less adequate the communication between them. Hence, as stated above, the observer's data are determined by the subjects' ability and willingness to report. Since he cannot duplicate their experience, he cannot draw his conclusions from his own marginal experiences. He always operates in the borderland of their experience and, hence is still faced with the problem of *imputing* meaning to their actions. Whereas his subjects base their own interpretations and evaluations on folklore, religion, myth, illusion, special and vested interests or even on the basis of local standards of social analysis, the social science observer-analyst uses the independent and extraneous standards of science.

The participant-observation technique has been offered as one of the best techniques on which to base prearranged obser-

[9] Roger G. Barker and Herbert F. Wright, *One Boy's Day* (New York: Harper & Bros., 1951).

vational and structured interview categories. The assumption is that, with his greater familiarity with the respondents' experiences and their meanings, the participant observer is in the best position to draw up meaningful categories. However, with the passage of time and the assumption and ascription of new roles and statuses, his perspective on the society is constantly changing. His marginal position allows him more social movement by virtue of which his perceptions will change with time, particularly as he gains greater and greater familiarity. Categories which initially seemed meaningful later on may appear superficial or even meaningless. Moreover, as long as he remains a participant observer, his social marginality undergoes continuous redefinition. As a result any categories he formulates in advance or at any given time will seem inadequate later when his social perspective has changed.[10] Attempts to establish categories into which directly observed action can be classified threaten to reduce the action to static entities which influence later observations, a condition which the technique of participant observation is designed to avoid. Indeed, it is this last condition which makes participant observation most suitable to the study of social change.

The technique of participant observation more than any other technique places the observer closer to social change as it takes place in a passing present. Change, as measured by the succession of days and hours rather than by years or arbitrary measures, takes place slowly. The desire of, and necessity for, individuals is to act in terms of what is possible in specific immediate situations. The immediacy of social change to those who are involved in the moving present tends to obscure their perspective on it: a continuous altering of his memories and definitions of reality makes the individual involved unaware of change. The participant observer is also involved in these changes, but, by his marginal position and his conscious effort to objectify himself, he achieves a measure of noninvolvement. Hence, his perspective is conditioned by considerations other than involve-

[10] These changes in circumstances refer not only to his position in the society he studies but also to the professional society with which he works and changes in research focus.

ment. If the participant observer changed his perspective in phase with continuous changes in reality, he too could not see the change. For as long as changes in perspective accompany changes in reality, the change is likely not to be recognized. The participant who studies change as an observer must therefore maintain a perspective outside and independent of change. Noninvolvement helps to prevent the alteration of memory structures and permits the observer to see cumulative changes.

To refresh his memory, the participant observer can turn to his records. But, if his perspective has changed with time, he may disregard or discount early notes and impressions in favor of those taken later. Field notes from two different periods in a project may, indeed, be one of the more important means of studying change. Instead, what probably happens is that the field worker obscures change by treating his data as though everything happened at the same time. This results in a description from a single perspective, usually that held just before leaving the field, but redefined by the rereading of his notes.

Conclusions

Data collection does not take place in a vacuum. Perspectives and perceptions of social reality are shaped by the social position and interests of both the observed and the observer as they live through a passing present. The participant observer who is committed to relatively long periods of residence in the field experiences a continuous redefinition of his position. In this context the respondent's basis of response, as conditioned by his image of the observer, changes in accordance with new images based on the changing definitions of the observer's position. These forces influence the data.

A valid evaluation of data must necessarily include a reasonably thorough comprehension of the major social dimensions of the situation in which data were collected. The social positions of the observer and the observed and the relationship between them at the time must be taken into account when the data are interpreted. To fail to take account of these conditions is to assume an equivalence of situations which does not exist and leads to distortion.

To the extent that a participant observer can participate and still retain a measure of noninvolvement, his technique provides a basis for an approach to the problem of validity. The background of information which he acquires in time makes him familiar with the psychology of his respondents and their social milieu. With this knowledge he is able to impose a broader perspective on his data and, hence, to evaluate their validity on the basis of standards extraneous to the immediate situation. To accomplish this, it is necessary that the participant observer be skeptical of himself in all data-gathering situations; he must objectify himself in relation to his respondents and the passing present. This process of self-objectification leads to his further alienation from the society he studies. Between this alienation and attempts at objective evaluation lies an approach to the problem of validity.

THE VALIDITY OF FIELD DATA[*][1]

Introduction

SCATTERED through the professional journals in fields commonly included in the social sciences—sociology, anthropology, social psychology, personality, public opinion—there is found an increasing concern with the reliability and validity of information secured for social science analysis. Much of this interest stems from or was stimulated by the now classical *Social Science Research Council Bulletins* on the use of personal documents,[2] or by work being done simultaneously in England.[3]

In recent years all manner of instruments and techniques—ranging from participant observations[4] and psychological tests[5] to public opinion and census-type surveys[6]—and the quality of

* Reprinted by permission of the Society for Applied Anthropology from *Human Organization*, Vol. 13, No. 1 (Spring 1954), pp. 20-27.

[1] This work was conducted under the sponsorship of the Department of Child Development and Family Relationships in the New York State College of Home Economics at Cornell University. It is part of a larger project entitled Cornell Studies in Social Growth, and represents an outgrowth of a study in the determinants of constructive social behavior in the person, the family, and the community. The research program is supported in part by grants from the National Institute of Mental Health, United States Public Health Service, and the committee on the Early Identification of Talent of the Social Science Research Council, with the aid of funds granted to the council by the John and Mary R. Markle Foundation.

[2] Allport, F., "The Use of Personal Documents in Psychological Science," *Social Science Research, Council Bulletin No. 49*, 1942. Gottschalk, L., Kluckhohn, C., and Angell, R., "The Use of Personal Documents in History, Anthropology and Sociology," *Social Science Research Council Bulletin No. 53*, 1945. These works, in turn, were a direct outgrowth of Blumer's critique of Thomas and Znaniecki's *The Polish Peasant*.

[3] Bartlett, F. C., Ginsberg, M., Lindgren, E. J., Thouless, R. H., *The Study of Society*, London, 1939. Harvey, S. M., "A Preliminary Investigation of the Interview," *British Journal of Psychology*, Vol. 28, 1938, 263-287.

[4] Kluckhohn, F., "The Participant Observer Technique in Small Communities," *American Journal of Sociology*, Vol. 46, 1940, 331-342.

[5] Mensh, Ivan N., Henry, Jules, "Direct Observation and Psychological Tests in Anthropological Field Work," *American Anthropologist*, Vol. 54, No. 4, 1953, 461-480.

[6] Hyman, Herbert, "Problems in the Collection of Opinion Research Data," *American Journal of Sociology*, Vol. LV, No. 4, 1950, 362-370.

the data they yield have been placed under critical scrutiny. Depending on the interests and immediate concerns of the observers, emphasis has been placed primarily on distortions in data due to the interviewer,[7] the interviewer-respondent relationship,[8] the technical wording of questions,[9] and the limitations following from the social position of the researcher.[10] Much less attention has been given to information variability and distortion due to the informant's motives and his position[11] in the social structure, although for the anthropologist negligent in reporting his methods,[12] this has always been a classical caveat.[13] On the other hand, in fairness to some clinical psychologists, and especially to the applied psychologists who play for keeps in industrial, or military, or educational selection procedures, we must note their sincere and intense and, by their own findings, warranted concern with fakers and the fakability of their tests.[14] Indeed, one is impressed with the frequent appearance of articles on validity in the *Journal of Applied Psychology*, and disturbed by their lack of success in achieving it in even the most elementary tests.

Mauldin, W. P., and Marks, E. S., "Problems of Response in Enumerative Surveys," *American Sociological Review*, Vol. 15, No. 5, 1950, 649-657.

[7] Shapiro, S. and Eberhart, J., "Interviewer Differences in an Intensive Interview Survey," *International Journal of Opinion and Attitude Research*, Vol. I, No. 2, 1947, 1-17.

[8] Donceel, J. F., Alimena, B. S., and Birch, C. M., "Influence of Prestige Suggestion on the Answers of a Personality Inventory," *Journal of Applied Psychology*, Vol. 33, No. 4, 1949, 352-355. Extensive work has also been done on differential response to psychological tests according to the ethnic origin, color and sex of interviewer and respondent.

[9] Mauldin and Marks, *Op. cit.*

[10] Merton, Robert K., "Field Work in a Planned Community," *American Sociological Review*, Vol. 12, No. 3, 1947, 304-312.

[11] Merton, *op. cit.*, Vernon, P. E., "The Attitudes of the Subject in Personality Testing," *Journal of Applied Psychology*, Vol. 18, 1934, 165-167.

[12] Stavrianos, B. K., "Research Methods in Cultural Anthropology in Relation to Scientific Criteria," *Psychological Review*, Vol. 57, No. 6, 1950, 334-344.

[13] The sources cited contain citations to other social science comment on this problem.

[14] Longstaff, H. P. "Fakability of the Strong Interest Blank and the Kuder Preference Record," *Journal of Applied Psychology*, Vol. 32, No. 4, 1948, 360-369.

In view of this increasing intensity of concern with the field methods and techniques which provide social science with its data for analysis, it seems pertinent to examine the character of the information secured with the instruments and techniques ordinarily used. Unless approached from a fresh perspective— the simultaneous comparison and evaluation of data secured from a wide variety of instruments in a given context—little can be added to what are already recognized as basic problems in collecting data for social science research.

In three years of field work, the Springdale Project has employed a wide variety of field techniques: census-type fact-finding surveys, check-list personality inventories, passive non-participant observation, tape-recorded interviews with spouses, depth interviews, participant observation, unstructured and guided anthropological-type interviews, and structured, semi-structured and unstructured attitude interviews. This background provides an excellent source for the comparison of implications of different field methods.

This continuous and persistent focus of attention—field work in a relatively small area with an adult population of 1,500— gives the *field worker* an excellent opportunity to evaluate and appraise the types of information gathered by the use of one technique with the perspectives and information gathered from the use of other techniques. Awareness of the differences in response according to instruments and methods used raises a number of questions concerning the validity of response in field research.

This article is exclusively oriented to some of the fundamental problems and questions which arise in attempting to secure valid responses. This is not to say that interviewer bias, instrument bias and the interviewer-respondent relationship are not commanding problems in their own right, but merely to recognize the abundance of work already done in these areas and the prior importance of the relatively neglected area of valid response. Indeed, securing a valid response consistent with the behavior and phenomenology of the respondent *in ordinary non-research situations* is a *sine qua non* of other forms of data control.

Although it has raised many fundamental problems, the

rather scanty literature available on the problem of such response has been positively so directed as to leave it deficient in one major respect. Its positive concern has been with psychological and organizational defenses against giving information,[15] with developing techniques to assure a flow of information from cooperative respondents,[16] with differentials in response according to position in social structure,[17] and with the mediating effects of situational factors.[18] Few, if any, of these approaches to the problem have been based on cross-checks of information secured through the use of a variety of techniques in a single given situation by the field worker. In limited instances, such as in Mensh and Henry,[19] two or more field techniques have been compared, but usually this is from the perspective of the independent use and yield of each technique. The excellent work being done at the National Opinion Research Center as reported by Hyman indicates a multiplicity of sources of error in field data. The work of the NORC has focussed on interviewer effects as these are related to the validity of data. Kendall and Lazarsfeld[20] have developed a system for introducing intrinsic checks into survey designs which provide the analyst with information on informant incompetency, conscious and unconscious evasion, the informant's inability to be objectively accurate and variabilities in meanings according to slight differences in wording. These are outstanding contributions to the problem of evaluating the validity of response in survey type data.

In all these examples, the deficiency involved in evaluating

[15] Argyis, Chris, "Diagnosing Defenses Against the Outside," *The Journal of Social Issues*," Vol. VIII; No. 3, 1952, 24-34.

[16] Kahn, Robert and Mann, Floyd, "Developing Research Relations," *The Journal of Social Issues*, Vol. VIII, No. 3, 1952, 4-10, and Blum, Fred H., "Getting Individuals to Give Information to the Outsider," *The Journal of Social Issues*, Vol. VIII, No. 3, 1952, 35-42, Vernon, Phillip E., "The Attitude of the Subject in Personality Testing," *Journal of Applied Psychology*, Vol. 18, No. 1, 1934, 165-177.

[17] Merton, Robert K., *op. cit.*

[18] Hyman, Herbert, *op. cit.*

[19] Mensh, Ivan N. and Henry, Jules, *op. cit.*

[20] Kendall, Patricia L. and Lazarsfeld, Paul F., "Problems of Survey Analysis," in *Continuities in Social Research*, edited by Robert K. Merton and Paul F. Lazarsfeld, 1950, pp. 133-196.

the quality of the information secured lies in an inability to observe, interview and participate with the respondent in a wide variety of contexts and over a period of time. This paper attempts to evaluate interviewee responses to a variety of techniques in the context of enduring and intimate contact.[21]

Sources of Error in Response

Because several field workers utilizing a variety of techniques were continuously able to check, re-check and cross-check information gathered from the particular respondent, a number of types of errors and sources of mis-information became apparent. These errors and misinformation may be classed as due to (1) purposeful intent, (2) the temporary role of "respondent," (3) the psychology of the respondent, and (4) involuntary error.

Misinformation Due to Purposeful Intent

Particularly in communities or other relatively self-contained orders which come under the pervasive scrutiny of social research but also, we are convinced, in almost any other context,[22] purposefully given misinformation is a common occurrence. In our experience, outstanding examples of sources of misinformation include the following:

(a) Slanted information resulting from attempts to influence the results of the research. This is especially true of community leaders who usually are concerned with giving a favorable impression of the town.

(b) Dramatized information designed to make the informant and the community seem less prosaic.

(c) Over-information given by reformers who want to use the research to expose and reform the community.

---

[21] The limitations of space prevent the inclusion of detailed illustrative Springdale materials. Few of the types of data distortion presented in the following discussion are new to the literature. They are well documented and can be found in the various books and articles cited throughout this paper. Further elaboration of already well-known case materials is not the purpose of this paper.

[22] This is true in studies of anti-semitism and inter-group relations and has been adequately shown to exist. See Hyman, *op. cit.*

(d) Blockages of attempts to gain information about the dynamics of certain institutional complexes such as sex, power and class. The denial of the existence of problems and local taboos are special forms of information blockage.

(e) Rationalizations of publicly unacceptable behavior ("you don't find people doing much drinking in this town"), and pseudo-definitions of the character and inner-workings of the community. ("One thing about this town, if you try to throw your weight around—I don't care who you are—you soon get cut down to size.")

(f) Information distorted to serve personal ambitions, self-aggrandizement, self-protection or to serve in working out personal feuds.

(g) Advance preparation of responses based on rumors and other types of inter-communication about the research, leading to stylized and stereotyped responses.

The Temporary Role of "Respondent"

In all interview situations, including the various types of self-administered techniques, the respondents attempt to form an image of the interviewer and the organization he represents, and to form a basis of response with respect to the interviewer. In an age of psychological tests, public opinion polling and the popularization of social science findings, the respondent is aware in part of the consequence of his response. Small Town and Middletown are social realities to a surprisingly large number of informants, just as monographs on the Navaho and Pomo are familiar to them.[23] The social meaning of research and the role of the research worker in our own society are becoming increasingly understood. The prevalence of this knowledge offers a basis for forming preconceptions concerning the image of the field worker.

As a result of this image (whatever the basis of its formation) and on the basis of it, respondents frequently provide in-

[23] The apocryphal stories of native groups who use anthropological monographs as guides to the more perfect performance of their own ceremonies and religious rituals, indicate an extension of the influence of research on further response. In doing field work in Palau, the author was frequently referred to Japanese monographs.

formation which, with the best of intentions, they hope will enable the researcher to solve his particular problem.[24] In a difficult joint interview between a husband and wife, which required them to discuss certain problems, respondents would remind their spouses of failures to fulfill the instruction to "discuss" with the remark that "this is not what they wanted!" When couples failed to fulfill the instructions and saw that they had failed, they frequently apologized for their "ignorance" or ineptitude, and usually expressed a hope that they might be of further help on another occasion. Respondents who feel the importance of social science, or think it will solve the problems of the town, frequently volunteer information which they feel is necessary to the understanding of a problem. Respondents who regard social science as a branch of social work are particularly apt to do this.

This problem is accentuated when the research worker consciously or unconsciously[25] communicates his image of the community or organization to the respondent. When the Springdale community became aware that the research project was interested in "constructive" social behavior, in constructive solutions to community problems, and in organizations and organizational participation, many community members not only

[24] Merton, *op. cit.*, has adequately provided illustrative and illuminating examples of respondent images of the Craftown Research. He states: "Although the interviews were 'standardized,' in the sense of involving a definite schedule of questions and although the procedures used by the interviewers were likewise 'standardized,' the interview-*situation* was experienced in strikingly different ways by informants. Informants supplied the most varied motivations for the interview; their images of the interview ranged widely and freely; they imported a rich assortment of personal contexts into the interview. Subjectively the interview-situation varied enormously." He goes on to provide the following selected definitions of the interview situation.
  1. As a democratic channel for the expression of opinion.
  2. As an intellectually demanding experience.
  3. As a moral inventory.
  4. As part of an institutional pattern of social surveys.
  5. As having an ego-building and status conferral function.
  6. As a catharsis.
[25] Either through publicity, his approach, or the form and content of his questions.

saw a causal relationship between organizations and constructive behavior but they began to provide information on the assumption of that supposed causality. People became so geared to organizational memberships that when we came to them with our survey questions they presented us with previously prepared lists of their organizational memberships, together with membership cards. The positive emphasis placed on the term "constructive" prevented the expression of critical opinion in formal interviewing situations, especially where a record was being kept, since this implied a destructive attitude. Organizations became anxious for research representatives to attend their meetings for observational purposes, and provided them with all manner of information relevant to the constructive purposes of the particular organizations. One newly organized community-wide organization, which was early recognized by the research project as the small town answer to constructive behavior, continues to survive partly for the purpose of fulfilling research expectations, that is, so the research project can continue to study it in an effort to solve research problems. Even when the research shifted its emphasis from organizational activity to other forms of activity, informants, trained to a previous definition of research interests, tended to think they were being more helpful if they could place their answers in an organizational context or, in the case of a hobby, for example, tried to show how keeping baseball records was socially constructive for the community at large. In general, it seems that the clearer an image a respondent has of the research, the more likely he is to try to provide the specific answers he feels will satisfy the research worker.

The field worker occupies a unique position in the society. By way of illustration we may take the research worker in a small town. After being in the town awhile, he is not a stranger, but nor is he an insider; as a result, respondents from different statuses accord him different statuses. Simultaneously, he may be respected because he is educated; feared because he is an outsider; disdained by the upper-class and envied by the middle-class; rejected as a long-hair by the uneducated and accepted by those of learning; a confidante to some, a non-involved friend to others, and a downright snooper to still others. He will inherit the friends and enemies of his intimate acquaintances and informants. Frequently, as experienced by many field workers, he is accorded the status of an F.B.I. agent or communist infiltrator, depending on his name, origin, dress or accent. The Springdale project and its individual representatives have experienced a gamut of differential status relationships with respondents. Local aristocratic elements of long lineage standing have tended to consider themselves above the purposes of the research. Concretely, they refuse to be interviewed formally. Among some groups, particularly the lower income groups, suspicion and fear of the research group can become so great as to result in open and organized hostility by entire kinship groupings. We have had three such kinship-organized resistances to a mass survey structured interview. One was penetrated by working into it through collateral relatives, but another continued to resist on the word of a paternal grandfather, even after he had been visited by our "diplomatic missions." The community-minded section of the middle class, however, has been eager to please and cooperate and has always affirmed its belief in the worth of the research. Many individuals, particularly a relatively large number with double occupations, who do not actively participate in organized community affairs, have taken a perfunctory attitude toward the research and have responded to interviews accordingly. On an individual idiosyncratic basis, some respondents are so sensitized to our presence in the community that they have a specialized role which they act out whenever we are present; one man invariably talks local history or gravestones to us, while with another the only subject ever discussed is the price of milk. Professionals, on the other hand, talk the language of the sociologist and, in formal as well as informal interviews, they like to talk directly to such sociological terms as class, status, power and the old aristocracy. These roles and relationships frequently determine the amount and quality, as well as the intimacy of information gathered. Hence, at a given time the interviewer may be receiving a response based on sincere impressions, conventional stereotypes, misinformation, accurate information, partial truths, or responses specifically designed to give favorable impressions or purposely intended as "inside dope."

Furthermore, as field work progresses and the interplay of personalities between interviewers and respondents progresses and develops, these role relationships are subject to continuous change. Under these circumstances new sources and new levels of information, and new types of respondents suddenly become available to the interviewer. These new sources, levels and types arise as a result of varying and changing conditions, characteristic of most research, such as the following: changes in research foci and research personnel; changes in the public image given to the project by researchers; changes in the interviewer's organizational affiliations in the community and his acquaintanceship networks. The passage of time allows initial suspicions and stereotypes to be broken down, confidence relationships to be built up, and sympathy responses to develop.

Let us illustrate how a change in the public image of the project, based on an expansion of research activities, may influence the formal collection of even factual data over a period of time. The research group had maintained contact with the community for more than a year prior to setting up a field headquarters manned by a participant-observer. Up to this time the chief contact with the community had been with a group of organizational participators and Main Street businessmen. Research relations with this group of about 100 people were excellent. Two months after the field headquarters were established, a mass survey, previewed in the local press and organizations, was put into the field. Within two weeks every household —about 750—in the township had come in contact with the research through a 20-minute census-type interview. For the first time, rumors were spread on a large scale variously describing us as F.B.I. agents or communist spies. In spite of our own and our local supporters' efforts, which successfully combated the rumors over the next few weeks, data collection was affected. Among people who thought we were connected with the government, there was for a period of time a general belief that one of the SES questions, which asked for the number of rooms in the dwelling and the number heated in the winter, was to get data on available local housing which, in the event of an enemy attack on New York City, would be used to place city dwellers into country homes where it was indicated there was space. This reasoning led many individuals to under-report the size of their houses, but it also led people who wanted to convert their homes into income property to over-report both size and heating potential. Farmers almost universally believed the research was either connected with the government or the data would be made available to the government. Hence their answers to questions on farm productivity, number of cows, and income, tended either to be grossly under-estimated or were the same answers as reported officially to the government. In contacts with some of these same farmers nine months later, data secured on their incomes, capital evaluation and production potential bore only a remote resemblance to their official replies. In the interviewing context, which was unstructured and highly personalized, they tended to exaggerate and report inflated versions of their financial standing; the 100 people with whom contacts had been built up over a period of a year seemed to answer the survey questions directly and straightforwardly with full confidence in the research group and its integrity. Over a period of time, therefore, public images of the research and specific relationships between researchers and respondents can be so variously shaped and altered as to produce information on one question at a variety of different levels at one moment in time from several respondents, or at different points in time from a single informant. People who suspected us of being F.B.I. agents or communists provided us with a different level of survey response than those who had confidence in us. People who once suspected us have since been interviewed on the most intimate level, while people who once had confidence in the research have since become bored or disillusioned, and are no longer positively motivated to provide information.

Almost as rapidly as new channels of information open up, old sources of information which were initially open begin to close up. The passage of time and the exigencies of research constantly create new problems in the accessibility of information:

1. At the inception of field work or at the beginning of interviewing, all manner of hopes and fantasies are raised by the possible direction and beneficial consequences of the research. As the research program crystallizes, or as results are slow to come forth, or as one rather than another of the expected channels is chosen, sources of information along unpicked and unpredictable lines dry up. We have had respondents who expected the research project to intervene in a school board dispute on the side of better education, and others who would want us to get them jobs or to look into the problem of adolescent immorality. While the research was for a time interested in local definitions of social problems, many dirt road farmers genuinely thought their road would be paved as a consequence of our questioning. Favor seekers, many of whom are good sources of information, quickly lose interest in the research. The respondent with the school board interest has refused to talk to us ever since we refused his request. Some rural families have lost interest simply because we do not promise practical results in terms of better roads. Some informants who provided excellent information early in the research have regarded our efforts to collect information on a broader base as a personal insult. Other types of approach, such as continued neutrality in a community, failure to state research objectives, and (consciously or unconsciously) picking sides, have essentially the same general effects.

2. Personal likes and dislikes are unavoidable and certain to develop, even in the most transient of contacts, and lead to total avoidance or a mechanized approach to the interview.

3. The community begins to take the research project and its interviewers for granted and to assume that they know more than they actually do. Information which might otherwise be given is withheld merely because it is viewed as common every-day knowledge known to all, especially the research worker whose business it is to know. Businessmen, for example, in conversations with the research worker about other business-

men seem to assume he possesses the same background of information on local businesses as other proprietors, who all seem to be familiar with each other's inventory values and gross volume of business. One businessman was appalled when we asked him about the causes of a recent business failure. His reaction was, "Well, now, I thought you were a college graduate, and you can't understand that? They ought to teach you that any man who spends money the way he did isn't going to stay in business very long. I thought you'd know that." It frequently happens that we are introduced to people whom we have never heard of with the comment, "He's from the Research Project, he knows all about you already."

4. The interviewer himself may become over-socialized and, hence, unable to probe for certain types of information because he himself accepts local taboos and, even more, premises. He finds himself unwilling to expose himself to certain kinds of information because he is afraid of having others know that he has it or because he does not see its immediate research relevance. Or, in other cases, as a result of personal values, he regards taking certain kinds of information as exploitative or disturbing to his own sensibilities.[26]

As a result of this constant interplay between respondents and interviewers, the substantive data given by a particular respondent even on such factual matters as income, or such unchangeable facts as previous marriages, will change through time. Perfectly reasonable data secured at one time will be invalidated by subsequent follow-up, chance remark, or confidential revelation in another situation and within the framework of a new relationship.

The Psychology of the Respondent

The respondent, like all other individuals, is subject to failure of and selectivity in memory and recall, to the implications of attitudinal set, to the individual and collective illusions and myths of his day, to the usual motivations of interest and dis-

[26] S. M. Miller discusses this general area in "The Participant Observer and Over-Rapport," *American Sociological Review*, Vol. 17, No. 1, 1952, 97-99.

interest, to the limitations imposed by preconception and perspective, not to mention his own fears and anxieties. All of Bartlett's work on remembering, the lessons of Gestalt psychology, and the pioneering work in phenomenology attest to the operation of such processes. In concrete terms, there is a tremendous qualitative difference in the response of an individual who literally sweats through an interview, as contrasted with one who is comfortable and garrulous. People who see a formal interview as the equivalent of an intelligence test (and there are many in Springdale who view it in this light), are under severe pressure in the interview situation to perform at their highest capacity. They will usually hazard an opinion before admitting they have none. Respondents' descriptions of their own motivations seem to be more related to interviewer expectations and the tone and set established by a sequence of questions than to the basis on which the respondent acts.

Frequently overlooked, although less so in some branches of public opinion polling and the U.S. census, are differences in symbolic meanings between the cultural worlds of those who make interviews and those who are interviewed. In our own experience working with a check list designed to measure degree of familiarity with national political figures, respondents frequently identified Joseph McCarthy as the ex-manager of the New York Yankees rather than as the senator, as it was assumed the name would be understood. Moreover, in this economically-marginal rural area, language styles and sheer vocabulary sizes place severe restrictions on introducing such terms as social class, social background, and power or influence. It would require differently worded questions to evoke the same image of class from a lawyer and a poor farmer. These few illustrations hardly demonstrate the seriousness and all-pervasiveness of this problem of differential mediums. Most interviewers will recognize the problem, however, as a failure in comprehension or communication and will confirm its presence in almost any standardized interview schedule.[27]

---

[27] An excellent example readily available is provided by Bartlett and highlights this problem as it occurs cross-culturally:

"For example, a few years ago Mr. A. T. Culwick asked Mr. E. Farmer and myself to collaborate with him in devising a set of tests which could be applied to natives in Tanganyika. We did this, taking

These psychological processes and cultural differentials constantly play into and determine the response received at a given moment. A slight change in wording, a rearrangement of the sequence of questions, length of pauses, sharpness and saliency of image called forth, all these conditions as they are related to the "mentality" of the respondent affect, alter and shape what he can and will say in a given context.

Involuntary Error

Respondents are frequently unable to provide information, not because they are unwilling or deceptive, but because they are not consciously able to respond to the demands of the in-

---

particular care, as we imagined, to choose test-material which would fit in with the social and material environment of the natives concerned. At the moment I am dealing with only one of these tests. A short story was constructed as follows: A lives in Kiberege village, and B, who has one toe missing from his left foot, lives at Sululu, three miles away. One night A, who is a very light sleeper, goes to bed, where he remains undisturbed by any noise until the morning. On going out he finds that his goat kraal has been broken open and his best she-goat is missing. Outside the kraal, which is close beside the hut, he sees the footprints of a man, who obviously has a toe missing from his left foot, and one of the footprints is obviously over the fresh spoor of a lion. He finds nothing else. Why, do you think, is the goat missing?

"This story was told to a selected group of natives in their own language, by experimenters with whom the subjects were extremely familiar and friendly. Not one native succeeded in solving the problem; 'not even,' says Mr. Culwick, the detective or men who can track difficult spoor and read in a wonderful manner the meaning of a patch of trampled earth or a few broken twigs. It was not that they reasoned incorrectly, but that they could not see how they were to deal with the problem at all. They did not grasp any of the significant points.'

"The fact is that problems used anywhere in the world to elicit mental processes must be placed in their immediately appropriate medium. To set before an African native a verbal difficulty in this story form and expect to learn from his way of dealing with it what his normal thinking processes are like, may be as unfair as it would be were we to wound an Englishman in the heel and then to describe his normal walk in terms of the resulting limp." Bartlett, F. C., "Phychological Methods and Anthropological Problems," *Africa*, Vol. X, No. 4, 1937, 410-411. The same problem is hinted at by Gordon Streib in "The Use of Survey Methods Among the Navaho," *American Anthropologist*, Vol. 54, No. 1, 1952, 30-40. He notes ". . . that the questions concerned subjects that were not elements of the aboriginal culture. This fact suggests the possibility that the structured interview may be most useful in societies in which the acculturation process is, or has been in operation." p. 36.

terview due to blockages, inhibitions, or constraints. Or on the other hand sincerely given self-revelations of motives and desires may be based on systems of thought whose logic lies in folklore, stereotype, or religion. In a small community, however, it is possible for the observer, at least in limited cases, to account for the behavior of the respondents better than the respondents can verbalize their own motives. The basis of all psychiatry attests to the fact that this is possible.

The observer, sensitive to the methods and standards of psychiatry, is able to make assessments which frequently go beyond the limits of the subject's verbal response. His ability to do this with certainty and to validate conclusively his assessment is a standard which he infrequently fulfills.

However, once the research worker begins to make such assessments he does more than record. He has begun to analyze answers as he gets them and to impute motives beyond that which is contained in the formal response. In order to do this, the interviewer-analyst must have confidence in his judgment; lack of such confidence will convert him into a mechanical recorder less efficient than a secretary or a machine. However, when large scale research involves a multitude of interviewers, and when no single standard of judgment can prevail at such intimate levels of assessment, mechanical recording is the only method to guarantee reliable but not valid response.

The Problem of Analysis for the Anthropologist

Given all these typical sources of error and mis-information, bias and deceit, and the effects of the various psychological processes, the problem confronting the analyst and interviewer is almost overwhelming. The data gathered at any particular time and by any particular instrument will be highly uneven and contradictory.

The particular level of information an interviewer obtains from a respondent is highly variable. Given all the idiosyncratic and frequently unknown factors and forces which play on a respondent at a given moment, it becomes obvious that a casual unanticipated remark by an interviewer may at times open up a flood of unexpected and highly important information; conversely, a witless remark may dry up a hitherto satisfactory flow of data. In an interview with a school teacher set up to get data on the role of teachers in a small town, our interviewer routinely asked the subject how she happened to settle in Springdale. She had settled there before she had married a local farmer. This fact played such a decisive role in her life that it led to an explanation of her significant familial relationships and her position and activities in the community. She had married beneath her class and her father had disapproved of her marriage and "written her out of his will." In her own words, her home, her garden and her community activities are to show her father that a farmer's wife can be a lady. Obviously this is a simplified version of a long interview, but before it was over the interviewer happened to mention the name of the resident participant-observer, whereupon the respondent said, "Oh, are you going to tell him all this?" and then stopped talking on a subject on which she had been elaborating a moment earlier. In other instances, the interviewer, without knowing it, may switch the direction of comment from one area or topic to another, or the psychological set from one position to another. Some interviewers are certainly more reliable and more successful than others, but such variability as this tends to hold even for the best and most highly trained interviewers.

Anthropologists have not been unaware of these problems. Clyde Kluckhohn has noted the problem of dishonesty, and non-western respondents' obsequiousness and anxiousness to fulfill interviewer expectations,[28] and has noted the effect which these can have on data gathered. Passin has dealt directly with the problem of prevarication.[29] Almost every anthropological monograph contains the oft repeated dictum that the data employed should be evaluated with references to the personal characteristics and social role of the respondent who was its source. Other social scientists have been unwilling to accept this method as valid. Yet their dicta essentially represents an

[28] Kluckhohn, "The Use of Personal Documents, etc.," *op. cit.*, see especially pages 111, 125, 131.

[29] Passin, Herbert, "Tarahumara Prevarication: A Problem in Field Method," *American Anthropologist*, Vol. 44, 235-247, 1942.

honest effort to appraise the validity of their data. While such a procedure is necessarily subjective, to do otherwise leaves the evaluation of credibility to the respondent and the problem of validity unanswered.

However, when the anthropologist does interpret it is based on the total impression and information of the community and respondents which he, as an interviewer and an analyst, brings to the particular interview. As a result of this type of analysis, the interviewer-analyst is likely to, and usually does, attach different weights to the responses of different respondents, and to the responses from a single respondent gathered at different times and under different circumstances. This does not mean that his theoretical preconceptions do not influence his evaluation, but merely that his background of information and knowledge allows him to make such judgments.[30]

The anthropologist is well aware that one informed respondent may be a gold mine of encyclopedic information while a dozen others may be worthless. He knows that some responses may be worthless except to tell the levels of defense, rationalization and illusion necessary to a respondent in a given situation. This he must accept as a condition for dealing with reality. However, he must also accept the fact that he can never be sure that those respondents who provided stereotyped or defensive responses might, in other situations and in response to other techniques and other anthropologists, provide new and different levels of data; and if a particular respondent opens up new levels of information to him in new situations, he must then evaluate the two levels of response in the certain knowledge that further probing might open up still further levels of information. Hence, even with the most informed of respondents, the anthropologist can never be sure that other procedures or further probing might not have yielded different information.

How, then, does an anthropologist gain a plausible approach

---

[30] The problem of frame of reference and its influence on interpretation and analysis of particular data is a separate problem important in its own right. Oscar Lewis in his *Life in a Mexican Village: Tepoztlan Restudied*, University of Illinois Press, 1951, has made a suggestive and careful inquiry into this problem.

to his data? He does so by being sophisticated in his evaluations and interpretations; by not being deceived by the surface meanings and circumlocutions of his data; by not being too anxious to find confirmations to his theories; and by employing artistry and integrity in obtaining and interpreting the data.[31]

The Problems of Analysis in Other Techniques

It is patently obvious, as is frequently noted by other disciplines, that the anthropologist is in grave difficulties in objectively supporting the validity of his interpretations. But the same difficulties which apply to the anthropologist using traditionally accepted field techniques also apply to other techniques. The social psychological apparatus which produces different levels of response in depth and free interviewing, also operates in other types of field instruments. The same errors, deception, misinformation, inhibitions and role playing operate even in check-list research, as is indicated by the differences in response by the same respondents interviewed by different techniques. This is equally true of attitude surveys, self-administered itemaires and fact-finding census-type interviews. In brief, *the central problem rests in the fact that all answers to the same question on a questionnaire are not of equal weight,* and cannot be treated as such.

Attaching equal numerical weights to all responses and adding them, as well as performing more complicated statistical operations on them, assigns to the responses gratuitous equivalences which are neither psychologically true of the respondents nor consistent with the area under investigation, that is, of the total picture seen from all the sources of data. The analyst adds up the conscious and unconscious misinformation, bias and accuracy and treats them all as equal. If such data distortion is admitted, it is frequently vaguely assumed that such errors either cancel each other out or are totally uncontrollable and, therefore, admissible.

However, this procedure in the analysis of relatively struc-

---

[31] Robert Redfield has discussed this more fully in his "The Art of Social Science," *American Journal of Sociology,* Vol. LIX, No. 3, 1948, 181-190.

tured techniques dispenses with the entire background of information and judgment which the trained field worker can give to his data. He can do this both in the design of structured techniques and in the evaluation of the data they produce. To our knowledge this interplay has been exploited in several projects, including the Springdale project. At best, when equivalence of response is assumed, the trained field worker can only superimpose his raw unchecked impression on the statistical results after the unevaluated data are processed and tabulated. At this stage, moreover, consummate skill and artistry are required and the demand made upon the trained field worker frequently goes beyond the limits of the statistical data.

This is not to say that structured techniques and census-type surveys are without value. Census-type data, even with its known and proven types of distortion, provides the best known method for learning the basic descriptive perimeters of a given population. This data is of inestimable worth in preventing distortions in the perspectives of anthropological "impressionism." Similiarly, structured questionnaire-type information is useful in the absence of other sources of data—small samples of large populations spread over great areas, preliminary stages of research in concentrated areas, etc. In short, they retain their utility, within the framework of limitations suggested in this discussion, wherever alternative forms of securing responses are either unavailable or impractical. As soon as other sources of information are available, a partial basis for checking and cross-checking is also available and, hence, there is a basis for estimating validity of response. In the absence of other sources of information, we operate on the tacit agreement that distortion either does not exist, is unimportant, or is beyond control; all of which are highly unsatisfactory scientific procedures.

Poll-type surveys, then, secure and provide information in specialized areas of mass society where such information is not otherwise readily available. Such surveys are extremely valuable when they probe relatively simple areas of choices among alternatives current and available at a public level—for example, presidential polls or radio and television polling. However, when the depth study of the dynamics of a community or institution is the object of research, and where the problem of social and psychological levels of response are crucial to the research problem itself, other techniques are indispensable. Thus, for example, in totalitarian societies even political and communications polling does not provide valid results since opinions which lead to such data are not admissible at the public level.[32]

A Perspective for Anthropology

Anthropological field work and community and institutional studies in depth, as well as more specialized studies of roles, are in intent and purpose and by their very nature different from the purposes to which large, cross-sectional surveys can be put. In such latter surveys, the very size of the sample, the differences in the life situations of individuals making up various segments of the sample, and the sheer mechanical complexity of the research, all force the field staff to rely on relatively simple and mechanical procedures in processing the data. In this situation, objectivity, in the statistical sense of qualification and comparability, is a necessity which is not exclusively virtuous.

In his depth studies, the anthropological field worker, because he limits the extent of his study, is able to penetrate in depth into various segments of the community and to weigh the relative importance of different institutional structures, roles, and individuals, and the linkages between them. While doing this he is able to check information from a respondent by other information given by the same respondent at later dates. He is

[32] Although not to the same extent, the monolithic Republican control of Springdale influences validity in the same way. The results of our presidential polling in the summer of 1952, indicated a much greater landslide for Eisenhower than actually occurred on November 4. In order to account for the actual vote, almost all the people who claimed to be undecided must have voted Democratic.

Some of our interviewers, all of whom were Democrats, have informed us that it became relatively easy to spot hidden Democrats. Their typical responses to the question: "Which party do you lean toward in the coming election?" was "undecided" or "none of your business." As interviewing progressed, interviewers developed and employed techniques for encouraging the hidden Democrats to come out in the open. These techniques varied according to the exact circumstances, of a specific case, but it is certain that sober-faced neutrality did not encourage the Democrats to admit their political leanings.

also able to check the information with that of other respondents and by observing the behavior of the informant himself. He is not forced to assume the equivalence of, or the equal validity of responses. Because of the multiplicity of sources of and checks on information available to him, the anthropologist acts as a detective or, literally, as an investigator. He does not have to assume that verbal responses are in and of themselves meaningful. Instead, his technique enables him to assess different levels of meaning in verbal response. Anthropological field work, then, is both a technique and an art which is peculiarly suited to the types of data to which anthropologists usually address themselves.

In the past few years anthropologists have begun to record the industrialization and mechanization of societies in all corners of the world. They are now in the position of joining their primitive cohorts in viewing the mechanization of anthropology. In the area of industry, however, there are technical and economical advantages which accrue from and account for the industrialization of the world. In the field of anthropology, the functional equivalents to the advantages accruing to industrialization are nowhere as apparent. There are virtues in conventional field work which should not be overlooked in the quest for mechanization.

SOCIAL THEORY IN FIELD RESEARCH*

IN THE last fifteen years a central concern of both sociology and anthropology has been the relationship between theory and research. One of the turning points in this discussion was Merton's comment on the position of sociological theory,[1] in which he calls for more attention to "theories of the middle range"—"theories intermediate to the minor working hypotheses evolved in abundance during the day-by-day routines of research, and the all-inclusive speculations comprising a master conceptual scheme from which it is hoped to derive a very large number of empirically observed uniformities of social behavior."[2] Other studies addressed to issues in the relationship between theory and research are represented in the work of Mills, Blumer, Becker, Abel, A. K. Davis, Becker and Boskoff, Znaniecki, Borgatta and Meyer, Coser and Rosenberg, and Goode and Hatt, to mention only a few. All these authors have criticized the hiatus between low-level theory dealing with factually exact minutiae and the world-sweeping generalizations of theorists who appear to fail to appreciate the time-consuming task of systematically gathering and interpreting data. In addition, the older classical theorists have been explicitly criticized for being more interested in probing specific problems than in developing theoretical systems, independent of specific cases. This has led to a movement to construct a general theory that can be independent of specific data, but for the most part the authors mentioned have joined the issue on the disparity between generalized theory and low-level theory.

Two methods have been developed to provide a link between empirical observations and higher theory:

1. Closed logical-deductive models which presuppose that *co-ordinates* can be established which will make possible linkages

* Reprinted, with permission of the University of Chicago Press, from the *American Journal of Sociology*, Vol. 65, No. 6 (May 1960), pp. 577-84.

[1] Robert K. Merton, "The Position of Sociological Theory—Discussion," *American Sociological Review*, XIII (1949), 164-68, republished in substantially the same form in Robert K. Merton, *Social Theory and Social Structure* (rev. ed.; Glencoe, Ill.: Free Press, 1958), pp. 4-10.

[2] *Social Theory and Social Structure*, pp. 5-6.

between the models and the open systems of the empirical world.[3] When the general dimensions of elements or units of systems have been specified, the investigator can develop complex models of systems based on the various combinations and relationships of the elements in them. It may be a personality system, a terminological system, a social system, a cultural system, a kinship system, a motivational system, etc. A fundamental method in the construction of such systems is the comparison of specific empirically open systems with the abstract, common elements necessary to any social system.

2. The "codification of theoretical perspectives,"[4] in which the researcher-theorist attempts to state systematically the relationship of existing theories to each other. Specific and discrete theories which have been used in the past on specific problems are examined, and the investigator attempts to discover the fundamental dimensions, implicit and explicit, of each, after which he compares them.[5] In making comparisons, the codifier discovers overlapping areas, convergences, different levels of generality and generalization, and different vectors of observation and perspective. He constructs paradigms and models of the various theories so as to offer a complete theoretical point of

---

[3] Edward Shils has described this process in a similar way as follows: "The role of general theory consists of a general systematic scrutiny of particular facts: then the theory is either disconfirmed by the facts and is replaced by one more adequate to them, or the hypothesis and corresponding theory are confirmed and the problem is settled" ("Primordial, Personal, Sacred, and Civil Ties: Some Particular Observations on the Relationships of Sociological Research and Theory," *British Journal of Sociology*, VIII, No. 2 [June, 1957], 130-45).

[4] Merton, *Social Theory and Social Structure*, p. 12. Also see James Olds, *The Growth and Structure of Motives* (Glencoe, Ill.: Free Press, 1956), pp. 21-22, on "the limited theory viewpoint" in which the position of H. G. Birch and M. E. Bitterman (in "Sensory Integration and Cognitive Theory," *Psychological Review*, LVIII [1951], 355-61) is used as an illustration.

[5] Best exemplified by Robin M. Williams, Jr., *The Reduction of Intergroup Tensions: A Survey of Research Problems of Ethnic, Racial, and Religious Group Relations* (Social Science Research Council Bull. 57 [New York: Social Science Research Council, 1947]), esp. chap. iii. Similar studies are Merton, "The Sociology of Knowledge," in *Social Theory and Social Structure*, pp. 217-45; R. Sarbin, "Role Theory," in Gardner Lindzey (ed.), *Handbook of Social Psychology* (Cambridge, Mass.: Addison-Wesley Press, 1954), pp. 223-58.

view which points to the data necessary to answer theoretical problems. The net product is a heuristic model which serves as a basis for future research.

Both these approaches to theory have been offered as corrections of the unsystematic uses to which theory has been put in the past. It is useful, however, to inquire what the older "unsystematic" and "specific" theory purports to do and how it focuses on the relationship between theory and research. Blumer has indicated that adherence to unsystematic theories sensitizes the theorist and the researcher who is familiar with a wide range of theories to a plurality of possibilities—to wide ranges of data.[6] Shils has specifically shown how the older, unsystematic theorists have helped him to locate and define one of the major problem areas in modern society, and he provides a vivid description of their part in the evolution of his own research and his perspective on society.[7] Blumer and Shils both show that the researcher-theorist can probe and check his data against a number of perspectives in theory and then discern the theoretical possibilities of them.[8] The researcher discovers novel and previously unspecified relationships in his data. Unsystematic theory, in this way, can lead to creative work.

To explore systematically one way in which unsystematic theories have been used, we will confine ourselves to specific research problems in which we have recently been engaged:[9] How is a small rural community related to the large-scale mass society? How does the mass society affect the public and inner life of the individuals of the community? How does the mass

[6] Herbert Blumer, "What Is Wrong with Social Theory?" *American Sociological Review*, XIX (1954), 3-10.

[7] Shils, *op. cit.*

[8] Shils's article (*ibid.*) is a case history of this procedure. He has shown how the interplay between his research experience and received theory has led him to discard, revamp, and reinterpret the different theorists with whom he has been concerned, accordingly as his experience with different sets of data has called forth and brought into perspective different elements and segments of the theorists with whom he has been concerned—mainly Tönnies, Cooley, Mayo, Schmalenbach, Lenin, Weber, Parsons and Sorel.

[9] The analysis of these problems is reported in the authors' *Small Town in Mass Society: Class, Power and Religion in a Rural Community* (Princeton, N.J.: Princeton University Press, 1958).

society affect the social structure of the town, particularly its class structure and the character of its institutional arrangements? What is the response of the small town institutionally and individually, to the institutions and agencies of the mass society that affect it?

Evocation of Theory From Observation

In response to the research organization's inquiry into possible sources of creativity among members of the community,[10] the observer's attention was directed to the locally owned and operated telephone company, whose management was considering a program of expansion. A newspaper's announcement of a proposed plan to instal a new telephone system, with underground cables, dial phones, and an automatic central switchboard, offered an example of creative activity in community life which seemed ideal for investigation.

It was discovered that the force behind the drive for expansion was not the local operator but the state telephone company. In fact, the elderly local owner and policy-maker would have preferred to keep the installation as it was, since he had neither the stamina nor the capital to undertake the expansion. However, he could not resist the expansion program because he was dependent on the state company.

The local system was linked to the state system, through connecting trunks and long-distance lines, to all neighboring towns and the state and the nation at large. In addition, the local company's installations and finances bound it closely to the state company, which provided it with an auditing service, engineering consultants, advertising layouts, etc. The responsibilities of the local company were for maintenance, collections, and ownership. The state company was interested in promoting the

[10] Cornell Studies in Social Growth, sponsored by the Department of Child Development and Family Relationships, New York State College of Home Economics, Cornell University, with the aid of funds from the National Institute of Mental Health, the United States Public Health Service, and the Social Science Research Council. The present study, as well as the original one upon which this one draws, is an independent by-product of Cornell studies and does not represent the authorized viewpoint of the project.

expansion program because it found the local installation cumbersome and awkward; incoming calls could not be handled easily or automatically, and much attention from outside specialists was required. All these irritants could be removed, and service could be improved, by modernization.

The state company did not want to buy the local company. It appeared that it wanted to retain this and other independents as "competing independent companies." The local owner could not close down, though he might have liked to, because the state Public Service Commission would not permit termination of a public service. Since the company existed and since some improvements had to be made, the local company announced and undertook the expansion program. Almost nothing about the expansion, however, could be attributed to local action.

When the various external influences in the local "spontaneous" action were noticed, the attention of the authors was directed to an entirely different range of problems from those which led to the original inquiry. Not only were state agencies, other bureaucracies, and a whole range of experts decisive in the case of the telephone company but similar connections and influences were at work in politics, education, religion, and the cultural life of the community. Local educational policy, religious affairs, public policy and politics—all were intimately related to policy-determining groups far removed from the town. The question then was: How is it possible to comprehend and interpret the relationships between local and external action in a way that is true to the basic facts and elements observed? We turned our attention to various unsystematic and unsystematized theories developed in the past to handle similar data and problems: those of Redfield, Weber, Tönnies, Veblen, Merton, Lynd, Warner, Mills, Sapir, and Tumin. In each case we applied their perspectives to our data. In effect, we asked: "What in their theories would permit us to comprehend our data?"

In the case of each theory which our initial finding made salient, we had a directive for data which could be elicited by further field research. Thus, for example, Veblen's study of the country town makes the point that the political conservatism of rural life rests in the rural village because economically it dominates the surrounding agricultural area. We did not find this to correspond with our observations and could only account for the difference by noting that Veblen wrote in a day when rural banks were strong and apparently autonomous agencies. While many things in Veblen's study of the country town rang true, it did not provide us with a basis for further investigation of our particular problem. On the other hand, Sapir's analysis of spurious culture, which emphasizes the role of cultural imports, directed us to view all phases of the cultural life of the community as a successive series of imports made at different times since 1890. In short, existing theory gave our field work a focus, and we could conduct it along the lines thereby suggested.

Theories were helpful in opening our eyes to specific facts about our problem. For example, Sapir called our attention to the agencies of cultural penetration; Mills and Selznick, to the agencies of institutional penetration and organizational co-optation. In some instances a theorist's minor point became a central point to us, while his central point seemed irrelevant. In no case did we view any theory as offering us a solution to our problem, nor did we use any one theory exclusively to direct our observations. Research, for us, did not demonstrate, document, or annotate theory, but rather it exhausted the theories that came to our attention. Sapir's theory of the genuine culture was exhausted when nothing was found in the cultural life of the community that was indigenous to it—when everything cultural could be traced to an external source. In our procedure a theory was exhausted if and when it either yielded little follow-up data or if the data suggested by the theory were not forthcoming.

The Exhausting and "Destruction" of Theories

If a theoretical perspective does not yield the expected data, the question to be raised is: What facts and what theories are necessary to account for the gaps left by the specific theory? When one set of theories does not exhaust the potentialities of the data, other sets can be employed to point to and to explain the facts which remain unexplained. Thus for any initial statement of the field problem a whole series of theories may be successively applied, each yielding different orders of data and each perhaps being limited by the special perspectives and dimensions on which it is predicated.[11]

The relationships between theories and levels, orders and vectors of analysis, are not resolved a priori but rather on the basis of the contribution of each perspective to the solution of the research problem. The order achieved (if the research is successful) is not the logical order of concepts but the order of uniformities in the social structure of the community. The value of these unsystematic theories is not in their formal order but in their heuristic usefulness.

Each of the theories provides a set of questions asked of the data, and the data lead to the continuous destruction of unproductive theories whenever the theories no longer yield new data or fail to solve the original problem. The reverse is also true: the theory may lead to the evocation of new data by focusing observation and its assessment.

The Substitution of Theories

However, it has been our experience that, when new data are evoked by a theory, they lead quite frequently to the reformulation of the research problem, sometimes in a way that leaves the original theories (in this case dealing with penetration, external influences, etc.) inadequate. This is the case in which the data evoked by the observation forces such a radical shift in perspective that new theories must be called forth. For example, in tracing both the impact of the mass society on the community and the response of the community to agencies of the mass society, it was relatively easy to discover that different social and economic classes responded in different ways. Farmers as a class, for example, were the only group directly protected and aided by federal legislation, but not all farmers responded similarly to the benefits it brought them. A farmer's reaction to federal legislation had an important effect on his

[11] Similarly Robert Redfield, in *The Little Community* (Chicago: University of Chicago Press, 1955), takes five different societies, each studied from a different perspective, and demonstrates how the perspective limits the data.

local class position. Small businessmen had lost their monopoly of the local market to the large urban chains, and they responded to the loss in a psychologically and economically defensive manner. The connections of the professional class to the outside world were almost exclusively cultural, but these enhanced their prestige in the local community, etc. In examining the problem of penetration, we could not look at the town as a unified whole but had to examine how each class was related to the outside world.

As a result of these observations it was necessary to recast our problem as a consideration of class. Class had to be considered, however, in terms not only of the specific problem of mass society but also of the general theories of class. In posing our problem as a class problem, again a whole range of new theories was evoked, including those of Warner, Lynd, Kaufman, Hollingshead, Weber, and Marx. However, again, theories of class were not considered *sui generis* but rather as pragmatic devices which would bring us to a solution to the original problem; that is, the alternative data which would be selected by different theories were considered initially only in terms necessary to solve the problem of the relationship of the local class structure to the mass society, using as many dimensions as theory would allow. The new focus meant making an examination of all relevant class data.

When the data had been re-examined and additional research had been conducted on class, theory was used in an additional way. The conception of the class structure of the community which we had developed in our research was criticized in the light of the class theories with which we were working.

Theories in the Criticism of Field Work

The procedure we followed was to take various theories of class and to postulate them as hypothetically fruitful and, then, to ask what would the hypothetical yield of each be toward exhausting the data then locally available. Some data that should have been elicited by certain of the theories were not present in the initial field work. The question was then raised: Is this a deficiency of the theory or of the field work? It was necessary to reanalyze the data already gathered and to make additional observations in order to make sure the fault was not the researcher's in these theoretical respects. This does not mean that all theories were equally productive or, in fact, productive at all. We found that the prestige associations reported in Warner's work were not to be found in the initial analysis of our data. We postulated Warner as a critic of our analysis and then found that we had to ask ourselves why our analysis had not revealed socially exclusive local groups based on prestige. However, while Warner's system forced us to find groups of the type he describes, the class system we had discovered and described did not appear in most other respects to fit his model.[12] This does not prove or disprove the validity of Warner's work, which might in other communities be more meaningful; however, it did not cover the whole range of our data. In the same way, the theories of Hollingshead yielded valuable data, but again the phenomena were not entirely the same.

Theories of class led to another refocusing of the problem, this time in the area of politics.[13] It became apparent that members of different classes played different roles in local political life. Accordingly, we considered the political theories of Weber, Centers, Marx, V. O. Key, Mosca, Neumann, Michel, and Mills.

Each successive application of theory, derived in each instance from stimulation given by the immediately preceding investigation, caused us to take into account new orders of data which in turn forced us to select different types of theory. Thus the method compelled us to consider not only politics but the relationship between political and non-political leadership, between the public ideology of the town and the private lives of its members, the role of religion in local life, and modes

[12] The ladies' book clubs, card-playing groups, men's clubs and associations, and "old American" families resemble groups found by Warner, but other classes in our study did not; e.g., "Old American" families, or what we called the "Old Aristocracy," occupied symbolically important positions but could not be called an "upper-upper" class.

[13] In our first work politics received only scant attention; only the role of the lawyer as an intermediary between local government and state agencies had been examined by us (Bensman and Vidich, *op. cit.*, chap. iv).

of personal adjustment to the social system. Our original starting point turned out to be merely a starting point for an examination of the major institutional and psychological problems of the community.

Thus successive modifications of our problem followed from the interplay of new data and new points of view. Only a portion of this process took place during the field phase; some was a result of the re-examination of field records, and some occurred during the writing-up of the data.

Let us summarize the functions that unsystematic theory can serve and the conditions under which it can be employed in research:

1. The specification of possible areas of field work as the researcher leans upon the educated perspective of his predecessors to guide him to important and significant areas of investigation.
2. The criticism of field work while doing it. Alternative perspectives in theory yield alternative perspectives in field observation.
3. The discovery of the limitations of one's original statement of the problem; the continuous discovery of new data compels new formulations of the problem.
4. The discovery of the limitations of one's own theory by its continuous confrontation with empirical observation.
5. The discovery of new dimensions of the problem.
6. The reconstruction of one's problem, field work, and past theory into a further limited and discrete theory to handle the problem. Such a theory is not final or general but adequate only to the specific problem in the specific field. However, this type of theoretical solution, in turn, provides raw materials for other research posing new problems, and these new problems as they are studied by other investigators in other settings contribute to the continuous cultivation of new theories.

The Relationship Between Heuristic and Systematic Theory

Heuristic theory as outlined above is operative at every level of research: the statement of the problem, the gathering of the field data, the analysis and evaluation of the findings, and the analyzing and reporting of the results. However, heuristic theory is highly limited in that it does not produce generalized findings valid beyond the statement of the specific original problem. The generalization of the findings after observation, analysis, and interpretation must depend on other types of theory. Theorists of systematic theory have assumed the function of generalization.

As an enterprise, systematic theory can integrate new research findings with established theory and findings, thus accomplishing a continuous evaluation and assessment of research and heuristic theory. However, this can be accomplished only if general systematic theory pays attention to the differences in the problems, in the levels of heuristic theories, and in the field situations in which the problem and the theory are specified. The attempt to seek the common features of all social systems or of a hypothetical "the social system" overlooks the specific validity and the specific character of most heuristic theory and all research. If systematic theory is at all possible as an aid to scientific research, it must reach out and establish its empirical co-ordinates to the empirical world. It can do this only if it takes into account the limited and specific character of heuristic theory.

The Codification of Theory and the Heuristic Approach to Theory

There is relatively little difference between the theoretical enterprise that codifies theoretical perspectives and heuristic theory as described above. The major difference—and it is very important—is in the timing of the integration of the theoretical perspectives brought up for consideration. Codification of theory attempts to bring together and relate the various theoretical dimensions that can be brought to bear on a problem by the rigorous logical analysis of received theory in terms of the theories themselves. All these theories are considered in one analytical operation; ideally, the composite perspective derived from them is applied as a unit to a field situation.

Contrary to codified theory, heuristic theory allows past theory to remain as a residue of latent possibilities which the research worker can bring to bear on his specific field problem.

He cannot know in advance exactly what orders of theory are relevant to his problem until he discovers its nature in the field and what resistances to his preconceptions emerge as his field work progresses. Totally new perspectives emerge as he discovers these resistances. New perspectives, new levels, new orders, and new dimensions of data become salient, regardless of what level of codification he has considered in the past; in the field, in the encounter with the world, the press of the data is manifold, continuous, and not easily amenable to preconceived selection. Moreover, the level of detail of data, the precision of analysis, and the concepts employed are functions of the merging perspectives of the field worker in the field. It can thus happen that whole areas, codified in the past, may prove worthless for coping with a specific problem, though the past codifications may be valuable for other problems. However, there is no level of codification sufficiently precise to be applicable when empirical data become the focus of attention.

To exhibit all possible dimensions of a problem in advance, codification would have to be extremely complex, cumbersome, and unworkable (e.g., in one problem the authors reached 256 formal logical possibilities of the data without ever reaching its substantive level, and, because of the complexity, one is, in effect, forced to work with heuristic concepts rather than with the full range of logically deducible possibilities. One deals with five or six major cells in a logical matrix and ignores a host of others which, for purposes of social science, are conceived of as logical but irrelevant. As a result, the researcher-theorist must continuously refine his theoretical analysis in terms of his problem and data.

Limitations of Heuristic Theory

Heuristic theory, as subjected to the rigors of specific substantive problems, has a number of limitations:

1. It cannot work if the research worker on a priori grounds is unwilling to entertain the possibility of using or seriously considering all or a variety of the available theories. Commitment to one school or theory means, in most instances, commitment to selected levels of data. These forms of commitment prevent the research worker from criticizing his findings from alternative

points of view and may blind him to the exhausting of his own favored theoretical approach. In the heuristic approach there is no guaranty that such standards of open-mindedness will prevail or that self-criticism can and will be made. Science, then—particularly social science—must depend not only on self-criticism but on the criticism made by others, willingness to accept which then becomes the basis of social science.

2. The *ad hoc* rotation of theoretical perspectives does not in itself guarantee the exhaustion of the empirical data if it is only ritual eclecticism. The only purpose in considering many perspectives is to solve or to redefine the problem. The listing of the alternative possibilities of different theories is not a solution, since listings are not a structural relationship of data. The end of objective of the procedure is not only to find what data are relevant to the problem but also to determine how they are functionally related. The only point that needs emphasis is that the functional relationships are products of the research and not of a priori theorizing.

3. These procedures of exhaustion and rotation of perspectives are dependent on the contingencies of field work, the investigator's background, and his sensitivity to his data; hence there is no guaranty that their use will assure success. There is no immutable deductive procedure which automatically guarantees the production of new concepts, theories, or findings. The research worker must face the possibility of failure in the knowledge that it may be due to the way in which he handled the problem.[14] Scientific inquiry means living an intellectually dangerous existence.

4. The method outlined here is amenable to not all types of research. Experimental studies assume that causes can be postulated in advance and that the problem in research is simply one of determining their conditions and efficiency. Large-scale surveys frequently telescope all the procedures of research described above into a single operation which does not and cannot allow for the continuous modification, substitution, and refinement of hypotheses and problems on the basis of field experience. The survey worker, in the absence of these intermediate checks on

[14] John Dewey, *The Quest for Certainty: A Study of the Relation of Knowledge and Action* (New York: Minton, Balch & Co., 1929).

his thinking, may be forced to pose all at the same time a wide range of theoretically possible alternatives resulting from a priori formulations and hunches, hoping that one or more of his theoretical dimensions will be productive after the field work is done and analysis is completed. He frequently finds that a limited number of areas are highly productive, but, since in the beginning he had to consider on a priori grounds a variety of alternative areas, time and funds limit the depth to which he can analyze those variables which finally proved productive. This is the familiar phenomenon of knowing better how to make a survey after is it done than at the beginning.

It is apparent from this discussion that in no case can the research worker feel that he has fully solved his problem. He must recognize that new levels of theory and new theories of which he may not have been aware at the time might have required new levels of data and further exhaustion of theory. At best, he can feel that he has advanced his problem along an infinite path so that his work need not be repeated. One must recognize that there is no final accumulation of knowledge and no final solution, in the usual meaning of these terms.[15]

[15] The following studies point to a similar conclusion: Max Weber, "Science as a Vocation," in *Essays from Max Weber*, trans. and ed. H. H. Gerth and C. Wright Mills (New York: Oxford University Press, 1946), pp. 129-56; Homer G. Barnett, "Comment to Acculturation: An Exploratory Formulation," *American Anthropologist*, LVIII, No. 6 (December, 1954), 1000-1002; Robert Redfield, "The Art of Social Science," *American Journal of Sociology*, LIX, No. 3 (November, 1948), 181-90; Herbert Blumer, *An Appraisal of Thomas and Znaniecki's "The Polish Peasant in Europe and America"* (New York: Social Science Research Council, 1939); Dewey, *op. cit.*; Allen H. Barton and Paul F. Lazarsfeld, "Some Functions of Qualitative Analysis in Social Research," *Sociologica*, I (1955), 321-61; Maurice R. Stein, *The Eclipse of Community: An Interpretation of American Community Studies* (Princeton, N.J.: Princeton University Press, 1960); Barrington Moore, Jr., "The Strategy of Social Science," in his *Political Power and Social Theory* (Cambridge, Mass.: Harvard University Press, 1958, pp. 111-59); and C. Wright Mills, *The Sociological Imagination* (New York: Oxford University Press, 1959).

Chapter 14

Ethical and Bureaucratic Implications
of Community Research

EDITORIAL—FREEDOM AND RESPONSIBILITY
IN RESEARCH: THE "SPRINGDALE" CASE*

A SMALL upstate New York village has now been immortalized in anthropological literature under the name of "Springdale." The local newspaper reports that the experience has not been entirely a pleasing one. We pass on this account:

> "The people of the Village [Springdale] waited quite awhile to get even with Art Vidich, who wrote a *Peyton Place*-type book about their town recently.
>
> "The featured float of the annual Fourth of July parade followed an authentic copy of the jacket of the book, *Small Town in Mass Society*, done large-scale by Mrs. Beverly Robinson. Following the book cover came residents of [Springdale] riding masked in cars labeled with the fictitious names given them in the book.
>
> "But the pay-off was the final scene, a manure-spreader filled with very rich barnyard fertilizer, over which was bending an effigy of 'The Author.' "

The account suggests that a good time was had by all—on this particular occasion. Nevertheless, local observers report that the disturbance caused by the book in the village has not been entirely compensated for by even such a ceremony carried out in the best anthropological traditions. The book and its aftermath raise some serious questions which, so far as we know, have never been publicly discussed. We feel that it is high time that these issues be raised:

* Reprinted by permission of the Society for Applied Anthropology from *Human Organization*, Vol. 17 (1958-59), pp. 1-2.

1. What obligation does the author of a community study have to the people of the community he studies, particularly when it comes to publication of his findings?
2. When the author is a member of a research team, what obligations does he have to the project director? And what obligations does the project director have to him?

Vidich spent two and a half years living in "Springdale" as field director of a Cornell project carried out in the Department of Child Development and Family Relations. The project was directed by Urie Bronfenbrenner, a social psychologist. As a result of this research experience, Vidich published several articles, but the official report in book form regarding the project did not materialize during his tenure at Cornell and is only getting into print at this writing. Some time after he left Cornell, Vidich began work on a book of his own, in collaboration with Joseph Bensman, who had had no previous association with the project.

The Vidich manuscript gave rise to considerable controversy between the author and the Springdale project director. In presenting the issues which arose between them, we are indebted to both Bronfenbrenner and Vidich for allowing us to examine their correspondence (from late 1955 to 1958) regarding the manuscript.

The points of controversy were essentially these:

1. Should individuals be identified in the book?
2. If individuals were identified, what—if anything—should be done to avoid damage to them?
3. Did Vidich have a right to use—or should he be allowed to use—project data which he did not gather himself? Who "owns" project data?

Before Vidich came onto the scene, Springdale people had been assured, when their collaboration was sought, that no individuals would be identified in printed reports. While all of the Vidich characters are given fictitious names, they can easily be identified within Springdale. The author argues that, when there is only one mayor and a small number of village and town officials and school board members, it is impossible to discuss the dynamics of the community without identifying individuals. He further argues that what he has reported in the book is "public knowledge" within Springdale. Even if this be true, is there a difference between "public knowledge" which circulates from mouth to mouth in the village and the same stories which appear in print?

In addition to his objections regarding the anonymity pledge, Bronfenbrenner claimed that certain individuals were described in ways which could be damaging to them. On this he submitted a long bill of particulars. One example (p. 97):

> One member of invisible government, in agreement with the principal's educational policy, has remarked that "He's a little too inhuman—has never got into anything in the town. He's good for Springdale until he gets things straightened out. Then we'll have to get rid of him."

Bronfenbrenner took the position that Vidich had no right to—and should not be allowed to—use project data beyond that which he personally had gathered. When Vidich wrote that, while he did not agree with Bronfenbrenner's reasoning, "wherever possible I will delete the material you consider objectionable," Bronfenbrenner responded by writing that, in this case, he would not object to having other project data used in this book. However, a comparison of the book with Bronfenbrenner's written objections indicates that, in most cases, changes were not made.

Beyond the specific questions raised by Bronfenbrenner, there is the more amorphous question of the "tone" oi a book describing a community. Vidich speaks throughout of the "invisible government." (For this reason, the characters in his book rode with masks in the Fourth of July celebration.) The words themselves suggest an illegitimate form of activity, a conspiracy to gain and hold power. While Vidich himself says in a footnote that this is not true, the use of such a phrase, and the tone of his treatment, presents the behavior in that light, and so it has been interpreted in Springdale.

The Springdale experience also raises a general problem regarding the relations of a staff member to the project director in a team project, especially when there is a long period between the initiation of the study and the publication of major research reports. The junior member of such a staff must naturally think about establishing his own professional reputation, which he can do primarily through publication. An article or two will help, but a book would help even more. Is he to be a co-author on a book which represents a major report of the study? In that case, he may have to wait some time for the appearance of the book, and, in the meantime, he has little in the way of credentials to offer as he seeks new teaching and research jobs. Furthermore, when his name does finally appear on such a book, many people naturally assume that the book is largely the creation of the project director. A junior member may feel that he does not, in this way, get adequate recognition. The project director, on the other hand, already owns an established academic reputation and so does not feel a strong compulsion to rush into print with the findings of the project. Furthermore, he has other involvements on the campus of his university, which is not true of the field director.

Is there some way in which the project director can promote opportunities so that the junior staff members win their own reputations—without encouraging each man to go off in a completely independent direction? It was hoped in the Springdale project that this could be accomplished. Experience so far indicates that the results have not met the expectations on either side of the controversy.

We will let the author have the next-to-last word on the controversy. Replying in the *Ithaca Journal* to a statement made by Bronfenbrenner, Vidich writes:

> "Strictly speaking, I take the position that in the interests of the pursuit of scientific truth, no one, including research organizations, has a right to lay claims of ownership of research data.
>
> "That is a violation of the entire spirit of disinterested research."

Asked whether he was aware that there would be a reaction in Springdale, Vidich replied:

"I was aware that there would be a reaction in the town when the book was published. While writing the book, however, it did not occur to us to anticipate what these reactions might be, nor did it occur to us to use such anticipations of reactions as a basis for selecting the data or carrying out the analysis.

"One can't gear social science writing to the expected reactions of any audience, and, if one does, the writing quickly degenerates into dishonesty, all objectivity in the sense that one can speak of objectivity in the social sciences is lost."

We do not have any firm answers to the various problems raised by this case, but we are quite convinced that the Vidich answer will not serve. He seems to take the position that he has a responsibility only to science. Has the researcher no responsibility to the people whom he studies? We are not prepared to state what the nature of this responsibility should be, but we find it strange indeed to hear a researcher argue that he assumes no responsibility at all.

We suggest that this is a field in which we all need to reflect upon our own experiences in an effort to clarify the responsibilities we should be prepared to assume. The editor would be glad to hear from our members on any of the points raised here. Perhaps in this way, to borrow a phrase from the motto of Cornell University, we shall arrive at a better understanding of "freedom and responsibility" in field research.

"FREEDOM AND RESPONSIBILITY IN RESEARCH": COMMENTS*

Arthur Vidich and Joseph Bensman

WE ARE pleased to be invited to join in the discussion of the issues which the Editor opened up in the editorial in *Human Organization*, Volume 17, Number 2, pp. 1-2. The editorial raises issues worthy of discussion both with reference to the specific problems connected with the publication of our book, *Small Town in Mass Society*, and, more importantly, to the general problem of the role of the researcher vis-à-vis both the community he studies and the research organizations which study human groups, organizations, and societies.

We feel, however, that his phrasing of the issues was too narrow, in that it was limited to the social and public relations problems of social science investigation. It failed to consider any of the problems related to the purposes of inquiry and to the scientific problems which social inquiry presumes to state and solve. For example, his editorial gave attention exclusively to the social scientist's responsibilities to the community and the research organization, and to his personal problems, such as career aspirations, rewards, publications, and the gaining of publicity. While all of these things are important as far as the organization of the discipline is concerned, they are irrelevant; progress in a science is somehow related to important substantive problems and issues, and the activities which lead to progress in the solution of the problems posed. This he altogether failed to bring up in his discussion.

His implication that publication in general is related only to career opportunism and that, specifically, this was our motive, is an extraordinarily limited perspective. In our case, we would feel that there are a large number of factors bearing on the writing of a book. All of these cannot be taken up in a brief reply such as this and, especially, they cannot be treated within

* Reprinted by permission of the Society for Applied Anthropology from *Human Organization*, Vol. 17, No. 4 (Winter 1958-59), pp. 1-7.

the range of possibilities suggested by the editorial. We had thought that our Springdale material offered us an opportunity to define some problems central to basic anthropological and sociological theory, in a way which would lead to some understanding of the development of contemporary society. In doing our work, we believe that these problems were worthy of inquiry and analysis, in and of themselves. We are gratified that almost all reviewers of *Small Town in Mass Society* have granted that we selected important problems and that we made some progress in stating and analysing them.

In order to describe how the research developed, we would like to present a short history of our work in relation to the Springdale project and the emergence of our book.

Vidich was employed by Cornell Studies in Social Growth, College of Home Economics, Cornell University, as a resident field director. His major duties in the field included administration of field surveys and supervision of field workers who interviewed the town's residents and observed the community's organizations. As an institutional obligation, he fronted for the project in the town and was responsible for maintaining rapport with all community members. As a result of this work, several thousand interviews were completed and three or four hundred protocols on meetings of community organizations were filed. In addition to these duties, Vidich acted as a participant observer in the community. In this capacity, he was allowed to do field work on his own initiative, using informal methods of research not subject to the formal mechanism of data collection.

In the course of this field work, Vidich and Bensman, who had worked together before on other problems, had occasion to discuss various aspects of the social structure of the community. Out of these conversations, which in the beginning were sporadic and almost aimless, there emerged a number of problems which we felt worthy of further thought and fuller exploration. The results of our work on these problems, as with all of the work which Vidich did alone or with others, were presented, as a matter of course, to project colleagues and were offered for discussion. By the end of the third year, a series of self-contained, separate papers, which both com-

mented on aspects of the Springdale community and had some
bearing on specific theoretical or methodological issues, were
written and presented to the director, the project staff, and
the head of the department. These papers consisted of an analysis of the participant-observer technique, a comparison of participant observation with survey data (in collaboration with Gilbert
Shapiro), an analysis of the problem of the validity of data in
social science, and an analysis of the relationships between the
town and mass society.[1] All of this work had been submitted
for publication while Vidich was still an employee of the project
and, in addition, upon the invitation of Professor John Dean,
the work on participant observation was presented to the Cornell
University Social Science Seminar. There were other papers
which we, Vidich and Bensman, had completed in draft form;
one was an analysis of the class structure of the town and the
other was a monograph-length analysis of the political structure
of the town. All of this material was presented to the project
staff while Vidich was still an employee. The project expressed
no particular interest in these writings, or in the ideas which
they represented, because they did not fall within the scope of
its research design and theoretical focus. A book had not been
envisaged by us at this time, although it was understood by
everyone concerned that the project was free to use the manuscripts and drafts and articles for the several volumes which the
project had planned at that time.

When Vidich completed his three-year appointment, the joint
work with Bensman continued. The monograph on politics was
entirely rewritten. The analysis of the role of the rural community in mass society was rewritten for presentation at a professional meeting. Again, all of this material, as it was completed and as a matter of course, was forwarded to the project.

[1] Published as "The Validity of Field Data," *Human Organization*,
XIII, No. 1/(Spring, 1954), 20-27; "Participant Observation and the
Collection and Interpretation of Data," *American Journal of Sociology*,
LX, No. 4 (Jan. 1955), 354-360; "A Comparison of Participant Ob-
servation and Survey Data," *American Sociological Review*, XX, No. 1
(Feb. 1955), 28-33; "Methodological Problems in the Observation of
Husband-Wife Interaction," *Marriage and Family Living*, XVIII, No.
3, 234-239.

During all this time, except for the articles on "Participant Observation" and "The Validity of Field Data," no objection to the work was presented to the authors and the objections to the articles were of a substantive nature.

Only when the authors thought that they had discovered a theme which could sustain a more extended and unified treatment, did the possibility of a book emerge. Their intention of doing a book was presented in conference to the project staff. There were no objections to this enterprise, and it was not only understood, but also specified, that all work was to be forwarded in manuscript form, as it was completed, to the project, which of course we did.

About a year and a half later, only after we had presented a manuscript, complete except for a few chapters, were any objections made. A project policy was then formulated:

> It is clear from your material that all of us must face a rather complex problem in terms of the identifiability of organizations and people within the Springdale community— a problem which cannot be avoided even with the care we are taking to disguise individuals and groups through deliberate alteration and recombination of important identifying characteristics. This problem is further accentuated by the fact that our research was sponsored by the New York State College of Home Economics. We have given the whole matter careful consideration and have agreed to the following procedure. Before any manuscripts are shown to outside representatives, such as publishers or their agents, we shall ask one or two persons within the college and possibly in Springdale, to read the manuscripts from the point of view of public relations. Although the final responsibility for deciding what we publish will rest with the project staff, the reactions of such readers would receive serious consideration and we would probably re-write and omit in accordance with their recommendations.

We did not accept this policy and said so. However, project members were given every opportunity to state their objections. We took such objections as were made under advisement and felt free to accept or reject them, doing so in relation to the necessity of treating the issues under consideration. We believed that it was impossible to discuss leadership without discussing leaders, politics without mentioning politicians, education without treatment of educators, and religion without ministers. In this sense, we violated the project policy of anonymity. At no point, however, did we gratuitously call attention to identifiable individuals beyond the necessity of treating the material and, when this was done, pseudonyms were used. In all cases, the decision of what material to accept and reject was our own.

The policy on the use of project material only emerged after the entire manuscript was completed:

"... your book should not utilize or make reference to any of the "official" data of the project such as survey results or observer and interviewer reports."

Previously, the project had let us use selected project data which did not fall within the purview of the project's central focus. When the project's permission to use their data was revoked, we went through the manuscript before typing a final draft and cut substantial portions of their data which we had used for illustrative purposes. These were observer's protocols which were used to illustrate the organizational operations of the political boards and the school board. We felt we were successful in these excisions in almost all cases, but we know that there are six quotations on pages 125, 151, 157, 161-163, 173-174, 182-186, and the two census-like tables on pages 17 and 18, which technically were the property of the project. If there is any feeling that we have not given due credit for the use of this data, we wish to do so now.

* * *

The particular fates of Vidich, Bensman, the project, the department, Cornell University, Springdale, etc. are of much less significance than the problems which the editorial raises for the future of scientific investigation in western society. Not that the Springdale example presents a new problem; on the contrary, negative reactions by organizations, individuals, and interest groups have been characteristic for the Lynds' study of Middletown, West's study of Plainville, Warner's study of Yankee City, Selznick's study of the T.V.A., Hunter's study of Community Power, and Whyte's study of Street Corner Society. In the latter case, Doc still suffers from the recognition he received in the book.

Historically, this problem has not appeared, or has appeared to a much lesser extent, in the anthropology of non-western society. This is because primitive populations have been less concerned, aware, and vocal in their response to the anthropological description of their societies. The life history, studies of native politics and organizations, etc., all invade the native's "privacy," subject his inner life to exposure, and strip him of the magic on which his existence rests. Because it was possible to do this with native society, sociologists and anthropologists have learned a great deal about social life which they could apply to western society. Now that so many primitives have become westernized and are aware of the implications of anthropological research, they, too, resent the invasion of privacy and descriptions of the inner structure of their society.

There is an interesting parallel between the license taken by anthropologists and that taken by sociologists who have studied crime, minority groups, caste groups, factory workers, prostitutes, psychopathic personalities, hoboes, taxi-dancers, beggars, marginal workers, slum dwellers, and other voiceless, powerless, unrespected, and disreputable groups. Negative reaction to community and organizational research is only heard when results describe articulate, powerful, and respected individuals and organizations.[2] We believe there would have been no objection to our study if it had been limited solely to the shack people.

We think all of the community and organizational studies mentioned above made important contributions. The problem is: *At what price should a contribution be made?*

One of the principal ideas of our book is that the public atmosphere of an organization or a community tends to be optimistic, positive, and geared to the public relations image of

---

[2] C. Wright Mills, "The Professional Ideology of the Social Pathologists," *American Journal of Sociology*, XLIV, No. 2 (1939), 415-435.

the community or the organization. The public mentality veils the dynamics and functional determinants of the group being studied. Any attempt in social analysis at presenting other than public relations rends the veil and must necessarily cause resentment. Moreover, any organization tends to represent a balance of divergent interests held in some kind of equilibrium by the power status of the parties involved.[3] A simple description of these factors, no matter how stated, will offend some of the groups in question.[4]

The only way to avoid such problems is not to deal with articulate groups who will publicly resist the attention which research gives to them, or to deal with the problems in such a way that they are inoffensive. Research of this type becomes banal, irrespective of its technical and methodological virtuosity.[5] We think this has always been the case and that the Springdale example presents nothing new.

What has changed since *Middletown* and *Street Corner Society* is the organization and financing of research. At the present time, research is carried on by large-scale organizations of a relatively permanent nature and it is financed by businesses, governments, foundations, research centers, and colleges which have vested interests apart from the research. The successful researcher in this setting is expected to be aware of, and to anticipate, these interests, regardless of whether a policy is ever explicitly made.

The researcher, working for a commercial firm, or even for a governmental agency, must develop an ethic of responsibility. He defines the problem on which he will work in a way which will be useful to his sponsors. He deals only with material which is salient to their defined needs and interests. He writes, edits,

[3] William Foote Whyte, *Street Corner Society*, University of Chicago Press (enlarged ed.), Chicago, 1954. See especially, Chap. VI, Section 6, "The Nature of Political Obligations."

[4] See the authors' "Validity of Field Data," *op. cit.*

[5] It is ironical that the very acceptance of research by all kinds of public agencies, businesses, managements, professions, unions, bureaucracies, churches, and other established and respected institutions tends to vitiate the power of research to deal with social issues for their own sake.

and censors his own material so that it will appear in a way which enhances the interests of his employers. There is no implication here of outright dishonesty. The researcher who did other than this would be violating his contractual obligation to his employers if he exposed them to an unfavorable limelight or to public attention which might cause embarrassment. This is only to be expected. If the researcher confines himself to research problems which are of immediate interest to these groups, and publishes only findings which are acceptable to his employers-sponsors-supporters, he meets his obligation.

If, however, as in our work, fundamental issues which are related to the basic problems of social science are raised, one cannot predict in advance the embarrassment which research may cause, including the embarrassment to oneself. If the social scientist wants to raise these kinds of issues, he has to risk the possibility of getting into these kinds of troubles. We foresaw this, as the research progressed, and there is no easy solution to the problem.

We think the social scientist can only answer the problem for himself, by asking himself what kind of research he wants to do. If he wants to do practical research which is important to some sponsoring body, he must accept the ethic of responsibility and give up the illusion of independent inquiry. If he wishes to do serious research on problems which are not practical (as practicality is now defined in modern society) he must almost certainly conclude that he must work outside the framework of large research organizations, large institutional grants, or research-servicing organizations. The choice he makes must then be a personal one and, in each case, he can preserve the ethical system he has selected.

However, if social science is to have some kind of independent problems and identity and, if a disinterested effort is to be made to solve these problems, a certain number of social scientists, presumably residing at universities, must be willing to resist the claims for planned, popular, practical research.[6]

[6] Bernard Rosenberg, *The Values of Veblen*, Public Affairs Press, Washington, D.C., 1956, especially Chap. I for similar structures.

410 *IMPLICATIONS*

*Robert Risley**

I have just read the editorial in *Human Organization* on the
Vidich incident and would like to congratulate the editor on the
manner in which he has set forth the fundamental issues.
As he knows, from our earlier discussions of this problem,
I find myself in an interesting dual role in this case. On the one
hand, I live in "Springdale," the community in which the study
was made, associate with the individuals about whom it was
written, and, in fact, was one of those interviewed in the course
of the study. On the other hand, in the course of directing
graduate students in their thesis work and in research of my
own, including particularly some work in the small business
area, I find it necessary to obtain community cooperation and
understanding in order to obtain participation. As a consequence,
my comments on the editorial relate, in part, to the knowledge
which I have of the reaction and attitudes of individuals in
"Springdale" to the study and its impact and, in part, to the
problems which it seems to me are inherent in this type of
research activity in the social sciences.

It seems to me that, if we are to be able to conduct research
within the world of reality in the social science area, there are
two principles which we have to accept. The first of these is
that it is essential that we arrive at a clear understanding with
those with whom we are to work concerning the nature of the
reports and the publications which are to grow out of the research and, in particular, concerning the degree to which the
specific situations or individuals in it will be cloaked with anonymity.

It may well be, on occasion, that, at an early stage of a
project, there is temptation to provide greater assurances concerning anonymity than are justified in view of any use of
data in published form. Sometimes this is done in order to "get
in," with the thought that, once in, matters can be resolved
later. It seems to me that this is not appropriate and if, in a
given situation, agreements cannot be arrived at which are

* Dr. Risley is Acting Dean of the New York State School of Industrial and Labor Relations, Cornell University, Ithaca, New York.

satisfactory to the researcher and to those individuals within the situation which is to be studied, research opportunities must be sought elsewhere. As a related point to this issue, it should, likewise, be clearly understood what review rights, if any, those being studied will have of the material prior to publication.

The second principle is that, if an individual in charge of a project has arrived at some understanding on these points in a given situation, those working with him are bound by the understanding as much as he. Possibly the director should make clear to the individuals who are planning to become involved in the project, the circumstances under which it is being undertaken. It seems to me clear, however, that the basic understanding arrived at by the director and the group being studied must be binding on all involved. Anything less than this provides no real standard of ethics which will be acceptable and will result in developing an unwillingness to permit research into lives and affairs of individuals, organizations, or communities.

As a corollary of this point, it seems to me that individuals who are hired to work on a project are not free to use data obtained from the project for their own purposes. Essentially, my position would be that the material accumulated by individuals assigned to the project belongs to the project. Consequently, no use should be made of data which a staff member of a project obtains, except in a situation in which the staff member has received authorization for its use from the individual heading the project.

I realize that my line of reasoning obviously will cause problems for junior members on the projects and might well be viewed as interfering with the freedom of a researcher. As the editor so well points out, however, "this freedom like other freedoms is balanced by responsibility." It seems to me, however, without the acceptance of some such mode of operation as I have suggested, there is no guarantee of this responsibility being exercised. What I am suggesting here seems to me to be consistent with the kind of ethics involved in other professions. Unless some such standard of ethics is generally accepted and acknowledged by those in the social science research area, access to individuals and groups for study will be severely limited.

Unfortunately, a violation of such ethics reflects, not only upon the individual concerned, but broadly upon the whole field of such research and upon individuals engaged in it. In the Vidich incident, I know that the feelings and distrust aroused will be generalized to a point where the feelings of the individuals and community involved are such that I suspect it would be many, many years before any type of social research undertaken by anyone could be conducted in this community. Further, the indictment in this particular incident has been, not only against Vidich as such, but against all the others involved in the study and, in at least the minds of some, against the academic profession and the university.

Raymond E. Ries**

It seems clear that social scientists are as culpable as other human beings in their failure to carry out in practice the implications of their theoretical positions. For many years now, American social science has been insistent upon a sharp distinction between the spheres of science and value. In the area of public policy, it has claimed that the knowledge of the economist or sociologist is instrumental only, that it can in no way determine the ends or values which the community or its individuals should choose. The social scientist may clarify alternatives in action, he may point out the consequences of intended actions, but it is only as a citizen that he can decide which course to take. With a heavy hand, the textbooks in social science point out repeatedly that objectivity requires the elimination of bias, prejudice, and values of the investigator. And it is more apparent today, than it was generally forty years ago, that science has come to a grinding halt at the threshold of questions of the meaning and values of human life and conduct.

But the intellectual heritage within which science and values were perceived as exclusive has not been entirely accepted by American social science. Perhaps the tragic implications of this view were muted by the characteristic optimism of the American. While it was accepted that scientific objectivity required the exclusion of judgments of value, scientific objectivity be-

** Dr. Ries is Assistant Professor of Sociology at Colgate University in Hamilton, New York.

came transformed into a value and meaning in itself. Somehow scientific objectivity became an object of faith and a road to salvation. When Lundberg posed the question: "Can Science Save Us?," his answer was "yes." But such a question is quite beyond science. As Max Weber pointed out forty years ago, science in itself is useful but meaningless, in the sense that it can give no answer to the question, "What shall we do and how shall we live?".

Activities conducted in the name of science can be morally reprehensible, but the pursuit of objectivity in no way tells us this. The dramatic illustration of this fact was found in the Nazi medical experiments. Less dramatic and, therefore, apparently less reprehensible, is the deliberate misinforming of subjects in the "experimental situation," which some social scientists like to employ. One should include the field research situation, in which, the informant is made a victim of his trust in the researcher. Analogous situations appear in "theoretical" writings. I am reminded of an innocent statement of R. K. Merton, in his discussion of latent functions performed by the political boss:

> Examined for a moment apart from any "moral" considerations, the political apparatus of the boss . . . performs these functions (economic regulation, help to the destitute, etc.) with a minimum of inefficiency.

Indeed, such a statement could remain morally neutral only for a moment. Vidich's justification for the community study publication, which exposed the privacy of persons and utilized some data gathered by a cooperative effort—namely, that it was done in name of science—likewise only holds for a moment. Science can provide no statement of meaning or value, in terms of which ends (in this instance publication), may be chosen. My reaction to Vidich's situation is generalized to a rejection of the principle that pursuit of scientific objectivity is a value to which questions of moral responsibility are subordinate.

In this world, there are few, if any, men who can live an ethic of absolute ends. However, men, and only men, are morally responsible for their actions. Neither the corporation, the state, nor any collectivity, including scientific institutions, can substitute for the integrity of the individual. As sociologists are fond of reminding us, these are, after all, mere abstractions, and the tradition of western civilization has been decisive here. The social scientist has to face the fact that he is morally responsible for his scientific activities and that his science and its objectivity is not evidence of sainthood.

This is nothing more than what Max Weber said forty years ago. To affirm that the vocation of a social scientist can be understood a "God's calling" is a mere pretense. At the same time, "value free" social science is, in itself, meaningless. A meaningful social science is one in which we recognize the value implications of our own behavior.

*Howard S. Becker****

In a certain sense, the three questions the editor raises can be regarded as irrelevant to the issue of junior staff-project director relations. In this sense, at least: although the questions are important, what does matter is that there should be a clear agreement on them between staff and director at the time of hiring. Troubles arise precisely when these questions are left up in the air and each party makes certain assumptions, which may not be true, about what their rights and obligations are. If Vidich and Bronfenbrenner had stated beforehand the positions they now take, Vidich might not have wanted the job and Bronfenbrenner might not have hired him. If they had stated their positions and worked out an acceptable compromise, they would each now be bound by it. All issues of what data would be available to what people, who would have publication rights, etc., should, in my view, be made very explicit at the time of hiring. In addition to these "standard" issues, there should be an imaginative and frank exploration of ideas about such questions as the researcher's obligations to those he studies, the balance to be observed between "scientific objectivity" and "avoiding damage to respondents," etc. This exploration should culminate in an explicit agreement as to the line which all project personnel will take with regard to these issues.

*** Dr. Becker is Research Associate on the staff of Community Studies, Inc., a non-profit social science research organization located in Kansas City, Missouri.

Now, of course, some of these questions require other kinds of answers than simple agreement between project director and staff because an entire project might agree on standards and procedures we would argue to be wrong. For instance, I agree that the researcher has some obligation to those he studies. This obligation is contained in the commitments he made to these people at the time of the study. If he promised, explicitly or implicitly, not to identify them, no appeal to "objectivity" can release him from his obligation to honor that promise. He is required to observe it, first, by the obligation he assumed with the promise and, second, by his obligation not to give social science a bad name (which obligation he assumes when he identifies himself to those he studies as a social scientist). If a man wishes to identify the objects of his study, all right; but he must not get his material by taking on obligations which he will not honor. He can state his intentions to the people he studies and can identify himself as a journalist, or a man who wants to write a book, and thus be free to publish whatever he pleases.

All I have said so far, really, is that people ought to be explicit about the bargains they make—with their employees, employers, and research subjects—and then stick by them; and that they must recognize the obligations they implicitly assume toward these people and toward their own colleagues. It seems to me that the Society (possibly in collaboration with other scientific societies in sociology, anthropology, and related fields) could make a great contribution by initiating some formal discussion on the kinds of bargains which social scientists can honorably make with one another and with their objects of study. I do not have in mind anything like writing a "standard contract" for all project directors to make with their employees for, obviously, there is great variety possible, depending on the people involved. But at least we could spell out the points which ought to be covered in such agreements and try to make it standard practice for these things to be discussed openly. I believe that, in the hiring situation, the project director often does not think of these points and the junior staff person is afraid to bring them up.

"FREEDOM AND RESPONSIBILITY IN RESEARCH": COMMENTS*

*Earl H. Bell***

I READ with great interest the editorial, "Freedom and Responsibility in Research: The Springdale Case." The problem relative to responsibility of authors to the community is one which always pushes itself into focus when I start writing a report. Personally, I have come to the conclusion that responsibility to the community does *not* conflict with responsibility to science. As a matter of fact, I have found frequently that attempting to state material cooly and objectively, rather than in terms of personalities and anecdotes, sharpens my understanding of sociological processes.

After writing the first draft of the Haskell County, Kansas Study, I took the manuscript to the community and went over it with my major informants. In many ways, this was the most productive part of the field work. It enabled the informants, for the first time, to understand what I was attempting to accomplish. This broader understanding brought to mind many things which they had not told me, largely because I did not have the knowledge of the culture and social system to formulate some significant questions. They also pointed out numerous errors of both fact and interpretation and thus saved me personal embarrassment and scientific error.

Douglas Haring also involved key informants in the review and criticism of draft copies of articles growing out of his field work in the Ryukyu Islands. He reports experiences similar to mine.

Ralph Linton used to say that we never would know the great errors in ethnological studies because non-literate people were not able to "talk back."

In summary, it seems evident to me that conscientiously fulfilling our responsibility to the community need not weaken

* Reprinted by permission of the Society for Applied Anthropology from *Human Organization*, Vol. 18, No. 2 (Summer 1959), pp. 49-52.
** Dr. Bell is in the Department of Sociology and Anthropology at Syracuse University.

our scientific integrity. Indeed, it may improve the scientific quality of our final product.

*Urie Bronfenbrenner****

In their comments on your editorial on "Freedom and Responsibility in Research," Vidich and Bensman state that a policy regarding "The indentifiability of people and organizations within the Springdale community" was not formulated until after Vidich had left the employ of the project and had submitted a manuscript of his book.

Ironically enough, the Springdale project is probably the only social research endeavor which went to the trouble of developing an explicit code of professional ethics prior to the initiation of major field operations. The following is a reprint of an article from *The American Psychologist*, Volume 7, Number 8 (August 1952), which presents this code in full. Although the code does not refer to publication specifically, the general implications are obvious. The implications were made explicit in frequent statements to residents of the community.

Vidich joined the staff in the fall of 1951, was shown copies of this code, and participated as a staff member in a training program for field workers in which the principles were a major focus of attention. What is even more important, residents of the community were informed on numerous occasions that no material would be published which might identify particular individuals or groups.

The principles had been developed prior to the hiring of a field director (Vidich) precisely for the reasons stressed by Becker in his comments on this same issue:

". . . What does matter is that there should be a clear agreement . . . between staff and director at the time of hiring. Troubles arise precisely when these things are left up in the air, and each party makes assumptions which may not be true about what their obligations and responsibilities are.[1]

*** Dr. Bronfenbrenner is in the Department of Child Development and Family Relationships, Cornell University, Ithaca, New York.

[1] Howard S. Becker, " 'Freedom and Responsibility in Research': A Comment," *Human Organization*, XVII, No. 4 (Winter 1958-1959), 6.

A number of the principles bear directly on the issues raised by Professor Whyte in his editorial. The code is included in its entirety since it may be of interest as one model for the ethical conduct of social researchers.

PRINCIPLES OF PROFESSIONAL ETHICS
CORNELL STUDIES IN SOCIAL GROWTH*

The "Principles of Professional Ethics" were developed by the members of the staff of Cornell Studies in Social Growth, a long-range program of team research sponsored by the Department of Child Development and Family Relationships in the College of Home Economics at Cornell University. Miss Doris Kells, a clinical psychologist, had the major responsibility for collating ideas and preparing drafts for staff discussion. The code represents an attempt to anticipate the ethical problems likely to arise in a community study (The Springdale Project) involving extensive interviewing and observation by specially trained graduate students working under faculty supervision. The present preliminary draft was drawn up before the most intensive phase of field operations had begun. Since that time, experience has underscored two important considerations.

1. A code of professional ethics defeats its purpose if it is treated as a set of rules to be followed without question. It is effective only to the degree that it provokes genuine consideration—and even conflict—in the mind of the individual research worker, who has a value commitment not only to professional ethics but also to scientific investigation. These two sets of values are not always harmoniously matched, so that the researcher must weigh possible scientific gains against the risks involved. Thus it is manifestly impossible to conduct meaningful social research which does not in some degree invade the privacy and security of other human beings. Therefore the responsible scientific investigator cannot avoid the conflictful question of whether the invasion which he proposes to undertake is really justified by the potential gain in scientific knowledge.

* Reprinted, with permission, from *The American Psychologist*, Volume 7, Number 8 (August 1952), 452-455.

2. This leads to a second and even more difficult dilemma, namely, that the social and psychological consequences of a particular research procedure often cannot be foreseen. Thus the only safe way to avoid violating principles of professional ethics is to refrain from doing social research altogether. It follows that the scientist, having tried earnestly to recognize and weigh the social consequences of his scientific activity, must always be ready to accept responsibility for and discontinue in midpassage procedures which prove more damaging than was originally anticipated and considered justifiable.

These two considerations, while they seem in their immediate consequences to be delimiting for scientific progress, may in the long run, through establishing more viable experimenter-subject relationships and sensitizing the investigator to hitherto unrecognized variables in the experimental situation, enrich rather than impoverish our scientific insights and experimental designs.

—Urie Bronfenbrenner

Preamble: A code of ethical procedures for research operations serves a twofold purpose. The first is to safeguard the integrity and welfare of those who serve as subjects for or who may be affected by the research study. The second is to give proper and necessary recognition in the research design to the variables introduced by the presence of the research worker in the field and the consequent awareness of community members that they are under study. We are operating then on a double premise: (1) The integrity and well-being of those studied are to be vouchsafed and respected in recognition of ethical human values. (2) The ethical values implicit in any research operation and their consequent procedural expressions must be made explicit and incorporated into the research design in the interests of sound scientific method, for otherwise they would represent unknown or uncontrolled variables. Only by taking into account the ethical import of research activities can the effects of the research upon those being studied be reckoned.

It will be noted that this document contains not only a section devoted to *General Principles and Ethics in the Field but also a section on Relationships among Research Workers (staff and trainees*). Here again the reason is twofold: (1) To take cognizance of ethical human values in the intragroup research operations. (2) To help insure the carrying out of the research design since the ethical values governing intragroup research relationships will tend to be reflected in the research relationships established with the community and also in the handling of data (e.g., matters of confidentiality).

I. *General Principles*

A. Professional ethics in research activities are a matter of first priority.

1. Progress in learning to establish adequate field relations and to apply ethical principles has first priority in evaluating trainees' continuation in the program and staff members' operations in the field.

2. Responsibility for the welfare of persons under study is a continuing one for all research workers (trainees and staff).

B. The social scientist views people as individuals, not as subjects to be exploited. Specifically, he takes every precaution to preserve the security and privacy of the individuals and groups under study.

1. Each technique developed for field use is carefully considered in terms of its potential for provoking anxiety or invading privacy. The research intent is to reduce maximally such threats.

2. The research worker in the practice of his profession shows regard for the social codes and moral expectations of the persons with whom he works.

3. To the maximum degree possible, the free consent of persons[2] involved is secured at each stage of research activity.

a. In requesting verbal consent, persons are given as direct and explicit an account as possible of research objectives and purposes. In requesting consent the investigator does not attempt

[2] Throughout this document "persons" refers to all those who serve as research subjects; e.g., residents of the community under study, persons being tested, college students used in pre-field trials, etc.

to evoke or capitalize on feelings of obligation or desires to please.

b. Consent can be secured only in relation to those experiences the consequences of which the person is in a position to appreciate; that is, consent to an unknown experience is not regarded as true consent.

4. The basic criterion for the investigator's interest in and inclusion of all data is that they have relevance to the problem under investigation.

a. Any material given to the investigator in his role as research worker is suitable for inclusion in research records. Material offered or secured in any other context is not suitable for the records. Examples of material not suitable are: (1) material given to the investigator on the assumption that he is a personal friend or counsellor, rather than a research worker; (2) material given with the specific request that it be kept off-the-record (i.e., not recorded or communicated to anyone else).

5. All data from the field are regarded as confidential and every precaution is taken to insure the anonymity of individuals and groups save as such knowledge is essential to the work of persons specifically charged with responsibility for those data.

a. Information secured about persons involved in research is used primarily for research purposes. With proper regard for anonymity it may also be used for training and instructional purposes. Information that can be *identified with* community, specific groups, or individuals is used *only* for research purposes including training. With proper regard for anonymity it may also be used for other instruction (e.g., university classes).

b. Staff and trainees have access only to those files containing data essential to their work.

c. Permission to use field data for special research problems (e.g., theses, term reports, etc.) is granted by the staff as a whole. Permission is contingent upon the worker's ability to comply with the principles of professional ethics here outlined. In each instance the worker shall be instructed in his responsibility for maintaining the confidentiality of the material with which he works.

d. Trainees are evaluated and screened with regard to their ability to be entrusted with confidential data before identifiable group or individual material is used for training purposes and before trainees go into the field.

e. Professional colleagues shall not be told the name of the community(ies) under study save as it is essential for their own work, and regard for anonymity shall be maintained in conveying information regarding research procedures, data, hypotheses, etc.

f. Research workers have the responsibility for informing and indoctrinating family members in the professional ethics of field operations.

(1) Family discussion of individuals or groups under study is to be kept at a minimum.

(2) Family participation in community affairs is to be carefully planned to enhance rather than inhibit research relationships.

g. Personal information about research subjects, whether or not these subjects are identified by name, is not an appropriate topic for discussion at social affairs, informal gatherings, conversations with friends, etc. Discussion of the purpose of the study, the research design, or any generalized findings do not, of course, come under this heading.

h. Field activities and data are not suitable topics for entertaining staff members, colleagues, visitors, students, etc. In like manner, persons or community are not exhibited as a curiosity to visitors, friends, etc.

II. *Ethics in the Field*

A. Role and responsibilities of field worker are clearly specified before the field worker goes into the field (campus, community, etc.) and changes in the conception of the job or of field worker's responsibilities are a matter for staff decision.

1. Whenever the field worker finds that circumstances require his adopting a role not covered by previous specifications,

it is his responsibility to bring this to the attention of the appropriate supervisor or staff group for discussion and decision.

B. In this project, the research design limits the role of the research worker to that of scientific investigator. He is not an agent for change, a therapist, or specialist who can serve as a resource person. There are two reasons for this policy: (1) To reduce the number of complicating variables by designing the research procedures to have minimal effect on the lives of the community members. (2) To keep at a minimum any activities by staff members which may evoke feelings of conflict or anxiety.

C. It is the field worker's responsibility to keep his field role in the dimension of scientific investigator.

D. Every reasonable effort shall be made to convey to the persons under study, the nature and limits of the job of the field worker.

III. *Relationships Among Research Workers (Staff and Trainees)*

A. No research member is asked to undertake any activity which is not in harmony with his personal ethics and beliefs.

B. Any reflections upon the personality or actions of a field worker by a person involved in the research studies are considered to be a private matter. Wherever this is of vital concern to the research project, the matter should be discussed with a staff member. If the incident is to be made a part of the field report, it should be done only after discussion and agreement with the field worker concerned.

C. The responsibility of staff member to trainee is that of training him in research activities.[3] The training program in all its aspects is to be job-oriented.

[3] The functions of academic advisor, teacher of a subject-matter field, or personal counsellor, if they occur between staff member and trainee, are in the context of the staff member's role as member of the faculty or as personal acquaintance.

D. It is staff responsibility to keep clear explicitly (in training) and implicitly (in office relations, etc.) the nature of the job and responsibilities of the staff and the nature of the job and responsibilities of the trainee.

E. It is staff responsibility to keep well-structured in the minds of the trainees their status-in-training and their responsibilities in the research project.

1. It is staff responsibility to convey to the trainee at the beginning of and throughout his training, the opportunities, limits, and trial nature of his participation in the research program.

2. It is staff responsibility to conduct planned evaluation conferences with trainees sufficiently frequently to provide them with a realistic awareness of their progress and status-in-training.

F. The basis for evaluation-selection of trainees for assistantships or other jobs on the project is their performance on the job.

G. In the event of evaluation-selection of trainee for assistantship or other job for which he has not had a previous trial, personal factors are considered in so far as they are pertinent to the job to be filled and have been evidenced in the trainee's performance during training.

1. Pertinent information known to a staff member by virtue of his activities and relationships outside of the research staff is not a proper subject for discussion with other staff members, but may properly influence the individual decision of that staff member in regard to the trainee's job qualifications.

H. It is staff responsibility to convey to the trainee, by precept and example, the professional ethics implicit and explicit in this document.

1. The area of professional ethics shall be included as an integral part of the training program.

"FREEDOM AND RESPONSIBILITY IN RESEARCH": A REJOINDER*

Arthur J. Vidich

IN HIS REPLY to the joint comment of Dr. Bensman and myself on "Freedom and Responsibility in Research," Professor Bronfenbrenner quotes me as saying that a policy regarding "the identifiability of persons and organizations within the Springdale community" was not formulated until after I had left the project and had submitted the manuscript of the book, *Small Town in Mass Society*. It is clear in the context of our reply that we made no such statement and that the project policy we quoted was one which was not in the code but a later one made with specific reference to our manuscript.

No mention of the code of ethics was made in our reply to Dr. Whyte's editorial because the project itself had never raised the issue of the code in the course of our three and one-half year correspondence concerning our independent writing and the publication of *Small Town in Mass Society*. Since the code has been introduced into the discussion, I would like to say a few words about its status in the project in the hope that the Springdale case may serve as a useful example for others.

At the time I was being interviewed for the job as resident field director and participant observer in Springdale, I was shown a draft version of the published code of ethics. It was my understanding that the code represented a statement of intent and I accepted it as such, agreeing in principle with what it contained. The code never had the status of a legal directive and so no one was ever asked to take oaths or sign statements. This was because the code did not purport to be a prescriptive guide for all future action. There were a number of reasons why this was the case:

1. The code had been built up on the basis of the project's preceding three or four years of research experience and was,

* Reprinted by permission of the Society for Applied Anthropology from *Human Organization*, Vol. 19, No. 1 (Spring 1960), pp. 3-4.

insofar as possible, an attempt to avoid certain types of interpersonal problems which had arisen in the past.

2. At the time the code was completed, the project entered
an entirely new phase of research operations which had not been
considered in the formulation of the code because they had not
been experienced by those who had formulated it.

3. Prior to setting up the field station which coincided with
my employment, the project had not had a participant observer
and so, understandably, there was no provision in the code for
this research role.

In fact, the very act of hiring a participant observer was a
violation of the code since it was his (my) job to get information on the life of the community in a way that would appear
natural and not part of the formal research. The community
was not told that my observations were research observations,
but the project regarded my observations as project data. The
carrying out of this disguise against the community as a matter
of policy was never accounted for in the code, nor was the code
revised to account for it.

The fact is that, once the code has been formulated, it was
never changed in spite of the fact that any number of unac-
countable issues arose which, in addition to the above example,
were inconsistent with the code. In practice we tended to act in
terms of what seemed right in specific situations as they were
encountered and did not refer back to the code as a guide. This
was done in good faith and is quite understandable since it is
very difficult to formulate codes which will anticipate situations which have not yet occurred.

When it came to the writing of our book, I continued to
follow the policy of trying to find solutions to new types of
problems as they arose. To this end, the project director, Professor Bronfenbrenner, and I carried on a three-year correspondence in which we considered the problems connected with
use of data, mention of public roles in the community, and
publication of the book. Throughout this correspondence no
mention was ever made of the code of ethics. Rather, as during
the years of the field study, the project staff formulated policies
to meet specific situations. It was just such an "uncodified"

policy which Bensman and I previously quoted and it was not, as Bronfenbrenner implies, one that was cited in the "code." According to the project's code of ethics as published in *Human Organization* (Volume 18, Number 2, Summer, 1959):

> . . . information that can be identified with community, specific groups, or individuals is used only for research purposes including training.

In no case did I use any information for purposes other than research. In addition, according to the code, every precaution was to be taken

> . . . to insure the anonymity of individuals and groups save as such knowledge is essential to the work of persons specifically charged with the responsibility for those data.

From the perspective of a social scientist engaged in a community study, I had understood this to mean that pseudonyms would be used whenever it was necessary to make reference to specific places or roles. In following this policy, I took my cue from the sociological tradition of community studies as exemplified by the Lynds' study of *Middletown*, Whyte's study of *Street Corner Society* and Hunter's study of *Community Power Structure*, etc. From my perspective, this approach seemed consistent with the idea of protecting the community while still making it possible to accomplish the scientific objective of doing the analysis and reporting the data. Actually, while this policy is consistent with the code, it was inconsistent with another policy which emerged as the research progressed. It is worth mentioning this latter policy because it seems to be the cause of many problems that have arisen since.

As the research progressed, the policy of anonymity came to be equated with "doing an entirely statistical report." It appeared to me that this happened in a curiously inadvertent way: on various occasions when the project was asked to explain its purposes in greater detail or when community suspicions had been aroused, the standard practice of some staff members was to assure members of the community that there was nothing to worry about because all individuals and specific events would get lost in the statistical analysis. At the time, these assurances were very successful in allaying the fears and anxieties of key members of the community, and so some members of the project, particularly those who were less trained and more prone to panic, began to give such assurance whenever resistances developed. I personally never gave such assurances, preferring not to get any information at all than to get it under this condition. Unfortunately, some key members of the community were left with the impression that the entire report would be statistical. As this impression became more prevalent in the community, it also became more prevalent in the research project until it was understood by many persons in both groups that no other than a statistical presentation of the data was to be made.

The equating of anonymity with a statistical report was unnecessary, and not called for in the code of ethics. Like other policies this one, too, emerged as a response to the exigencies of the field situation. It was never discussed at a policy conference during the three years I was with the project, and the research implications of concealment of identities through the use of statistical aggregates was never brought up for discussion.

I personally did not accept the policy of preparing only a statistical report and, for that matter, the expectation of the project was that I, as the participant observer, would be responsible for doing the historical and social structural analysis of the town. The policy of the statistical report was one which, in practice, was always accepted more by the town than the project. Among the project members it tended to receive more acceptance while in the town than in the central offices. To me, as the staff member who had offices in both places, this contradiction became readily apparent, but I, like everyone else, did not raise the issue and in this I was culpable in perpetrating a fraud on the town.

When the field work was going on, no one really faced the problem of what form the report would take. This was because it was not known in advance what the data would be nor how it might be presented. Thus it happened that there was never any immediate pressure to come to workable terms with what anonymity meant and, in writing the book, I followed the sociological tradition of using pseudonyms.

Only a year and a half later—after I had left the project, and after the first draft of the book had been written—was any other policy formulated. This was a policy which was not mentioned or even considered in the code—a policy of

. . . disguising individuals and groups through deliberate alteration and recombination of important identifying characteristics.

Bensman and I felt at the time, and still feel, that alteration and recombination—"fixing" of our data—to please a few people was not consistent with scientific procedure, and would becloud precisely those elements in our analysis that were theoretically most relevant to the understanding of the underlying theoretical issues in the study.

In these terms I can only reiterate our previously stated general conclusion that the obligation to do scientific justice to one's findings quite often conflicts with the social obligation to please all objects of research. One can accept a "scientific ethic" or a "social-contractual ethic." It is not easy to accept both.

THE SPRINGDALE CASE: ACADEMIC BUREAU-CRATS AND SENSITIVE TOWNSPEOPLE*

Arthur J. Vidich and Joseph Bensman

SINCE THE ADVENT of large-scale research and large-scale financing of research, the community study has come to be thought of as a "project" for which it is necessary to have a systematic statement of problem, a staff, legitimate sponsorship, and a budget. One of the first steps in setting up project research is making application for the research grant, a procedure requiring a formal statement of the problem, an explicit theory, and a specific methodology that will be used as the operational procedure in conducting the research. The dignity of scientific enterprise is attached to the whole of the project structure.

In this essay we report on the consequences of carrying out a community research study that ignored all the procedures of the scientific project research. The community study which we reported in *Small Town in Mass Society*[1] was unintentionally unplanned, had no budget, no a priori theory, no staff, no research stages or phases, and was not conceived as a study or a project until it was almost over.

Although the research and writing that resulted in *Small Town in Mass Society* were informal and unprogrammed, the work was actually carried out within the formal structure of an organized and programmed research project known as Cornell Studies in Social Growth, sponsored by the Department of Child Development and Family Relationships of the College of Home Economics, School of Agriculture, Cornell University. We must note that our study could not have been done except as a by-product of this formalized and organized research structure.

Our study of Springdale was related to the Cornell Studies in Social Growth project by the accident that one of the collaborators was hired as a resident field director to observe and

* Reprinted, with permission, Arthur J. Vidich, Joseph Bensman, and Maurice Stein, eds., *Reflections on Community Studies* (New York: John Wiley and Sons, 1964), pp. 313-49.
[1] Princeton University Press, 1958.

participate in the life of the community, to maintain liaison between the community and the research organization, to administer and supervise mass surveys, and to provide background social structural data for the project's formal study of modes and qualities of community participation and leadership.[2]

The responsibility of the field director was to collect the data necessary to the formal study with a minimum of embarrassment to all parties concerned while not compromising the quality of the data. For this reason all research activities in the town were highly calculated and restricted to those areas of investigation and community personnel that had a direct bearing on the project design at the time each specific field operation was being carried out.

Administratively, the field director was a temporary employee of an annually renewable, long-range research project housed in and "supported" by Cornell University. The job requirement was that the field director live in Ithaca for several months until he could become familiar with the project and that he then move with his family to Springdale where he would live as if he were a resident of the town working for the university which was doing a study of the town. This was thought to be a reasonable approach to the town because other Cornell employees, including a professor, a graduate assistant and extension agents, already lived in the town, thus giving the role some legitimation. These administrative and residence arrangements had a number of implications pertinent to nonprogrammed research.

Simply by being present in the town and by being interested in the day-to-day nonresearch life of the community residents, a great deal of material which was not encompassed by the Cornell Studies in Social Growth study design inevitably came to the attention of the field director. In some instances highly personal information was acquired from personal friends in the town, and this information remains as part of the personal experience of the field director. In other instances the field director was advised or directed to join organizations and activi-

[2] This study has been published as "Leadership and Participation in a Changing Rural Community," in *The Journal of Social Issues*, Vol. XVI, No. 4, 1960.

ties for purposes that were not directly related to the project design. For example, it was a joint staff decision that the field director should go to church, but be given a personal option on teaching Sunday school. Although the project was almost exclusively interested in the participational structure of church life, the field director, by participating in the church himself, became familiar with at least some dimensions of all aspects of church life.

Theoretically the project research design allowed for all levels of information, but only on the grounds that anything and everything that could be known might be relevant. This was why the field director was put into the town. Practically, however, there was a project tendency to regard as data only the information that found its way into a formal protocol or an interview schedule, so that even within the framework of the official research, the material that came to the attention of the field director exceeded the limits of the formal study. By being in the town it was difficult not to see more than could be contained in field reports. The general, informal experience resulting from continuous exposure left an image of the town that was never quite summed up in staff and field reports. As a result of these differences in the quality of information possessed by different researchers on the staff, different images of the town were held by researchers who occupied different positions in the research organization.

These differences in imagery were further complicated by the difference in intellectual starting points of the different members of the research staff. Data became relevant to the field director simply because he had previous theoretical interests and field experiences in "primitive" and other rural communities which were independent of the research design. For example, the field director's earlier field experiences left him with the impression that Springdale was as much a "colony" as Palau in the Western Carolines and as deeply penetrated by central bureaucracy as Kropa in Yugoslavia. So compelling were the similarities among Palau, Kropa, and Springdale that all points at which Springdale had a relationship to the rest of American society began to stand out as especially salient data. This orientation resulted in semisystematic observation and collection of data on a number of peripheral issues which seemingly had no relationship to any formal design or, least of all, to the project design. At this stage of the informal research, the continuity and structure of these observations was given by the personal life history of the field director.

Both of the authors had been interested in some of these peripheral issues from previous collaborative work, and out of this mutual interest and a continuing personal friendship came discussions of some of the implications. of these early observations. The project had no interest in the ideas that evolved from these observations because it was from the project's point of view that the ideas were peripheral. As a result we explored the ideas as a personal project which we conducted informally in the form of conversation.

After we had explored what seemed to us to be all the implications of Springdale's relationship to the external world, we discovered that certain dimensions of the class and status structure of the town could not be explained by external factors. The social and economic position of prosperous farmers, for example, could only be explained partially by subsidy programs and price supports; part of their status in the community rested on the productive mystique of agriculture for other members of the community. This and other leads forced us to look into the internal dynamics of the community in a way which otherwise would not have been accessible to our consciousness. It was at this point that the field director secured permission from the project director to conduct twenty special interviews focusing on the social structure of the town. These interviews (conducted with Jones, Flint, Lee, Peabody, several merchants, ethnic leaders, religious leaders, and industrial workers) were specifically aimed at discovering some of the internal dimensions of community life as seen by the individuals interviewed.

Though it is apparent from the selection of informants that the interviews focused on special themes, at that time there was no notion of doing a study, a project, or a book independent of the formal project.

As the informal work progressed, a number of ad hoc memoranda, outlines, and analyses of specific problem areas were submitted to the project as relevant theoretical themes implicit in the situation of the small town. We had thought of these analyses as bearing a direct importance for the theoretical foundations of the project's research design and as offering a basis for its conceptual reformulation in a way that would account for the total situation of the small town in the modern world. The project was interested in these formulations but did not feel they were of crucial importance to its central study design. The authors continued to work on these problems simply because they were fascinating.

After two more years of continued informal work, a series of other areas had been explored on an ad hoc basis, and it was only then that it occurred to the authors that they were actually doing a community study which not only had a unified theoretical focus, but which could actually become the object of an extended and integrated monograph. At this point, which coincided with the field director's termination of his employment with the project, we asked for and received permission to do an independent study with the understanding that our work be submitted to the directors of the project as it was being written and revised so that it would be available to the project staff while its members were making their analysis of the formal survey data.

PROGRAMMED VERSUS UNPROGRAMMED PROJECT
ADMINISTRATION[3]

It was our experience that by and large the logic of a problem has its own internal dynamic which means that once one has embarked on the pursuit of the problem and is willing to follow

---

[3] We have discussed two other dimensions of unprogrammed research, namely, undesigned field work and heuristic theorizing in essays otherwise available. See the authors' "The Validity of Field Data," *Human Organization*, 13, No. 1, pp. 20-27 (reprinted in *Human Organization Research*, Homewood, Ill.: Dorsey Press, 1960), and "Social Theory in Field Research," *The American Journal of Sociology*, 65, No. 6 (May 1960), pp. 577-584 (reprinted in M. Stein and A. Vidich, *Sociology on Trial*, Englewood Cliffs, N.J.: Prentice-Hall, Spectrum Series, 1963).

its logic, he must *administer* in terms of where the problem leads and not in terms of prearranged schedules.

It is in the structure of project organization that termination p ints must be set, deadlines must be met, production schedules must be set, annual reports must be made, production functions must be distributed among staff members, and so on. Bureaucratic structure and staff organization in and of themselves impose on project research a flow whose direction is not easily redirected. Staff and organization become significant functions of research in programmed studies.

In the Springdale research we observed a variety of tensions arising from the conflict between research functions and bureaucratic functions.

1. Staff distribution of field functions leaves each staff functionary with a uniquely specialized view of individual informants and of the dimensions of community life. There are as many images of the community in circulation as there are staff functions in the research organization. This means that staff conferees are continuously involved in discussions whose major latent function is to reduce the community to a single bureaucratically acceptable image, so that for the project research purposes a major objective of the committee process is to reach a mutually acceptable fictional definition of the community which all staff members can work with while playing their project roles.

2. Since each interview is a source of standardized as well as subliminal information, all standardization of observational or interview procedures necessitated by quality control requirements arising from the uneven distribution of skills and interests among the staff has the effect of destroying all but formal information.

3. Staff execution of research, which must necessarily be guided in part by time and logistic factors relevant to other organizational and personal responsibilities (teaching, committee meetings, staff discussions, travel, vacations, family, etc.), prohibits continuity of contact between informant and researcher: the informant meets a variety of researchers and the researcher infrequently meets any informant in depth. Under this system the simple building up of personality profiles and sketches in-

volves vast amounts of filing and collecting of information by clerks whose final product is always less than the cumulative impression that is acquired by the continuous observation by one person of another over a period of time.

4. Once the research machinery is committed to securing a certain type or level of information, it is difficult for the research organization to accept, absorb or acknowledge data which might threaten to undermine that commitment. In accepting a "fixed" statement of the project problem, it is both psychologically and bureaucratically risky to move in directions that might deviate from the last agreed-upon plan.

In the Springdale research the project was committed to finding solutions to what makes for constructive, positive, community functioning. The project thus directed itself to a study of creative activity and to the locating of leadership and participator types of local citizens who could exemplify constructive activity.

Because it was assumed that there was creative activity in the community, it was psychologically difficult for those committed to the research design to acknowledge the absence of creativity where it might have only appeared to be at first glance. Thus the case of the telephone company's expansion program which was to have been a major illustration of community creativity was simply abandoned as an illustration when it was found that the modernization program had nothing to do with the local town except insofar as the local town was a front for the state telephone company.[4]

In the same manner the research organization made a major commitment to the local community club as a creative community activity. When it was found that the community club involved only a few hundred persons and that nine-tenths of the community was excluded from participation in spite of the club slogan that all were invited even if they did not pay dues, the research project continued its commitment for research reasons. Even after the practical limitations of the club's role in com-

[4] See Vidich and Bensman, "Social Theory in Field Research," *op. cit.*, pp. 578-579 for a discussion of the telephone company.

munity affairs were acknowledged by all research personnel, it was not possible to ignore the club because ignoring it would have been a violation of the previous commitments to the club. The community club represented a handful of activists and a shifting number of aspirants. It excluded all shack people, the marginal middle classes, and major portions of all other classes including the middle class. In short, the community club represented the minor segment of the middle class that was most attuned to social affairs and the outside world. The inspiration for the founding of the club was initially provided by community organizers and extension specialists hired by the same institution and the same college as those who were studying it as a creative community activity. Acknowledgment of these observations would have constituted a major embarrassment for the project since it would have meant in effect a reformulation of the study design. Instead a number of defenses were invoked which allowed prior commitments to be upheld. The defenses were:

1. A blindness to the existence of all community groups except the middle class, and an equating of creative activity with middle-class activities.

2. Failure to see any relationship between social club activity leaders and the community's economic and political structure.

3. The necessity to see the town only in terms of itself and without reference to anything located outside it, especially Cornell University and the research project itself.

4. The unwillingness to acknowledge all critical groups in the town and especially the refusal to listen to other outside experts who were the project's counterparts in the town. Thus the 4-H agent became the enemy of the project because he was a concrete counterimage of what the project "expected" of the town even though the original idea for a community club had come from the 4-H agent.

The foregoing illustrations indicate a fundamental tension between research as a bureaucratic enterprise and the perceptual freedom that nonbureaucratic research usually involves. As a bureaucratic employee the functionary has the responsibility of following those problems which are bureaucratically defined by authority as the purpose of the project. The project directors are obliged to stay with the problem for which they received money. The problems must be approached with the previously specified methods, and, moreover, official interpretations of what constitutes a finding come to pervade the entire project structure. Individual discoveries may be expressed so long as this is done with due caution and within the previously agreed-upon framework.

The research perspective of an individual who is independently pursuing knowledge is quite different from the one that prevails in bureaucratic settings. The perspective of independent investigation is based on whatever concatenation of theoretical background and experience the researcher brings to the field, and on his discovery of problems while he is in the midst of the field experience. He devises means to follow those insights that appear to him to be appropriate to the insight and the data, and he tends to push his explorations to their logical conclusion (whether they result in failure or success) to the point where he is satisfied he has made all efforts possible in examining the problems that stimulated inquiry.

The existence of external and formalized bureaucratic constraints may:

1. Deflect the worker from seeing the problem except perhaps as a minor deviation from a central plan since the preordained design acts to funnel his vision. Thus, there is always the possibility of a number of leads that were not followed up which then constitute the fund of anecdotes about the project.

2. Force the investigator to systematically avoid pursuit of such insights even if they are central to his own theoretical and perceptual apparatus. To accomplish this form of avoidance involves complicated intellectual self-manipulation.

3. May make it necessary to find ways of reporting findings which are not relevant to the agreed-upon research design even though such findings are actually acknowledged by the investigators to each other.

4. Force the investigator to find devices such as aesopian language to sneak in the point in the report.

The result of all of this for the bureaucratic researcher is that he must build up a complicated apparatus to justify the neglect of the perceived issue when he felt that bureaucratic loyalty was more important than the issues that he himself once felt were more important. The pressures "to play ball" are enormous, and ways are found.

Most of the issues that were developed in *Small Town in Mass Society* were issues that did not fit the formal design of the project study. The issues we saw were:

1. The relationship of the community to the society at large.

2. The analysis of social and economic class as central to the community.

3. The analysis of power and politics.

4. The inclusion of economic data as relevant to the design.

5. Reporting on the actions of individual institutional leaders in the exercise of their institutional roles.

6. Reporting on "negative" or not affirmative aspects of community life[5] as necessary to an examination of the social and psychological basis of community participation.

Our pursuit of these issues as issues that were personally interesting to us could be carried out without conflict or tension within project administration so long as our work was not made public. As we shall later note more fully, however, it is difficult for programmed project administration to tolerate public discussion or publication of non-programmed issues. Under ordinary circumstances, the structure of project administration with its hierarchy of control, committee meetings, and other forms of maintaining discipline prevents the individual from developing an independent perspective. This has a number of

---

[5] It was the project that introduced the idea of positive as opposed to negative ways of evaluating the facts: "We agree with most of what these authors (i.e., Vidich and Bensman) say about the facts of community life in Springdale, but our evaluation of these facts tends to be positive rather than negative." See "Leadership and Participation in a Changing Rural Community," *op. cit.*, p. 53, footnote.

consequences for both the intellectual development of the individual and for the project bureaucracy.

In the extreme case the inability on the part of an individual to find a way of developing his theoretical perspective or of pursuing what he regards as valid insights results in double-think wherein language publicly sanctioned by research officials defines "research realities" as opposed to "normal" realities. In other instances it results in forms of research and nonresearch language, ironic detachment from one's own work, or compliant work as a "team man" who moves intellectually in phase with project policy changes. The net result of all this for the individual is various forms of conscious or subliminal self-hatred, so that all of the categories that are found in Merton's description of bureaucratic self-hatred are found in bureaucratic research.

The failure of the foregoing techniques to function adequately leads to personnel crises, demoralization of staff, bickering, feuds, and stalemates. The measure of the failure of these techniques is the rate of labor turnover of project personnel. The unsuccessful project never quite succeeds in repressing intellectual individuality and thus is fraught with tensions and impasses, whereas the successful project succeeds in achieving organizational stability, regulated production schedules, and so on at the cost of repressing the individual idea.[6]

In the face of these dynamics, a large part of project research becomes the reconciling of differences of viewpoints and insights and arriving at formulas of consensus which are quite similar to those described for village politics in Springdale. This is to say issues disappear, problems lose their sharpness, and talking and memo writing define the dominant ethos of the research enterprise until no individual insight embarrasses the smooth functioning of the organization of the project. In terms of organizational operations, this means:

1. When there are differences of opinion between research-

[6] The problem of repressing original ideas can be solved in advance by personnel recruitment policies: when only like-minded social scientists are hired, agreement is assured. It is for this reason that recruitment policies in bureaucratic research may be a decisive factor in determining the success or failure of the project.

ers, especially between subordinates and supervisors or project heads, endless meetings ensue.

2. If the differences are fundamental and irreconcilable, there may be a suppression and postponement of an accumulating pile of differences.

3. Self-imposed conscious and begrudging suppression of differences of opinion and hostility, especially on the part of subordinates, and the development of factions and private gossip groups build up around stylized forms of suppression.

4. The development of diplomatic styles of language and other linguistic formulas which allow different views to be expressed in the same sentences, paragraphs, or chapters.

5. The building up of long, drawn-out feuds, political factionalization of the research organization, all of which is usually covered over on public occasions and always concealed from the view of the financial backers of the research.

6. The factions and feuds embellish the research with various forms of bureaucratic chicanery.

7. There is a continuous possibility for the occurrence of shifts in the direction of the project problem and in the research design as different individuals become predominant in the organizational structure over the course of the history of the project. As a result a project can have dozens of false starts, none of which is pursued because no one individual or faction ever achieves a clear victory.

8. There is always the chance for publication of multiple reports, a solution which in our opinion is the best method of resolving differences.

Retrospectively, it appears to us that only two things can be concluded from all this. First, it seems that the best bureaucratic research is achieved when one man is able to set himself up as an absolute dictator, almost no matter on what basis he gains his power. Then at least *his* point of view comes through in the work, thus giving the project a focus, even if this denies "democracy" to the other participating academicians. Second, it appears that the primary qualities necessary to doing bureaucratic research lie in the fields of statecraft, diplomacy, and group work techniques by which consensus can be engineered. From the perspective of the individual researcher, all group and bureaucratic research is a form of torture.

PROJECT FOREIGN AFFAIRS AND THEIR EFFECT ON RESEARCH

Just as a community exists in a social matrix larger than itself, so any formal research project operates in an institutional context that encompasses more than itself. This fact may or may not determine the direction of research. The individual researcher who lacks plan and design and who has no staff or budget can ignore almost all problems of "foreign affairs" if he has the time and resources to pursue his demons as and where they may emerge. Programmed research finds itself in a much more complicated situation. The programmed project always faces outside publics and, moreover, must come to terms with them, make agreements with them, and reach an understanding on problems and issues defined by the publics. In university-connected community research these publics include the sponsor, the community, and the university. Each of these publics is a reference group, and each poses his own problems for scientific research investigation.

The Sponsor as Reference Group. The first problem facing the prospective researcher is to find a project for which a potential sponsor exists. Since it is only in extreme cases that a researcher will completely phrase his problem to meet sponsorship requirements, the usual tactic is to find a sponsor who will be interested and willing to provide funds to support a study that is still in some way related to the researcher's interests.[7]

[7] The problem is more complicated than this. We have seen researchers whose interests have changed in phase with changes in sources of available funds. When a large number of individuals in a scientific community do this, we witness the phenomenon of research fads, for example, the mental health and organizational research which are popular at the present time. Available pools of money determine the dominant emphasis of the over-all research enterprise. More recently the directors of the philanthropic foundations and bureaus have come to conceive of themselves as possessing an explicit managerial function in choosing the direction of research investments. That is, a decision is made to invest in a given area, problem, or place, and proposals that fit the predefini-

The sponsoring agency, as is clearly understandable to every-one, wishes to support research within an area or within a range of problems related to its fundamental purposes as specified in its brochure. For a sponsoring agency to do otherwise is a breach of trust and is sometimes illegal as well. The researcher, then, begins his research by conducting research on sponsoring agencies which are likely to support his research.

Although basic research on sponsors has itself progressed to the point where directories of sponsors and synopses of their interests are published, the existence of these research tools does not solve the researchers' problems. Sponsors are suspicious of claimants, first, because there are so many of them and, second, because some of them from the sponsor's viewpoint are quacks whose ideas are inadmissible. This then leads to the necessity for finding "respectable, clean-cut, stable, responsible" direc-tors and negotiators to meet with their foundation counter-parts. The requirements for creative research are only acciden-tally related to the talent for negotiating with foundations. If and when the smooth, pleasant negotiator gains actual author-ity in the project (on the basis of his access to funds), any value of the research findings is also likely to be accidental.

In spite of all basic research on sponsors, the project re-searcher is still faced with:

1. Making contacts with the potential sponsor either through third parties or by hiring personnel because they bring the con-tact with them, or by directly hiring the sponsor's personnel. The choice of technique depends on stage of research, level of organization, and quality of connections.

2. Defining the project in terms of language, theories, and hypotheses that will be congenial to sponsor views as indicated in their statement of purposes and as expressed by specific ad-ministrative agents of the sponsor. A higher level of complexity is introduced where multiple sponsors are involved, for this means finding linguistic and theoretical compromises that will

---

tion are supported. It is perfectly understandable that fund dispensers should try in this way to make their work interesting and creative.

breach the differences between sponsors and that will yet appear to leave no contradictions in the statement of the problem. A field of expertise has grown up around this function.[8]

It is part of the rhythm of the total research cycle that the sponsor recedes as an important reference group after the grant has been received and is only again reasserted as a significant other when findings are to be discovered, written, and reported. No matter what happens between the time the money is given and the research operations are completed, at the time of writing and reporting the analyst must address himself to the original problem statement because the sponsor is still thinking in its terms in spite of the passage of time and the new experiences gained by the researcher from carrying out the research.[9] As a result the researcher is obliged to come up with findings that in some way relate to the original problem statements as worked out with and for the sponsor. Maintaining trust with the sponsor is as important for this kind of research as the research itself because, apart from other considerations, specific projects are always part of a larger career pattern which requires future sponsors.

Faithfulness to the original statement of the problem is only one of a number of problems that arise in the later stages of project research.

1. A report discharging, at least at formal levels, the obligation to the grant must be delivered. The pressures at this point make the successful project director a virtuoso at putting something between two covers.

2. The production of the report may not be as simple as it

[8] In a fund-raising experience recently encountered by one of the authors, a team of two incompatible applicants agreed not to disagree with each other until funds could be secured from two incompatible agencies, each of which had "other" reasons for desiring to give research funds. Almost all of the negotiators to this transaction were experts who understood the fundamental contradictions between the pariticipants but who also realized that it was necessary not to mention these differences during the monetary negotiations.

[9] Researchers who attempt to keep sponsors informed of every change in direction of the research find themselves involved in endless negotiations with sponsors and with little time for research.

appears to an outsider or even to the sponsor. Since the project's inception there have been many changes in project personnel: people who carried out crucial research operations have moved to other positions and universities, and important project officers who may have had little contact with the actual research data remain. As if this were not enough, all of the data may not bear a relationship to the stated problem since some of them at least will reflect "hunches" that were followed but did not produce the desired results—during the heat of data collection the formally stated problem sometimes loses its saliency. As a consequence of factors such as these, there is the institution known as the "rescue operation" wherein no one on the staff is willing or able to write a report, so the last man hired is hired specifically to piece together all the bits, to create the appearance of a unified structure to the data, and to write all this in a form that can be bound, even if it is only a mimeographed, hectographed, or subsidized publication.

The salvage expert may be a junior project member who happens to have literary skills; he may be a specialized expert who moves from project to project because he can write, but lacks the organizational stature and competence to get his own grants; or he may be primarily a writer who has little specialized competence in the research field. The rescue operation has become so standardized in project research that (1) salvage skills are a recognized professional ability, (2) men may build reputations only on the fact that they have never failed to submit a report, and (3) at times the mimeographed and the heavily subsidized publication has more prestige in some circles than real books because it is understood that the hectographed report represents a large cash investment which a book may not.

3. In final form the report must eliminate all embarrassing findings and, more specifically, all mention of specific people and instances that might otherwise be necessary to illustrate a point. The definition of what is an embarrassing finding of course is always related to the ideology of the audience to which the report is directed, but at a minimum the report is written with at least one eye to the sponsor, and at a maximum an attempt is made to create a unified and pleasant image of the

whole project. The major value conveyed by the report is academic and research respectability. Any "rocking the boat" becomes a major crime against the sponsor, his values, and those whose careers are identified with the project.

The Community as a Reference Group. From the inception of the first contacts with the community, the town wants to know what the research is about and how the town will be affected by it. The answers to these questions define the project and the research to the townspeople and add up to a set of future promises to the town.

As in most research, many people in the community are un-enthusiastic if not suspicious about being investigated. Springdale, in upstate New York, was a Republican-dominated, conservative town which had previous experiences, not all of them happy, with researchers from Cornell University.[10] In order to secure acceptance by the community in the face of its suspiciousness, its past experiences with research, and a certain amount of hostility and resentment it had toward the University simply because it was a big and dominant institution in the area, the research project presented itself to the town as an upholder of rural values. Scientific investigators regularly attended meetings of the Community Club and told jokes and played games with its members in order to get in exchange their adherence to the research project.

By the terms of its own past the project was committed to studying socially creative activity, and at the time of the Springdale phase of the research it had elected to study this creativity in the form of socially constructive community activities. Springdale was selected for study because the directors of the project thought it was more "constructive" than other towns surveyed as possible choices. Even after the selection of the town and the hiring of a field director it was not entirely clear what was con-

[10] Several years prior to our research, a division of the agricultural school had made a land classification survey which rated all land from bad to excellent depending on various criteria of soil content. Farmers in low-rated areas remembered and resented this survey because it had tended to set relative real-estate values on land so that prospective buyers could point to Cornell's survey and argue land prices on the basis of its authority.

structive activity. This was natural enough, of course, because if it had been known in advance the research would have been unnecessary.

Nevertheless, without knowing exactly what we would be studying, we were pressed by the community to tell what the study was about, who it included, what its purpose was, and what kind of book would be written. In response to these inquiries, the project developed a line that included:

"We are not interested in the negative features of the town because too much fruitless work on that has been done already."

"A positive approach is needed."

"We are interested in constructive activities because from this we feel we can help other people in other communities to live better lives. Springdale is a laboratory which may help us find important solutions."

"We are especially interested in the Community Club because it is a democratic organization that brings *all the people* together and there are no restrictions on membership and no entrance fees."

"We have to get back to the older values of the individual, neighboring and the neighborhood, and Springdale seems to provide an opportune setting for this. We enlist your cooperation in helping us to solve this scientific problem."

All of these commitments were made as a way of selling the project to the townspeople at a time when no one knew what the project would be studying or where it would locate the community's constructive activities. In giving "nonexistent" answers to community inquiries when the project's methods and results are indefinite, the project, unfortunately, becomes committed to those answers.

The greatest concern of some townspeople was with how they personally would be portrayed in the "book." In some instances this concern bordered on anxiety and in other instances an exhibitionism, with a desire only to appear in a favorable light. In the field work the statement, "I hope you're not going to quote me on this," seemed to demand a reassuring answer, and again the issue of community relations played a role in shaping policy. Let us illustrate this with an example presented in another paper.

> As the research progressed, the "assurance" of anonymity came to be equated with "doing an entirely statistical report." This happened in a curiously inadvertent way: on various occasions when the project was asked to explain its purposes in greater detail or when community suspicions had been aroused, the standard practice of some staff members was to assure members of the community that there was nothing to worry about because all individuals and specific events would get lost in the statistical analysis. At the time, these assurances were very successful in allaying the fears and anxieties of the key members of the community, and so some members of the project, particularly those who were less trained and more prone to panic, began to give such assurances whenever resistances developed. Unfortunately, some key members of the community were left with the impression that the entire report would be statistical. As this impression became more prevalent in the community, it also became more prevalent in the research project until it was understood by many persons in both groups that no other than a statistical presentation of the data was to be made.[11]

This was not an explicit policy of the project. It was an implied promise always accepted more by the town than by the project. Among the project members it tended to receive more acceptance when they were in the town than in the central offices, but as time progressed it became difficult for project members themselves to think of any kind of report other than a statistical one, even though it was always also assumed that there would be an analysis of the social structure of the town.

The idea of doing only a statistical report grew out of the project's promise to the community not to identify any of its members in a recognizable way. When people asked how identi-

[11] A. Vidich, "Freedom and Responsibility in Research: A Rejoinder," *Human Organization*, 19, No. 1 (Spring 1960), pp. 3-4.

ties would be concealed, the easiest answer was, "It'll be all statistical." In the writing and analysis, however, the problem of identity concealment could not be handled so easily. In the writing of *Small Town in Mass Society*, we decided we would use the solution used by community sociologists in the past, namely, the use of pseudonyms.[12] When we published our book we were criticized in *Human Organization* and by Cornell University for following that policy. However, when the staff of Cornell Studies in Social Growth later came to write its report, it discovered the same dilemma.

. . . We were all very much disturbed by the reaction of our major Springdale informants to your book. The essential problem was that they had been promised in their initial contacts with us that in any report out of the research they would not be personally identifiable. This was true of the kind of report which we foresaw at the time, and I think it will be true of the *Journal of Social Issues* number. However, it is certainly not true of your book, so we were naturally asked the question, "What about this?" The line we took with the support of the college administration and the Social Science Research Center was that we had expected you to be bound by the same promises which were made to the Springdale people before you appeared on the scene, that we were very much disappointed by the amount and kind of information about clearly recognizable Springdale individuals, which was included in your book, but that we did not have any control over what was finally published. However, we made it clear that we disapproved of this type of publication and wished to dissociate ourselves from it as much as possible. We are now faced with the problem of producing a report which will meet the criteria which was laid down in the original contacts with the Springdale residents. I do not know how well we will be able to do this . . .[13]

[12] Our reasons for doing this have been stated more fully in *Human Organization*, "Freedom and Responsibility in Research," 17, No. 4, and "Freedom and Responsibility in Research: A Rejoinder," *ibid*.
[13] Personal communication from project official, January 1958.

In the final official project report[14] on the town the following solution to the problem of identification was reached.

The main problem which publication presented was, of course, the one of identifying the individual participants in the community. We became convinced that you were right in thinking that it is not possible to provide a meaningful discussion of community action without describing at least some of the principal leaders in a way that makes them readily identifiable to others in the community. Consequently, we decided to use your (Vidich and Bensman) code names in our account, at least the code names Jones, Hilton, Lee, and Flint. The other main participants centering around the repair of the mill dam were people who did not seem to us to require accurate placement in the community power structure; consequently, we used pseudonyms for these people which, I think, would not allow them to be identified by their friends and neighbors—except, of course, those who were themselves involved in the dam project. My present interpretation of the basic reason for the difficulty between you and the project over the write-up of your material is that the project made promises to the people in Springdale which were compatible with the kind of report which was originally planned . . . , but which was not compatible with a report which would deal in any realistic fashion with the social structure of the community.[15]

It is in the nature of the social structure of a community that a project can never have a relationship with it as a totality. It is necessary from the beginning to deal selectively with specific persons in order to secure and sustain some acceptance. The Springdale project worked on the theory that admission to the community would be best secured by working through the important social and organizational leaders. The logic of this action was that since leadership and social organization were the important dimensions of the study, gaining support and accept-

[14] "Leadership and Participation in a Changing Rural Community," *op. cit.*
[15] Personal communication from project official, July 1961.

ance from these sources would both secure legitimacy quickly and efficiently and give access to a strata of important respondents. In practical field terms this strategy was effective—the doors to the community members and organizations were opened—but in scientific terms the implications of this identification with the town fathers and social respectability had far-reaching implications.

1. Because of the organizational importance of particular individuals, these individuals came to be regarded as more valid sources of information than others. As the work progressed it was assumed that, before starting field-work plans for new research, activities would be presented to the executive officers of the Community Club and then to the entire club. The club became a major sounding board for the project and some of its members were used as "consultants" on matters concerning project-town relations. The more the project began to depend on selected informants, the more it became committed to and dependent on their perspective of the town. An operating structure of images of the town was built up which would be violated if other informants were to be used. In practice critics of the Community Club and community leaders were dismissed as "bad citizens."

2. The project's image of the town thus came to coincide with the image held by the town's leadership strata. This created its own problems. Since the official, dominant image of the town was not held by all members of the community, the problem arose of disposing of the unacceptable counterimages in circulation in the community. Two methods of disposition were found. (*a*) minority images could be dismissed as being irrelevant to the project because they did not fall within its purview. This was the case with the world view of the shack people as a whole who were not regarded as instrumental in promoting community mindedness. (*b*) They could be dismissed as representing a deviant or ridiculous viewpoint. The project's attitude to West, the potato and gladiola farmer, became the same as Lee's; West was laughed off the stage. Though West almost became a major innovator by his near successful political cam-

paign to oust the town powers from office, it never occurred to anyone in the central research offices to consider this as creative activity or even leadership.

After three years of contact with the community, the members of the project and "The Project" as an official organization had established many personal and official contacts, commitments, friendships, and confidences. This was inevitable simply because of the duration and closeness of the contact. The problem was how these personal and official relations relate to scientific reporting. In the Springdale case the project director took the position that certain materials were questionable from the point of view of ethics and possible injury to persons.

I have just finished reading the manuscript of you and Bensman and, in response to your request, am giving concrete examples of material which, though it may represent public knowledge, is, in our judgment, highly questionable from the point of view of professional ethics and possible injury to the persons involved. Since there are many instances of this kind, I shall confine myself to a few outstanding examples.

1. There are many references to the enmity between Flint and Lee . . . Since, as you yourself have emphasized, these two persons will be immediately recognizable to anyone familiar with the community, assertions that Flint "has been excluded from town politics by Lee" who harbors "resentment" against him are fairly strong accusations. Moreover, the discussion of their personal antagonism is not really central to your analysis of the way in which the community operates and hence you would not lose much by omitting mention of the matter.

2. The whole discussion of Peabody, the school principal, and his relation to the community could, if it remained in its present form, do a good deal of harm and arouse justifiable resentment. For example, consider the possible impact on him and others of reading the following direct quotation attributed "to a prominent member of invisible government": "He's a little too inhuman—has never gone into anything

in the town. He's good for Springdale until he gets things straightened out. Then we will have to get rid of him." Potentially equally damaging are the statements quoted from the observers' report, but these, along with all excerpts from the project files, would of course no longer appear in the manuscript.

3. In pointing out that the Polish community is controlled by political leaders through intermediaries who are willing to do their bidding in exchange for acceptance, is it necessary to point the finger so visibly at Kinserna? You do this very pointedly . . . where you go so far as to assert that the upshot of his activities is "to get the Poles to accept measures and policies which are disadvantageous to them."

4. Personality descriptions of the ministers . . . are likewise conspicuously on the *ad hominem* side. For example, you refer to one as "awkward, condescending, and not of the people" and to another as a "cantankerous trouble-maker." Also, I wonder whether the description of the Episcopalian minister as trained in "one of the 'radical' Eastern seminaries" is not subject to misinterpretation by Springdale readers despite your use of quotations around the word radical. Given upstate New York's climate of opinion, such a statement may have some unfortunate consequences for the man concerned.

5. The clearly uncomplimentary remarks about Grainger . . . have especial importance for not only is he likely to read them himself, even though he is no longer living in the community, but they are also likely to be read by his colleagues and superiors in the Extension Service. It would be particularly unfair and unfortunate, especially in view of Grainger's whole-hearted cooperation with the project, if any statement made by you jeopardized Grainger's professional future. As the manuscript now stands, such a possibility is by no means out of the question. . . .[16]

The issue here is not the specific items of censorship, but rather the assumption of protective attitudes toward specific

[16] Personal communication from project director, July 1956.

community members on the basis of personal attractiveness, entangling commitments, respondent's earlier cooperativeness, and other nonresearch considerations. As a result of personal, social, and organizational commitments, the project finds itself in the position of writing its findings with an eye to other than research or theoretical interests and issues.

As a final step in viewing the community as a reference group, the project decided that:

> . . . Before any manuscripts are shown to outside representatives, such as publishers or their agents, we will ask one or two persons within the college and possibly in Springdale to read the manuscripts from the point of view of public relations. Although the final responsibility for deciding what we publish will rest with the project staff, the reactions of such readers would receive serious consideration and we would probably rewrite and omit in accordance with their recommendations. . . .[17]

In this instance, to avoid personal responsibility for the project's research reporting, selected nonresearch respondents would be invited to pass on manuscripts purely as a way of avoiding bad public relations, so that aspects of community life that may be theoretically relevant can be censored by local individuals on nonresearch grounds. Moreover, the local individuals to be selected would be specifically those who constituted the project's dominant reference group in the town, namely, the town's official leaders and spokesmen who represented most forcefully the stereotyped image of the positive-minded community which the project has absorbed as its own image of the town.

The identification of the project and its personnel with the town's interests and with the feelings and sentiments of individuals and groups being studied leads to a subtle adaptation of the research to the problems of the community even though those problems are not the problems of the research. In an extreme instance this policy would lead to no point of view except the point of view of the community. Acting Dean

[17] Personal letter from project director, January 1956.

Grisely[18] of Cornell University seems to take this position as the only viable one for social science.

The first thing that happened with a book like this has to be taken in the context that people are not very happy to be studied. I don't know to what extent you may find yourselves, those of you who are becoming involved in the social science field, are likely to find that one of the most difficult things that you will have to do is to sell a project to a group, an organization, by getting them to permit you to come in and ask questions, observe them, write them up, interfere with their time, and in most cases for uses that they don't know or understand, and they are somewhat suspicious and concerned with this whole process. This particular project (Cornell Studies in Social Growth) was introduced to the community through the Extension Service system of the College of Agriculture. People in the community who had confidence in the university for a variety of reasons accepted and sponsored the project and the individuals connected with it. Now Mr. Vidich, as he points out, lived in the community and was accepted in a real sense as one of the people in the community, with people making an effort to see that he was introduced to various groups and so on. Now when this book came out with some of the characterizations and implications, I think there were several kinds of reactions.

In the first place it made people mad. It made those people mad who had brought the study in, who had been responsible and had participated in it. It was in total violation of the understandings which they felt existed between the university and themselves and the community. Second, it made other people feel very badly and hurt them, some of them I'm afraid considerably because they felt that the friendships and confidences they had extended to Mr. Vidich and his family had been violated. Further, I think the distortion of the characterization of these people, many of whom were friends of

[18] Since the Dean is a resident of the Springdale community, we have, in accordance with past practice, invented this name in order to maintain the anonymity of our informants.

his and some of whom were very good friends during the time he was in the community, created a self-consciousness of these individuals which they found very discomforting, which lasted for a time, but from which they recovered. Fourth, I think that the community itself could not particularly welcome the outside attention that it received, especially those people who were in a variety of ways related to outside activities and they found that they were being examined and cross-examined about the community by outsiders with whom they came in contact.

There was a problem of some loss of faith and disruption of university relationships, and I suspect there is an increase in suspicion of outsiders, particularly inquisitive outsiders.[19]

At certain stages the community may become a more important reference group for the project than is the scientific community to which the research is ostensibly addressed. In Springdale, for example, the study of constructive activities in the community gradually came to include the ideology that the project and its members assume constructive attitudes toward Springdale in all phases of work including community relations, field work, participation, analysis of data, and reporting of scientific results.

The highest form of project identification with the town is when the research organization attempts to take responsibility for the actions of all its agents who act in and on the town. The Springdale field work was carried out by more than one hundred people who at a variety of organizational levels participated in the work at different times over a period of three years. Simply by sending large numbers of people into a town, a large amount of public relations is required; new field operations have to be announced, results of preceding surveys must be tentatively reported, newspaper stories have to be written, apologies must be made for field workers' errors, the project's local landlord must be placated when the field director fails to cut the grass, and so on. In order to avoid public-relations errors, field per-

[19] From a tape-recorded address delivered to a group of sociology students at Harpur College, 1962.

sonnel begin to be selected on public-relations grounds. Can you send a foreign student into an upstate New York community? In what positions is it advisable not to have a Jew? What about the Negro who is the husband of a staff member? Some members of the project are excluded from the town completely because they are too "argumentative," too "controversial," or too "unreliable" in some way as defined by the project.

When research workers in their field work provoke a complaint from a community member or a local official, the complaint is sent to research headquarters, and, by the act of accepting the complaint, the project assumes responsibility for rectification either to the individual in question or to the "community as a whole." This means the project is placed in the position of apologizing for its research workers and on occasion publicly reprimanding and punishing its research staff. Punishment of staff usually takes the form of revoking privileges to enter the field; complaints from community members can jeopardize sociological careers.

Standard practice is for the project to make a scapegoat of the last man who left the project, so that all the project's ills in the community will be attributed to him; the man who is no longer there to defend himself serves the purpose of absorbing all of the free-floating resentment the town has against the project. In the same measure as the departee acts as a scapegoat, so his ideas, insights, and knowledge of the community can be safely ignored and forgotten. The project's offering of scapegoats to the town is always a concession to the ideology of the town.

As already indicated the officials of the Springdale project were placed in the position of taking a policy stand before the opinion of the community on the existence of our book. There could be no question to anyone who had any familiarity with the town that *Small Town in Mass Society* would be a provocative experience for Springdale. So far had the project commitment to the community and its values become entrenched that, almost as a reflex response, the publication of *Small Town in Mass Society* evoked a public project apology[20] published on page one of the Springdale *Courier*.

February 6, 1958

The Editor
Springdale *Courier*
Springdale, New York
Dear Sir:

We at Cornell have read the book by Vidich and Bensman entitled *Small Town in Mass Society* and wish to make clear that this work in no sense reflects the intentions or views of the Cornell Project. The book was written after Dr. Vidich had left our employ. Mr. Bensman, of course, never had any connection with the Cornell Project. The general orientation of the work, as well as the material with which it deals, stands in direct contradiction to our policies regarding confidentiality of data and the publication of identifiable information.

Upon learning of Dr. Vidich's plans, we requested him to eliminate or, at least, modify the materials in the manuscript which we felt to be most objectionable, and received his assurances that he would do so. Accordingly, we were doubly shocked to find that much of the objectionable material had been retained.

Since Dr. Vidich entered and lived in the community as a member of our staff, we must accept some indirect responsibility for what has happened. Unfortunately, we know of no way to undo what has been done but can only express our sincere regrets.

Sincerely yours,

Project Director
Cornell Studies in Social Growth

This project apology, addressed though it is to the community at large, is clearly meant to placate those particular in-

[20] Letter to the editor of the Springdale *Courier* published as a lead article shortly after the publication of *Small Town in Mass Society*.

dividuals and groups in the community who might have taken offense. First and foremost, these are the official leaders and the middle class. It must be recalled that the community is composed of individuals and groups who do not see eye to eye on all issues, and that not all community members would be equally offended or even offended at all by the publication of this book. However, it was in the logic of the project's commitment to the community, namely, that it was tied to certain individuals and groups, that it must necessarily condemn, disavow, and dissociate from the study of *Small Town in Mass Society*. The scientific enterprise had come to fully reflect the ideology of the rural community.

Insofar as the ideology of the community grew in salience and became the basis of project reactions, all project actions more and more came to be addressed to it. In due course any offense against the community ideology became a risk to the project and a major crime for the project members.

Once the point was reached that an offense against the town was a crime, the project began to spend more and more time attempting to avert both the crime and the risk of the crime. This could be done only by making a major effort to control the town, the movements of research workers within it, and, finally, by controlling the town's image of the project by organized public relations. Because of this a large part of the field director's activities were devoted to maintaining project-community harmony. This same process apparently was carried out in just as intensive a form at the time of the publication of the book.

At this point I found myself [Dean Grisely] in the interesting position of becoming a liaison between the director of the study who was greatly concerned with this thing being published over which he could not exercise any control really, and the community. I transmitted messages back and forth and so on. I thought you might be interested to know that I received during the process of this a lot of notes from people in the community, and one from an elderly lady who was a retired teacher. I just want to give you a sampling of this. She wrote the note to my wife and said, "I'm so glad your husband gave that Cornell report at the Community Club because now I feel better towards Cornell." I attempted to explain that this was not a Cornell study, it was not an official study, but it was a violation of the study itself.[21]

Once the cycle has reached this stage, there is little left of research except diplomacy and public relations. When project diplomacy and public relations win out, it means converting the town into a rat lab, that is, the project converts the community into so many actors for the research project, and the research investigators respond like actors to the roles they have created.

The reactions of both the town and the University to the book's publication reflected their accumulated public-relations expectations. A number of people, particularly those officials who had collaborated most closely with the project, felt that their trust had been betrayed, and they lodged complaints with the project staff and Cornell University. Since we were not participants to that scene, others will have to report that aspect of the problem. The official position of Cornell as already noted was to dissociate from the book and its authors and to identify with the town. At the time of publication, Vidich was privately reprimanded as follows:

> Having read your book, we, no less than the people of Springdale, are surprised and shocked. Despite your assurances that, wherever possible, you would delete material that we considered objectionable, you have made little more than a token effort in this direction. . . .
>
> It is yet too early to judge how serious the effects of your book will be on Springdale and Cornell. We already have indications, however, that a number of people have been badly hurt, and at least one of Cornell's programs in the area

[21] From Dean Grisely's address to the sociology group at Harpur College, 1962.

has encountered resistance and resentment directly attributable to your publication.[22]

We find it difficult to believe that, in choosing to retain objectionable material, you were not well aware of what you were doing. In any event, we wish to make it absolutely clear that we regard your actions in this matter as a breach of faith and professional ethics both with ourselves, and, what is much more important, with the many people of Springdale who granted us the privilege of their hospitality and confidence.[23]

The town itself came to its own defense in reviews of the book which appeared in Springdale and neighboring towns. For example, the *Times* in the county seat:[24]

THE SMALL TOWN IN MASS SOCIETY—[SPRINGDALE]
SAYS IT ISN'T SO

Small Town in Mass Society, by Arthur J. Vidich and Joseph Bensman (Princeton University Press, $6.00)

An accurate review of this book should be from the viewpoint of a professional sociologist since it is intended as a textbook for the social sciences.

Lacking that point of view, our interest in the book stems from the fact that it is written by a former resident of [Springdale] and concerns itself with "class, power and religion" in [Springdale], called Springdale in the book.

[22] So far as we know this was one of Dean Grisely's projects on small businessmen. If true, we refuse to take full responsibility for the resentment because, in terms of our analysis, the small businessman will seize on any easily available object of resentment so long as the object in question absolutely lacks defenses.

[23] Personal communication from project director, February 1958.

[24] We were not able to secure a copy of the issue of the Springdale *Courier* which carried the review of the book. Though we wrote to the publishers asking for copies and enclosed funds to cover costs, no one ever replied to our request. Our relations with Cornell have been so strained that we have not asked to see their files on the matter. Reviews appeared in other regional papers like the Ithaca *Journal*, but we have made no effort to collect these.

Mr. Vidich is currently about as popular in [Springdale] as the author of *Peyton Place* is in her small town and for the same reason—both authors violate what Vidich calls the etiquette of gossip.

During the three years he lived here, Vidich was engaged in a research project. "Cornell Studies in Social Growth" sponsored by the New York State College of Home Economics and with the aid of funds from the National Institute of Mental Health, United Public Health Service and the Social Science Research Council.

He then proceeded to use portions of the survey material, making Cornell very unhappy, added a considerable amount of misinformation and gossip and drew certain conclusions based on the three sources.

The Cornell survey material is fairly accurate and pertains to economics and population trends. The misinformation indicates that Vidich is something less than a scientist and has either deliberately distorted facts to prove his personal conclusions or has failed to inquire into basic facts. For example, he states that the railroad running through the village has not made a stop there in years: this misstatement seems immaterial except that he uses it to bolster his conclusion that local business is at a standstill.

He discusses the failure of ecumenicalism in [Springdale], stating that Episcopal and Congregational churches failed to merge because of the opposition of powerful members of the older generation who were fearful of losing the traditions of their churches. Actually, no merger was ever contemplated and the temporary arrangement of sharing one minister ceased when his superior decided he was being overworked.

The inference is that [Springdale] is living in the past, unable to accept new ideas of mass society, and, further, that it is run by certain individuals.

The theme of control runs throughout the book. [Springdale] citizens will be amazed to discover that practically every phase of daily living is subject to the whims of one man and his cohorts. They run local government, including the school, decide church policies and influence the economic life of the community.

No attempt is made to disguise the individuals who may be readily identified by anyone having any knowledge of [Springdale]. In this field, Vidich seems to have resorted to pure gossip as his source of material.

The author is shocked by the fact people settle their differences in private rather than resorting to public argument; economy in government becomes "the psychology of scarcity"; he arrives at the conclusion people work fantastically hard to avoid coming to terms with themselves.

He finally sums up the whole picture by proclaiming that the entire population is disenchanted, has surrendered all aspirations and illusions. But, says he, Springdalers are too stupid to realize they are frustrated. To a certain extent (they) live a full and not wholly unenjoyable life. "Because they do not recognize their defeat, they are not defeated."

"Life consists in making an adjustment that is as satisfactory as possible within a world which is not often tractable to basic wishes and desires."

It should not have taken 314 pages of repetition and technical language to discover that life, as so defined, is not a problem peculiar to a small town.—CC[25]

The reactions of some of the people in the community were recorded in one part of a three-part feature story about the book which was carried by the Ithaca *Journal*. The varied reactions indicate that the town's response was not monolithic, and, moreover, that not all persons had equally absorbed the public relations.

BOOK'S SALES SPIRAL IN SUBJECT VILLAGE
Here is the last of three articles about a book and
its effect on the town about which it was written.

By Donald Greet

For a book that costs $6 and is "slow" to read, "Small Town" proved to be a best-seller in [Springdale].

[25] Owego *Times*, January 31, 1958.

Elmer G. Kilpatric, proprietor of a main street store, sold more than two dozen copies. He says only "Peyton Place" in a half-dollar paperback did better.

Mrs. Mary Lou Van Scoy, librarian at the village library (which does not have "Peyton Place"), says two copies "have been on the move since we got it."

One copy, she says, "got bitten up by a dog."

There is evidence, then, that a good many people in [Springdale] have read the book and a good many more have been treated to certain salient passages by their friends.

Ask a waitress in the local restaurant if she is acquainted with "Small Town" and she will say, "Oh, yes, that book."

The three persons who felt the chief impact of the book are called in its pages Sam Lee, Howard Jones and John Flint.

Villagers know these men respectively as C. Arthur Beebe, C. Paul Ward and Winston S. Ives. Beebe is the retired head of the [Springdale] *Courier*, Ward is a partner in Ward & Van Scoy Feed Mills and Ives is an attorney.

All three have been and are active in local politics. The book refers to the threesome as the "invisible government," a term that has provoked both merriment and anger in [Springdale].

All three proved real enough to give their impressions of "Small Town." Says Beebe: "People have talked over every situation in the book. They have not felt generally that the book was fair.

"It was not as objective as it was supposed to have been. It was only one man's opinion. He (author Vidich) was judging a small community by big city standards. We felt it was sneaky."

Ward comments: "The whole thing is based on gossip and is not a true study. He (Vidich) didn't find it out by any bona fide investigation.

"The book could just as well have been written from New York (City). It was not a scientific study, which is what it purports to be."

Attorney Ives is somewhat more generous:

"Two-thirds of the book is probably alright but he (Vidich) got into his biggest difficulty with personalities and in dealing with certain recent events.

"My principal objection to the book is that there are unfortunately a number of factual inaccuracies which in some cases create a distinctly misleading impression.

"Another objection is that the book suggests 'invisible government' had no motive but control. In my experience and to my knowledge leaders have been motivated to do what they thought best for the community."

Others in town added their comments. The Rev. V. F. Cline, minister of the Baptist Church for 14 years, said: "It (the book) has caused a suspicion between individuals and groups."

Funeral director Myron Miller puts it succinctly: "Much ado about nothing."

Off-the-cuff statements, not intended for quoted publication, indicate that some portions of the book struck pretty close to home and gave [Springdalers] the chance to see themselves as others see them.

Said one observer: "The book did more to allay apathy in [Springdale] than anything in a long time."

Perhaps it is just coincidence, but interest in a village election this spring shot up from the usual two dozen votes to 178.

The village's two fire companies, needled in the book for pursuing their separate ways over the years, recently joined forces.

One thing is certain: Walk into [Springdale] and mention "Small Town" and you won't get away without a reaction. Those reactions range from horse-laughs, to polite smiles to the angry bristle of a porcupine.[26]

Later when the town held its annual Fourth of July parade, several floats were addressed to the book. It is clear from the following account of the event that the community had managed to reassert its image of itself.

[26] Ithaca *Journal*, June 13, 1958.

[SPRINGDALE] CALLS IT EVEN

The people of the village of [Springdale] waited quite a while to get even with Art Vidich who wrote a "Peyton Place" type book about their town recently.

The featured float of the annual Fourth of July parade today followed an authentic copy of the jacket of the book *Small Town in Mass Society*, done large scale by Mrs. Beverly Robinson. Following the book cover came residents of [Springdale], riding masked in cars labeled with the fictitious names given them in the book.

But the pay-off was the final scene, a manure-spreader filled with very rich barnyard fertilizer, over which was bending an effigy of "The Author."

Vidich, who lived in the town and won confidence of the local citizenry over a period of two years, worked under the auspices of Cornell University to complete a survey of typical village life. The survey was made available to village planners.

However, Vidich in collaboration with Joseph Bensman decided to capitalize on the material in a way that would benefit themselves financially.[27]

With this final defeat of the book in terms consistent with the psychology of the town's residents, the community was able to continue as if the book had never been published or, more exactly, that it had now been consigned to its proper place in the town's imagery. The community could return to its former self-image and to the project's definition of rural life.

Public relations is a form of promise to a public. All the public-relations attitudes and postures of the town will focus the report to the point of view that the town holds on the project in response to the project's prior public relations. Even if research administrators are quite conscious that they are using public relations to get the work done, they are forced into reporting their findings on the basis of past promises. At this point all of the accumulated public relations stand as a barrier

[27] Springdale *Courier* press release, July 4, 1958.

to reporting anything but the *bon homie* which the project projected onto the town beforehand. The project leaders then have the choice of either making a bland, pleasant report, or of violating a trust relationship which they have purposely created to further the carrying out of the research. Since it is difficult for the researcher to see beforehand all of the ramifications of a public-relations program at the time it is instituted, he may find himself paralyzed by the task of writing a report consistent with public-relations commitments. Due to these dynamics many reports are never written.

The University as a Project Reference Group and Pressure Group. The relationship between the university and the project rests on the consideration that each has some value for the other.

The university is interested in the research project because it helps in the financing of the institution. Project budgets contain standard overhead items, help to cover staff salaries, and help with the purchasing of equipment. Frequently the project will bring to the university additional staff members who otherwise could not be brought because of lack of funds, because the number of departmental positions is limited, or because salary rates are too low to attract the research stars. As a rule research projects allow universities to grow, if not painlessly, at least easily.

Also, the project brings prestige to the university in its competition for prestige with other universities. A university without projects is regarded as not doing any research, and without projects is is not possible to get other projects. In addition to all this, there is at least the ideology that there should be a coincidence of interest between research and the idea of the university; that is, teaching, research, and knowledge are thought of as related to each other positively and as being necessary to the idea of the university.

For their parts the individual project members and the project director receive status in the university because they bring money to it in the form of overhead write-offs, because the staff underwrites its own costs and because the project brings additional staff to the university at little or no cost. If looked at only in the form of statistical aggregates, the student-teacher ratio is improved and the standing of the university, with the accrediting agencies and other interested publics, is given a more solid foundation by project research.

In addition, the project brings a promise of prestige in the form of a future publication which will be linked to the name of the university. Not only is there the promise of publication as such, but the research may receive rewards from professional associations, and individual project members may be cited for the importance of their work by relevant reference groups. In its early stages, at least, almost any project is full of hoped-for gains to the university.

Personnel connected with the project receive short-range esteem within the university for different reasons. If the project is heavily financed by "respectable" money and staffed by prestigious "leaders of the field," almost all personnel connected with the project may absorb some of the surplus prestige as their own. At times researchers may elect to be or not to be associated with a project accordingly as it possesses surpluses of prestige. Up to a point, at least within the world of projects, project reputation is personal and institutional prestige. For this reason projects address themselves to project prestige competition within the university.

To the university community at large, project personnel receive esteem because they are busy, because they publish, because they possess a whole range of anecdotes which enliven the life of the university with something different (especially something that appears to have some relevance to the "real" world), and because they can talk knowingly about research designs and the other apparatus of scientific research. An occasional trip to Washington or upper Fifth Avenue can be an added embellishment.

In the research project there is a general evidence of activity which appears to be in the pursuit of knowledge, and this knowledge is different from the general run of routine teaching or "unreal" knowledge that otherwise appears to inhabit the university. Project members can hold their own in campus conversations and, the face they present to the campus world is that they are getting things done, not just teaching the standard stock of knowledge, but actually expanding its frontiers and producing what will later appear in the textbooks. The research project lends a certain excitement and importance to campus life.

Whosoever brings a research project to the university enhances his department's prestige in relation to other departments in the university, and helps to advertise his department to the outside world, especially in relation to the competition between departments in different universities. Gaining a competitive edge over competitive departments is important to the university administration not only because it helps the recruiting of students but more importantly it creates a generalized image that important research is taking place which can then become a basis for recruiting other research funds. Economically speaking, the total corpus that is the university can reach the point where, if it has *enough* research, it can ideally live off itself.

Research projects tie in with the expansion of graduate training programs since they bring in funds to support graduate students who otherwise would not come to the university if it did not provide them with a livelihood while they are studying. The graduate student who is being subsidized by the research project considers himself fortunate to be able to continue his education without monetary cost to himself. At the same time as he is being subsidized, he is available to the administration as an item of display to potential sponsors of other research projects. The university must have projects, staff, and graduate students in order to get more projects, staff, and graduate students.

In exchange for allowing projects to settle in its territory, the university expects in return to place certain constraints on the way projects conduct their business. At a minimum the project sponsor must be respectable within the terms of respectability adhered to by the administration of the university. Sometimes size of grant helps to establish the donor's respectability.

Since the university has an obligation to the community and to prestigious sponsors, there are a number of political obligations that must be met. Nowadays these political obligations are organized under the university Social Science Research Center, an institution which seems to be based on the model of the historic Agricultural Extension Services: the Social Science Research Center is to the bureaucratic age what the Extension Service was to the agricultural age. This is not to mention that the university president himself as well as second level officials in the university bureaucracy have personal communication with the foundations, government, segments of the business world, and with the alumni who are themselves connected to these agencies and foundations.

Because of whatever complex network of interconnections exists between the university and the outside benefactors and supporters, the university places certain requirements on research. The major requirement is that specific findings should not alienate any group of benefactors or sponsors, including political figures in the town or the state. At the political level there is a great deal of variability between the social and physical sciences and within the social sciences. Different schools may be connected to different reference groups with different ideologies and positions. The only point being made is that for any specific school there will usually be some correspondence between research lines and the line of the higher administrative officials of the school as a whole, which means that for the research project:

1. Specific findings should not alienate any groups of sponsors or benefactors or the general line of political commitment.

2. Pressure will always be placed by the school to see that the project is at least in a minimal way fulfilled. The report must be written in a way and in terms that are acceptable to the sponsoring foundation.

There is always a point at which the report is unacceptable, and this point is discovered only when a project overreaches the prevailing line of the institution in which it is located. At other stages there are always points at which people who might cause embarrassment are either not hired or are fired. At every stage it is embarrassing for the project to embarrass the administration.

3. At all points the university administration maintains a public-relations-type supervision over the operation of its projects and this supervision in the fully bureaucratic university is embodied in the University Research Center.

4. Apart from all this, even under ideal conditions, the project director must be aware of the consequences of research for the public-relations position of the university. One might go so far as to say that in the pure case he enacts public-relations functions without knowing it, and that to the extent that the pure case prevails all research is a function of public relations.

When one adds up all of the pressures, conflicts, tensions, and contradictions which are functions of bureaucratic research, one can only ask how all of this effects the quality of the "official" research report. What does it mean in concrete terms when an analyst-writer responds to the public-relations requirements of the town, the politics of the university, and the internal contradictions of the bureaucratic research organization?

The official Springdale report, "Leadership and Participation in a Changing Rural Community,"[28] is available to us as a case illustration. This is to be criticized less for its viewpoint than for its lack of a focus or an organizing idea. When one has read this booklet, one is aware of having read six essays, each reflecting the interests of the given author or combination of authors. The lack of a central problem or, rather, the succession of different problems and theories introduced on an ad hoc basis mirrors the failure of any one project point of view to develop or prevail.

For lack of a consistent point of view or a problem, the report cannot present a consistent or integrated portrait of the community along several or even any single dimension of its institutional organization. From reading "Leadership and Participation" one is left with the impression that neither leadership nor participation has any relationship to the economic and political life of Springdale. The Community Club emerges as a central institution which exists largely outside the framework of other social realities as if it were conditioned only by itself

[28] *Op. cit.* (see footnote 2).

and by the project's conception of the neighborhood structure of the township. When specific roles and their incumbents are mentioned, they are mentioned not to describe their structural position in the town, but only to clarify their participation in an important Community Club project, the repair of the dam. This is not the place to provide an analysis for why the project did not develop a consistent theory for leadership and participation. For present purposes it is only necessary to note that the substantive limits set by the project for itself stay well within the limits of what the community and the university administrative officials expected. No one need be offended because everyone's feelings have been taken into account in advance. In short the report achieves such a level of blandness and neutrality that after reading it any reader can go on as if nothing had happened to him. Nothing is said sharply enough to give anyone in the community a pretext for complaining to the university administration, and those who are dissatisfied because the report does not make any points do not complain because there is nothing to complain against.

One might speculate that the absence of a central problem, the absence of a central theory, and even the absence of the sense of the social structure of the community may be due to the inability of the project leaders to see and pose issues sharply in order to avoid offending significant members of the community.

The Ethos of Research. From the foregoing discussion it is apparent that there are at least three different criteria by which the fundamental values in research can be evaluated:

1. By the ethic of scientific inquiry—the pursuit of knowledge for the sake of knowledge regardless of its consequences.

2. By the ethic of bureaucratic inquiry which we have already outlined.

3. And by the ethic of Christian human relations—for the sake of helping or at least not hurting others.

Every organizational structure imposes its own set of ethics on the individuals who work in it. This is largely because ethics have largely come to be work rules. Knowing that bureaucratic research is here to stay means also that bureaucratic ethics are here to stay, and that, furthermore, they will be elaborated in formal codes as part of the bureaucratic rules. All current trends in bureacuratic research point in the direction of ethical and professional codes which try to specifiy codes of research conduct that will be consistent with the exigencies of the bureaucratic method of research.

Much of the current concern with ethics in the social sciences is simply a working out of an attempt to resolve some of the contradictions between individual responsibility and corporate group responsibility. The general trend is toward statements of viable rules for specifying the canons of individuals working in a bureaucratic setting. Actually this is not a new problem. It is the same problem that has been confronted by business and industry and government for the past two hundred years, since the beginning of the bureaucratic trend in all phases of life. These trends are only now beginning to emerge in the research process itself because research itself has come to occupy a unique position with a halo of its own, no matter how far behind the times it may actually be.

However, the ethic of independent and disinterested research with regard only for the creation of new theories and the discovery of new facts is much older than the modern bureaucratic ethic. At some point almost everyone is willing to accept the ancient Greek ideal of personal integrity, especially after an individual scholar produces valuable and useful results.

Even in modern times the advocates of bureaucratic research ethics are themselves at some point perfectly willing to accept the findings of individuals whose work was conducted in violation of the bureaucratic ethics, so that we assume that some value is still placed on independent research.

It is our opinion that the basic conflict in research ethics is not only a conflict of values but also a conflict in the very structure of the research enterprise. Therefore, if bureaucratically organized research is necessary and if it is the esteemed form for carrying out research activity, it appears that the conflict between the two ethics is a permanent part of the research scene which will never be resolved by any further explication of ethics. It would be dangerous for the freedom of inquiry if the formalized ethics of bureaucracy prevailed or predominated in all research. At the same time it does not seem likely that bureaucratic research will disappear just because a few individual scholars dislike its methods and results. Therefore, pluralistic, conflicting research ethics are likely to exist so long as adherents to both types of research exist and so long as individuals have the spontaneity and the insight to see an unanticipated problem, to pursue a new insight or hypothesis that contravenes the formal design and expectations of whole series of administrators, sponsors, officials, respondents, politicians, and seekers for prospects for grants from foundations who are presold in another direction.

Fundamentally, then, the problem is not one of ethics, but of what type or method of social research is most likely to be productive.

Large-scale bureaucratic research has the advantage of being able to mobolize vast funds and large numbers of researchers in relatively narrow problem areas. It is weak in allowing the unplanned, unplannable, unanticipated, and unpredictable operation of insight, curiosity, creative hypothesis formulation, pursuit of incongruous and inconvenient facts—all of which may challenge the validity of received theory or evoke the possibility of a new theory.

Only the individual scholar working alone—even in the midst of a bureaucratic setting—has the possibility to raise himself above the routine and mechanics of research. If, when, and under what circumstances this happens is not predictable in advance.

Bureaucratic constraints make it all but impossible for the individual to follow the insights he otherwise would because such constraints are central to the plans and obligations that are the heart of large-scale organization.

As a result large-scale research organizations are most effective at gathering and processing data along the lines of sharply defined hypotheses which have standardized variables, dimensions, and methods of analysis.

The work of the individual scholar, no matter where he is

located, and no matter how he is financed, organized, constrained, or aided, is perhaps the sole source of creativity. The successful placing of limitations on individual scholarship under the guise of "ethics," work rules, institutional responsibility, or higher considerations forces a society to live off the intellectual capital of its independent thinkers.

Afterword

Arthur J. Vidich

———◆◇◆———

I. Springdale: An Accidental Odyssey

BEFORE I TOOK a job in 1951 as field director in Springdale for the Cornell project Studies in Social Growth, I had studied a variety of communities and had learned something of how they functioned. Before I arrived at Ithaca, I had lost any illusions I might have had about life in small towns.

Having grown up in West Allis, an ethnic industrial suburb of Milwaukee, I knew that Allis Chalmers—a major producer of tractors and turbines—and several other machine tool industries not only dominated the life of the community but also held its repeatedly reelected and incompetent mayor in virtual hostage to the requirements of industry. To be aware of this sociological datum did not require research in the usual sense; everyone in town knew that the political life of the community was dominated by major economic interests.

My second exposure to an American community came in the summer of 1947, two years after World War II had ended, when I returned to graduate school at the University of Wisconsin: John Useem and Peter Munch hired me as an assistant in their study of Viroqua, a Norwegian community in west central Wisconsin. While in Viroqua, I conducted my own study, later submitted as an M.A. thesis, on the success aspirations of small-town young men, who, I learned, held illusions far in excess of any reality principle. Despite challenges to these illusions, they still believed they lived in the best of all possible worlds.

On that same field trip, I had an opportunity to interview Gerald L. K. Smith, hometown hero, editor of *The Cross and the Flag*, America Firster, and advocate in the 1930s of an American version of proto-fascism. His appeal to his constituencies in the postwar period had largely evaporated. In

Viroqua's centennial year, the town fathers had tried but failed, because of the opposition of the state and regional press, to celebrate Smith as its outstanding citizen. I interviewed Smith and learned from him the moral values and political foundations of Lutheran fundamentalism. Viroqua was a solidly Christian community that upheld, simultaneously, the values of competitive business and the ethical stricture to be thy brother's and sister's keeper. One of my teachers, Hans H. Gerth, in his efforts to educate me, had suggested that I read Thorstein Veblen's essay "Christian Morals and the Competitive System," which maintains that "Western civilization is both Christian and competitive (pecuniary)" and describes the contradictions between these two institutional norms. How these norms might come to terms with each other posed some fundamental questions, not easily resolvable.

The contrasting images of community life given me by Viroqua and West Allis were at that time beyond my capacity to reconcile. But if I learned anything from these experiences, it was an understanding of the standards of public etiquette in community life: one learned to abide by a community's rules and not to question their validity.

The third community I studied was Palau, one of the Western Caroline Islands. John Useem invited me to join a group he had assembled under the sponsorship of the National Science Foundation. During World War II, the Americans had captured Palau from the Japanese and were administrating it as part of a trust territory. Earlier, Palau had been successively colonized by Spain, Germany, and Japan. Each change in colonial administrators and policies sent shock waves through Palauan society and led to changes in leadership, economy, and culture. For example, the colonizers' recognition of non-traditional leaders undercut traditional authority; the introduction of a money economy competed with the values of an indigenous "monetary" system; and bi- and trilingualism became a new basis for making status claims and opening up access to economic opportunity. The interactions between the American colonizer and the Palauan colonized and their consequences for Palau's institutions were the focus of my research.

I had discovered that Palau's social structure had been radically transformed several times over as a result of bureaucratic decisions made elsewhere.

In 1948, I was admitted to Harvard University's Department of Social Relations, where the anthropologist Clyde Kluckhohn became my senior professor. It was at Harvard that I completed my report on Palau for the National Science Foundation.[1] In 1950, after I had been at Harvard for two years, Kluckhohn sponsored me for a Fulbright Fellowship to University College of the University of London to study with Daryll Forde and John Barnes. It was there that I began to convert my Palau report into a dissertation. When in London, I had occasion to make several visits to Kropa, a small town in Slovenia's Julian Alps from which my parents had emigrated to the United States. My observations in Kropa gave me another angle on small-town life. Kropa had been a wrought-iron-working town since the twelfth century, and during World War II, its inhabitants had sided, at great risk to themselves, with Tito's partisans against the German invaders. As a reward for its wartime loyalty, the central government in Belgrade, holding to Kropa's iron-working tradition, awarded it a new factory for the production of cold-pressed nuts and bolts. The postwar prosperity of the town—and of my relatives—was entirely a consequence of this political favor, even though there was no rational economic reason to build such a factory there since all its raw production materials and presses had to be imported. Nevertheless, the status and the class systems of the town were determined by the existence of the factory. Although accessible only by a dirt road, there was nothing isolated about Kropa. In the early years of the cold war, local residents could listen to radio broadcasts from Moscow, England, and the Voice of America (just as some Palauans had in 1948).

While I was still in England and on the job market for a position in an American university, a series of unexpected events led me to be hired for the job in Springdale. David Schneider, in England at the time as an instructor at the London School of Economics, and I exchanged notes on our respective job prospects. Schneider had done field work in 1947 on Yap, an island adjacent to Palau, under Kluckhohn's sponsorship. We both knew an opening existed in Harvard's Department of Social Relations and speculated about who might be appointed to it. Clyde Kluckhohn, for reasons that puzzled me, never responded to my letters asking him for leads on jobs. Schneider won the appointment to Harvard, and I returned to Cambridge jobless. When I went to visit Kluckhohn, I was summarily rebuffed. Kluckhohn, as it turned out, had developed personal grievances against me in my absence. He himself never spoke to me about them except to say that I had spread a vicious rumor about him, something I had not done. Only later did I learn that the reason was something deeply personal and unknown to me while I was in England. Kluckhohn had suggested that I apply for a position at the Johns Hopkins Operations Research Center. In desperation, because by then I had a family of two children, I interviewed at Johns Hopkins, only to discover that the job entailed small group research then of special concern to military planners. In this case, it was to conduct a study of two-man firing groups on the frontline in Korea. This left me with no options until Peter H. and Alice Rossi, then at Harvard, suggested I see Talcott Parsons about a job at Cornell. Parsons gave me the information I needed to apply for the Cornell position, and despite Kluckhohn's efforts to block my appointment, I was hired.

I tell this story because, in my rather nebulous career plan, I had never expected to be a field director for Cornell's College of Agriculture and never thought that I would study an upstate New York rural community for three years. From the beginning, *Small Town in Mass Society* was the result of an unanticipated set of circumstances, what Hermann Broch calls "the nameless loneliness of chance." In retrospect, Kluckhohn's rejection was the best thing that could have happened to me, and I owe him for the chance he gave me to do the Springdale study.

II. Living and Reliving Springdale

In Springdale, the personal, professional and theoretical could never be separated.

It was understood as part of my job specification that I was to find a place to live in the town and take up residence with my family. An opportunity to rent a farmhouse arose when its owner sold it to a neighboring farmer, who, wishing to expand his operation, bought it on the strength of the rental income I could pay him for the duration of my Cornell contract. My rental transaction with the dairy farmer gave me a house without central heat, a large garden plot, an unusable outhouse, and a chicken coop.

The house, which became field headquarters, was located on Route 17 across the road from the residence and farm of Mr. Jones. Its setting, fortunately, protected from the village residents' scrutiny the innumerable interviewers and researchers who visited and slept over in spare bedrooms. The one-on-one rental transaction with the dairy farmer authenticated me: I had become a community resident who paid his way independently of Cornell University. My status in the town was therefore comparable with that of a local extension agent on the payroll of the New York State Agricultural College at Cornell University.

When my wife and I moved into town, we already had two sons, aged three and one, who became, if not observers, participant residents of the town. In 1953, the arrival of another son created something of a nursery atmosphere in the household and helped reinforce my identity as a responsible family man. Of course, while everyone seemed to pretend that I was just another Cornell employee (a Cornell dean also lived in the town), the reality was quite different.

My wife, a trained sociologist and interviewer, worked part-time for the project. She made her own research observations but shared those with me. She also attended the Congregational church and enrolled the children in its nursery school. In an effort to patronize local commerce, we bought our groceries at the local store and often ate at the restaurant. We attended community club meetings, where we met other members of the community, some of whom became friends with whom we socialized, visiting their homes. Our pattern of sociability did not, however, include visits by our local friends to the field headquarters. The only villager who regularly entered the field headquarters was a housekeeper who cared for the children and cleaned the house. Student field workers and interviewers also became part of the household. When senior staff members visited the town to attend community club functions, they did not come to the field headquarters and generally kept their distance from its day-to-day operations. The field headquarters was the site of a mixture of family and business activities and the place where information about the town was exchanged; field workers neither entered nor left the town without my knowing it.

After almost fifty years, my memory of specific experiences in the town is highly selective and tends to focus on colorful instances. The school's guidance counselor and I entered into a joint venture to raise a pig on my garden plot. One day the pig escaped and was seen running down the highway, whereupon the housekeeper and I gave chase to it. Luckily she knew—although I didn't—that the way to immobilize a running pig is to grab one of its hind legs. My effort at pig farming endeared me to no one, but it has given me the raw material for many reminiscences. Another season, I allowed our postman, at his request, to graze his geese on my plot. This effort at communal cooperation ended tragically when my dog broke loose and killed all the geese. On the same rampage, our pet also killed one of Jones's sheep. Unaware of the gravity of his action, he was regarded as a criminal by the owners of his victims. According to local mores, there was only one solution for this problem, namely, to have the dog put down, a service provided for me by Cornell University's Department of Animal Husbandry. My image as a responsible citizen was upheld, but, in the eyes of my family, I was the criminal. No claims were made against me by the owners of the dead livestock, nor were these incidents ever mentioned to me by members of the community. My status as field director and my affiliation with Cornell University gave me a form of protection not available to an ordinary citizen of the town.

On another occasion, my landlord, who was unhappy with what he regarded as the unkempt condition of the part of my lawn facing the highway, complained about this to project headquarters. One of the project directors visited the landlord and intervened on his behalf, advising me that I was not maintaining respectable appearances, an action that struck me as violating my rights in my relationship with my landlord. Again this confirmed the ambiguities of my role as a resident of Springdale.

When I left Springdale, there were farewell gatherings and fond remembrances. Yet all of this, even friendships and friendly relations in the homes of some members of the community, was part of the research enterprise: the personal and the professional always were intertwined. Effective field research depends on researchers' successful integration into the community they want to understand. Each community has its own criteria to judge integration and acknowledge acceptance, and in the case of Springdale, as elsewhere, the community always remembered that I was a researcher.

I approached Springdale with the same attitude I had used to examine Palau–that of acceptance of the town on its own terms, observing its rules of etiquette, while objectifying myself in relation to them whenever I was not acting in the field. Performing the social acrobatics to maintain this dual consciousness was made easier for me by the requirement that I make regular reports to project headquarters in Ithaca about what I was seeing in Springdale; when making such reports, I had to be objective about my life in the town. The same split consciousness obtained in my discussions with field workers at field headquarters. Splitting myself into two halves was an occupational requirement and quickly became a matter of habit.

My first field work assignment was to supervise, from my home, a staff of graduate student interviewers in a census-like survey of the 750 households in Springdale. The interview schedule was short, six or eight pages, and included items requesting information on the names of members of the household, occupations, education, religious affiliation, household appliances, income, and the like. I did some of the interviews myself and read and edited all the others. All this information went into my head before it was machine processed at project headquarters.[2] By the time the survey had been completed, I had memorized the names, places of residence, and the occupations of most of the members of the community.

During this period, Joseph Bensman (1922–1986) was a sociologist employed as a mechanic in an aircraft factory on Long Island. Both of us felt a sense of professional isolation, so when Bensman and his family visited me in Springdale, our discussion of the town evoked our recognition of a genuine sociological problem for us to investigate. This was the beginning of our joint attempt to understand the functioning of Springdale. We entered this project out of curiosity and for our own edification. Bensman had not expected to be diverted from a career as a sociologist, and I had not expected to be hired as a field administrator in an upstate New York town where I was expected to be a participant observer and not the academic anthropologist I had hoped to be.

Bensman and I had originally met while we were undergraduate students at the University of Wisconsin. After the war, we both returned to Madison to continue graduate studies in the Department of Sociology and Anthropology, where we had collaborated on a report in John Useem's seminar on social systems. Bensman was then Hans H. Gerth's student, helping Gerth edit some of his Max Weber translations, and I was studying anthropology and attending Gerth's lectures. In 1946, when Gerth and Mills published *From Max Weber: Essays in Sociology,* the book opened up a new way of looking at social analysis. For me, reading Weber presented intellectual problems because his anthropology was difficult to square with what I was hearing from my anthropology professors. The exposure Gerth gave us to Weber and to himself provided a common ground for Bensman's and my approach to the problems posed for us by Springdale, and for this reason we dedicated *Small Town in Mass Society* to Gerth.

Viewing the town from a sociological perspective, we initially turned to the question of isolating and differentiating the groups and classes into which the residents of the town could be sorted. Attempting to grasp the contours of Springdale's class structure, we had to find categories that would allow us to place every family in a typology of classes. In the Weberian sense, certain common features among individuals, but not necessarily all features, make up a type. To classify each household, I impressionistically sorted the 750 interviews into different piles on the floor of my office, each pile differentiated from the others by social and economic characteristics.

The first sorting produced thirty or forty discrete piles. I then asked myself why I had included the given schedules in the same pile—what did they share in common? After completing this exercise with all the schedules, I began a process of regrouping and combining until each pile was distinguished from the others by such categories as income, occupation, consumption patterns, life styles, social status in the community, and orientations to savings, investment, and consumption. Our footnote on pages 51 and 52 explains what we mean by *class* and the multidimensional elements used to define the groups into which we put the residents of Springdale.

This primitive sorting process could not have been accomplished by a machine because it depended on observations and impressions not contained in the interview schedules. Chapter 3 of this book describes the class groupings that resulted from this research process and specifies the underlying values that distinguish each class from others. This formulation of the class system made it possible for us to examine how the social-psychological orientation of each class was played out in the daily life of Springdale. Our chapters on classes and politics—including the politics of education, religion, and leadership—analyze the functioning of community institutions in relation to the town's class system. While still grappling with the class structure, and after more than a year in the field, I began to formulate my ideas about the processes by which external agencies penetrated the town.

I then wrote a paper, "Introduction to Springdale's Social Structure."[3] From the beginning, it was the project's expectation that I was to analyze the town's social structure and that somehow my observations would be integrated with the project's focus on community creativity and social growth. When I wrote this paper, my mind was on Palauan colonialism (I was still finishing the dissertation); this fix led me to look for all conceivable external influences on the town. The paper was an attempt to find a theoretical framework for linking local institutions and social processes to their connections with the larger economic, political, and cultural processes. To this end, I itemized all these interconnections and their significance for the functioning of the town. The paper begins with "The Colonial Position of Springdale in Relation to the Larger Society and Its Consequences for the Microcosmic Social Structure" and continues: "In the recent past–20 to 50 years–the structural relationships between Springdale and the larger society have been drastically altered. These changes are largely a consequence of changes which have occurred in the major institutional complexes of the larger society. A description of these latter changes and their psychological correlates is necessary for an understanding of the microcosmic social structure."

It goes on to identify the forms of institutional penetration and specifies their carriers. The paper never elicited a response from my project supervisors, but Bensman, with whom I shared it, thought it was a good statement. He said in a letter to me that it was "one of the best things I have seen on the analysis of rural society." However, he had a number of reservations:

the criticisms I . . . make are based upon the fact that you are presenting so much material in so small a space that you give the reader constipation. You have an element of mixed empiricism and theoretical analysis which in a small space does not do justice to either. A great many problems would disappear, if the form for this were a large book and your paper was a conclusion. . . . You presented a picture of the causes and dynamics of the community without presenting the community behavior itself. . . . One of the problems that interests me is that in terms of the daily fabric of life the appearances are completely different from your analysis.

Bensman, who had grown up in Two Rivers, Wisconsin, in a farming and industrial region, was familiar with life in a small town. His response gave me the assurance that I was on the right track; this was the conscious beginning of our formulation of a theory for the sociology of Springdale.

In the first place, the term *colonialism* was inappropriate for the case of Springdale inasmuch as there were neither colonial administrators nor a system of indirect rule. The institutional means of penetration were largely invisible, and external cultural influences were simply regarded as the American way of life. If one participated in the life of the community, however, the invisible became visible and cultural penetration transparent. For example, during the early hysterical stages of the cold war and after the Soviet Union had successfully produced an atomic bomb in 1949, military planners initiated policies of civil defense designed to prepare the population for a possible nuclear attack. These plans included a network of aircraft warning sites throughout the East operated by the volunteer civilian Ground Observers' Corps. Springdale, chosen as one of the sites, responded by constructing on a hill a hut with a telephone and had it manned twenty-four hours a day. I volunteered my services, and during the midnight watch, to which I was assigned, I was to look out for enemy planes. From a military standpoint, the entire project was meaningless—even if any plane were spotted, the untrained observer could not identify it—but from the point of view of civil defense policy, it was a propaganda campaign designed to assure Springdalers that we were participating in the defense of the nation. Somewhere in Washington, D.C., in the office of a civil defense planner, Springdale existed and had been selected to play a role in a national propaganda campaign.[4] Springdale responded on cue to this propaganda campaign, just as it did to the policies and programs created by central educational, agricultural, and political party bureaucracies.

One of the ironies of Springdale's cultural penetration was that the project focused on the community club as an example of creative community action, but the community club had actually been instigated by Cornell's extension agent, Jack Grainger, who became its first president. Nonetheless, the project seemed to assume that this had been an autonomous community creation. Other forms of cultural penetration included state-mandated educational requirements for the consolidated school and the introduction of the new medium of television. Also, in the Sunday school classes that I taught in the Congregational church, at the invitation of the local pastor and with the approval of project headquarters, all instructional materials were imported from church headquarters.

A perspective that focused on external penetration of the town posed a theoretical problem not treated in the existing literature. The traditional sociological dichotomies of rural and urban and secular and sacred societies, then in fashion, inevitably narrowed and distorted an observer's perception of the local reality. By connecting the class and leadership systems with the forms of penetration, Bensman and I had found a way to bridge the space between the "isolated" community and the larger society.

Without an analysis of the systems of class and penetration, the dynamics of the social processes could not have been explored. As Bensman had noted in his critique of my paper, the problem this analysis presented was that our portrait was completely different from the appearances of the daily fabric of life in Springdale. This discrepancy posed the question of how to reconcile phenomenological appearances and sociological analysis, that is, how the daily fabric of community life and its underlying illusions conceal the dynamics of social processes that are related to the invisible structures. We resolved this issue in chapter 11, where we introduce psychological variables to reconcile appearances and institutional realities.

During the third and last year of the field work, I conducted thirty "social structure" interviews as the project termed them. After two years of living in Springdale and thinking about, observing, and administering innumerable specialized surveys, I knew by then what I did not know and where to get it. My list of interviewees included a local historian, an editor of the town's newspaper, political leaders, the lawyer, the extension agent, small businessmen, successful and marginal farmers, owners of the mill, and clergymen. These were unstructured, open-ended interviews, which I recorded in shorthand form and later edited and made legible; I can still remember the names of most of these respondents. I had advised the project director that after the completion of these interviews and at the conclusion of the third year of my contract, I would seek employment elsewhere. It was understood that the data collected on the field, including the copies of my thirty interviews, were the property of the project. Nevertheless, by this time I had completed and submitted to the project drafts of chapters on local and school politics that contained information taken from project protocols. When I left Springdale to take a job in Puerto Rico, I took with me only copies of the drafted chapters, leaving all protocols, interviews, memoranda, and draft chapters with the project.

To this day, except for my "Introduction to Springdale's Social Structure," I possess none of the primary data that I collected while in Springdale. Since I did not have any of the primary data, we had to finish writing the book as quickly as possible while my memories of the data and the town were still fresh. Within a little more than a year, in continuous communication with Bensman, who was in New York, he and I completed a first draft of the manuscript published in 1958.

When *Small Town in Mass Society* was published, the contradiction between the personal and the intellectual could no longer be concealed. Many in the town, especially those who had become friends, were shocked and felt betrayed when they read the book. I knew this would be the case; the publication of other community studies had produced similar reactions. I had not, however, allowed this knowledge to act as an anticipatory form of censorship on our description and analysis of the data. My job in Puerto Rico at the time of the writing had distanced me from the immediacy of the town, detached me from my personal relations, and immunized me from the town's potential reactions. I believed that this circumstance enhanced the objectivity of the analysis, even though I knew that publication of the book would cause a stir in the town.

After the second edition of *Small Town in Mass Society* was published in 1968, the book became an institution in its own right. The conflict between the authors and Cornell over questions of ethics, although never resolved, lost its salience. The book became an artifact of history, no longer charged with the emotions evoked by the first edition.

However, no erasure can wipe out the consequences of my residence and work in Springdale. My children, knowing that Bensman and I had written *Small Town,* were curious to know where they had been during that portion of their lives. I was never able to clarify fully for them their sojourn in Springdale until my fourth son, born in Puerto Rico and reared in Connecticut, decided to study in the School of Arts and Science at Cornell University. His choice led me to take several trips to Ithaca via Springdale, and, upon his graduation, the entire family revisited the farmhouse and its environs, finally completing a circle in the family history. For me, the name of the town is still Springdale because, by agreement with the ethical rules of the project, candor in the use of its real name would be a violation of the project's understanding with the town. Even some of the pseudonyms I invented to refer to public figures in the town seem more real to me than their real names. The three years of my life in Springdale are bracketed apart from my life before and after the research. Despite the bracketing and the necessity of engaging in such linguistic juggling acts, my family and I have been tied to the town throughout these years as if by an umbilical cord that refuses to be cut. For example, when I first moved to Greenwich Village in New York, my second wife went to pick up a prescription for me at McKay's drugstore on Sixth Avenue and Fourth Street. The pharmacist asked her if she was related to the same Vidich who had written the book. He then informed her, "I saw your husband hung in effigy." In the same vein, I've had telephone calls from friends in different parts of the country who told me they met someone who knew me in Springdale. My children tell me that while they were in college, their names identified them with *Small Town.* In 1982, I was invited by Jones's son, Howard, to spend a summer restudying Springdale. When I first met Howard in 1953, he had returned to the community after a successful career as an engineer. His letter of invitation read in part as follows:

> Art, we became friends in 1953 when we came back to [Springdale] and you were completing your notes and observations on life in "Springdale." . . . Though the community reaction

to your book . . . was violently adverse, I knew you had assessed the community . . . accurately except for one thing–motive. Here you were wrong. You assigned selfishness as a motive for most actions when community welfare was the actual motive. I think you owe it to yourself and to the community to correct that mistake. Why don't you spend the summer here . . . and reassess the situation.

In my letter–of which I do not have a copy–replying to this invitation, I demurred and told Howard I could not accept. I tried to explain to him that the analysis of the community club, whose concern was the welfare of the community as a whole, might be an indirect answer to his criticism that we stressed selfishness as a motive. But, in sociological analysis, interpretations of motives are notoriously difficult to substantiate, since actors themselves are frequently unaware of their own motives or are unwilling to reveal them. This invitation was received thirty years after the fact; by this time, I was thinking about other things and lacked the inclination and emotional stamina to face my friends in Springdale.

To this day, the book continues to have a life of its own. Several symposia have been dedicated to it. One at the New School, sponsored by Ahmad and Mahmoud Sadri, was attended by a former resident of Springdale. The Texas affiliate of National Public Radio made a documentary on small towns, for which I was interviewed and televised. Not being much of a television viewer, I've never seen this show, but every now and then friends and relatives call to tell me they saw me on T.V.

A few years ago, I received a telephone call from a Vietnam War veteran who had chosen Springdale as a place to live and to open a restaurant. When the restaurant failed and he lost his investment, he bitterly condemned all of Springdale for its hypocrisy, but he actually was expressing resentment against Springdalers for not patronizing his establishment. By agreeing with me that the book's description was accurate, he wanted me to support his gripes against the town, putting me in the odd position of defending the mores of Springdale.

On January 20 and 27, 1988, the thirtieth anniversary of *Small*

Town, the *Tioga County Courier* ran a two-part series entitled "Small Town in Mass Society Revisited." These articles reviewed the initial reactions of the town and Cornell to the book and repeated comments about the authors that appeared in the local press. The author of this series, Michael Golachok, also visited the town and interviewed Jack Grainger, the county agent; Kinserna, the Polish farmer; Henry Hanks, the Tioga County legislative chairman; and several other Springdale figures. Golachok's articles repeated much of the content and tone of the press reports published just after the first edition of *Small Town* appeared. They rejected the book's major conclusions and once again vindicated the authenticity of small-town life.[5]

III. The Book and the Profession

The process of getting *Small Town* into print for its first edition included many difficulties, not the least of which was how it might be assimilated as a work in the professional mainstream of sociology, but it also illustrated the many vagaries and problems of publication itself.

Finding a publisher proved to be difficult. Four commercial presses to which we submitted the manuscript in seriatim rejected it for such reasons as "already . . . recently published a community study," "lack of a market for such a specialized work," and "its excessively technical language." Discouraged because we had not been able to find a publisher for more than a year but persistent, we decided that each of us would submit the book independently in the hope that one of us would come up with a publisher. We simultaneously submitted it to two university presses, Bensman to Princeton and I to Harvard. We learned with surprise, in the light of our earlier failures, that both presses accepted the book: Princeton at the urging of Melvin Tumin, whom Bensman had contacted, and Harvard under the sponsorship of Barrington Moore Jr., whose graduate assistant I had been and who had served as my dissertation supervisor. However, both presses' readers were critical and requested revisions, extensive ones in the case of Harvard. Princeton's primary reader savaged the manuscript, seeing nothing whatsoever worthy in it:

The style of this manuscript is painfully inadequate. There are two styles . . . one is the plodding style of simple declarative sentence, jacked up with the offensive jargon of the Sociologist; the other style, which has more changes of pace, is souped up with offensive jargon of the Psychologist. The clumsy structure of the sentences might serve as a microcosm of the clumsy structure of the entire manuscript.

. . . These collaborators brought to their task certain standards of measurement which made it inevitable that they should arrive at their findings, such as they are, before they began their measurements.

Princeton's acquisition editor also had doubts about the manuscript: "The authors' methodology, focus, and on the whole their presentation seemed good as I went along, but I was bothered by what might be excess of detail in certain spots (discussion of the political structure, for example), by some repetition, and, in particular, by the lack of reference to the findings of comparable studies."

Despite these assessments, Bensman and I were convinced that we had written a good book. Moreover, despite its primary reader's dismissive treatment of the manuscript, Princeton published the book. The review process seemed to matter less than the intervention of Melvin Tumin, whose informal defense led to its publication.

Harvard's primary reviewer, an anthropologist who had also published an American community study, offered a qualified endorsement of the manuscript but insisted that publication depended on substantial revisions:

I recommend the publication of [the] book, but with a certain lack of enthusiasm. I believe that there is value in the manuscript but that it would be much improved by careful re-examination and some perhaps rather far-reaching changes. . . . There are two major flaws in the manuscript. The first and most important is conceptual and stems from the particular nature of the community and the particular emphasis of their self-imposed problem. . . . The second major objection is the failure of the authors to adduce adequate evidence to support many of their statements . . . no chapter is entirely free of this fault. . . . I am not so much asking for proof as for specific illustrations . . . I want to see the evidence. If the authors spent as much time in the field as they indicated, they must have far more data than they can possibly encompass within a single volume. . . . The third objection is perhaps of a lessor order, but still seems significant to me. The book purports to be a case study, presumably offering insight into an aspect of American society—at least broader than the immediate community of Springdale. Nevertheless, the authors frequently resolve problems on a purely local basis, and fail to draw the sociological generalizations that might have usefulness for understanding social processes in the U.S.

This reviewer's assessment required the addition of considerable material that was in the possession of the project and entailed a much longer and unwieldy book, bordering on an ethnography and diluting the theoretical framework. Barrington Moore Jr. came to the book's defense, rejecting the need for more illustration, but he made some criticisms of his own:

The manuscript has more than its share of annoying typographical errors. . . . I am dubious about its thesis that village gossip seldom poisons friendly relations. Finally, I think the book would be greatly strengthened by a concluding chapter that would tie the findings into a broader intellectual stream interpreting the processes of change in American society. . . . [The] manuscript is after all, a careful sociological study of the impact of modern industrial society on the rural scene. . . . The authors should make clear the broad implications of their findings.

Moore's comment about the typographical errors was accurate. The manuscript had been typed at the University of Puerto Rico in its College of Social Sciences typing pool by Spanish-speaking typists; that it needed editing was indisputable. In retrospect, I believe Moore was right in his criticism of our treatment of gossip, but because I was an outsider to the town, I was rarely admitted into this relatively private sphere of social relations; in fact, I was also protected from whatever gossip there was about me. Moore's request that we write an additional chapter would require generalizations about American society from a specific case study that we preferred to leave as a self-contained case from which readers might draw their own conclusions.

As is evident, neither press expressed unqualified enthusiasm about publishing our manuscript. Still both presses accepted it for publication. Harvard's acquisition editor "definitely wanted to publish [our] manuscript, provided that it is seriously and quite drastically revised," adding that it "needs a good deal more work than we can cover in our budget." This editor continued, "I think it is clear that you and Mr. Bensman have produced an important book about the social attitudes of a certain large group of people. Thus, we are very anxious to have it put into shape so that we can publish it. At the same time it has the faults of many books of this sort. It falls apart and it is not nearly as well written as it ought to be. What do you and Mr. Bensman think you can do about it?"

This editor seemed to think that the book was mainly about social attitudes and did not respond to what we thought was its institutional framework. He groped for a way to accept it but, unsure of the ground he was on, told us that the book "falls apart," leaving us equally unsure of what ground we stood on.

Princeton's editor expressed more enthusiasm and noted, "Our acceptance of your work does not depend . . . on your revising your manuscript. . . . However, we have asked you to forego royalties on sales up to 1,700 copies . . . because we shall be investing funds in publication at some risk and will break even only when sales have reached 1,700 copies. When I say that there will be a risk, it is because of the fairly technical nature of the work; we feel sure it is high *quality,* or we should not be willing to publish it."

With this assurance, we accepted Princeton's offer. However, this was not the end of the affair. Harvard regarded our withdrawal of the book from its consideration and our acceptance of a contract from Princeton an insult and a breach of publishing ethics; we had not informed either press of the double submission. Harvard's editor took umbrage at our withdrawal of the manuscript because it had been accepted by Princeton without a request for revisions. In his view, we had violated publishing ethics by setting his press in an unseemly competition with Princeton. However, instead of complaining to us, he complained to Princeton. Informed of this by Princeton, we accepted an ever-so-slight slap on the wrist from Princeton for our misdeed.

The birth of *Small Town in Mass Society* was difficult, protracted, and almost unwanted. Finding a publisher and cleaning up the manuscript took more than two years and taught us a few things about the practices of the publishing business. A reviewer, we discovered, can write with personal pique and ignore the substance of a work or, as in one case, can respond competitively and negatively when he himself had written a book in the same general area. Yet despite reviewers' reports, editors who receive the most negative reviews may still decide in favor of publication; there seemed to be no logic to the process. We also learned that with perseverance a book can get published despite rejections and negative reviews.

In its first run, Princeton printed 2,500 hardcover copies, but many of the books in that run were lost in a warehouse fire. When positive reviews by Dennis Wrong and Harold Rosenberg appeared in New York magazines, Princeton subcontracted the book to Doubleday Anchor, which, during the ten years it held the rights, sold 137,672 copies. Princeton regained its rights in 1968, and in seven printings of a second edition, sold 86,296 copies,[6] taking it out of print in 1997 as *Small Town* reached its fortieth birthday.[7]

The readers of these editions were largely graduate students and undergraduates in sociology, political science, and American studies; Protestant ministers and administrators; and, of course, residents of Springdale and the region surrounding Cornell University. The readership also included students who had read chapters that had been excerpted in scores of anthologies. Judging from the number of inquiries I have had from sociologists from abroad, the book has had an active life in Scandinavia, Western and Eastern Europe, and Russia. Many of these inquiries focused on the methodological essays and the conflict over ethics reported in the second edition, but others responded to its theoretical implications. In 1991, Thomas Luckmann, who used *Small Town* as a text in his course "Soziologische Theorie II: Empirische Wissensoziologie" at the University of Constance, sent me a copy of a student paper devoted to an analysis of the book's theoretical perspective, saying, "[Y]ou might be pleased to see that your book with Joe Bensman is still being intensively studied."

Its readership did not, however, include the anthropologists. This surprised and bewildered me because I thought that *Small Town* was written with the attitude of an anthropologist, that is, the study of Man (as it was then known) without regard for time or place. I thought I had done an anthropological study comparable with my work on Palau, except that Springdale had a written history going back to the westward expansion of New England. Moreover, there was an ethnographic literature of community studies, not only that of Thorstein Veblen's chapters on the country town in his book *Absentee Ownership* but also such sociological case studies as the Lynds' Middletown books and the Yankee City series, conducted by the anthropologist W. Lloyd Warner. Such materials gave anthropologists studying their own society access to cases and theories from which to draw an orientation of their own.

Yet when the book was published, it did not penetrate professional anthropology in the United States. The view of Stanley Diamond, who treated the book as a study in rural sociology, was representative. Its failure to make an impact on anthropology led me to reassess my relationship with that field. Palau had already taught me to give up some of the sacred beliefs of the profession; for example, that by studying natives we could learn about ourselves, or that there was some urgency to complete the task of studying primitive societies before they disappeared, or that the natives were incapable of rational action. As I saw it, there was no difference between studying Palau as an anthropologist from the United States and studying Springdale as if I were an anthropologist from Palau. For me, the barriers between sociology and anthropology had broken down, and I decided that I no longer knew what made anthropology a distinctive discipline. This led me to drift back to the comparative and historical sociology of Max Weber, which I had originally learned from Hans H. Gerth. However, because I needed to have a professional label, I decided to call myself a sociologist-anthropologist, not knowing that I had chosen a designation that was too general to fit into any of the increasingly specialized branches of either field.

Some were also unable or unwilling to deal with the economic foundations of our sociological analysis. So far as I know, economists did not read the book, perhaps because econometrics dominated that field. Sociologists had largely abandoned an economic conception of class structure and were mainly concerned with prestige, omitting an inquiry into its economic foundations. Among sociologists, Marxism later became a cultural phenomenon that did not include the analysis of class as central to an understanding of culture.

But the fate of the book in the hands of American sociology's arbiters of respectability deserves more extensive comments. Even occasions of honor for *Small Town* can reveal an effort to dispute its lasting value to the mainstream of sociological work. In 1987, Ruth Horowitz, the chair of the Helen and Robert Lynd Award Committee–an award given for contributions to sociological research on communities of the American Sociological Association's Community Section–presented the Lynd award to *Small Town in Mass Society* (shared with Maurice Stein for his book *The Eclipse of Community*). At that same gathering, Dennis Wrong, speaking on behalf of Jonathan Reider's *Canarsie: The Jews and Italians of Brooklyn against Liberalism,* took the occasion to observe that Reider's book had displaced or superseded the importance of *Small Town,* as if to make this commemoration a burial ceremony. Wrong's remarks surprised me because his review of *Small Town* in the *New Leader* shortly after it was published lauded the book and helped make it a success. Wrong's estimate seemed gratuitous and disturbed me–in part, perhaps because his reviews of some of my later books were also negative–but I believe that in this case Wrong was wrong.

Of course, it is understandable that our essay "The Springdale Case: Academic Bureaucrats and Sensitive Townspeople," republished in the second edition,[8] would endear us neither to university officials concerned about their relations with constituencies in academia nor to leaders of the organized academic professions. As far as I know, the book has no standing in the

American Sociological Association's Citation Index. Perhaps it is difficult to categorize, but there may be other reasons as well. For example, a working paper summarizing community studies published by the Historical Studies Program at the New School refers to *Small Town* as a "C. Wright Mills type study" and lets it go at that. Apparently, the book is difficult to fit into conventional categories and caused some embarrassment to the upholders of academic respectability when the controversy with Cornell University erupted.

Our controversy with Cornell University over the ethics of publishing *Small Town* cast a shadow over our careers in American academia because it implied a disloyalty to university employers and had a negative effect on the public image of sociology. As a consequence of this controversy, questions of ethical norms in community and ethnographic research are now widely discussed. A recent issue of *Lingua Franca* contains an article reviewing a number of sociological reports that have raised ethical questions. Entitled "Spies like Us: When Sociologists Deceive Their Subjects," it notes that "the ethics of deceptive research did not become a controversial topic in the profession until 1958. The occasion was a massive Cornell University study of participatory democracy in a local community and its unanticipated spin-off book *Small Town in Mass Society.* . . ." The article, written by Charlotte Allen, continues:

> For many years afterward, sociologists who feared that Vidich's conduct had jeopardized the field's newfound respectability, argued over whether he had done anything wrong. On one hand, everyone in [Springdale] knew he was the director of a Cornell research project. On the other hand, many [Springdale] residents might have thought (and been encouraged by Cornell to think) that the project consisted of the fieldworker's ethnographic survey. In the end, sociologists failed to resolve the ethical questions that Vidich's course of actions raised.[9]

At a time when many sociologists are employees of organizations attempting to project a positive public image, issues of ethics become muddled with those of public relations. In consequence, the sociologist is left with several options: accept the censorship of the organization, engage in self-censorship, or disregard all forms of anticipatory censorship and take the consequences for reputation, career, and professional stigmatization. In my case, I had already been left without the sponsorship of my senior professor at Harvard and could never ask for references from my Cornell employers. Finding jobs for myself was a problem that was not solved until 1960, when the Graduate Faculty of the New School for Social Research hired me on the strength of the book and asked for no references at all from my previous sponsors and employers.

An entirely new dimension of my tether to Springdale appeared a few years ago when Paul Piccone, whom I have known for many years, bought one of Springdale's stately houses, took up residence in the town, and became one of its new immigrants. Piccone is also editor of the journal *Telos*. Learning, apparently for the first time, that I had co-authored a book on Springdale, he wanted to read it, and I supplied him with a copy. What he read did not conform to his image of the town and displeased him. In the spring 1995 issue of *Telos*, in an essay titled "Postmodern Populism," he took the occasion to defend Springdale against our interpretation of it: "Contrary to the dark forebodings of New Class Sociologists, modernization has not overwhelmed whatever 'organic communities' there ever were in the U.S. Rather their survival and continued viability is a function of their ability to resist or otherwise avoid modernizing procedures."[10] Selectively quoting from our essay "A Theory of the Contemporary American Community," which appeared in the second edition and was intended not as an analysis of Springdale but as a sketch of some possibilities for the future of the United States, he wrote:

> In their mid-1950s study of a paradigmatic rural (organic) community, Vidich and Bensman not only projected the imminent obliteration of such communities, but, in typical "end of ideology" style, warned about the potential fascist implications of what they saw as "fundamental and perhaps irreversible trends" in the very structure of American society. . . . Four decades after the study was completed, "Springdale" has yet to succumb to these "fundamental . . . irreversible trends." The village has still no fast food facilities or other obvious signs of irreversible "moderniza-

tion," and it still runs pretty much as it did in the 1950s by the direct descendants of those very people Vidich and Bensman ridicule in their "scientific" treatise and, more importantly, by scores of new villagers who have moved in since and who, contrary to dark foreboding of "populist" intolerance, . . . have become integral members of an ever changing dynamic organic community.[11]

In Piccone's view, Springdale is one of the last organic communities in the United States, one that he found and moved into. However, his is an effort, like that of Howard Jones, to affirm the authenticity of public appearances against unappealing realities. Actually, there are many communities like Springdale. That they are similar to what they were fifty years ago indicates that small-scale farming is still a viable business, that opportunities exist to commute to work at white-collar and industrial jobs in the surrounding region, and that fast food chains do not see in them a mass market for their products. Despite Piccone's assertion of the community's organicism, it would surprise me if the culture wars and their political implications have not penetrated Springdale. In fact, Bensman and I made no predictions that the town would be obliterated but only suggested that its dilemmas and contradictions were solved by complicated patterns of social and personal self-deception that permitted Springdalers to retain their systems of beliefs, while at the same time acting within the framework of social realities that denied these beliefs. Perhaps these same mechanisms are available to and utilized by intellectuals. If one considers the history of the treatment of the Springdale study by the American sociological establishment, this would seem to be the case.

IV. Springdale at Rest

In our introduction to Princeton's second edition of *Small Town,* Bensman and I referred to our forthcoming book, *The Third American Revolution.* Though we had thought the book would be published under that title, it was published as *The New American Society: The Revolution of the Middle Classes.*[12] When writing this book, we had in mind Barrington Moore Jr.'s suggestion that we add a chapter to the original edition that would locate Springdale in a macroscopic framework. As we conceived of *The New American Society,* the connecting link between it and *Small Town* was our conception of Springdale's new middle classes, whose ideas, cultural forms, and life styles ran counter to most of the town's traditional values. Although we began with this idea, we treated *The New American Society* as an independent macro-analysis of changes in American society from the postbellum period to the 1960s. Recognizing that we had not directly addressed Moore's suggestion, we wrote a new chapter, "A Theory of the Contemporary American Community," for the 1968 edition of *Small Town.* This chapter extrapolates our Springdale findings to the then newly emerged middle-class suburbs, university towns, and urban middle-class enclaves. We stressed the potential for a clash between traditional American values and the new life styles that had gained currency among the upcoming generations in the 1960s. In our conclusion, we wrote that

> the new life styles are not based on un-American ideas but rather have evolved out of fundamental organizational, economic, educational, and demographic changes in American society. . . . Whether one likes the direction of these trends or not, they cannot be wished away, abolished by law or reversed by going back to the past without doing violence to the emergent society. . . . A direct confrontation based on these opposing orientations will have to be avoided if the United States hopes to cope with its other problems.[13]

We could not then know how that confrontation would work itself out, but it is apparent that it is now taking place. On one side are those who uphold the sanctity of the family and of the nation as a community requiring reverence for quasi-sacred traditions and support for the moral sentiments of kinship, fidelity, and patriotism. On the other are the realities of racial and ethnic tensions, new family norms, sexual styles that do not conform to older standards, novel forms of entertainment, and varying consumption patterns. Commitments to these competing values and moralities are expressed in legal struggles, propaganda campaigns, and the direct use of violence.

Moral and life-style issues are also played out in national politics and legislative confrontations in Congress and between a multitude of think tanks on the Washington Beltway. What is at stake is no less than the soul of American society.[14] Our original discoveries in Springdale revealed incipient cultural tendencies that later became paradigmatic for the society at large. Although we may now declare that our relationship with Springdale is at rest, it is unlikely that the same claim can be made for the book.

Notes

I thank Larry Carney, Guy Oakes, Stanford M. Lyman, Marilyn Bensman, and Robert N. Wilson for editorial advice on an earlier draft of the manuscript and Larry Carney, Guy Oakes, Robert Jackall, and Mary Vidich for criticisms on the final version.

1. Arthur J. Vidich, *Political Factionalism in Palau: Its Rise and Development,* Co-ordinated Investigation of Micronesian Anthropology, National Science Foundation Report 23 (Washington, D.C.: Pacific Science Board, National Research Council, 1949).

2. Since the social growth project had intended to present its conclusions in statistical terms, all protocols collected in the field were machine processed and cross-run for correlations between different variables. As the data from surveys began to accumulate, the number of variables increased and the cross-runs for correlations multiplied. It had been hoped that the machine process might provide leads to significant variables from which community creativity and leadership could be understood. But the pile of printouts resulting from this procedure became unmanageable, leaving the project analysts without a specific theme or problem. As a result of this style of investigation, the project never produced a full-length monograph on Springdale.

3. Listed in project files under the designation D-4.

4. A full-scale study of cold war civil defense policy is found in Guy Oakes, *The Imaginary War: Civil Defense and American Cold War Culture* (New York: Oxford University Press, 1994). See also my review of this book, "Atomic Bombs and American Democracy," *International Journal of Politics, Culture and Society,* 8, no. 3 (1995), 499–506.

5. A more recent journalistic comment appeared in the July 14, 1999, issue of the Springdale newspaper. Reporting on the winning floats in the town's Fourth of July parade, it mentions that under the category of "prettiest," the Springdale Historical Society received first place for its entry "Small Town in Mass Society."

6. Herbert Gans's essay "Best Sellers by Sociologists: An Exploratory Study," *Contemporary Sociology*, 26 (March 1997), 131–35, does not list *Small Town in Mass Society* as one of his bestsellers. His research for this study also failed to produce data for C. Wright Mills's *White Collar, the Power Elite,* and Hans H. Gerth and C. Wright Mills's *From Max Weber: Character and Social Structure,* each of which is still in print.

7. In the original edition of *Small Town,* Bensman and I deliberately said nothing about the source of theory that guided our analysis. In the second edition, we included an essay we had already published entitled "Social Theory in Field Research," which describes how we heuristically employed the theories of others to arrive at the interpretation of our data. When the second edition went to press, we had not completed the essay "Social Theory and the Substantive Problems of Sociology," which until 1991 remained as "Some Notes on Social Theory" originally drafted by Bensman and expanded and completed by me. This essay, published in *International Journal of Politics, Culture and Society,* 4, no. 4 (1991), 517–34, makes explicit the sources of our intellectual orientations and how they influenced our choices of problems.

8. Originally published in Arthur J. Vidich, Joseph Bensman, and Maurice Stein, *Reflections on Community Studies* (New York: J. Wiley and Sons, 1964), 313–49.

9. Charlotte Allen, "Spies like Us: When Sociologists Deceive Their Subjects," *Lingua Franca* 7 (November 1997), 5.

10. Paul Piccone, "Postmodern Populism," *Telos,* no. 103 (Spring 1995), 54n19.

11. Ibid.

12. Joseph Bensman and Arthur J. Vidich, *The New American Society: The Revolution of the Middle Classes* (Chicago: Quadrangle, 1971). A second edition entitled *American Society: The Welfare State and Beyond* was published by Bergin and Garvey in 1987 with a new foreword and two additional chapters.

13. Page 347 herein.

14. For a later and more detailed examination of some of these issues, see my edited book *The New Middle Classes: Life-Styles, Status Claims, and Political Orientations* (New York: New York University Press, 1995), esp. 281–99; "The New Conservatism: Political Ideology and Class Structure in America" (contributed by Michael Hughey), 300–334; "The Politics of the Middle Classes in a National Crisis: The Case of Watergate," 335–63; and "Class and Politics in an Epoch of Declining Abundance," 364–86.

Index

————◄◉►————

rural preference 202. *See also*
politics, state, roads
statistics, informal census data,
15-19
status, social: concept of, 52n. *See
also* prestige
stereotypes of economic evaluation,
42-43; of equality ideology,
39-40; of "bad folks," 36-37, of
"good folks," 37-38; of gossip,
negative, 42; of intellectuals,
38; of the good minister, 240-
241; of rural-urban relationships, 80-81; of shack people,
36; of success, 71; of urban
life, 31-32; of work as ideology,
41
subsidies: attitude towards, 295;
and local politics, 198-202; and
town roads, 139-140; and village board, 113
success, *see* values, success as

taxes: and assessments, village,
123; rebates, attitude toward,
59; low-tax ideology, 116-118;
and new middle class, 331, 338;
and representation, 20; and
roads, town tax structure, 138n,
139n; town rates vs. village
rates, 142
teachers: class description, 60;
agents of cultural importation,
83; and specialized leadership,
266; as technical leaders, 270;
school board attitudes toward,
195; automatic tenure, 197;
and work, 50. *See also* professionals
television; and leisure and consumption, 84
theology, *see* ecumenicalism, religion
theory: and empirical observations,
383-396; "exhaustion" of, 388-
389; and the solution of research problems, 385-394; systematic, 383-385, 392-394; sub-
stitutions of, 389-392, 394-395;
unsystematic (heuristic): func-

tions of, 385-392, limitations of,
394-396, and systematic theory,
392-394
town board, *see* politics, town
town clerk, *see* politics, town, Lee
traffic, 3, 4

Ukrainians, *see* ethnic groups
unanimity, of decision-making:
and village board, 110-112:
formula, 128, and social basis of
issues, 127, 134; and public
position of Jones, 276; social,
and minister's policies, 239; and
school board, 172-173
urbanism, 325-326. *See also* mass
society, rural-urban relationships, stereotypes
urbanization, 325-326

validity, 359-365, 377-382
values, public: ambivalence in,
105; and defense mechanisms,
319-321, normalcy, 292: and
goals, substitution of, 298; independence as: and illusion
and reality, 286-287, of lay advisors to school, 191, 192, in
rural self-image, 32, of traditional farmers vs. prosperous
farmers, 68-69; and institutions,
conflicts of, 285-287, 319-321;
moral, of "folk," 30; and leaders, specialized, 272; and professionals, substitute for economic immobility, 88-89; and
religion, 158, 258; religious, of
ministers: and congregations,
234-236, and local values, 238-
239, and personal behavior,
239-241; and shack people, 290-
291; and science, 412-414; success as: ideology of, in public
conversation, 44-45; for businessmen, 54; and conversational
level, 303-304; and expanding
farmers, 71; and illusions, 302;
and illusion and reality, 286-
287; and Poles, 271; and professionals, 89; of hard work,

Author Index

University of Illinois Press
1325 South Oak Street
Champaign, IL 61820-6903
www.press.uillinois.edu